Richard Saul Wurman

WASHINGTON
DC
ACCESS®

Cover photograph: Joel Katz ©1984 Katz Wheeler Design

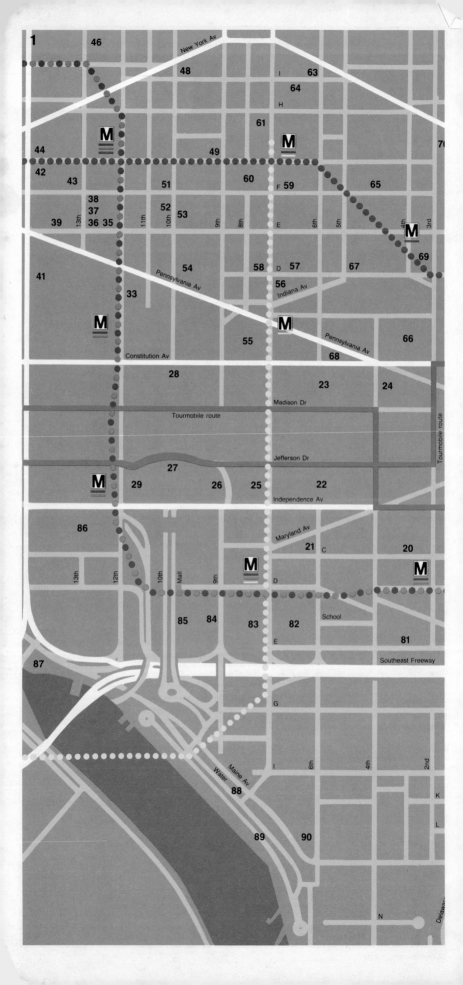

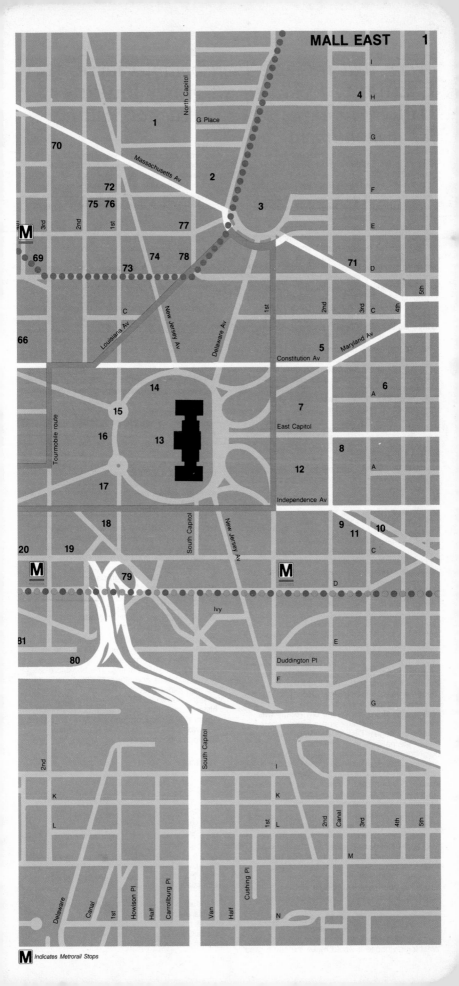

When that irascible Frenchman, **Pierre L'Enfant**, looked up at grassy **Jenkins Hill** in 1790, he saw "a pedestal waiting for a monument."

What he put atop it was the **Capitol** of the new republic. It is from there, the heart of the city he planned, that one can still best see the outlines of this **last of the Baroque cities.**

Not all the subsequent builders and planners of the national capital have seen the city through L'Enfant's eyes. Indeed, virtually the whole of Washington, but especially the area around the Capitol, has been a touchstone of city planning as that concept has changed through the years. Whether planners have been called upon by the nation to build—or rebuild—the capital, or whether they have assigned themselves the task, no other American city so reflects the nation's changing sense of itself. A walk from the would-be Napoleonic grandeur of the **Library of Congress** to the starkness of the new **Hart Office Building** is a brief tour through the national character.

The Hill, as Washingtonians know it, is full of stops. Along with the Capitol, which includes both the **House of Representatives** and the **Senate,** there are also the **Supreme Court Building** and the multiplying **Office Buildings of Congress.** The **Folger Shakespeare Library** was placed on *The Hill* by its founder, Standard Oil executive **H.C. Folger.** Noteworthy from the exterior is **Daniel Burnham's Union Station,** a bit northwest of the Capitol. Here he, for one, succeeded in marking his credo into stone, counseling *"Make no little plans."* Shops and restaurants, for the inevitably foot weary, can be found by walking north a couple of blocks on Pennsylvania Avenue.

The city's planners, be they legislators, architects, or charlatans, have not had an easy time turning their dreams into marble. Washington, after all, soon grew off the drawing board and into a real city. Behind the picture postcard views from Jenkins Hill, these 2 forces—*the planned city vs. the real one*—have been engaged in a long struggle that continues today.

Pennsylvania Avenue, for example, may be the *Parade Ground of the Republic* for most Americans, but for Washingtonians it was for many years merely *Main Street.* They used to— and many still do—know it as just *The Avenue.* Where today the stately **Archives Building** stands, reminding passersby, perhaps suggestively, that *Past is Prologue*—there once stood the city's major produce market. Where the new **National Place** has just risen, there stood for years infamous **Rum Row** (around the corner, if it explains anything, from old **Newspaper Row**), where the *Gin Rickey* was first concocted. Just across the street, where stands the august **District Building,** was once one of the nation's most infamous neighborhoods. So great an offense to 19th-century public morality was it that one of the Union's foremost commanders, **General Joseph Hooker,** was ordered to clean it up. *Hooker's Brigade,* the area came to be called, and its denizens merely *hookers.*

Pennsylvania Avenue today is being rebuilt. The **Old Post Office** has been saved and turned into a public shopping and eating pavilion. Saved also is the **National Theater,** on the same site since 1835, and where Washingtonian **Helen Hayes** watched her first play. Most of The Avenue is lined with massive governmental structures such as the **J. Edgar Hoover (FBI) Building,** which gives one of the city's most popular tours.

Washington's **Southwest waterfront,** south of The Hill, is the one-time working class neighborhood where **Al Jolson** grew up. George Washington hoped it would make the city a great commercial center, and years later, in the 1950s, Congress saw it as a showcase in **Urban Renewal.** Neither plan worked out as expected, but in the meantime Washington's famous **Arena Stage** has made its home there. So have a string of locally popular seafood restaurants and riverside hotels.

The Mall itself has not been spared. Here was a true urban innovation: a non-commercial street around which a city was to grow. Yet for its first half century it was completely ignored; railroad tracks, of all things, were laid across its middle. Later planners decreed that it should be surrounded only with white marble buildings (the **Department of Agriculture** is a survivor of this plan) and the **Smithsonian Castle** destroyed.

Today, of course, The Mall cuts its green swath through the monumental core of Washington, approximately as L'Enfant planned in the first place. It is surrounded with museums and galleries, including the **National Gallery of Art,** the **National Air and Space Museum,** the **Freer Gallery,** and the **Hirshhorn,** to name only a few.

Actually, the much-contested city tradition of planning and replanning started with L'Enfant himself. When one of the city's very first residents built himself a house, Pierre L'Enfant discovered that it stood in the way of one of his proposed streets. At the time, there were not yet any streets at all, and virtually no people. Nor would the city amount to much of anything for another three-quarters of a century. But no matter. L'Enfant had the house torn down in the night. *He had a Plan.*

1   Government Printing Center & Bookstore. A mecca for information freaks, the center publishes 1.4 billion volumes a year. According to the *Guinness Book of World Records,* it's the world's largest in-plant printing operation (5000 workers) and uses enough paper yearly to fill 25 miles of train cars. Main offerings include *The Congressional Record* (sent to Capitol Hill bound in Moroccan leather with marbled end papers) and *The Federal Register,* the daily trade paper of the federal government.

Thousands of consumer-information books and booklets are published here. The all-time best-seller, *Infant Care,* has sold 17 million copies since its first 1914 printing. The bookstore stocks over 3,000 titles and offers 17,000 more in its catalog, plus NASA and National Park Service posters, how-to books, government guides, histories and most government publications. Tours run am and pm on weekdays. Of course, you won't see the restricted areas where passports, postal orders, etc. are printed.

The main building (1901) is a massive Romanesque Revival edifice composed entirely of handmade brick. *Morning and afternoon tours M-F; call at least one week in advance (275-3541). Bookstore open M-F 8am-4pm; other branches in the Dept. of Commerce, Health & Human Services, and Pentagon (274-2091). 710 N. Capitol St. NW (between G & H Sts.).*

2   Main Post Office. (1914, **Graham & Burnham**) Designed to complement nearby Union Station (also by Burnham), this smaller and less opulent Beaux-Arts building is rendered in white Italian marble and trimmed with an Ionic colonnade. *Massachusetts Ave & N. Capitol St.*

Introductions/Theaters/Narrative black
Hotels purple
Museums/Architecture blue
Parks/Open spaces green
Shops/Galleries violet

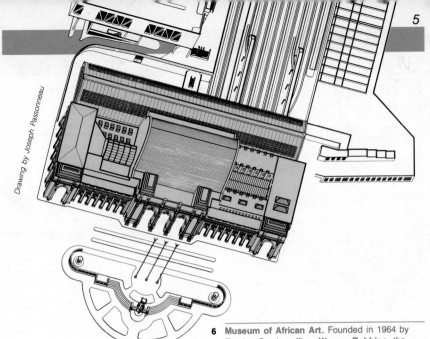

Drawing by Joseph Passonneau

3 **Union Station.** (1908, **Daniel Burnham**) Burnham's trademark was a robust romanticism that found full expression in this remarkable Beaux-Arts monument to the railroads. Built of granite and based on the Arch of Constantine (outside) and the Baths of Diocletian (inside). Reconstruction will keep the main building closed for several years. However, there is a fully operational facility behind it. At Capitol Plaza, you'll find bus, subway and taxi service. *Massachusetts Ave. at Delaware Ave. NE. Metrorail red line. Amtrak info., 484-7540.*

Columbus Memorial Fountain. Columbus stands on the prow of a ship; figures on either side represent the old and new worlds. Sculpted in 1912 by **Lorenzo Taft.** *Union Station, Massachusetts, Louisiana and Delaware Aves. NW.*

4 **Capital Children's Museum.** Learning and playing finally meet in fine hands-on children's museums such as these, where it's equally amusing to see the grown-ups getting involved with the touchy-feely gizmos, play clothes and climb-ons. Here children learn how to use the city by play-riding in a bus or taxi; they explore other cultures by putting on the clothes and trying the food of foreign lands. They learn by doing, whether it's computing, building or painting. The **Penny Exchange** gift shop sells all kinds of toys, most as educational as they are fun.

Admission charge. Open Tu-Sa 10am-4pm, Su 1-5pm. 800 3rd St. NE (H St.). Metrorail red line. 543-8600.

5 **Sewall-Belmont House.** The National Women's Party has turned this house into a museum of American women's political achievements. The original structure dates from the late 1600s-early 1700s. Sewall added to the house in 1800, and parts were burned by the British in 1813. Numerous remodelings have made it a crazy quilt of architectural styles: Queen Anne, Georgian, Classic and French influences are evident. **Albert Gallatin,** Jefferson's and Madison's Secretary of the Treasury, is purported to have worked out the Louisiana Purchase deal here.

In 1929 the NWP bought the house. Today it serves as their headquarters. Displays commemorate **Alice Paul,** author of the Equal Rights Amendments, and trace the history of the women's movement from suffrage to the present. *Open Tu-F 10am-2pm; Sa, Su, some holidays noon-4pm. 144 Constitution Ave. NE. Metrorail blue/orange/red lines. 546-1210/546-3989.*

6 **Museum of African Art.** Founded in 1964 by Foreign Service officer **Warren Robbins,** the museum's creation was really a labor of love by a private citizen. Though it received immediate acclaim as the only museum of its kind in the nation, it struggled financially. In 1979 the museum was taken over by the Smithsonian Institution, ensuring its survival as an educational center, museum and cultural ambassador. The museum makes its home in a row of beautifully restored Victorian townhouses; one was once occupied by **Frederick Douglass,** noted author, abolitionist and former slave.

Thirteen galleries show traveling exhibits as well as items from the museum's 8,000-piece collection. Over 35 tribes are represented by headdresses, masks, jewelry, bronze figurines, tools, weapons and musical instruments.

The museum has a well-deserved reputation for its skillful presentations. Though the objects are powerful and very dramatic, the exhibitions—in small homey galleries—tend to stress the religious and cultural significance of the works rather than their value as curios or primitive objets d'art. All exhibits are labeled in English and Swahili.

On permanent display are an exhibit of drums and musical instruments; an exhibit showing the influence of African art on modern masters like Picasso, Matisse, Modigliani and Klee; and a faithful recreation of Frederick Douglass' study.

The late photographer for *Life Magazine,* **Eliot Elisofon,** endowed the museum with thousands of photos and slides. Some of the slides have been arranged in a stunning 15-minute sound and light show about the people and cultures of Africa.

The museum gift shop has wonderful African craft items, some at very reasonable prices. There is also a large assortment of books and catalogs on African art and history. The museum frequently has special programs on African folk tales, music and craft workshops.

Admission free. Open M-F 11am-5pm; Sa, Su & holidays noon-5pm. 316 A St. NE. 287-3490.

In 1979, Congress authorized plans for one of the most complex yet beautifying mergers on behalf of the American people: the Smithsonian consolidation of the Museum of African Art, the Arthur Sackler Collection of Art, and a new International Center into a unique 4.2-acre combination called **The Quadrangle.** To be called the **Center for African, Near Eastern and Asian Cultures,** it will stand as the Smithsonian's response to a growing need for an understanding of non-Western cultures, giving more than 20 million visitors yearly an appreciation of the ancient civilizations of the Eastern hemisphere. The Center, slated for a September 1986 opening, is also regarded as

the crowning achievement of **S. Dillon Ripley**, former secretary and director of the Smithsonian Institution, who helped guide the Institution during a 20-year period of enormous technological change and development in US history. Ripley retired in 1984.

Ninety percent of the $75 million complex will be constructed underground to help maintain an unobstructed view of the Smithsonian Castle as the Institution's official landmark. Ground level will extend 60 feet below the surface. The first 2 levels in the right wing will house the African Museum of Art, with several new acquisitions added to its present 8,000-piece collection. The complete Arthur Sackler Gallery, predominantly Chinese art, will receive a permanent home in the first 2 floors above and below ground on the left side of the structure. A brand new facility, the International Center, has been designed to occupy the entire basement level. It will provide the mall area with great foreign art exhibits, positions for fellowships and studies based on grants, donations of scholarships and facilities for scholarly conferences.

Other plans within the department include a vast research library and a possible center for Islamic studies. Due to the labor-intensive activities of relocating the already existing collections, the Museum of African Art is expected to be closed from February 1986 until the new 360,000 square-foot building opens its doors 7 months later.

Director's Bests

Warren Robbins
Director Emeritus, National Museum of African Art

The **9 restored 19th-century row houses** which the museum occupies—each with its own Victorian character on the outside but interconnected on the inside.

The **period room** that reflects the life and times of **Frederick Douglass,** the great abolitionist whose one time Capitol Hill residence contains the public galleries of the museum.

The **intimate scale of the galleries,** which create a special ambience for the sculpture to come alive in.

•

The dynamism of **African tribal sculpture**—one of the great art traditions of mankind. Some of my favorites in the museum's collection:

The stately **Chiwara,** representing a mythological figure—half antelope, half man—of the **Bamana** people of Mali.

The imposing male and female pair of figures of the **Senufo** people of the Ivory Coast.

The graceful Brancusi-like rearing python, a water spirit of the **Baga** people of Guinea.

The small but queenly maternity figure of the **Yombe** people of Zaire, one of the true masterpieces of African art.

•

The **magnificent color photography** of the late *Life* photographer and principal museum patron **Eliot Elisofon.**

The **beautiful beaded aprons** of the **N'Debele-Zulu** people of South Africa and their spectacular geometric color murals replicated on the walls of the museum's courtyard and of the alley which runs for a block to historic Constitution Avenue.

Boutique Africa, featuring beautiful contemporary craft objects, textiles and jewelry.

The **daily story telling and drumming sessions** for children led by African members of the museum's staff.

Shepley Bulfinch Richardson and Abbott

7   Supreme Court. (1935, **Cass Gilbert**) Armed only with the US Constitution and a carefully fashioned authority, the Supreme Court determines the complexion of American Society more than almost any other single power. For this reason a session at the Supreme Court is one of the most rewarding experiences for those who come to Washington DC, as a pilgrimage to honor and explore the federal government.

The Court's 9 justices are called into session the first Monday in October. They hear cases for 2 weeks, then retire to formulate their decisions for 2 weeks, continuing to work through the end of June. During the in-session weeks, the Court is open to the public during hearings *(M, Tu, Th 10am-3pm; W 10am-noon)*. No passes are needed to attend, but there are only 100-150 seats available to the public, so you must come no later than 9:30am—possibly earlier—to get a seat. The *Washington Post* will report the cases due for review on days the Court is in session, and you will be able to anticipate the crowd. Monday is the day that decisions are generally handed down, so if possible make that the day of your visit and feel the true drama of the nation's highest court.

When the Court is in session, in-courtroom lectures are given M-F 3:30-4pm. When the Court is out, lectures are given 9:30am-3:30pm every hour on the half hour. In addition, there is a half-hour film featuring the Chief Justice and others on the bench explaining the history and day-to-day workings of the Court.

The Supreme Court began hearing cases in 1790, but so little was thought of its prestige that the first Chief Justice, **John Jay,** resigned to become governor of New York. It took almost a century and a half before it was deemed worthy of its own home, a dazzling white Neo-Classic edifice fronted by 16 *Iowan* corn-capital columns of Vermont marble. Though restrained and commanding, there is evidence that Gilbert perhaps didn't take the commission as seriously as he could have: He and some of his non-judicial contemporaries are among the robed figures in the main pediment.

The massive building has one of the best government cafeterias, open for breakfast *M-F 7:30am-10:30am, for lunch from 11am-2pm. Court is free to the public. Open M-F 9am-4:30pm. 1st St. at E. Capitol St. Metrorail blue/orange/red lines. 252-3000.*

In his Pulitzer Prize-winning novel, *Advise and Consent,* **Allen Drury** wrote the following about DC: *"Like a city in dreams the great white capital stretches along the placid river from Georgetown on the west to Anacostia on the east. It is a city of temporaries, a city of just-arriveds and only-visitings, built on the shifting sands of politics, filled with people just passing through."*

During the Civil War, Washington was the capital of the Union. The Confederacy was established in Montgomery, Alabama, but moved its capital to Richmond, Virginia soon after.

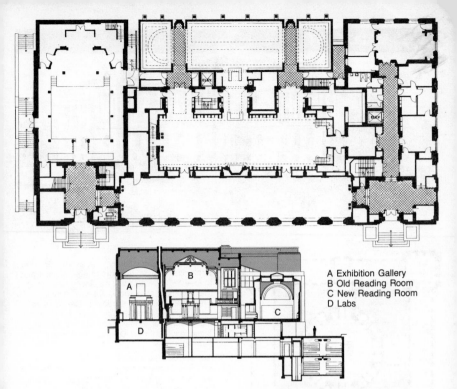

A Exhibition Gallery
B Old Reading Room
C New Reading Room
D Labs

8 Folger Shakespeare Library. (1930s, **Cret & Trowbridge;** remodeling 1979, **Hartman-Cox**) This shrine of serious theater students contains the largest and most varied collection of Shakespearean memorabilia in existence. If you have a soft spot for the master, you'll enjoy the collection of manuscripts, including first editions and those annotated by the stage's most famous Hamlets, Lady Macbeths and star-crossed lovers. There are costumes and props, photos, musical scores, and every other implement used to commit Shakespearean drama. The collection includes works by *The Bard's* contemporaries and an excellent collection of artifacts from the England of his lifetime. The building, which successfully reconciles a Greek-influenced Art Deco exterior with an Elizabethan interior, is considered among Paul Philippe Cret's finest designs; the late-1970s additions are sensitive and well-done.

The **Folger Theater Group** presents both Shakespearean classics and contemporary plays in an authentic 16th-century theater; the resident **Renaissance Musical Group** also performs here. Take special note of the 9 marble relief sculptures depicting favorite Shakespearean scenes on the East Capitol St. side of the building (1932, **John Gregory**). **Puck Fountain,** a delightful statue of the mischievous sprite from *A Midsummer Night's Dream,* was sculpted in 1932 by **Brenda Putnam.** Written on the pedestal: *"What fools these mortals be."* Perhaps it is no accident that Puck seems to be turning away from the Capitol. *West Facade.* A small gift shop sells all kinds of things with Shakespeare's face or words printed on them.

Admission free. Open M-Sa 10am-4pm, open Su 10am-4pm Apr-Labor Day. 201 E. Capitol St. NE. Metrorail blue/orange lines. 544-4600/Box Office, 546-4000.

---

9 209½. ☆ ☆ ☆ ☆ $$$ One of Capitol Hill's finest restaurants, and an exemplar of new American cuisine. Small, pretty, fresh flowers abounding, 209½ boasts a polished staff, a nice selection of wines and aperitifs, and a fixed-price menu that changes with the seasons. Specialties include zucchini-parmesan pancakes, soft shell crabs with hazelnuts, grilled duck, cold dishes like vegetables with pesto, and figs marinated in wine. *Original American. Open M-F 11:30am-2:30pm, 6-11:30pm; Sa 6-11:30pm. Closed Su. Reservations suggested. Coat and tie recommended. 209½ Pennsylvania Ave. SE.* 544-6352.

10 Timberlakes. ☆ ☆ $$ Good American staples: burgers, onion rings, omelets. *Bar & grill. Open M-Th 11:30am-midnight, F 11:30am-1am, Sa 10:30am-1am, Su 10:30am-midnight. 231 Pennsylvania Ave. SE.* 543-8337.

11 Sherrill's Bakery. ☆ ☆ ☆ $ One of the few authentic coffee shops in Washington. Narrow, filled with wooden booths, a long counter, and bakery cases stocked with homemade pastries, cakes, pies and cookies, Sherrill's offers cheap, tasty breakfasts and good sandwiches and platters. *American. Open M-F 6am-8:30pm; Sa & Su 8am-8:30pm. No reservations. 233 Pennsylvania Ave. SE.* 544-2480.

---

12 Library of Congress. (Main building 1897, **Smithmeyer & Pelz;** Adams Building 1939; Madison Building 1980) Here are some figures, though they're impossible to grasp: 80 million items, 400 more added every hour; nearly 6,000 books printed before the year 1500; 1,500 flutes, 5 Stradivarius violins; the world's largest collections of comic books; 3.5 million pieces of sheet music; recordings of traditional songs of the Sioux; one of only 3 remaining perfect vellum-printed Gutenberg bibles, circa 1455. At the time of its completion, the main building was the most expensive structure in the world. There is no doubt that this is the world's largest library and collection. Primarily it is a collection, unbounded by fashion, ideology or language.

Funded in 1800 with $5,000, the library began as a 1-room reference collection for Congress. When it was burned in 1814 by the British (we had just burned theirs in Canada), **Thomas Jefferson,** retired and in need of money, offered his fine private library as a replacement.

The main building is an ornate Italian Renaissance/Beaux-Arts confection designed after the Paris Opera House. Most striking is the Main Reading Room, a soaring, domed octagon built in 3 colors of veined marble; the copper roof of the dome was once gilded. Twice in the last 40 years the library has been forced to expand, first into the white Georgia marble **John Adams Building** at *2nd St. and Independence Ave. SE;* then into the new 9-story, 46-acre **James Madison Memorial Building,** *101 Independence Ave. SE,* where you can see a part of the library's collection of over 1 million photos and prints. Most of these were obtained as copyright submissions and span the history of photography. **Mathew Brady's** work is well represented and the entire photo collection of *Look* magazine is here.

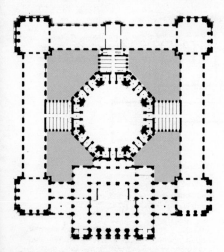

This is the nation's library, and as such is open to all citizens over 18 years of age. A good place to lose the inevitable first-day intimidation is at the 18-minute slide show, *America's Library,* which shows every hour, *M-F 8:45am-8:45pm; Sa, Su and holidays 8:45am-5:45pm.* Follow this with a tour that will take you into the stacks; these leave from the **Orientation Theatre** *9am-4pm daily.*

The library's cafeteria is on the top floor of the Madison Annex and offers a fine view. There is also a small gift shop in the main building which sells books, cards and crafts.

Admission free. Open M-F 8:30am-9:30pm, Sa 8:30am-5pm, Su 1-5pm. Jefferson (main) Building, 1st St. at E. Capitol St. SE. Metrorail blue/orange lines. 287-5000/Reference: 287-6500.

Special collections include **Rare Books,** which comprises volumes from many of the presidents' private libraries; the **History and Genealogy Room,** where family records may be researched; extensive **Asian and European collections;** and the **National Library Service for the Blind and Physically Handicapped.**

From April through September, stop by and view the annual photo exhibit of the White House news photographers, an excellent retrospective of the past year. Concerts are offered from October through April and include those by the Juilliard String Quartet, which plays the library's collection of Stradivarius and other fine stringed instruments to keep them from being ruined by disuse. Literary events run October through May and feature poets and authors of note.

Director's Bests

Daniel Boorstin
Director, Library of Congress

The Giant Bible of Mainz

Staff of the Library of Congress

View of the Capitol from my office in the Madison Building

Swann Collection of Political Caricatures

Hans Kraus Collection of Francis Drake Materials

Collections of **birds eye views** in the Geography and Map Division

Great Hall in the Jefferson Building.

Listening to the **Stradivarius** in the Library of Congress

---

13 The Capitol. **Pierre L'Enfant** picked the hill on which the *Congress House* would sit. It was designed in 1792 by **Dr. William Thornton,** a physician with a passionate interest in architecture. **George Washington** officiated at the cornerstone-laying ceremony in 1793 (the sandstond for the building came from his Aquia Creek quarries), but it was not until 22 November 1800, at **President John Adams'** insistence, that the House and the Senate moved into the Capitol and officially called the first joint session of Congress to order. The building at this time was a 2-story square structure. By 1807 a second similar edifice had been built for the House of Representatives. A wooden walkway linked the 2 buildings.

In 1814 British troops invaded Washington and convened in a little session of their own in the Senate building. The decision that day was to burn the Capitol along with the city's other federal buildings. Only a sudden summer rainstorm spared the building from total destruction. Five years later, the structure repaired, Congress returned home, and what you see today is an outgrowth of the 1819 Capitol. Most visitors enter the building via the **East**

Portico, where every 4 years on 20 January, the presidential inauguration ceremonies take place. As you walk up the steps toward the magnificent bronze **Columbus Doors,** keep in mind that it was here that **William Henry Harrison** delivered the longest inaugural speech on record (1½ hours) in a drizzly downpour, only to die of pneumonia 3 weeks later. Here too **Franklin Delano Roosevelt** reassured a nation beset by Depression, declaring that *"the only thing we have to fear is fear itself."* On the East Portico steps in 1961, **John F. Kennedy** set the tone for his presidency with the immortal words, *"Ask not what your country can do for you, but what you can do for your country."*

Inside the **Rotunda,** 180 feet beneath the 9-million-pound iron dome, visitors can join one of the free Capitol building tours which leave every 15 minutes, or you can launch your own tour.

There had once been a small wooden dome sheathed in copper atop the Capitol, but in the 1850s, Congress decided it was unsafe and badly proportioned. They commissioned a much bigger one designed by **Thomas U. Walter** and raised with the engineering expertise of **General Montgomery Meigs.** Erratic financing and then the Civil War plagued the progress of construction, and when the Secretary of War wanted to divert the iron and manpower to the war effort, it looked like the project would be scrapped entirely.

At the time, Washington was a shambles and morale was very low. The Capitol itself had been forced into double duty as a field hospital. **President Lincoln** appraised the situation and decided that construction must go on *"as a symbol that our nation will go on."*

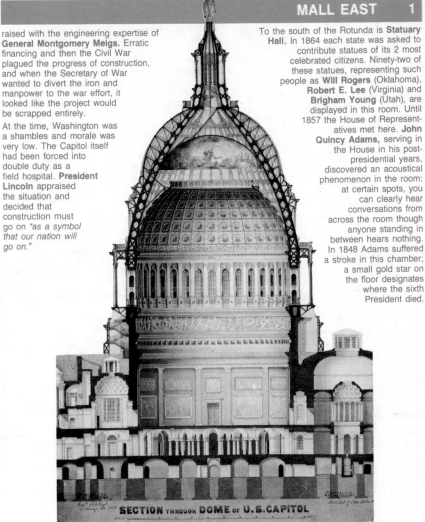

SECTION THROUGH DOME of U.S. CAPITOL

To the south of the Rotunda is **Statuary Hall.** In 1864 each state was asked to contribute statues of its 2 most celebrated citizens. Ninety-two of these statues, representing such people as **Will Rogers** (Oklahoma), **Robert E. Lee** (Virginia) and **Brigham Young** (Utah), are displayed in this room. Until 1857 the House of Representatives met here. **John Quincy Adams,** serving in the House in his post-presidential years, discovered an acoustical phenomenon in the room: at certain spots, you can clearly hear conversations from across the room though anyone standing in between hears nothing. In 1848 Adams suffered a stroke in this chamber; a small gold star on the floor designates where the sixth President died.

And so, while doctors and chaplains ministered to the wounded, workmen hammered overhead. Late in 1863, amidst tremendous fanfare, the 19½-foot **Statue of Freedom** was raised to the top of the Capitol dome. From the distance the figure looks like an American Indian: She wears a helmet rimmed by stars and finished with an eagle's head, actually symbols from ancient mythology. But when first designed by **Thomas Crawford** in the late 1850s, she wore a *Liberty Cap,* the hat worn by freed Roman slaves. **Jefferson Davis,** then Secretary of War and in charge of construction, objected to the anti-slavery implication and had the design changed.

Ironically, Davis left Washington in 1861 to become president of the Confederacy, and the Statue of Freedom, sculpted in Italy, was shipped to America and cast in bronze by slave labor.

Much of the artwork in the Rotunda and throughout the Capitol is a testament to one man: **Constantino Brumidi.** A political refugee, Brumidi spent 25 years (1852-77) painting the Capitol's interior as a way of thanking his adopted homeland. The fresco in the dome's eye, with its 15-foot-high colonial statesmen mingling among classical deities (they look life-size from the Rotunda floor), is Brumidi's work, as is the frieze, which from the floor looks deceptively 3-dimensional.

Four of the 8 large historical paintings lining the Rotunda walls were done by **John Trumball,** an aide to (then) General George Washington. Trumball did not paint from second-hand reports; he was an actual witness to each of the scenes he depicts.

North of the Rotunda, the public areas include the **Old Senate Chamber,** the **President's Room** and the **Old Supreme Court Chamber.** If you wish to sit in the **Visitors' Galleries** in either the **Senate Chamber** or the **House Chamber,** and you're not on the official tour, you'll need to stop by the office of either your senator or congressperson (depending on which chamber you wish to observe) and pick up a gallery pass. If you don't know your representative's name or office location, call the Capitol switchboard at *224-3121.* (For easy access from the Rotunda to the representative's office, use the subway—a must for children!—which links the Capitol with the surrounding office buildings.) Foreign visitors can enter the galleries by showing their passports. Space is reserved in each gallery for handicapped visitors.

Be sure to check beforehand to verify that Congress is in session and, if so, what's on the day's schedule. You can do this by calling *224-3121* or by checking the *Washington Post's* daily *Activities in Congress* column. If an American flag is flying over the chamber you wish to visit (south: House, north: Senate), that legislative body is in session, and if a lantern glows from the Capitol dome, at least one of the chambers is at work.

The action on Capitol Hill builds in intensity in December as the elected officials attempt to tie up loose ends and still make it home for the holidays. If your visit to Washington is primarily to see Congress in action, this is the time to come. Throughout the year if you're looking for drama and pacing, a visit to the chamber galleries is protocol. But the real place to be is at the committee meetings. Schedules are also listed in the *Washington Post*. Just make sure it's an open meeting and show up on time.

When you visit the Capitol, do not be intimidated by it. If you're an American, you're one of the owners.

Open daily except Thanksgiving, Christmas and New Year's 9am-4:30pm. Capitol Rotunda and Statuary Hall open in the summer until 10pm. When the House or Senate is in night session, that wing remains open. Daily tours lasting between 30-45 minutes leave from the Rotunda every 15 minutes. Free. Write your senator or congressperson well in advance to arrange a VIP tour of the Capitol. East Front Entrance at E. Capitol St. on Capitol Hill. Metrorail blue/orange/red lines. 224-3121.

To write your senator:
Senator (name)_____
Senate Office Building
Washington DC 20510

To write your Congressperson:
Congressman (-woman) (name)_____
House Office Building
Washington DC 20515

During the summer, the Capitol's **West Terrace** sets the stage for free evening concerts, beginning at 8pm:
M   US Navy Concert Band
Tu US Air Force Band
W   US Marine Band
F   US Army Band
Special concerts are offered on Memorial Day, July 4th and Labor Day. The West Terrace also affords an incredible view of the city.

If you hear bells ringing while visiting the House of Representatives and its office buildings, it's not an auditory hallucination but a complicated code that tells the representative what's happening on the House floor and if he's needed for a vote. There are 13 different codes and many congresspeople never master them, preferring to call the office of the Clerk of the House to find out what's going on.

1 ring: A teller vote. Congresspersons walk past the Clerk for a simple *yes* or *no* vote. Typically used for less controversial issues since individual votes are not recorded.

2 rings: A formal, electronically recorded vote is in progress. Representatives have 15 minutes to get to the floor and vote.

2 rings-pause-2 rings: A manual roll-call-type vote. This is used only when the electronic voting system is down. Hardly anyone recognizes this signal as it's only been used 3 times in the last 10 years.

2 rings-pause-5 rings: First vote under Suspension of the Rules. This is a procedure in which many bills will be voted on in a hurry, without debate. After the first vote, only 5 minutes are allowed for each succeeding vote.

3 rings: A quorum call. A full 218 members (more than one-half) must be present for business to continue. Members who are not present are marked as absent on their voting records. A quorum call often preceeds an electronically recorded vote on important issues. At other times it may be used as a parliamentary delaying procedure.

4 rings: Adjournment of the House at the end of the day.

6 rings: Recess of the House, for a Joint Session of Congress, for instance.

12 rings: Civil defense warning, nuclear attack.

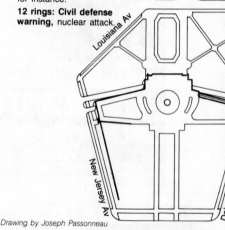

Drawing by Joseph Passonneau

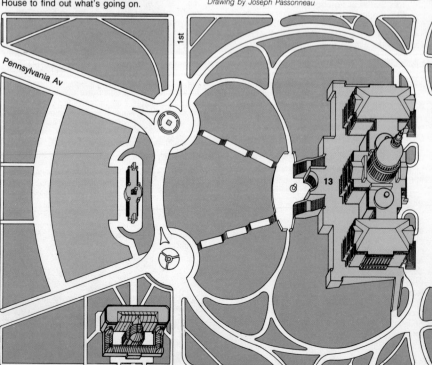

Director's Bests

Elliott Carroll, FAIA
Executive Assistant, Architect of the Capitol

The Cast Iron Dome 1858-1865, **Thomas U. Walter.** Favorite thing: That it couldn't have been built had not cast iron technology advanced, making it possible to bear the new, larger, cantilevered dome on Bulfinch's old masonry drum (1817-1829) which had supported the old copper-covered wooden dome. The old drum is 20 feet back of Walter's stage-set base of ½-inch cast. All inspired by Leningrad's St. Isaac's Cathedral, not St. Paul's or St. Peter's, as popularly supposed.

The Rotunda 1817-1829 **Bulfinch,** 1858-1865, **Walter Trumbull** paintings, 1819-1824. **Brumidi** paintings 1865-1880. The grandest space of all.

Old Senate Chamber 1793-1829, **Latrobe** covered by **Bulfinch.** Restored 1975.

Old Supreme Court 1800-1810, **Latrobe.** Restored 1975.

Tobacco leaf and corn-cob capitals 1800-1810, **Latrobe,** following **Thomas Jefferson's** direction. Survived the British fire of 1814. Tobacco blossoms are white but these are painted red! Artistic license.

The Grotto 1879, **Frederick Law Olmsted,** the elder. A lovely spring house in a glade.

The **view from the West Terraces** (or any window) 1872-present. **Olmsted, Burnham,** et al.

The *Brumidi* **corridor** and stairs 1855-1880. **Walter** and **Constantino Brumidi**

Burial Vault 1817-1829, **Bulfinch** and **Lincoln Catafalque,** 1865. Designed to receive the bodies of **George** and **Martha Washington,** the family refused their removal from Mt. Vernon.

The **Capitol dome** is cast iron painted to look like marble. It must be repainted every 6 or 7 years, a job requiring 600 gallons of paint.

Parks/Open spaces green
Restaurants/Nightlife red
Shops/Galleries violet

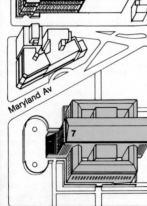

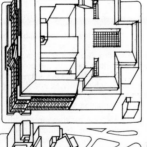

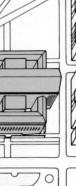

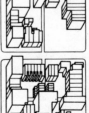

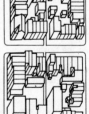

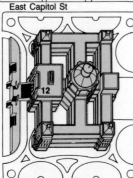

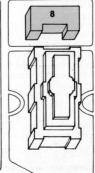

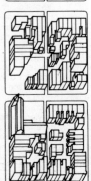

D St

Maryland Av

7

East Capitol St

8

12

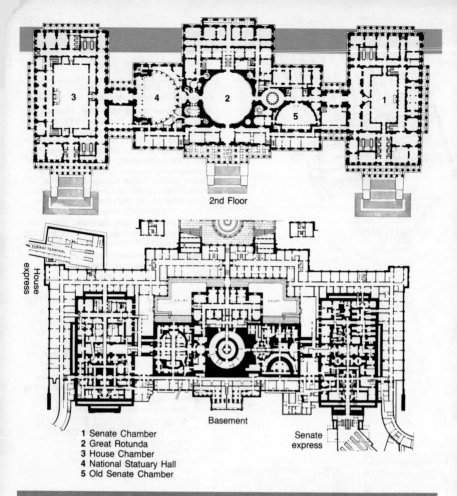

2nd Floor

Basement

1 Senate Chamber
2 Great Rotunda
3 House Chamber
4 National Statuary Hall
5 Old Senate Chamber

Senate
express

The Continental Congress first convened in 1774. From then until 1800, when they moved into official headquarters in the District of Columbia, they resembled nothing so much as a roving band of bedouins in knee breeches. During that time they met in 8 different cities, each having the right to call itself the capital—at least for a moment. Congress was so transitory that in 1783 when a statue in honor of **George Washington** was proposed, **Francis Hopkinson**, a representative from Pennsylvania, suggested that it be mounted on wheels, the better to follow Congress in its wanderings.

Philadelphia was the capital more frequently than any other city, but in 1777, with the British closing in, Congress hightailed it to the town of **Lancaster**, Pennsylvania, which became capital-for-a-day. From Lancaster, Congress moved across the Susquehanna River to **York**, where it remained until June of 1778. **The Articles of Confederation** were passed there, and **Benjamin Franklin** had his press moved up so he could print $1 million worth of much-needed Continental money. Congress moved back to Philadelphia, but was again threatened by the British and moved to **Baltimore**, Maryland, in 1779.

In 1783 the Revolutionary War was over, but the nation was broke and the union tenuous. Congress was once again meeting in Philadelphia and might have continued to do so had a group of soldiers not invaded the city and rioted for back pay. Congress fled to **Princeton**, New Jersey, where it met in **Nassau Hall**, still part of the **Princeton University** campus and then the largest building in the country. However, there wasn't enough room in town for the growing bureaucracy, which soon moved on to **Annapolis**, Maryland, where there was presumably more hotel space. In Annapolis, Congress decided that the new government needed its own city, but no one could agree on the site.

Every town in the country immediately began lobbying to be named capital, including **Trenton**, New Jersey. Congress met there briefly in 1774 before rejecting the proposal. In 1774 the capital was in **New York City**, and in 1789 George Washington was inaugurated there. Later that year Congress moved back to Philadelphia and remained there until 1800.

Debate on where to put the capital was fierce. Northerners wanted it near a financial center, while agrarian Southerners feared the power of northern financiers and special interests. It took a political compromise between **Alexander Hamilton** and **Thomas Jefferson** to decide the issue in 1790. During the Revolutionary War the South had managed to pay her soldiers, but the North had not. Led by Hamilton, the northern states wanted Congress to absorb their debt. The South, led by Jefferson, was opposed. Finally the 2 men worked out a deal whereby the North was relieved of its debt and the South gained the prestige of a national capital.

Congress specified the size of the site and that it be somewhere on the Potomac River, but the exact choice was left to Washington, who had once been a surveyor. Though he was hounded by land speculators, he made a good, independent choice, picking a diamond-shaped area where the Potomac and Anacostia rivers merge. He hoped the Anacostia would provide a deep-water naval port while the Potomac would be a link to western provinces by way of the proposed **Potowmack Canal**. Perhaps it was also no accident that the Capital would be an easy day's ride from Washington's home at **Mt. Vernon**.

Mrs. John Adams, the first First Lady to live in Washington, got lost trying to find the place. She wandered aimlessly for hours until a tramp directed her. In a letter to her daughter, she wrote, *"Woods are all you see, from Baltimore until you reach the city, which is only so in name."*

14 **Spring Grotto.** (1875, **Frederick Law Olmsted**) A cool and quiet hideaway best visited on a hot summer day, designed by the creator of New York's Central Park. *North of Capitol.*

15 **The Peace Monument,** sculpted by **Franklin Simmons** in 1877, is a marble memorial to sailors slain in the Civil War. The figure of America weeps on the shoulder of History. Inscribed in her book: *They died that their country might live. Pennsylvania Ave. at 1st St. NW.*

16 **General Ulysses S. Grant Memorial.** Scores of statues in Washington commemorate wars, great leaders and fallen warriors, yet none is as striking in its realism and so strongly a condemnation of war as this monument in Union Square.

In the center of the installation is the 17-foot bronze of Grant. To the north is the **Cavalry Group.** Seven mounted men prepare to charge. Their officer holds up his sword, his mouth is open as he shouts the advance. To his side a horse has stumbled, pitching its rider headlong onto the mud. The soldier behind pulls desperately on his mount's reins, trying to avoid the fallen man. The group seems alive with tension and movement.

To the south is the **Artillery Group.** Three horses, one with a rider, pull a cart holding a cannon and 3 soldiers. The horses are rearing back in response to a sudden order to turn. Each soldier shows a different face of battle. One is ready another frightened, another weary to the bone.

The sculptor, **Henry Schrady,** was only 31 years old and largely unknown when he was chosen by a jury of the most respected sculptors of his day, including **Augustus Saint-Gaudens** and **Daniel Chester French.** Despite the consternation of the artistic establishment and his own poor health, Shrady plunged into his work, dedicating the remaining 20 years of his life to this single project. The completed memorial was finally dedicated in 1927, 2 weeks after his death. *Union Square, east end of Mall.*

17 **US Botanic Gardens.** (1902, **Bennett, Parsons & Frost**) The 19th-century greenhouse style, epitomized by Syon and Kew Gardens in England, lives on in this tropical mall retreat. The cast-iron and glass Victorian novelty houses ferns, succulents, cacti and the occasional botanical guest; it also provides plants to Congressional offices. Group tours available; call for information. *Admission free. Open daily 9am-5pm. 1st St. at Independence Ave. SW. 225-8333.*

18 **Bartholdi Fountain.** This 1,500 pound cast iron extravaganza (a prize-winner at the 1876 Centennial) was designed by **Frederic Bartholdi,** who also gave us the **Statue of Liberty.** Three colossal women hold up the main basin, which is rimmed with fanciful electric lamps. One of the first public displays of electric illumination, the fountain was a big hit with turn-of-the-century audiences. *Independence Ave. at 1st St. SW.*

19 **Hubert H. Humphrey Building (Department of Health & Human Services).** Completed in 1976, this vigorous, energetic **Marcel Breuer** design is often compared favorably to his nearby HUD building. The carbon monoxide funnels for I-395 (which runs under Capitol Hill) are incorporated into the structure, so sometimes the building appears to smoke. *Independence Ave. between 2nd and 3rd Sts. SW.*

Federal workers make up 36 percent of DC's work force, with service and trade industries also contributing highly. Tourism, DC's second largest industry, brings in over $1 billion every year, and generates about 45,000 jobs.

Introductions/Theaters/Narrative black
Hotels purple
Museums/Architecture blue
Parks/Open spaces green
Restaurants/Nightlife red
Shops/Galleries violet

20 **Voice of America.** This special radio station is charged with broadcasting objective news and facts about the US and its stand on the issues. Some 76 overseas and 34 North American transmitters disseminate the US's views plus cultural programs in 42 languages and to all parts of the globe. On this tour of VOA's headquarters, you can hear broadcasts in Bengali, Slovak, Urdu or Albanian. Tours explain the role of VOA and its parent organization, the **US Information Agency.** *Admission free. Reservations for groups of 4 or more. 30 min. tours M-F except holidays 8:45am, 9:45am, 1:45pm, 2:45pm. 330 Independence Ave. SW, 2nd floor. Metrorail blue/orange lines. 755-4744.*

21 **Vie de France.** ☆ $ Domestic concept of French—fast and furious. Emphasis on baked goods and buttery croissants in the self-service section; the cafe has a variety of sandwiches, omelettes and pseudo-Gallic specials. Perfect for breakfast or a quick lunch. *Americanized French. Open M-F 7:30am-7pm (self-service), 11am-8:30pm (cafe). 600 Maryland Ave. SW. 544-7870*

The Smithsonian Institution. Without a doubt, Washington DC's most quoted understatement is, *"You could spend a week just seeing the Smithsonian."*

Fun Fact: If all the Smithsonian treasures were lined up in one long exhibit and you spent just one second looking at each item, it would take you more than 2½ years of 24-hour-a-day, non-stop touring to see them all—and by then, the Institute would have acquired an additional 2½ million more items.

The Smithsonian collection, which attracts more visitors than any other tourist center in the nation (far outshining Disneyland), is in fact so big that only one percent of its inventory can be displayed at any one time, despite the Institution's 14 museums, galleries and parks in Washington, DC.

Of course, the Smithsonian is in no way limited to exhibits encased in buildings. It is both a seeker and source of education—the patron of thousands of global expeditions, the publisher of over 300 books and monographs each year. Its 9 research centers host scientists ranging in age from the pre-school to the post-graduate level.

When **Thaddeus Lowe** successfully convinced **Abraham Lincoln** to use hot air balloons to observe Civil War military movements and conflicts, the Smithsonian was there. When **John Wesley Powell** led his party of wooden rafts through the raging white waters of the Grand Canyon in 1869, it was under the sponsorship of the Smithsonian. Each time a satellite circles the globe, it owes a part of its history to the Smithsonian and a young experimenter named **Robert Goddard,** who found an encouraging sponsor and publisher in the Institute when no one else would listen. Goddard is today recognized as the father of modern rocketry and of the US space program.

Whatever the field, if the acquisition and propagation of knowledge is involved, so too, undoubtedly, is the Smithsonian Institution.

The criteria for the Institute's work was established in 1826 in one of history's most unusual wills. **James Smithson,** a highly regarded British scientist, decreed that if the nephew who was his only heir died childless, the Smithson fortune would go to the United States of America *"to found at Washington, under the name of the Smithsonian Institution, an establishment for the increase and diffusion of knowledge among men."* The irony of the bequest was that Smithson had never even visited the United States!

Stigmatized through life as the bastard child of a duke and a descendant of **King Henry VII,** Smithson had fought to overcome that albatross by excelling as a scientist. Sadly, despite his many professional accomplishments, including the isolation of zinc carbonate (smithsonite), Smithson never broke free from 19th-century Britain's restrictive obsession with illegitimacy. *"The best blood of England flows in my veins,"* the scientist wrote, *"but this avails me not."*

Smithson's nephew died childless in 1835; 2 years later, to Washington's amazement, the US capital learned that it was heir to more than a half million dollars, a vast sum in that day. Congress appointed **Joseph Henry,** America's most distinguished scientist in the mid-1800s, to act as the Smithsonian's first secretary. Henry's principles still govern the Institution: *"The great object is to facilitate...the promotion of science...the fostering of original research, and enlarging the bounds of human thought."*

By Joseph Henry's decree, no branch of knowledge should be excluded from the Smithsonian's attention. Today, the Institution's channels for disseminating knowledge are almost as varied as its collection of treasures. If you are curious about an object's historical importance or an art work's origin, write to the Smithsonian, and they'll give you their researched opinion. If you have an appetite for astrophysical observations, feed your hunger by calling **Dial-a-Phenomenon** at 357-7000. To get in on a special museum exhibit or event, just **Dial-A-Museum** at 357-2020.

Parking in and around the Mall is extremely limited, and public transportation is recommended (see **Transportation**). On the Metrorail line, convenient stops are at L'Enfant Plaza, the Smithsonian, and the Federal Triangle.

1 Smithsonian Museums
2 Smithsonian Institution Building (Castle)
3 National Air & Space Museum
4 National Museum of Natural History
5 Freer Gallery of Art
6 Hirshhorn Museum and Sculpture Garden
7 National Museum of African Art
8 Anacostia Neighborhood Museum
9 National Museum of American Art
10 National Portrait Gallery
11 National Museum of American History
12, 13 National Gallery of Art
14 Arts & Industries Building
15 Renwick Gallery
16 National Zoological Park

Eight of the Smithsonian's 14 museums and galleries are located on the Mall, forming the hub of the world's largest museum complex.

Introductions/Theaters/Narrative black
Hotels purple
Museums/Architecture blue
Parks/Open spaces green
Restaurants/Nightlife red
Shops/Galleries violet

A system of **information kiosks** and symbols representing major attractions is used throughout the Mall. Each of 37 pagoda-shaped kiosks has a 3-D relief map where points of interest are located with an identifying symbol and accompanied by a written description. Bus-subway and auto routes are on the side panels. To further orient you, graceful Mall lampposts (designed by **Frederick Law Olmsted** are hung with blue and white steel banners, each painted with the identifying symbol of the attraction you are near.

22 The National Air and Space Museum. (1976, **Hellmuth, Obata & Kassabaum**) is the world's most popular museum, and for good reason. Here, in 23 exhibit areas, are reminders of aviation's finest hours: the **Wright Brothers'** 1903 Flyer, **Goddard's** early rockets, **Lindbergh's** *Spirit of St. Louis* (an old story says the aviator himself stopped by one evening to pick up something he'd left in the glove box), a 1927 mail carrier, **Amelia Earhart's** Vega (she made her record-setting transatlantic solo flight in this one), a Douglas DC3 transport plane, **Chuck Yeager's** Bell X-1 (first plane to break the sound barrier), the Mercury *Friendship 7*, the Apollo 11 Command Module *Columbia*, the studio model of Star Trek's *USS Enterprise*, the *Gossamer Condor* (the first successful man-powered aircraft), the list goes on....

Here the difference between education and sheer pleasure is a mighty fine line. You can touch a rock brought back from the lunar surface, feel the excitement and thrill of being on an aircraft carrier's flight deck as the planes take off and land in an all-too-real simulation, walk through an actual *Skylab*, and learn about jet propulsion from a puppet troupe.

The building, which first opened on 4 July 1976, is appropriate to the idea of flight. Huge and hangarlike, with steel frames and trusses supporting both the structure and the aircraft suspended from it, its vast glass curtain walls let in light and splendid Mall views.

This is also the best place to see the *Best Film of the Decade,* as voted by the Independent Film Producers of America. **To Fly** is a 30-minute voyage across America via various methods of flight. Thanks to the **Langley Theater's** innovative *IMAX*® system on which the show is recorded, and the 5-story wide screen, you do indeed feel as if you've left the ground for a very special, unforgettable trip. The film runs several times a day, beginning at 9:30am. Tickets are available on the day of the performance and for the first screening the following day. The box office charge is nominal.

The Langley Theater also screens other films related to air and space travel throughout the day. **Charles Eames'** short film, *Powers of Ten,* narrated by **Philip C.K. Morrison,** is not to be missed. A fascinating multi-media show runs daily at the **Albert Einstein Spacearium** on the second floor. *Nominal admission charge.*

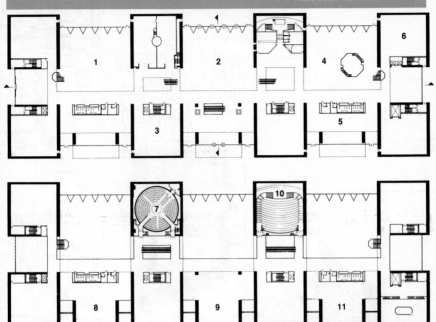

First Floor
1 Air Transportation
2 Milestones of Flight
3 Early Flight
4 Space Hall
5 Satellites
6 Rocketry and
　Space Flight

Second Floor
7 Spacearium
8 Balloons and Airships
9 Pioneers of Flight
10 Theater
11 Apollo to the Moon

Over 36 percent of DC's population—nearly a
quarter of a million residents—is single.

Director's Bests

Walter J. Boyne
Director, National Air and Space Museum,

The **look of a senior citizen as they
touch a rock brought back from the surface
of the moon**—it seems to mean more to them
than it does to a school child, to whom the idea
of space travel is commonplace.

The **juxtaposition of the Wright Flyer of 1903**,
the very first airplane in the world, just 30 feet in
distance and 66 years in time from the **Apollo
11 spacecraft** *Columbia*, in which **Armstrong,
Aldrin and Collins** went to and from the moon.

The **sense of understanding that people seem
to have in looking at Lindbergh's** *Spirit of St.
Louis;* there is awe at the bravery of his
33-hour flight across the Atlantic, from New York
to Paris, as well as a sense that, unlike the
spacecraft, the *Spirit* would be an achievable
thing to master.

The **care with which the handicapped are
attended to.** There are ramps, wheelchairs,
elevator service to all floors, accessible
restrooms and water fountains, material for the
sight or hearing impaired, plus a very courteous
guard force and docent staff which enjoy being
of assistance.

The **crowds waiting eagerly to get in to the
theater** to see *To Fly*, although most of them
have already seen it several times. (The record
holder is supposed to have seen it several
hundred times.)

Walking through *Sky Lab*, the Orbital Workshop
which was really America's first space station, its
gold-covered exterior reflecting the crowds
waiting to pass through.

Looking across an upper gallery, through the
Gossamer Condor, the first successful
manpowered aircraft which is covered in
transparent Mylar, past the *Pioneer 10*, the first

man-made object to leave the solar system, to
the orange and white *Bell X-1* in which **Chuck
Yeager** demonstrated the right stuff in breaking
the sound barrier.

Looking upward at the suspended aircraft
through the glass bubbled roof; the movement
outside of the clouds imparts an illusion of
movement even to the fully-equipped Douglas
DC-3, which, like all the other aircraft, sways
gently in the breeze.

Strolling through the jet age gallery, past
lethal looking jet fighters, into the theater where
a section from **Sid Caesar** and **Imogene Coca's**
Show of Shows depicts Sid *busting the sound
barrier.*

Listening to the dads explain to the kids how
they flew this or that aircraft *during the big war.*

Bending down to look through the sighting
holes in the exhibit on Stonehenge.

**Walking along the galleries and hearing the
polyglot mixture of comments;** seeing that
children and adults from all over the world react
with the same sense of humanity to the triumphs
of modern technology.

Delving into the background of the various
artifacts and realizing that they all proceed from
the same central source of human invention, and
that they are all expressions of human dreams.

Going up to the library on the third floor to do
research in one of the greatest collections of
aviation documentary material in the world.

Taking the short ride out to *Silver Hill*, the Paul
E. Garber Facility where Cellini-like craftsmen
restore 70-year-old aircraft which are little more
than *basket cases* to perfection.

In 1981, per capita income in Washington, DC
was just over $13,000 per year—higher than
any other metropolitan area in the country.

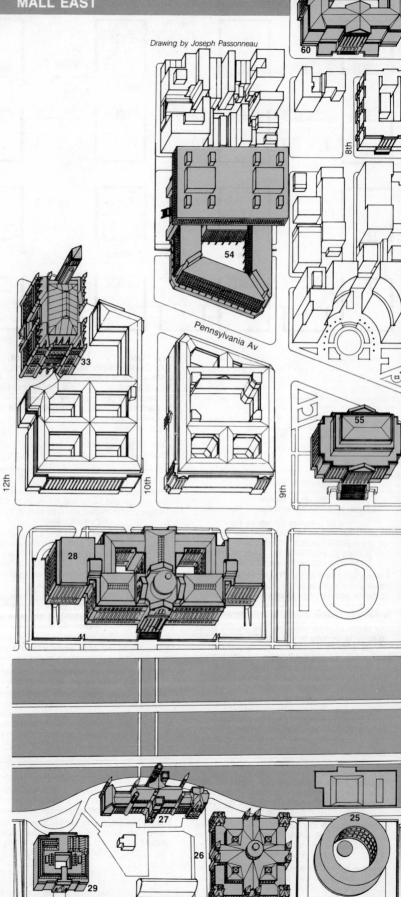

Drawing by Joseph Passonneau

Pennsylvania Av

Independence Av

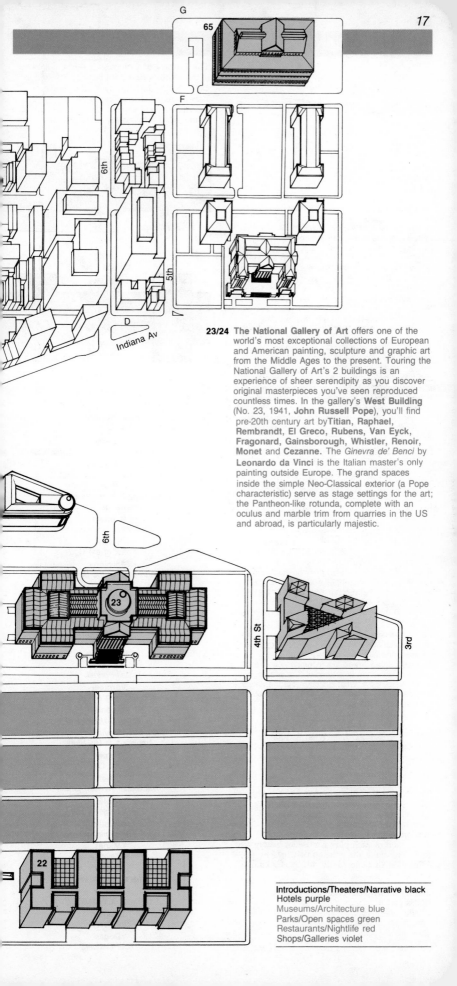

G

65

F

6th

5th

D

Indiana Av

23/24 The National Gallery of Art offers one of the world's most exceptional collections of European and American painting, sculpture and graphic art from the Middle Ages to the present. Touring the National Gallery of Art's 2 buildings is an experience of sheer serendipity as you discover original masterpieces you've seen reproduced countless times. In the gallery's **West Building** (No. 23, 1941, **John Russell Pope**), you'll find pre-20th century art by **Titian, Raphael, Rembrandt, El Greco, Rubens, Van Eyck, Fragonard, Gainsborough, Whistler, Renoir, Monet** and **Cezanne.** The *Ginevra de' Benci* by **Leonardo da Vinci** is the Italian master's only painting outside Europe. The grand spaces inside the simple Neo-Classical exterior (a Pope characteristic) serve as stage settings for the art; the Pantheon-like rotunda, complete with an oculus and marble trim from quarries in the US and abroad, is particularly majestic.

6th

23

4th St

3rd

22

Introductions/Theaters/Narrative black
Hotels purple
Museums/Architecture blue
Parks/Open spaces green
Restaurants/Nightlife red
Shops/Galleries violet

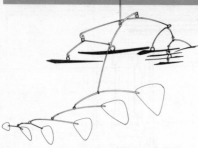

East Building (No. 24). Across the National Gallery Plaza, connected by an underground concourse, is the **East Building** (1978, I.M. Pei). Here you'll find more than a sampling of 20th-century art, including **Alexander Calder's** last major mobile, *Untitled*, and **Joan Miro's** dramatic tapestry *Woman*. **Henry Moore's** ever-changing sculpture, *Knife Edge Mirror Two Piece*, is stationed outside at the entrance portico. The East Building also showcases numerous temporary exhibits throughout the year. One of the best new buildings in the city, the twin triangles fit together to fill the oddly shaped site, leaving only a narrow greenbelt around the perimeter. The old quarry in Tennessee that provided the stone for the West Building's exterior was reopened for this project; Pei carefully designed the new gallery to blend with the mathematical harmonies of the older one—height, color, even the size of the marble blocks reflect the example of the West Building. Inside, the gallery spaces are strong and dramatic, and the roofline is a wonderland of space frames and towers.

Sunday lectures, given in the East Building auditorium at 4pm, feature art historians discussing their own research or part of the Gallery collection. Sunday evening concerts, performed by the **National Gallery Orchestra** or guest artists, are free and begin at 7pm (seating begins at 6pm) in the East Garden Court of the West Building (no concerts in July, August or September).

Free 50-minute introductory tours meet at the main floor entrance M-Sa 11am & 3pm; Su 1pm & 5pm. The **Tour of the Week** takes an in-depth look at one type of painting or one special exhibit; this 50-minute tour begins Tu-Sa 1pm, Su 2:30pm. A **Painting of the Week** is featured in a 15-minute lecture Tu-Sa noon, 2pm; Su 3:30pm & 6pm. Special tours can be arranged by calling 737-4215.

For inexpensive postcards or poster reproductions of works from **Leonardo** to **Picasso**, the **National Gallery Book and Museum Sales Areas** are incomparable. An excellent collection of art books is available, both in the shop in the West Building and the newer one near the *Cascade Cafe* in the underground passageway.

Admission free. Gallery open daily except Christmas and New Year's. Open M-Sa 10am-5pm Su noon-9pm. **West Building:** *Constitution Ave. at 6th St. NW or Madison Dr. at 6th St. NW.* **East Building:** *4th St. between Constitution and Madison Drs. Metrorail blue/orange/red lines. 737-4215.*

The National Gallery of Art has gone high-tech in the form of an interactive laserdisk. The size of an LP, it features crystal clear still frames of 1,645 paintings, sculptures, drawings and prints from the museum and a brief description of each plus a museum history and tour. On sale at the giftshop or write, VPI/VIDMAX Suite 734 E. 4th St., Cincinnati, OH 45202.

Introductions/Theaters/Narrative black
Hotels purple
Museums/Architecture blue
Parks/Open spaces green
Restaurants/Nightlife red
Shops/Galleries violet

The Library of Congress is the proud owner of the **world's first cookbook**, published in 1475. Written in Latin by Vatican librarian **Bartolomeo Platina**, one of the recipes describes a good version of ravioli, to be boiled as long as it takes to say 2 Our Fathers.

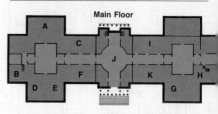

Main Floor

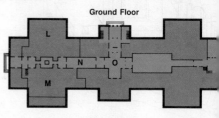

Ground Floor

Director's Bests

J. Carter Brown
Director, National Gallery of Art

West Building:

Duccio
Nativity
The Calling of the Apostles Peter and Andrew

Fra Angelico
The Adoration of the Magi
(with Fra **Filippo Lippi**)

Leonardo da Vinci
Ginevra de' Benci

Raphael
The Alba Madonna

Bellini
The Feast of the Gods

Giorgione
The Adoration of the Shepherds

Titian
Venus with a Mirror

van Eyck
The Annunciation

El Greco
Laocoon

Rembrandt
The Mill
Self-Portrait

Vermeer
The Girl with a Red Hat

Fragonard
A Young Girl Reading

David
Napoleon in His Study

Turner
Keelmen Heaving in Coals by Moonlight

Stuart
The Skater (William Grant)

Cole
The Voyage of Life

Whistler
The White Girl

Manet
Gare Saint-Lazare

Monet
The Artist's Garden at Vetheuil

Renoir
A Girl with a Watering Can

Gauguin
Self-Portrait

Degas
Four Dancers

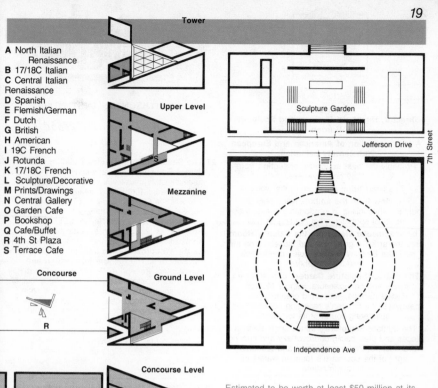

Tower

A North Italian
   Renaissance
B 17/18C Italian
C Central Italian
   Renaissance
D Spanish
E Flemish/German
F Dutch
G British
H American
I 19C French
J Rotunda
K 17/18C French
L Sculpture/Decorative
M Prints/Drawings
N Central Gallery
O Garden Cafe
P Bookshop
Q Cafe/Buffet
R 4th St Plaza
S Terrace Cafe

Upper Level

Mezzanine

Concourse

Ground Level

Sculpture Garden

Jefferson Drive

7th Street

Independence Ave

Concourse Level

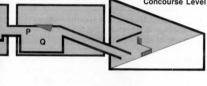

Ground Floor:

Kress bronzes
Garbisch paintings
Widener rooms

East Building:

Picasso
Family of Saltimbanques
Kandinsky
Improvisation 31
Matisse
Large Composition with Masks
Pollock
Number 1, 1950 (Lavender Mist)
View from the Mezzanine
looking west to the West Building
View from the Upper Level Bridge to see both
Calder and Miro

The Hirshhorn Museum and Sculpture Garden
(1974, **Gordon Bunshaft/Skidmore, Owing &
Merrill**) For the modern art enthusiast, this is the
stuff of which dreams are made. The museum is
in fact the dream child of American immigrant
and self-made millionaire **Joseph Hirshhorn.**
The industrialist spent over 40 years indulging
his love of art and championing the cause of
many yet-to-be-discovered American artists at a
time when most Americans still looked to Europe
for artistic legitimacy.

Estimated to be worth at least $50 million at its
premiere, at that time the Hirshhorn collection
consisted of over 6,000 items, including some
2,000 pieces of sculpture. Under the
Smithsonian's guidance, the collection has
continued to grow and now boasts such
sculptors as **Rodin, Brancusi, David Smith,
Calder** and **Henry Moore.** The museum's 19th-
and 20th-century painter credits list such noteables
as **Winslow Homer, Mary Cassatt, John Marin,
Josef Albers, Georgia O'Keeffe, Andy Warhol,
Jim Dine, Kenneth Noland** and **Jackson
Pollock,** to name just a few. The Hirshhorn also
mounts several major loan exhibitions each year,
concentrating on a particular artist, medium, style
or theme.

The controversial doughnut-shaped building (all
the circular forms look concentric, but they're
actually very slightly off-center) was designed to
maximize wall space while minimizing sun
damage to the art. Hence there are no exterior
windows, but the third-floor balcony offers a
breath-taking view.

Be sure to spend at least a few moments in the
sunken garden adjacent to the museum: the
terraces, reflecting pool and works by master
sculptors make it one of the city's most
evocative settings. One of the most rewarding
stops in the sculpture garden is the **Burghers of
Calais.** This haunting piece dramatizes the
moment when the town fathers of Calais, France,
gave themselves up to British invaders so that
their town might be saved. The 6 proud,
anguished men wear nooses around their necks
as they prepare to hand over the keys to the
city. Sculpted in 1886 by **Auguste Rodin,** it's
worthy of a moment's reflection. Thursday and
Friday evenings the Hirshhorn sponsors
independently produced film shorts, representing
the best work of both local and national
filmmakers (admission free; not held during
summer).

*Free guided, walk-in museum tours are available
M-Sa 10:30am, noon and 1:30pm; Su 12:30, 1:30
and 2:30pm. Special tour arrangements can be
made by calling 357-3235 at least 2 weeks in
advance. Call also to find out about free films
and lectures held periodically in the auditorium.
No baby strollers are allowed in the galleries—
exchange them for an infant backpack loaned at
the checkroom. Museum shop. Cafeteria open in
the summer months. Museum open daily except
Christmas 10am-5:30pm (open till 7:30pm in the
summer). Independence Ave. at 8th St. SW.
Metrorail blue/orange lines. 357-1461/357-2700.*

Director's Bests

Abram Lerner
Director, Hirshhorn Museum and Sculpture Garden

A great **collection of American and European 20th-century paintings.**

Probably the **best sculpture collection** from 1850 on, anywhere.

The **least tiring museum** in the world.

The **view from the ambulatories** onto the fountain while lolling in comfortable chairs; these are ideal spots for quiet reading as well.

The **spectacular view from the Balcony Room** onto the array of great national museums on the mall; the Balcony Room's quiet, comfortable, restful atmosphere.

The outdoor **Sculpture Garden,** a must for art lovers and connoisseurs, with its Moores, Rodins, Smiths, etc., amid greenery-lined pathways; the Garden's reflecting pool and the splattering sound of its fountain.

The outdoor **Sculpture Plaza's** large abstract pieces and their *backgrounds* of sky and curving architecture; the dramatic roar and refreshing sight of the courtyard's fountain waters in summertime.

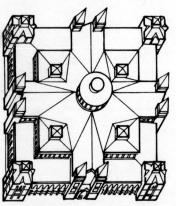

JP

26 **The Arts & Industries Building** (1880, **Cluss & Schule**) was restored in 1976 to house one of the most extensive collections of American Victoriana in existence. Many of the items, collectively called *1876: A Centennial Exhibition* , are the same items displayed in the Philadelpia Exposition of 1876: horse-drawn carriages, French lace, pistols, silverware, furniture and unusual objets d'art, all celebrating the exciting brass glory that typified America 100 years ago. Even the building, built as a partner to the administration building next door, is a Queen Anne Victorian fantasy: an elaborate polychrome brick affair with giant industrial trusses and meandering iron balconies. The museum shop includes many Victorian temptations as well as a photo booth where visitors, dressed in period costumes, can be captured in a daguerrotype portrait.

The Discovery Theater, open Wednesday through Sunday (admission charge), offers a changing series of programs, ranging from puppet shows to mimes to dance troupes.

Admission free. For show times, tickets and reservations, call 357-1500. For tour information, call 357-1481. Museum open daily except Christmas 10am-5:30pm (open till 9pm in the summer). Jefferson Dr. at 9th St. W. Metrorail blue/orange lines. 357-1300/357-2700.

The Algonquin Indians who lived along the lower river called it Potowmek—the trading place.

SMITHSONIAN INSTITUTION

Washington, D.C. 20560
U.S.A.

27 **The Smithsonian Institution Building.** (1849, **James Renwick**). Popularly known as *the Castle* because of its marvelous roofline collection of spires, towers, turrets and crenellated parapets, this was the Smithsonian's first building. Built of red Seneca sandstone and widely recognized as one of the finest Gothic Revival buildings in America, its occupants include the Institute's administrative offices as well as the headquarters for the **Woodrow Wilson International Center for Scholars.** The **Visitors Information and Associates' Reception Center** in the **Great Hall** makes an excellent departure point for a tour of the Smithsonian's Mall complex. A slide show, available in 4 languages, covers some of the Smithsonian's best-known treasures. On the way out, stop by the **Crypt Room,** the tomb of the Institution's benefactor, **James Smithson.** *Admission free. Open daily except Christmas 10am-5:30pm, till 7:30pm during summer. 1000 Jefferson Dr. SW at 10th St. Metrorail blue/orange lines. 357-2700.*

28 **The National Museum of Natural History** (1911, **Hornblower & Marshall**) and the **National Museum of Man** is a treasure chest of natural sciences. Here you will see the models, live and mounted specimens, dioramas, recreations, prototypes and artifacts used to study man's evolution, human cultures, dinosaurs, fossils, amphibians, reptiles, birds, sea organisms, mammals, insects, plants, rocks, minerals and meteorites—in short, the entire planet Earth!

There's really too much here to digest in one visit, but some of the highlights are: **Uncle Beazley,** the life-size model of a Triceratops dinosaur that greets you at the Mall entrance; a 13-foot-tall African bush elephant (you can't miss him; he's the largest known specimen of the largest land animal of modern times); a 3.1 billion-year-old fossil of a South African fig tree; dinosaur skeletons; an audio-visual show describing Ice Age glaciation's effects on the earth's surface; a freeze-dried Ice Age bison recently discovered by Alaskan gold miners; and one of the Easter Island's famous stone heads. And that's only the beginning!

There is also a life-size model of a 92-foot whale; a living coral reef community housed in a king-size aquarium complete with waves; and in the mind-boggling **Hall of Gems,** more than 1000 precious and semi-precious stones, the star of which is the legendary and infamous **Hope Diamond,** a 45.5-carat dazzler with a curse to match its beauty.

Another must-see is the **Insect Room** which features thousands of live insects going about their daily routines, oblivious to the funny-looking people on the other side of the plexiglass.

Think that's everything? That's not even the icing! The Museum of Natural History has a catalog of over 60 million objects, but only a fraction of that inventory is on display at any one time. Especially if you have children, you'll want to visit the **Discovery Room,** where you can touch, smell and in some cases even taste hundreds of natural history specimens ranging from elephant tusks to crocodile heads to herb seeds. Discovery room open M-Th noon-2:30pm, F & Sa 10:30am-3:30pm. One adult for every 3 children is required. For group reservations or information call 357-2747.

The median age of Washington residents is 31.8 years.

Free lectures are offered every Friday at noon. Reservations required. Free concerts sponsored by the **Smithsonian Performing Arts Series** also take place at the museum. Call 357-2700.

Free walk-in tours of the museum are available daily at 10:30am and 1:30pm. Special afternoon adult tours are given occasionally. Group tours, including those for school children, should be booked well in advance by calling 357-2747. Receivers for a self-guided audio tour of the exhibits are available in the second floor rotunda (charge).

Admission free. Open daily except Christmas 10am-5:30pm (till 7:30pm in summer). Cafeteria and excellent museum shop. Museum located at Constitution Ave. at 10th St. NW. Mall entrance: Madison Dr. between 9th and 12th St. NW. Metrorail blue/orange lines. 357-2700.

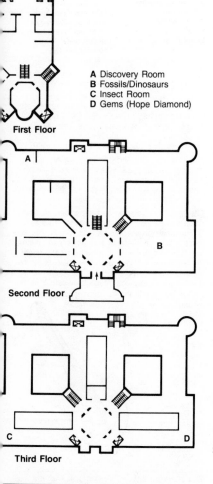

A Discovery Room
B Fossils/Dinosaurs
C Insect Room
D Gems (Hope Diamond)

First Floor

Second Floor

Third Floor

Hsing-Hsing and **Ling-Ling,** the only 2 pandas in America, can be found at the National Zoological Park, where they feast daily on rations of 60 pounds of domestic, fresh-cut bamboo. Any offspring, expected since their US arrival in 1972, will weigh no more than 4 to 5 ounces at birth and reach full maturity, 250 pounds, at age 7.

JUST FOR KIDS

1 Leave the kids to **Uncle Beazley** for a while—he's a 25-foot-long replica of a Triceratops, a dinosaur from the Cretaceous Period. Kids can climb all over the sculpture by Louis Paul Jones at the Smithsonian's National Museum of Natural History.

2 Let the kids loose on the mall between the Smithsonian museums to **chase pigeons.**

3 Buy a bag of peanuts and let the kids feed the hundreds of **polite and amusing squirrels** that abound on the lawns of the Capitol grounds.

4 Visit the **Lincoln and Jefferson memorials** in the evening, as these monuments are lit up and especially memorable for a young person.

5 Don't forget to **explore the water fountains and mossy cave** that are half hidden behind trees and bushes on the right side of the Capitol lawn facing Pennsylvania Avenue—a secret hiding place guaranteed to delight the young adventurer.

6 Make sure you **visit the sidewalk** that connects the National Gallery of Art with the East Building. The neat thing is that it's underground!

7 Paddle-boats are always fun, and you can find them at the Tidal Basin. Rent from Thompson's Boathouse, 15th St. and Maine Ave. SW. Open late April to mid-October. 484-3475; rentals, 333-9543.

8 Equally exciting and less strenuous are the 2 **boat trips that run down the Potomac.** Washington Boat Lines offers a cruise to Mt. Vernon daily, which includes a sightseeing stopover there. There's also a cruise departing from the Lincoln Memorial Dock or from Georgetown at the end of Wisconsin Ave. NW. There are light snacks available on board, and passenger parking available at the dock's parking lot. For schedule and fare information call 554-8000.

9 For some fast-paced excitement, take the kids to **Skelterama,** which offers safe go-carts on an outdoor track. The carts go about 12 mph, and adults must ride with children under 8 years of age. Admission charge. 301-864-0110 for directions.

10 Horseback riding is available all year round at the Rock Creek Park Horse Center, located on Military and Glover roads NW. The center is experienced with children, and handicapped children as well; a call ahead is recommended if special attention will be needed. 362-0117.

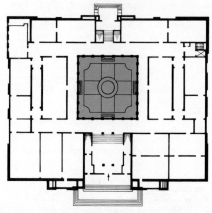

29 The Freer Gallery of Art (1923, **Charles Platt**) is a highly specialized collection dominated by oriental art but including late 19th-century to early 20th-century American art which shows a Far Eastern influence. What may seem to be an unusual combination is in fact a reflection of the tastes and passions of one man. **Charles Lang Freer,** a wealthy Detroit businessman, began studying and collecting Eastern art on the advice of his close friend, American artist **James McNeill Whistler.** The vibrant *Peacock Room,* permanently installed in the museum, is the work of Whistler and is worth a visit.

Only about 8 percent of the collection—which includes over 1,400 drawings, paintings and prints from its American catalog and over 24,000 articles from the Orient—are on display at any one time, but requests can be made to see anything in the collection. According to Freer's 1919 will, no addition is to be made to the American collection and nothing is to be loaned to or from either collection. This ensures visitors who have come to see a particular object that it will in fact be in-house.

The Oriental collection has been augmented, per Freer's instructions, with over 10,000 pieces since the benefactor's death. All were carefully chosen as being of the highest quality and an unquestionable complement to the core collection. Freer's will also included funds for the museum building, a subtle granite Florentine palazzo which provides an elegant and quiet background for the art, and for an endowment for the study and care of the collection, as well as for further research into Eastern art.

Since its 1923 opening, the Freer Gallery of Art has become a mecca for students and scholars of Oriental art. Their primary congregating point is the lower level library which contains more than 30,000 volumes, half of them in Oriental languages.

Admission free. Free guided tours are given daily. Special group tours can be arranged by calling 357-2104 at least 2 weeks in advance. Free lectures are given throughout the year. Gallery open daily except Christmas 10am-5:30pm. Jefferson Dr. at 12th St. SW. Metrorail blue/orange lines. 357-2104/357-2700

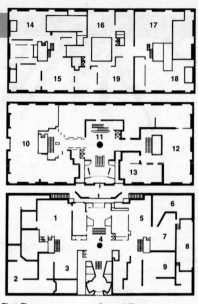

First Floor
1 Atom Smashers
2 Medical Sciences
3 Mathematics
4 Foucault Pendulum
5 Farm Machinery
6 American Maritime
  Enterprise
7 Vehicle Hall
8 Railroads
9 Electricity

Second Floor
10 A Nation of Nations
11 Star-Spangled Banner
12 We the People
13 First Ladies' Gowns

Third Floor
14 Ceramics
15 Printing and Graphic Arts
16 Money and Medals
17 Armed Forces History
18 Ordnance
19 Photography

NATIONAL MUSEUM
of
AMERICAN HISTORY

30 The **National Museum of American History.** (1964, **McKim, Mead & White;** completed by **Steinmann, Cain & White**) is filled with all the things Americans love too much to throw away, even though we're not sure why we got a few of them in the first place.

The museum collection began in 1858 when the US Patent Office transferred its overcrowded cabinet of curiosities to the Smithsonian. Then in 1876 came a windfall of exhibits from Philadelphia's Centennial Exposition. What you see today is an excellent cross-section of America's scientific, political, cultural and technological histories.

Behind the pink Tennessee marble exterior, the box-like building stores such highlights as the **Country Store Post Office** from Headsville, West Virginia, circa 1861 (you can still post your mail here, and it'll go out with a special Smithsonian Station postmark); the **Foucault Pendulum** which demonstrates the earth's rotation by knocking down red pegs, to the delight of visitors; farm machinery from a time when farming was strictly a family business; a **Conestoga wagon;** a 1913 **Ford Model T** (manufacturer's suggested retail price: $325); one of **Thomas Edison's** first phonographs; the first typewriter (1829); a 1790 chemistry lab which includes equipment used by Joseph Priestly; **George Washington's** false teeth; and a 280-ton steam locomotive. And that's just the first floor.

On the second floor, among many other things, you'll see the original **Star Spangled Banner,** the one **Francis Scott Key** saw *by the dawn's early light* over Fort McHenry in 1814; original home interiors dating from the 1600s to the 1900s and ranging from a colonial Virginia parlor to a California rancher's kitchen; campaign paraphernalia; a pocket compass used by **Lewis and Clark;** the table and chairs used when **Robert E. Lee** surrendered at Appomatox;

gowns worn by every first lady since **Martha Washington;** and...well, you get the idea.

The **first floor** showcases sciences and technology, the **second floor** concentrates on social and political history; the **third floor** focuses on stamps, coins, glass, ceramics, musical instruments, photography, communication and graphic arts.

The Navy's jazz band performs every Wednesday on the **East Patio** at noon (in the auditorium during inclement weather). Traditional American musical instruments are played in the museum from 11-noon weekdays.

The recently relocated and expanded Museum Shop features current titles published by the Smithsonian presses as well as handicrafts and items—from needlepoint and pottery to children's folk toys and jewelry—that authentically relate to the exhibitions. The shop's new false entrance, located opposite the museum's popular pendulum centerpiece, leads browsers to a bridge that overlooks the expanded basement location. *Admission free. Open daily 10am-5:30pm except Christmas & New Year's. Extended hours during summer. Free walk-in tours and group tours are available, but the schedule is not a permanent one; call 357-1481 for information. A special quilt tour takes place every Tuesday at 11 am. 356-2700.*

The beautiful city of Washington was not always so breathtaking. In 1801, a traveler characterized it as *"a capital of miserable huts."* Fifty years later a Senator decried *"the abominable nuisance of cows, horses, sheep and goats running through the city."* Today, its more than 250,000 registered motor vehicles have a similar clogging effect!

Director's Bests

Roger G. Kennedy
Director, National Museum of
American History

With regard to this Museum, I do have some favorite spots. They are the **radio shack** next to the engine room in the great ocean liner where one can lean back, listen and imagine oneself on board any of the *Queens* or the *Normandie;* the quiet place where the fountain runs in the **Ceramics and Glass Hall** where the glazed and transitory serenity of a thousand households comes together and imposes a tiptoeing reverence; the **alchemists' chamber** where one does not have to be a Jungian to feel a deep sense of mystery; the **drug store** that out-drug stores any other drug store; and the **Palm Court** that out-Palm Courts any other Palm Court outside of San Francisco. I like the feeling of America's town square centering around the **Jacksonville, Illinois bandstand** at the west end of the building, with the Washington Monument looming above us to remind us of our aspirations. There are other things around town which I like: **the way in which the dome of the Jefferson Memorial tips its hat** to the dome of the National Gallery, and both remind us of the dome there should have been on the City Hall, now the District Courts Building; the **pink color** that appears in the flesh of the National Gallery building when it has just taken a bath in the rain; the second Washington Monument, that is, **Arlington House; George Hadfield's Van Ness Memorial** in Rock Creek Cemetery and the splendid reluctance of Old Town Alexandria to become Georgetown. That ought to hold us for a while.

Infinity, a gleaming strip of stainless steel stretched into a lyrical loop that turns in on itself, was sculpted by **Jose de Rivera** in 1967. It is the first piece of abstract art commissioned by the government. The sculpture makes a full revolution on its base every 6 minutes. Madison Dr. NW at Museum of American History.

Departmental Auditorium. (1935, **Arthur Brown, Jr.**) The unusually dynamic sculpture in the exterior pediments hints at the opulence within. Although the Neo-Classic/Beaux-Arts theater style appeared in movie houses nationwide at the time, this is one of the few where all

the rich materials you see—gold, marble, crystal—are the real thing. The 1300-seat auditorium is used mainly for ceremonial events. Constitution Ave. between 12th and 14th Sts. NW.

Pavilion at the Old Post Office (original building, 1899, **W. Edbrooke**; restoration, 1983, **Arthur Cotton Moore**) The **Evans Development Company** was the power behind a first-class mix of 50 specialty shops, 5 restaurants and cafes and 16 food kiosks that serve quick cuisine from tacos and curries to crepes and ice cream. It's the capital's newest and most inspired indoor mall, built into an old and

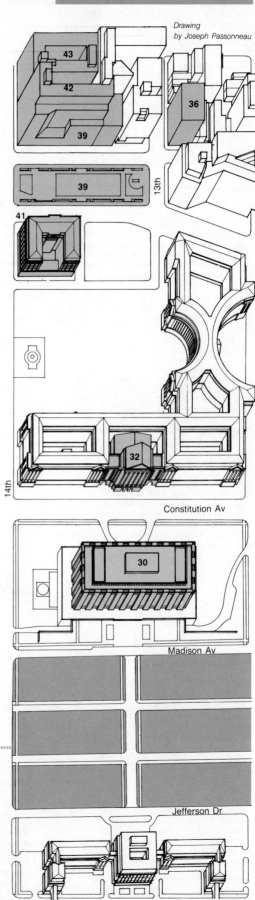

Drawing
by Joseph Passonneau

13th

14th

Constitution Av

Madison Av

Jefferson Dr

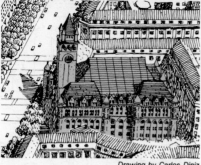

Drawing by Carlos Diniz

significant Romanesque Revival chateau that had been threatened by demolition. The 315-foot clock tower is the third tallest structure in DC. The stunning atrium is accented with Victorian brass fittings, red oak woodwork and frosted glass; the retail and restaurant arcade is bustling, skylit and filled with the aroma of international foods. The interior focal point is the stage, where free live entertainment—dancers, musicians, magicians—is a pleasant diversion for afternoon shoppers out for a fast lunch.

A feisty example of urban revitalization, the Pavilion is pumping new life into the staid and bureaucratic **Federal Triangle**. Because the Old Post Office is a federal building, retailers had to wait for the 1976 *Cooperative Use Act* to share open space with the government offices housed in the top 7 floors. But the 3 lower levels now form an impulse-shopper's paradise, offering a diversity of merchandise from penny postcards at **Penn Station** to designer jewelry at **Impulse**. **Gifts at The Pavilion** offers high-ticket items by **Boda, Seiko** and **Kosta**. **Kinder Haus Toys** features imported children's playthings while **Modigliani** caters to adults with its silky lingerie and sultry perfumes. **Have a Heart** specializes in anything in the heart motif, and **The Upper Duck** favors themes having to do with our web-footed friends.

Open daily. 1100 Pennsylvania Ave. NW. Metrorail blue/orange lines. 289-4224.

34 The Bread Oven. ☆☆$ Now that downtown Washington has been revitalized, this branch of the popular 19th St. restaurant should attract the theater-and-museum crowd. The airy, basket-filled dining room, gracious service and nicely prepared French fare—bouillabaisse, pates and terrines, salade nicoise—provide a delightful dining experience at a reasonable price. *French. Lunch M-Sa 11:30am-3pm; dinner M-Th 5:30-9pm, F & Sa till 11pm. Closed Su. Reservations required for 5 or more. 1201 Pennsylvania Ave. NW. 737-7772.*

35 Danker's. $$ It'll do in a pinch due to its central location. *American. Open daily 11am-midnight. 1209 E. St. NW. 628-2330.*

The latest presidential ratings, by the Journal of American History, ranks our chiefs of state as follows:

Greats	Kennedy
Lincoln	Madison
F.D.R.	Monroe
Washington	John Q. Adams
Jefferson	Cleveland
Near Greats	**Average**
Teddy Roosevelt	McKinley
Wilson	Taft
Jackson	Van Buren
Truman	Hoover
Above Average	Hayes
John Adams	Arthur
Lyndon Johnson	Ford
Eisenhower	Carter
Polk	Benjamin Harrison

Jacqueline Kennedy, on her first night in the White House: *"I felt like a moth hanging on a windowpane."*

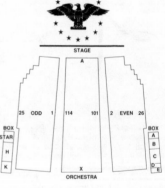

36 Warner Theater. The 2,000-seat theater opened in 1926 as a vaudeville showcase then served as a movie house during the '30s. The Warner Brothers bought it in 1948 and turned it into a major Washington playhouse. The classic theater's gilded ceiling and art deco fixtures add to the magic of the evening's concert or play. *513 13th St. NW. Metrorail blue/orange/red lines. 626-1050.*

37 Hunan Taste. ☆☆$$ Exciting Hunan-Szechuan dishes are featured on the mile-long menu. Recommended for those adventurous in both palate and mind. *Chinese. Open M-Sa 11:30am-11pm. 519 13th St. NW. 347-5281*

38 Thai Room. ☆$ Forget the garish decor and attend instead to the intricately spiced and frequently flaming soups, skewered meats and *pad thai*, a heavenly mixture of thin noodles, shrimp and vegetables. *Thai. Open M-F 11:30am-2:30pm, 5-10pm; Sa 5-10pm. Closed Su. Reservations accepted. 527 13th St. NW (F St. NW). 638-2444.*

39 National Theater. (Seats 1672) Established in 1835, the National's stage has seen more performances than any other theater in the country. Recently purchased by the Shubert organization, the theater can now offer Broadway's best, giving the Kennedy Center some strong competition. It has also just undergone a $6 million renovation in which designer **Oliver Smith** recaptured the original building's aura with Federal period furnishings. The theater reopened with David Merrick's *42nd Street*. Saturday programs for children. *1321 E. St. NW. 628-6161.*

WASHINGTON CONVENTION CENTER

Welton Beckett Associates Architects

Dion Building. (1984, **David Childs**) This huge, sparkling new building is a modern salute to the monolithic old office blocks that surround it. Heavy columns, Roman barrel vaults and a limestone facade give it a Baroque flair, but its sheer size (12 stories, 1.2 million square feet of office space, and over 1200 windows) puts it squarely in the 20th century. Inside, over a quarter acre of Greek and Italian tile paves the Grand Court, and a waterfall plunges down from the skylight 6 stories overhead. *1201 Pennsylvania Ave. NW. 393-1400.*

Western Plaza. (1980, **Venturi, Rauch and Scott Brown**) The block-long piazza was built to resolve the disrupted axis between the Capitol and the White House. Engravings in the raised marble terraces form a map of L'Enfant's original plan for the city, including details of the floor plans for the White House and Capitol; seating, statues and greenery frame the park and add human scale. *1300 block of Pennsylvania Ave. NW.*

J.J. Mellon's. ☆ ☆ $$$ First-class American food at its most earnest. Barbequed swordfish, fresh seafood, dry-aged prime beef and milk-fed veal are raw materials for the upscale Yankee cuisine. Reliable wine list with a few pleasant surprises. *American. Open M-Th 11:30am-9:30pm, Fri 11:30am-11pm, Sa 4:30-11pm. Closed Su. 1201 Pennsylvania Ave. NW. 737-5700.*

District Building. (1908, **Cope & Stewardson**) Once reviled as a monstrosity, this overblown classic Beaux-Arts edifice is now finding many fans. *Pennsylvania Ave. at 14th St. NW.*

J.W. Marriott. *Moderate/expensive.* Washington's newest convention hotel is located next door to the National Theater; ask about special theater packages when the National's stage is hosting Broadway shows. The acclaimed **National Center** collection of specialty shops, a **Rouse Company** development, is accessible through the hotel's lobby. Health club for guests. *1331 Pennsylvania Ave. NW. 393-2000/800-228-9290.*

National Center. The newest of downtown Washington's impulse malls: 125,000 square feet of retail shopping pleasures—more than 100 boutiques (from **Casual Corner** to **Joyce Selby**), fast food shops and restaurants (from **Roy Rogers** to **American Cafe**). The dark wood and brass interior opens to the lobby of the **J.W. Marriott's** new flagship hotel and extends to the newly restored **National Press Building** at the east end of the block. Fall '84 completion date. *13th & F Sts. NW.*

Colorado Building. (1922, **Ralph Townsend**) A wild array of garish ornamentation encrusts the facade, but sleek, modern influences still shine through. *14th & G Sts. NW.*

German Deli. ☆ $ Classic home-cooking of Valkyrian proportions—landjaeger sausage, *kalbschnitzel,* sauerbrauten and sauerkraut— served with oom-pah-pah piano music on Saturday nights. *German. Open M-Sa lunch 11am-4pm, dinner 4-10pm. 1331 H St. NW. 347-5732.*

Franklin School Building. (1868, **Adolph Cluss**) The ornate brickwork, mansard roof and Italianate window arches of this building brought new prestige to public schoolhouses and influenced their design citywide. The children of presidents **Andrew Johnson** and **Chester Arthur** studied here, and **Alexander Graham Bell** made his first light-transmitted, wireless telephone call from the building. *13th & K Sts. NW.*

Bus Stations. Greyhound. *1110 New York Ave. NW, 565-2662.*

DC ranks Number 1 in number of women in the workforce, with 761,480-plus working women, or 47.50 percent.

Introductions/Theaters/Narrative black
Hotels/purple
Museums/Architecture blue
Parks/Open spaces green
Restaurants/Nightlife red
Shops/Galleries violet

48 Washington Convention Center. This sparkling state-of-the-art meeting hall has come to symbolize downtown DC's intensive urban renewal effort. After 2½ years and $99 million, the center opened in 1983. Since that time it has hosted 7 major national conventions and trade shows and over 30 public shows—from car, boat and RV exhibitions, to antique, flower and travel shows, political rallies and the local high school district's graduation ceremonies. All this is estimated to have brought in over $30 million in spending by out-of-towners—proof that Downtown DC is worth the spruce-up efforts. The Convention Center provides 378,000 square feet of show and exhibit space, 40 meeting rooms, and ultra-modern facilities—from audio/visual support to language translation, to satellite conferencing. *New York Ave. to H St. NW, 9th to 11th Sts NW. Metrorail red/blue/orange lines, exit Metro Center; or Metrorail red line, exit Gallery Place. 789-1600.*

49 Martin Luther King Library. (1972, **Ludwig Mies van der Rohe**) The main branch of the DC public library system is more than just a stack of books. Besides sponsoring a citywide arts program, the library's permanent collection of paintings, sculpture and photographs is on display in the **Anteroom Gallery** and throughout the building. There are programs for children, poetry readings, theatrical performances and music concerts. But back to the stacks: Among the system's vast offering are the **Washingtoniana Room,** the largest collection of DC-related information in the world, including books, newspapers, registers, photos, etc. from the beginning of the 19th century; and the **Star Library,** masses of information from the old *Washington Star* newspaper. The simple black steel and glass box epitomizes Miesian design and was among his final works. Underground parking. *Open daily M-Th 9am-9pm, F & Sa 9am-5:30pm, Su 1-5pm. 901 G St. NW. 727-1111.*

50 Riggs Bank. (1891, **James G. Hill**) One of the few Chicago School buildings in a city which preferred European Beaux-Arts styles over the sinuous, clean look of the American Midwest. *9th and F St. NW.*

51 Woodward & Lothrop has been Washington's dependable, full-service department store since 1880, successfully catering to both the haute couture and budget-minded shopper with a wide range of styles and merchandise. Its 16 satellite stores in the metropolitan area underscore the popularity of *Woodies,* as Washingtonians call it. *Open Tu, W, F 10am-7pm; M, Th 10am-9pm; Sa 10am-6pm; Su noon-6pm. 11th & F Sts. NW. Metrorail blue/orange/red lines. 347-5300.*

52 Petersen House. This house, across the street from Ford's Theatre, is where government leaders carried the dying **President Lincoln** in 1865. The parlor where **Mary Todd Lincoln** waited through the night, and the back room where the president died, are furnished with period authenticity. Only the first floor is open. *Self-guided tours daily 9am-5pm. 516 10th St. NW. 426-6924.*

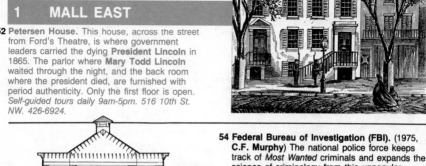

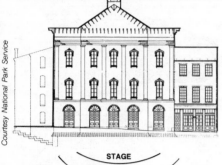

Courtesy National Park Service

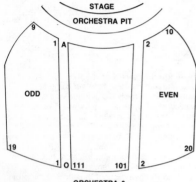

STAGE

ORCHESTRA PIT

ODD   EVEN

ORCHESTRA & PARQUET CIRCLE

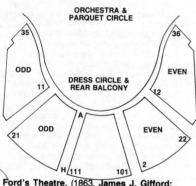

ODD   EVEN

DRESS CIRCLE & REAR BALCONY

ODD   EVEN

53 Ford's Theatre. (1863, **James J. Gifford;** restoration 1968, **Macomber & Peter, William Haussman**) **Abraham Lincoln** was shot here on 14 April 1865 during a performance of *Our American Cousin*, and the building was closed out of shame for over 100 years. The basement has a small but select museum of personal mementos of both the president and his assassin. On display are the suit of clothes in which Lincoln died and the flag which covered his casket, as well as the derringer that **John Wilkes Booth** used to commit his crime and the diary in which he recorded his conviction to do the deed. Upstairs you can view first-hand the flag-draped box where the president was sitting when Booth crept up behind him.

Family productions now light the Ford's stage. The National Park Service maintains the building, along with the Peterson House across the street, and conducts tours every hour on the half hour.

Sometimes closed during matinees and rehearsals, so call ahead. *Admission free. Open daily 9am-5pm. 511 10th St. NW, between E and F Sts. Metrorail blue/orange/red lines. 426-6924.*

Recipients of **The Smithson Medal**, established in 1965 in memory of the Institution's founder, have included **Queen Elizabeth II** (1976) and **Pope John Paul II** (1979).

54 Federal Bureau of Investigation (FBI). (1975, **C.F. Murphy**) The national police force keeps track of *Most Wanted* criminals and expands the science of criminology from this unpopular, brutalistic beige concrete building (rumor has it that **J. Edgar Hoover** himself helped design it). Created in 1908 by **Teddy Roosevelt** to fight political corruption, the FBI began to realize its powerful potential after 1924, the year Hoover was appointed director. You'll learn more about *the Bureau* in an introductory video presentation, then tour the high tech laboratories and see exhibits tracing the FBI's history through the gangster years to the Cold War decade of espionage to its current science fiction-like crime-fighting techniques. The tour wraps up with a firearms demonstration by a special agent. *Admission free. Tours M-F 9am-4:15pm. Reservations suggested for large groups. J. Edgar Hoover Bldg., 10th St. at Pennsylvania Ave. NW; enter on E St. (9th to 10th Sts.). Metrorail blue/orange/red lines. 324-3000.*

The FBI has fingerprints—about 164,756,933 sets of them—and they maintain that they still haven't found 2 sets alike.

The fingerprint cards are divided into criminal and civil files. The *criminal file* contains the prints of anyone arrested for a serious crime or felony (over 21 million people). The *civil file* contains the prints of military personnel, federal workers, those who have passed through immigration and naturalization, etc. The file is rounded out by another 5 million or so prints called *Personal IDs*. These are prints sent in voluntarily by citizens across the country, and they have proven useful in finding amnesia victims and missing children.

The **Latent Fingerprint Analysis Unit** is the unit that examines evidence—guns, car doors, etc.—for fingerprints. These are the guys you see in the movies spreading powder everywhere. When it comes to actually matching prints, a computer called the *Automatic Fingerprint Reader System* is used. All matches are then verified by a human being.

Under the *Freedom of Information Act* you may find out if the FBI has a file or fingerprint card for you. Request the information in a notarized letter. Send it to: *Director of the FBI, J. Edgar Hoover Building, 9th & Pennsylvania Ave. NW, Washington, DC 20535.*

The photos of 10 fearsome faces that grace the walls of your local post office are an outgrowth of the **Public Enemy Number 1** phenomenon, largely a creation of the media in the 1930s gangster era. The FBI discovered that all the publicity was instrumental in capturing criminals, so in 1950 they created the **Ten Most Wanted List**. To make the list, a criminal must meet 3 specifications: He must have broken federal law; he must be seen as a particular menace to the public (armed, fleeing, a history of violence, etc.); and the agency must believe that publicity will aid in his capture. Fugitive **Patty Hearst**, for instance, wasn't put on the list because the FBI thought her face was sufficiently well known.

When a spot opens up on the list—due to death, capture, or in rare cases, expiration of federal warrants—it's quickly filled by one of several thousand people in the Identification Order or *I.O. File*. New pictures are sent out to field offices, local police stations and media outlets across the country. The policy has proven very effective. Since the 1950s, 384 people have been on the list (6 of them women) and 109 have been caught with the aid of citizen identification.

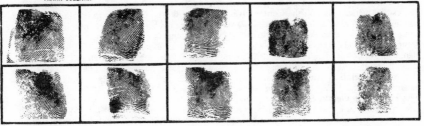
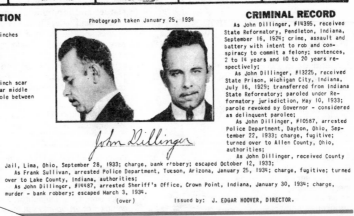

Joseph Passonneau

5 National Archives. (1935, **John Russell Pope**)
Fifty years ago, after the documents that serve
as the foundation for our government were
variously lost, mistaken for worthless paper,
threatened by advancing armies and left to
crumble in dark vaults, a suitable home was
finally created for the **Declaration of
Independence** and its **Bill of Rights**, and the
US Constitution.

The National Archives serves as the nation's
safety deposit box, a 21-floor collection of
treaties, laws, maps, land claims, bills of sale,
letters and speeches of important people, films,
sound recordings and other important
documents—enough to fill 250,000 4-drawer filing
cabinets!

The stories and memorabilia in this collection are
endless; one story researched here was **Alex
Haley's Roots. Richard Nixon's** letter of
resignation is kept in the Archives, as are the
Emancipation Proclamation, the surrender
documents of Japan's World War II government,
and a letter from the **King of Siam** to **Abraham
Lincoln** expounding the efficiency of elephant
labor.

Main attractions, though, are familiar to every US
schoolchild: the Constitution, Bill of Rights and
Declaration of Independence. These profoundly
influential documents are on permanent display
in the Archives' domed **Rotunda,** accessible via

the Constitution Avenue entrance. They are
sealed in protective helium to guard against
aging and lowered into deep vaults at night and
in case of emergency. Encircling the display
overhead, **Barry Faulkner's** massive murals
depict the forging of these papers.

In the Archives' **Exhibit Hall** encircling the
Rotunda, changing exhibits are displayed. Most
are thematic, celebrating an aspect of the
American people such as the inventive Yankee
genius, or a single remarkable person. Many of
the exhibits use photographs and engravings from
the collection's extensive pictorial records. The
collection spans the history of photography and
includes many historic pictures, such as **Mathew
Brady's** Civil War photos. Moving
pictures—140,000 reels—and miles of sound
recordings, from **FDR's Fireside Chats** to **Tokyo
Rose's** propaganda messages, are also on file.

The National Archives serves the public as more
than a museum; access to important records and
research assistance are available for
genealogical searches. Immigration records,
ships' logs, slave transit and ownership records,
treaties with American Indian tribes, and masses
of information on taxes, military service, births
and deaths help families uncover their roots.

The building which houses so much American
minutiae has a shimmering white exterior
trimmed with Corinthian columns, evidence of
Pope's facility with classical forms. The
Pennsylvania Avenue entry is a welcome change
from all the raised, rusticated bases supporting
other buildings in the Federal Triangle area.

Special *Behind the Scenes* tours by appointment,
preferably 2 weeks in advance. Tours weekdays
only, free of charge. Gift shop sells document
facsimiles, cards and books.

*Admission free. Rotunda and Exhibit Hall open
Apr 1-Labor Day 10am-9pm, Sept-Mar
10am-5:30pm. Closed Christmas. Research areas
open M-F 8:45am-10pm, Sa 8:45am-5:15pm.
Constitution Ave. at 8th St. Researchers use
Pennsylvania Ave. entrance. Metrorail yellow line.
523-3000/Tours: 523-3183.*

Although the **Zero Milestone** on the Ellipse's
northern tip is the legal center of the District
of Columbia, the actual center is also the
center of the OAS building.

The 18 acres of the **White House grounds** known as the *President's Park* contain more than 80 varieties of trees planted throughout the years by almost every presidential family. The giant American Elm on the **Center Oval** was first a seedling from **John Quincy Adams** home in Massachusetts. **Andrew Jackson** brought a magnolia from Tennessee as a memorial to his wife. The other magnolia near the east entrance to the White House was planted by **Warren Harding,** in memory of the animals killed during WWI. More recent trees include the **Gerald Ford** family's white pine, a giant sequoia set by **Richard Nixon** in the Center Oval, and little **Amy Carter's** tree house, built on poles and shielded by a magnificent Silver atlas cedar. Perhaps the most famous part of the park is **Ellen Wilson's Rose Garden,** planted in 1913 and redesigned by **Mrs. Paul Mellon** at the request of **John F. Kennedy** in 1962. The rendition of an 18th-century garden shows osmanthus and boxwood hedges, tulips, narcissus, chrysanthemums and heliotrope. The grounds are closed to visitors except during the White House garden tours and the annual Easter Egg Roll.

56 Temperance Fountain. (1880) **Henry Cogswell,** an eccentric California dentist, liked to dedicate these fountains—on which his name would be prominently inscribed—to any city that would have one. He hoped the pedestrian would slake his thirst with cool water rather than booze. Prohibition has since been repealed and the city long ago stopped maintaining the obsolete cooling system hidden in the fountain's base. So, while America may no longer be dry, Cogswell's fountain is. *Pennsylvania Ave. at 7th St. NW.*

57 d.c. space. ☆$ In a city decidedly lacking in things avant-garde, this new wavy bar and cafe stands out. Narrow, noisy and neoned, it's home to denizens of nearby rock'n'roll clubs, Corcoran Art School students and other nouveau bohemian types. Good burgers, salads, vegetarian dishes. Music or cabaret acts on some weekends. *American. M-Sa 11:30am-2am. Closed Su. 443 7th St. NW (D St. NW). 347-4960.*

58 406 Group. Located in the middle of the impressive Smithsonian art museum/gallery aggregation, this building at 406 7th Street NW (Metrorail yellow line) is a bonus for the visitor with spare time: 4 first-rate art galleries occupy the building's 3 floors, adding richness to the downtown 7th Street *cultural corridor.*

Jane Haslem shows contemporary American art and is well known for its extensive collection of prints and drawings; **Gabor Peterdi** is a particular star. *Open Tu-F 11:30am-3:30pm, Sa noon-5pm. Closed Su & M. 638-6162.*

Osuna exhibits contemporary American works, with occasional forays into European and Latin American realms. Its stable includes 2 of Washington's strongest artists, **Manon Cleary** and **Rebecca Davenport.** *Open Tu-Sa 11am-6pm. Closed Su & M. 296-1963.*

B.R. Kornblatt focuses on contemporary American paintings and sculpture, often showing big-name artists such as **Motherwell, Noland** and **Stella.** *Open Tu-Sa 10:30am-5:30pm. Closed Su & M. 638-7657.*

David Adamson, owned by a master printer, not surprisingly emphasizes graphics. **Kevin MacDonald** and **Michael Clark** are notable artists shown by the Adamson gallery. *Open Tu-Sa 10am-5:30pm. Closed Su & M. 628-0257.*

The **Washington Monument** runs in different veins for a good reason: When construction of the shaft was interrupted and resumed after more than 20 years, the Army Corps of Engineers were unable to obtain the exact same marble used for the first 150 feet of the monument. They used matching marble from Massachusetts for the next 26 feet, and then marble from a similar vein in the original Maryland quarry. Take a closer look at the shaft—there is a ring about one third of the way up.

Yearly, $116,000 are allocated to a quarterly **cleaning of the Capital's 56 principal statues and monuments,** including the Lincoln and Jefferson memorials, the Juarez statues and the DC War Memorial. The process consists of a 5-man crew, operating a steam-pressure-system hose. This is attached to a mobile tank truck filled with 1,500 gallons of pure water. A complete 5,000-gallon washdown of the Lincoln Memorial takes 6 working days and nights.

American author **Henry James** called Washington, *"the city of conversation."*

Flanking the 406 Building is the **Washington Project for the Arts.** An extensive ground-floor shop features artists' books. Galleries are upstairs. *Call 393-9619 for information.* On the other side is the **Lansburgh's Building** with a complex of art operations, including resident visual arts groups. The extensive display windows of the former Lansburgh's department store provide the largest ongoing display of art in the city. Inside, the **Washington Women's Arts Center** is a gallery/school/networking source. Call for information on special exhibits, classes, lectures, films, theater, etc. *Gallery open Tu-Sa 11am-5pm; office open 9:30am-3pm. 420 7th St. NW. Gallery: 393-0197/Office: 393-8364.*

59 Hecht's. This third of the downtown department store troika is showing its years and would lose a beauty contest to both Woodies and Garfinckel's. That's why a new, modern and more compact Hecht's is under construction a couple of blocks away (between 12th and 13th Sts. at G St. NW), attached to the **Metrorail Center** station and slated for completion in 1985. Meanwhile, the old one will continue to attract moderate-income shoppers with its trendy stock. *Open Tu & W, F & Sa 10am-6pm; M & Th 10am-8pm. Su noon-5pm. 7th and F Sts. NW. Metrorail blue/orange/red lines. 626-8000.*

60 National Museum of American Art & National Portrait Gallery (Old Patent Building). (1836-67, **Robert Mills**) When it served for 92 years as the US Patent Office, this building held an archive of American technical ingenuity. Now the arched and pillared marble hallways display American artistic talent in 2 proudly patriotic collections.

The **Old Patent Office** building itself is a century-old replica of the Parthenon rendered in Virginia freestone, a dignified home for the art it houses. The building's saddest role was as hospital and morgue after the battle at Antietam; **Clara Barton** and **Walt Whitman** ministered to the wounded. Today a pair of Civil War-era palms enliven the cool courtyard between the 2 great museums. Bring your own snack and picnic here, or eat at the pleasant **Patent Pending** restaurant within the building.

The **National Museum of American Art,** on the building's north side, celebrates 2 centuries of native talent. A recent reinstallation of the entire museum, with the works more chronologically ordered, makes it easier to trace the development of native styles and movements. This is the first major refurbishment of the museum since its move to the building in 1968.

Washington rates 8th among US cities in population density, with nearly 10,400 people per square mile.

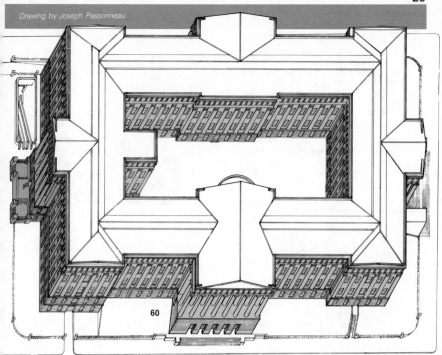

Drawing by Joseph Passonneau

60

This is the country's oldest art collection; it now owns over 30,000 pieces, including works by **Georgia O'Keeffe, Andrew Wyeth, Winslow Homer, James McNeill Whistler** and **Benjamin West. George Catlin's** 455-painting gallery depicting North America's original inhabitants is here, as are selections of **Hiram Powers'** sculpture, oils by **Albert Pinkham Ryder,** and the country's largest collection of New Deal art.

The subjects preserved on canvas and in bronze lead visitors on a walk through America, past and present: the wild landscapes and frontier lifestyle depicted by **Frederick Remington** and **Albert Bierstadt;** wildlife chronicled by **J.J. Audubon** and his disciples; portraits of Americans both common and uncommon painted by **Mary Cassatt** and **Charles Wilson Peale.** Finally the energy of the 20th century is captured in the works of **Franz Kline, Willem de Kooning, Robert Rauschenberg** and **Alexander Calder.** Some 25 major exhibits are mounted yearly.

The third-floor **Lincoln Gallery,** the site of the 1864 inaugural ball, now holds modern artworks. The museum has a large collection of miniatures and, for good measure, a small collection of European and Asian masterworks that are instructive as influences on American art as well as pleasing in and of themselves. **Explore Gallery** and **Discovery Gallery** are filled with special exhibits and activities for children. Also at the Museum is a 40,000-volume library and the **Archives of American Art,** which also serves the National Portrait Gallery.

The **Renwick Gallery** (see District 2) of the NMAA exhibits American craft and design arts. The **Barney Studio House** at Sheridan Square (see District 4) depicts a turn-of-the-century artists' home and studio.

Besides permanent and rotating exhibits, the NMAA hosts lectures and film series; call for information, *357-3095.*

Admission free. Open daily except Christmas 10am-5:30pm. Walk-in tours M-F, Su 2pm. 8th & G Sts. NW. Metrorail red line. 357-3176/357-2700.

Introductions/Theaters/Narrative black
Hotels purple
Museums/Architecture blue
Parks/Open spaces green
Restaurants/Nightlife red
Shops/Galleries violet

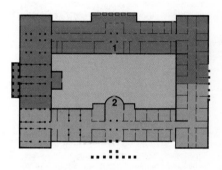

1 National Museum of American Art
2 National Portrait Gallery

The National Portrait Gallery, on the Old Patent Office's south side, is full of old friends: images of **George Washington** we first saw on our schoolroom walls; portraits of the explorers, military heroes and heroines, thinkers and doers in the arts and sciences, philanthropists and first families that people our history books. It's both humbling and inspiring to stand face to face with so much greatness.

The federal government unwittingly began this collection when it commissioned a series of presidential portraits in 1857. Now the Gallery comprises paintings, sculpture, etchings, photographs and silhouettes. Works by artists such as **John Singleton Copley, John Singer Sargent, Thomas Scully, Augustus Saint-Gaudens** and **Charles Wilson Peale** can be found here. Call for information on special exhibits and lectures.

Admission free. Open daily 10am-5:30pm. Closed Christmas. F St. at 8th St. NW. Metrorail red line. 357-2920/357-2137.

Washington has the **largest black population** (by percentage) of any US city. Over 70 percent of its citizens are black (compared to 66-plus percent in Atlanta and 63-plus percent in Detroit). The figure emphasizes the capital's symbolic and actual importance to newly freed slaves who flocked here for federal protection following the Emancipation Proclamation.

Alan Fern
Director, National Portrait Gallery

In some ways, **the building itself** is one of the great treasures of the National Portrait Gallery and National Museum of American Art. These 2 Smithsonian museums were fortunate enough to have been given the opportunity to move into the original Patent Office Building in 1962, shortly after the structure (built under the supervision of Robert Mills in the 1830s) had been saved from demolition. This Greek revival building was the fourth important structure—after the Capitol Building, the President's House, and the Treasury—completed for the United States Government as Washington was transformed from a village into a capital. Placed on the spot designated in L'Enfant's plan for a national cathedral or national pantheon, it was used both for the offices of the Patent Office and for the display of patent models, artworks and other objects of a museum nature owned by the federal government. When the Smithsonian was established, and the original Smithsonian building erected, the museum objects were placed on view there.

In the **Grand Hall, President and Mrs. Lincoln** received their guests at the second inaugural ball; the festivities continued in the adjoining **Lincoln Gallery** (now part of the National Museum of American Art), which was the largest interior space in Washington at the time.

The Patent Office was used as a hospital during the Civil War, and, in his writing, **Walt Whitman** commemorated its appearance both as a hospital and inaugural site.

The collections of the National Portrait Gallery are as diverse as the people who have shaped America. It has been the intention of the Gallery to find portraits painted from life, whenever possible, by the finest artists, of the most significant Americans. Considering that the Gallery began assembling its collections only in 1962 (long after the establishment of many major institutions elsewhere in the United States), and has been open to the public only since 1968, it is remarkable how many excellent works the Gallery has been able to acquire. Among the most notable are the American *icons,* the **Gilbert Stuart Athenaeum** portraits of **George and Martha Washington,** which the Gallery owns jointly with the Boston Museum of Fine Arts. When the Washington portraits are in Boston— as they are for 3 years, every 3 years— another superb Stuart is on view: the *Edgehill* portrait of **Thomas Jefferson,** jointly owned with the Thomas Jefferson Foundation at Monticello. The Gallery owns portraits of all the presidents, and some are particularly noteworthy as works of art. My favorites are the spirited **Anders Zorn** painting of **Grover Cleveland,** Jo Davidson's large stone sculpture of **Franklin Delano Roosevelt,** and the *cracked plate* portrait of **Abraham Lincoln** made by **Alexander Gardner** just days before Lincoln's assassination. The Gardner photograph is the only early print in the *Meserve Collection,* a group of more than 5,000 glass plates by **Mathew Brady** and his associates, from which a small selection of choice, modern albumen prints is on view at all times in the Gallery.

Among other notable portraits in the NPG collection are the moody and elegant *self-portrait* by **John Singleton Copley,** the brilliant painting of **Tallulah Bankhead** by **Augustus John,** a sensitive *self-portrait* in plaster by **John Frazee,** and 2 large composite portrait groups by **Christian Schussele:** *Men of Progress* and *Washington Irving and his Literary Friends at Sunnyside.*

In addition to showing a substantial portion of its permanent collection at all times, including originals for *TIME* cover portraits, and prints and photographs and drawings, the National Portrait Gallery has an active schedule of temporary exhibitions. In these, works on loan from public and private collections are brought together to explicate an aspect of American history or show the work of a significant portrait artist.

---

61 Golden Palace. The splendid red-gold dining room compensates for the sometimes uneven performance of the kitchen. Stick to *dim sum* or plain Cantonese standbys and you'll enjoy a pleasant meal. *Chinese. Open Su-Th 11am-10pm, F-Sa 11am-midnight. 720 7th St. NW. 783-1225.*

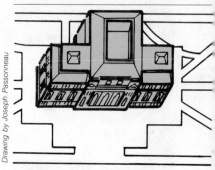

Drawing by Joseph Passonneau

62 Old Central Library. (1902, Ackerman & Ross) A grand Carnegie-funded Beaux-Arts triumph, now the library for Federal City College. Well-placed windows light the reading rooms inside. *8th & K Sts. NW.*

63 Szechuan. ☆ ☆ ☆ $ Probably your best bet for inexpensive Chinese food. Enlist your waiter's help in choosing from the vast menu of often-fiery appetizers and main courses. Excellent hot and sour soup, stir-fried vegetables, chicken with wine sauce and garlicky jumbo shrimp. Tea brunch served on weekends. *Chinese. Open Su-Th 11am-11pm, F & Sa till midnight. Reservations suggested. 615 I St. NW. 393-0130.*

64 Chinatown. Urban redevelopment, creeping east from Downtown, is whittling away the autonomy of this small neighborhood. There are still good ethnic eateries along restaurant row on H St. between 6th and 7th Sts. NW, well-stocked oriental groceries for those who cook their own exotic dishes, and colorful festivities on Chinese New Year. At 7th and H Streets NW, a large mural tells the story of Chinese immigration to the US.

64 China Inn. ☆ ☆ $$ For over 40 years, this brightly hued, bustling mainstay of DC's tiny Chinatown has offered a seemingly endless array of satisfying Cantonese dishes: steamed chicken with Chinese sausage, roast duck, rice noodles with roast pork, spare ribs in black bean sauce. Try the house specialties, especially the sea bass and other seafood preparations. *Chinese. Open M-Th 11am-3am, F & Sa till 3:30am, Su till 1:30am. No reservations. 631 H St. NW. 842-0909.*

64 China Doll. ☆ $ Basic Cantonese menu with a smattering of Szechuan delectables will help desperate noodle-junkies and starving insomniacs get through the night. Excellent *dim sum* for those who face the day. *Chinese. Open M-Th 11am-3am, F & Sa till 4am, Su till 2am. 627 H St. NW. 842-0660.*

64 House of Seven Stars. ☆ $ Judging by the large number of Chinese patrons, this recently opened storefront must be doing something right. Szechuan specialties are for those who like very hot food, Cantonese fare for the less adventurous palate. Avoid the beef dishes. *Chinese. Open Su-Th 11am-2am, F & Sa till 3am. Reservations accepted. 817 7th St. NW (I St. NW). 371-1711.*

64 Ruby Restaurant. ☆ $$ *Dim sum*—Chinese dumplings of all shapes, textures and flavors— are this restaurant's forte; order a selection. Take your chances on an otherwise hit-or-miss menu. *Chinese. Open daily 11am-3am, F & Sa till 4am. Reservations suggested. 609 H St. NW. 842-0060.*

Introductions/Theaters/Narrative black
Hotels purple
Museums/Architecture blue
Parks/Open spaces green
Restaurants/Nightlife red
Shops/Galleries violet

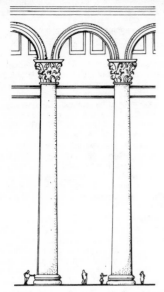

65 National Building Museum/Old Pension Building. (1883, **General Montgomery Meigs**) For years this low-budget Victorian version of the Palazzo Farnese in Italy was ridiculed as a white elephant. Its central court (the city's largest indoor space) and offices held 1,500 clerks processing pension payments for pre-WWI veterans and their families. Over some 40 years the clerks doled out 8 billion dollars, unaffected by the splendid setting of their humdrum jobs.

In the middle of this century the building was threatened with destruction, then happily rediscovered. In 1980 it became the home of this museum.

The NBM is dedicated to documenting and explaining the US's vital building trade, from the craft of hardhats to the art of architects. Along with conventional exhibits, it highlights controversial building and design issues with film and video. It has put together an archive/data bank of thousands of models, drawings, blueprints and documents.

The building's most stunning display, though, is itself. The central court is as long as a football field and approximately 16 stories high. Four tiers of balconies—some supporting ornate iron grillwork—climb its interior walls. In the center are the *8 largest Corinthian columns* in the world—each one required 85,000 bricks to build and measures 76-feet high and 25-feet in diameter.

The building was designed in 1883 by Army engineering past master General **Montgomery Meigs,** who had also engineered the White House dome and served as Quartermaster of the US Army. The inspired design—with offices radiating off the central court and its balconies, and hundreds of windows—eliminates dark, stale hallways typical of early office buildings and provides natural light and ventilation without the heat of a conventional skylight.

One architect remarked that the only 2 things capable of filling the vast space would be a thunderstorm or an inaugural ball. In fact, the inaugural celebrations of **Cleveland, Harrison, FDR, Nixon, Carter** and **Reagan** were held here.

Admission free. Open M-F 9am-5pm. Tours Tu 11am, Th 12:15pm. Special evening candlelight tours available, call for dates and times. 440 G. St. NW. 783-0690/272-2448.

66 District of Columbia Courthouse (Old City Hall). One of the earliest Greek Revival buildings in the city, it was designed in 1820 by **George Hadfield** and took over 30 years to complete. *4th and D Sts. NW.*

Director's Bests

Bates Lowry
Director, National Building Museum

On the exterior:

The **great frieze of soldiers, sailors and wounded warriors** that has been encircling the building for over 100 years. Its design was due to the architect of the building, **General Montgomery C. Meigs,** who dictated its subject and encouraged the sculptor, **Casper Buberl,** to study the recent photographic evidence produced by Muybridge about how horses moved, but to take at the same time the Parthenon frieze as a model for artistic expression. The meaning of the frieze as described by Meigs makes it a very moving national monument. He wished it to be a memorial to *all* men who believed so deeply in an ideal that they would willingly give their lives to defend it. Spoken at a time so shortly after the divisive Civil War, these words make the frieze a symbol of the bonds that had to be refashioned to make our nation whole.

After entering:

Once the visitor has overcome **an initial experience of the vast size** of the central court (316 feet by 116 feet) and begins to try to compare it with other space it is well to remember that a) it is higher than the nave of Notre Dame in Paris, b) the columns are higher than those at Baalbek, usually thought of as the tallest columns in the world, c) the square footage exceeds that of Hagia Sophia by over 9,000 square feet, d) the Pantheon of Rome could be fit within its walls, e) a contemporary 15-story building could be erected in its central court. All of these statistics, except for the latter, were known and described by General Meigs.

(See **Architecture section** for more *Bests.*)

With **a lively imagination and a keen ear** one should be able to hear any number of historic pieces of music that still linger in the Great Hall from the many Presidential Inaugural Balls held here, beginning in 1885 before the building was totally finished. They continue to be held here today, although **Victor Herbert** has long since been replaced as the bandleader.

When visiting the museum galleries, one should realize that these open, flowing **spaces represent the architect's goal of bringing fresh air and natural light into offices and they make marvelous museum galleries!**

In climbing the stairways, note their gentle rise and generous size. One is ascending the first stairways especially designed for the handicapped, a feature introduced by the architect because many of the employees of the Pension Bureau were maimed veterans.

The **sky blue ceiling of the Great Hall** results from the architect's desire that it appear to be an open courtyard like its Italian prototypes. The surrounding arcade—another typical feature of the Renaissance palace—serves the functional purpose of being a circulation corridor within the building. The architect opted for this design to avoid the central corridor circulation pattern used in earlier government offices which produced dark, gloomy and fetid areas.

The **richness of the colorful, decorative scheme** reflects the architect's belief that bright colors set off good architecture by adorning and emphasizing it. The lavish use of bronze coloring was much admired by early users of the building, one of whom believed that there had been nothing so splendid since Solomon's Temple. In the center court the series of plaster busts that enrich the upper cornice were intended by Meigs to achieve "a variety of forms, lights and shadows."

67 Darlington Fountain. Dedicated by **Joseph Darlington's** lawyer friends, this lovely Art Deco sculpture of a naked nymph standing beside a fawn created quite a stir among the barristers' Baptist co-religionists in 1923. In a pompous retort, the sculptor **Carl Jennewin** said that the lady was *"direct from the hands of God instead of from the hands of a dressmaker." Judiciary Sq., 5th to D Sts. NW.*

68 Mellon Fountain. Sculpted by **Sidney Waugh** in 1952, this elegant fountain is made of 3 concentric bronze basins; the outermost is the largest ever cast. A 20-foot-high plume of water gushes from the center. *Constitution and Pennsylvania Aves. NW.*

69 US Tax Court. (1982, **Victor Lundy**) This building is a showpiece of engineering. Granite and bronze-tinted glass sheath the exterior; the third-floor court chambers are each suspended from the ceiling by over 100 3-inch steel cables. The building was originally designed to span the nearby freeway, and although the plan was abandoned, the building's form still reflects the original intent. Concrete and teak lend texture to the interior surfaces. You can't just wander in—ask the guard at the entrance for permission to look around. *3rd St. between D and E Sts. NW.*

70 Jewish Historical Society. (1876) Housed in a modest red brick structure that was built for *Adas Israel,* the city's oldest synagogue, the society keeps records and oral histories of the community's Jewish heritage, and mounts special exhibits of Judaica. The building is a National Historic Shrine. *Admission free. Open Su 11am-3pm or call for special appointment. 701 3rd St. NW (G St.). 789-0900.*

71 American Cafe. ☆☆$ This spacious and relaxed branch of a trendy chain of restaurants includes outdoor cafe and take-out emporium. Choose from regional American specialties such as lobster pie, Hawaiian chicken and ribs. The baked beans are spicy sweet, the soups thick and creamy, the croissants gigantic. Leave room for a slice of pecan pie or a rich chocolate brownie. *Original American. Open Su-Th 11am-1am, F & Sa till 3am. Reservations suggested for large groups. 227 Massachusetts Ave. NE. 547-8500.*

72 Georgetown University Law Center. (1971, **Edward Durell Stone**) Designed at the same time and by the same architect as the **Kennedy Center,** the Law Center has been widely criticized as an inhospitable mass of brick. *600 New Jersey Ave. NW.*

73 Hyatt Regency Capitol Hill. *Expensive.* Not wanting to be upstaged by its ponderous Capitol Hill neighbors, the well-appointed Hyatt Regency offers both an art gallery and Atrium Park (the lobby filled with exotic vegetation) to create its own lovely niche in the neighborhood. There are 20 different meeting and banquet rooms and a variety of restaurants and lounges in cafe-like settings. Indoor parking available. *400 New Jersey Ave. NW. Metrorail red line. 737-1234/800-228-9000/Telex: 897432.*

74 Quality Inn Hotel Capitol Hill. *Moderate.* The 341 newly decorated rooms offer one of the best accommodations values in town, including special family and weekender plans. Each spacious room features a pair of double beds and free HBO movies. There's also free indoor/outdoor parking. The **Coach and Parlor** restaurant offers traditional American food; the **Whistlestop** lounge serves cocktails and complimentary hors d'oeuvres. Tour buses leave from the hotel to historic sites. *415 New Jersey Ave. NW. Metrorail red line. 638-1616/800-228-5151/Telex: 710-822-0153.*

75 The Irish Times. ☆☆$ A boisterously Irish restaurant and bar that caters to a regular crowd of Capitol Hill staffers and embassy employees. Generous portions of Irish stewed chili and Irish fish'n'chips are favorites during the busy lunch hour. Spirits are reasonably priced, so expect the 45-foot-long bar to be jammed during happy hour. Jukebox plays Irish hits non-stop, from Molly Malone to U2. *Irish. 14 F St. NW, between N. Capitol & 1st Sts. 543-5433.*

76 Tiber Creek Pub. ☆$$ Located in Capitol Hill's tiny **Bellevue Hotel,** this polished, wood-paneled restaurant/lounge offers hearty steaks, burgers and daily specials. Live jazz on weekends. *American. Open M-F 11:30am-2am, Sa & Su 5pm-2am. Reservations suggested. 15 E St. NW. 638-0900.*

77 The Dubliner. A bit o' Ireland, where pints of Guinness (on tap) follow shots of Jameson and Paddy's, where each night Celtic bands encourage customer sing-alongs and plenty of blarney. Saturday afternoons, too. Dinner menu. No cover or minimum. *Open Tu-Th 11am-2am, F & Sa till 3am. 520 N. Capitol St. NW. 737-3773.*

78 La Colline. ☆☆☆$$ This elegant brasserie a few blocks from Union Station offers one of the best values in town. Choose from a fixed-price menu, or go a la carte with a smoked salmon appetizer and entrees such as duck breast with cassis sauce, *coq au vin,* a tender veal cutlet in mushrooms and cream, or fresh fish. The dessert cart should definitely be investigated, as should the extensive wine list (order individual glasses from a selection of featured wines changed weekly). *French. Open M-F 7am-10pm, Sa 6-10pm. Closed Su. Reservations suggested. 400 N. Capitol St. NW (D St. NW). 737-0400.*

79 Basil. ☆☆$$$ This elegant establishment is frequented by senators, but don't let the snobbish airs intimidate you. Try the daily fresh fish special, chicken or brochettes of marinated meats. A special summertime treat is relaxing on the veranda with a slice of cappuccino pie—it's flown in from Texas. *Continental. Open M-F 11:30am-midnight, M-Sa during summer. 400 1st St. SE. 546-4545.*

80 Market Inn. ☆$$ Settle into the noisy, music-filled dining room, or opt for a darker, quieter booth nearby. Then choose from a huge selection of fresh seafood, homemade soups, and other entrees. *Seafood. Open M-Sa 11am-1am, Su 4pm-midnight. Reservations suggested. 200 E St. SW. 554-2100.*

81 Wax Museum. Your only chance to rub elbows with **Ronald Reagan** during a rock concert may be in the lobby of the Wax Museum. Well known for its layout and great acoustics, this 1,000-seat nightclub still houses about 30 historical celebrities from its former days as the real **National Historical Wax Museum.** For those who cannot abide rock, there are always the perpetual paraffin parking attendants to see in the adjacent public garage—**John Wayne** and **Albert Einstein.** *4th and E Sts. SW. Metrorail orange line. USA-0000.*

Abigail Smith Adams

Dolley Madison

Sarah Polk

Lucy Hayes

Frances Cleveland

Caroline Harrison

Helen Taft

Edith Wilson

Eleanor Roosevelt

Jacqueline Kennedy

While the Chief of State is usually the focal point of the nation's attention, several First Ladies have managed to capture the public's imagination and the press' headlines. Whether due to a flamboyant fashion or radical political stance—or even just for speaking up in public way back when—the women in the White House left their mark on the capital and the country.

1801—Wife of one president and mother of another, **Abigail Smith Adams** rarely stifled a political opinion, discussing current events freely with her male dinner guests. Despite her outstanding intellect, Abigail Adams remains best known for stringing clotheslines through a vacant White House audience room.

1809—While journalists continually tried to rename her Dorothea, **Mrs. James Madison** insisted her true name was just plain *Dolley*. She furthered the Adams style of drawing room diplomacy well past her days as First Lady. Her White House successors—as well as their husbands—sought her social and political opinions until the day she died (1849). Always a style setter, Dolley's trademark was a turban highly decorated with flowers and feathers.

1845—At 41, the young and popular **Sarah Childress Polk** took her religion and her role as First Lady seriously, gaining great respect for what today seem conservative standards. The Polks banned dancing and serving wine or liquor at the White House—the first considered frivolous, the second somewhat sinful. On inauguration night, when the Polks arrived, the dancing was ordered stopped. Following the First Couple's 2-hour stay, the music resumed and guests danced freely.

1877—The first First Lady with a college degree, **Lucy Webb Hayes** was an alumna of Wesleyan Female College in Cincinnati, Ohio. Mrs. Hayes brought the Easter Egg Roll to the White House grounds when Congress banned it from the Capitol lawns. Referred to as *Lemonade Lucy*, Hayes forbade even wine to be served at the White House.

1885—The first First Lady to be married in the White House was **Frances Folsom Cleveland.** The president insisted on a small private ceremony inside, but crowds were allowed to peek through the windows.

1889—While replacing a china closet, **Mrs. Benjamin Harrison** became interested in the bits and pieces of china she found. She began a White House collection of past president's china. Active politically, in 1891 she was elected the first President-General of the newly-formed Daughters of the American Revolution.

1909—Not a woman to hide in the president's shadow, **Helen Herron Taft** set a precedent by riding beside her husband in the inaugural procession down Pennsylvania Avenue to the White House. Mrs. Taft set other precedents as well, by allowing her cow, named **Mooly-Wholly**, to graze the White House lawn, and by introducing musicales to state dinners. She also suggested placing cherry trees around the Washington Tidal Basin.

1915—The second wife of President Woodrow Wilson, **Edith Bolling Galt Wilson** proved invaluable to him and the nation during his failing health. She allowed few to bother the president during his illness, serving as a *de facto* president, sending news and policy from the president to his administration.

1933—Often criticized and always controversial, **Anna Eleanor Roosevelt** traveled 38,000 miles her first year, 42,000 the second, and kept up the pace throughout her tenure. Called *The First Lady of the World*, Mrs. Roosevelt spoke her mind freely in her syndicated column *My Day*, radio broadcasts and special press conferences for woman reporters.

1961—Setting the fashion trends for the sixties, **Jacqueline Bouvier Kennedy** was the first First Lady to appoint a personal dress designer. Women all over the world wore copies of her suit dresses and pill-box hats. Mrs. Kennedy also brought culture to the mansion—by inviting distinguished guests to perform and to be honored.

1974—Known for her outspokenness on social issues, **Betty Ford** brought new candor to her office. She opened up the issues of breast cancer and chemical dependency for public discussion.

You can see all the First Ladies' inaugural gowns on display at the Smithsonian's **National Museum of American History.**

82 **Department of Transportation (Nassif Building).** Edward Durell Stone's insistent vertical lines and thin slab roof, rendered this time in Carrera marble. The building was privately built and leased to the Federal Government. *7th and D Sts. SW.*

83 **Department of Housing & Urban Development.** (1983, **Marcel Breuer**) The grid pattern in the beige concrete exterior walls is relentless, despite the open ground floor. The unique double-Y layout (also used in Breuer's design for the NATO building in Paris) improves circulation within the building and helps minimize the alienation of endless miles of office corridors. *7th St. at D St. SW.*

L'Enfant
PLAZA

84 **Loews L'Enfant Plaza Hotel.** *Deluxe.* This 4-star hostelry is popular with both sightseers and convention-goers. The hotel overlooks L'Enfant Plaza: a splashing fountain is surrounded by cool red granite, greenbelts and, nightly, the yellow glow of the plaza's trademark lamp globes. Spacious, contemporary rooms and suites. **Club 480** offers VIP service, including express check-in and out, concierge service, meeting parlor—even fresh fruit, cheese and Godiva chocolates waiting in your suite. Special convention/business accommodations include meeting and banquet rooms, catering, audio-visual services. Also ask about weekender specials. The **Apple of Eve** restaurant, **Greenhouse** cafe and **Quorum** lounge offer in-hotel refreshment. One flight below the hotel lobby is the L'Enfant Plaza shopping promenade—more than 50 shops (from **Hallmark Cards** to **Fannie Mae Candies, Flag**

Men's Shop to **The Unlimited** women's clothing) and services (including cleaners, beauticians, drug store and copy center). Deli snack and cafe foods. *480 L'Enfant Plaza SW. Metrorail yellow line. 484-1000.*

85 **L'Enfant Plaza.** (1966, **I.M. Pei**) Acres of red granite were to be the soil of a garden of urban delights watered by a splashing fountain; so far, nothing's grown. The surrounding office buildings are badly placed and all the shopping action is below plaza level. One of the few highlights is the US Postal Service's **Philatelic Sales Center,** located on the ground floor of their West Building.

85 **Intelsat.** The International Satellite Organization oversees the network of man-made devices circling the planet and which bring us instant news from around the globe. There are 102 member nations. Half-hour tours are free. *Open M-F 9am-5pm. 490 L'Enfant Plaza, SW. 488-2687.*

86 **Department of Agriculture.** (1905, **Ranking, Kellogg & Crane**) The first building erected by the McMillan Commission, which was charged at the turn of the century with resurrecting L'Enfant's plan for a gracious and ceremonial capital city. It was not completed until 1930. *14th St. & Independence Ave. SW.*

87 The Fish Market turns its share of noses on hot summer days, but locals swear by it for freshly caught and reasonably priced bounty trucked in from the lower Potomac and Delaware rivers, and Chesapeake Bay. Fish peddlers by the dozens set up shop along the Potomac's edge, some off the back of their boats, selling bushels of blue crabs, rockfish, oysters, shrimp, almost anything edible that swims in the region's waters. *Maine Ave. SW near the 14th St. Bridge.*

88 Barley Mow. ☆ $$ One cut above average steakhouse, serving Olde English roast and American prime rib in a country-style atmosphere. *American. Open for lunch M-Th 11:30am-2:30pm, F from 11am; open for dinner M-Th 5-10pm, F & Sa 5-11pm, Su 4-9pm. 700 Water St. SW. 554-7320.*

89 Channel Inn. *Expensive.* Decorated in elaborate nautical themes, this is the District's only waterside hotel located in the Washington Channel. All rooms have balconies. The **Pier 7 Restaurant** is a local landmark, famous for its fresh Chesapeake Bay seafood specialtes such as rockfish, swordfish, bouillabaisse and Maryland crab. There is live entertainment in the **Engine Room** lounge. Added to its list of pluses are free parking and a metro stop just a 10 minute walk away. *650 Water St. SW. Metrorail yellow line. 554-2400/800-368-5668.*

National Park Service. Located in East Potomac Park, near the Jefferson Memorial, the National Park Service (NPS) is the visitor's number one source for essential information. Part of the Interior Department, the Park Service offers free information and brochures on almost every aspect of Washington—and beyond.

The NPS maintains much of DC's great outdoors. It manages the **Chesapeake & Ohio Canal**, the **Petersen House** where Lincoln died, **Dyke Marsh**, the **Old Stone House** and the **Art Barn Gallery** in **Rock Creek Park**. Of special interest are NPS's Bird Walks through Dumbarton Oaks, Nature Walks through Rock Creek Park and Historical Walks through famous buildings. The NPS also co-sponsors, with the Association of Concert Bands of America, a series of concerts at **Wolf Trap Farm Park**.

During summer months, the Service offers tours through the various parks and DC hotspots every Sunday afternoon. Other walking tours are available daily. Check the NPS monthly newsletter, *Kiosk*, or call the NPS office for each week's meeting places and tours. Main events are advertised on the National Mall.

You can request information from or visit NPS at *1100 Ohio Drive, SW, Washington DC, 20242, 426-6700.* They also have staff members at the **Visitors' & Convention Bureau** in the Department of Commerce building (see District 2), phone 789-7000.

You would expect many creaks and knocks in an old mansion like the **White House**, but some residents and visitors claim that there's more to the noises than the house settling on swampy Potomac riverbank soil. The White House's most famous ghost is **Abraham Lincoln**, who commonly frightens the domestic staff, as **Harry Truman** noted in his diary. **Eleanor Roosevelt**, it has been reported, was visited by Abe's ghost on more than one occasion.

Willy Lincoln, the 11-year-old son of Abraham, died at the White House when his father was in office. His ghost was sometimes seen during the Grant Administration, but hasn't appeared since. Visits have also been reported by apparitions resembling **Dolley Madison** and **Abigail Adams**.

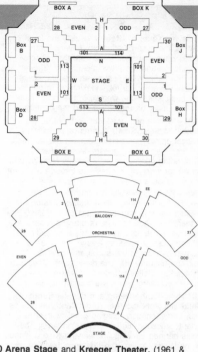

90 Arena Stage and **Kreeger Theater.** (1961 & 1970, **Harry Weese**) Since its first production in 1950, the **Arena Stage Repertory Company** has maintained a reputation as one of America's best resident theaters. Plays are carefully chosen for their ability to observe and capture life with clarity, empathy and passion. Founder and producing director **Zelda Fichlander** has brought plays such as *The Great White Hope, Animal Crackers* and *K2* to the Arena. Architect Weese won a great deal of recognition for his 800-seat Arena Stage and 500-seat Kreeger Theater designs, which use low-cost materials (concrete, sheet metal and paint) to achieve a stunning effect; the imagination, spatial clarity and attention to detail make them worthy of their illustrious tenants. **The Old Vat Room** (seats 180) was the first home of the company. Located adjacent to the waterfront, the complex permits one to easily combine an evening of fine dining and theater. *6th & M Sts. SW. 488-3300.*

In 1956 **John Zweifel**, a designer of miniatures and animated exhibits for department stores and amusement parks, took his own White House tour, but he only saw 5 out of 132 rooms. Miffed and curious, Zweifel decided to build his own White House—one that he and the public could look at as much as they wanted.

Zweifel applied to the Kennedy administration, which gave him limited access to the Executive Mansion. **Lyndon Johnson** and **Richard Nixon** weren't at all interested in his project. **Gerald Ford** gave him run of the building. Now the designer's sketches and photos fill almost 300 files.

For several years, Zweifel painstakingly built his one-twelfth scale model of the White House. It's 60 feet by 20 feet and weighs 8 tons. About half the interiors are completed, accurate to the last detail. Lights work, fountains spurt and phones ring. He spent 150 hours just carving the rosewood table in the Lincoln Sitting Room. When the model goes on national tour it's hauled by a 40-foot tractor/trailer.

The Secret Service, whose job it is to guard the president and foreign heads of state, also has plans for a White House model. This would be a life-size facade, or false front, of the White House, a facade of Blair House, where foreign dignitaries stay, and a complete recreation of Lafayette Park. The super-secret facility would be built at Secret Service headquarters in Beltsville, Maryland, and would be used to train agents to guard against terrorist attacks.

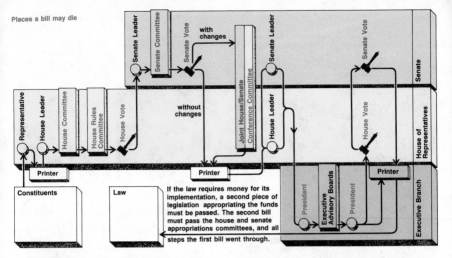

Places a bill may die

Together, the Senate and the House of Representatives form the 2 chambers of Congress called for in the Constitution. Congress makes federal law, sponsors studies and investigations, assesses taxes and appropriates funds for government projects. Though every new law must pass through both chambers before going to the president, the 2 chambers do have some powers exclusive of the other.

In general, the **Senate** plays a stronger role in foreign policy. It ratifies treaties and approves presidential appointments. It also sits as a court of impeachment on federal officials.

All legislation having to do with taxation or appropriations must be initiated in the **House of Representatives.** In addition, the House alone has the authority to bring charges of impeachment.

Big numbers have a way of blunting their own significance, but in the interest of showing how monumental is the task of governing America, here are a few big numbers. In 1983, 2,795 measures were proposed in the Senate, and 5,642 in the House of Representatives for a total of 8,437 Five hundred were passed by the Senate and 611 by the House. Of these, only 215 became public law; the rest ended up somewhere in the National Archives.

When one considers the many possible paths a piece of legislation may take—each with its own set of potentially fatal obstacles—it's amazing that even many make it. What follows is a simplified explanation of how a bill, originating in the House of Representatives, might become law.

The initial impetus for a bill may come from a wide array of sources: the president and his advisory commissions, congressional committees, lobbyists, private citizens, your congressperson. No matter its origin, in order for a bill to be considered, it must be sponsored by at least one senator or representative.

The **first step** is the drafting of a bill. This may be done by an individual citizen, but more frequently it's done by executive commissions, congressional committees, the Legislative Reference Service of the Library of Congress or an individual congressperson's staff.

The **bill is then** dropped into a box (hopper) on the desk of the **Clerk of the House.** It's assigned a number, read into the *Congressional Record* and sent to the **Government Printing Office,** which makes and distributes copies. The **Speaker of the House** then assigns the bill for study to a specific committee or sub-committee, depending on what the bill concerns—agriculture, defense, judicial matters, etc.

A **committee hearing** is really the first trial by fire for any new bill. The committee can table the bill, effectively killing it before it ever comes to a general vote. The committee may also revise the bill and or report it out. In that case the committee's report of recommendations is printed up and distributed and the bill is eligible to be voted on by the full House.

Before the vote, the bill must make its way through the **Rules Committee.** This group decides only on matters of procedure but its decisions can be a matter of life or death for proposed legislation. The committee determines what type of amendments, if any, will be allowed and what type of debate procedure will be followed; it also assigns the bill a place on the calendar. A lot of very important lobbying goes on between sponsoring representatives and members of the Rules Committee, for they can bury a bill so deep it will never see the light of day while Congress is in session. If that happens, the whole process must begin again—starting at the hopper.

The bill eventually comes up for **Second Reading** in front of the House. Any debate or amending takes place at this time. Majority and minority opponents and proponents of the bill are busy marshalling forces, persuading, and determining who will speak for their side on the floor of the House.

Finally, the bill gets a **Third Reading,** though in fact all that is read is its legislative number. A vote is then taken. In most cases only a simple majority is needed to pass a bill.

It's possible that while a bill has been moving through the House, a similar **companion bill** has been going through pretty much the same procedure in the Senate. In the event that both bills are passed, any differences between them are hammered out in a **Joint House-Senate Conference Committee.**

If there is no companion bill, a bill passed by the House moves across the Capitol building to the Senate where it starts a new round of committee hearings and votes. Any changes are put before a Joint Committee, and in most cases, a compromise version is arrived at. The revised text is printed and then goes before both chambers of Congress for another vote.

If the bill is passed in both houses, it is **enrolled.** This means a special copy is typeset on parchment. It goes to the Speaker of the House and the President of the Senate for signing, before it is sent to the president.

The president has 10 days in which to act on the bill. If he signs the bill it becomes law, and it automatically becomes law if he lets 10 days pass without taking any action. In the event that he vetoes the bill, ⅔ majority of the House and Senate are needed to **override** his decision. A rarely used third option is the **Pocket Veto.** If the bill comes to the president when there are less than 10 days left to the session of Congress, and the president declines to sign it, it dies.

Washington is the 15th largest US city, with 638,000 citizens. The DC metropolitan area has 3,060,240 people.

When the US government moved from Philadelphia to the new capital in 1800, the entire federal staff consisted of 150 people.

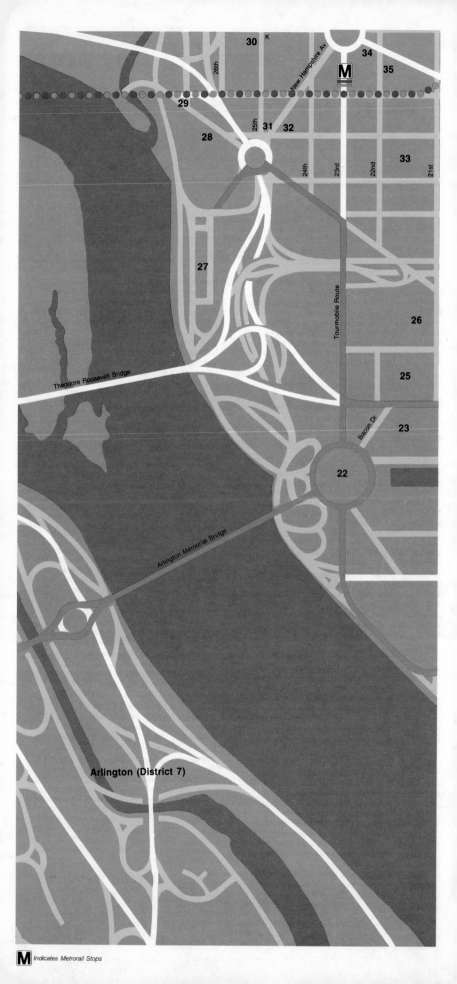

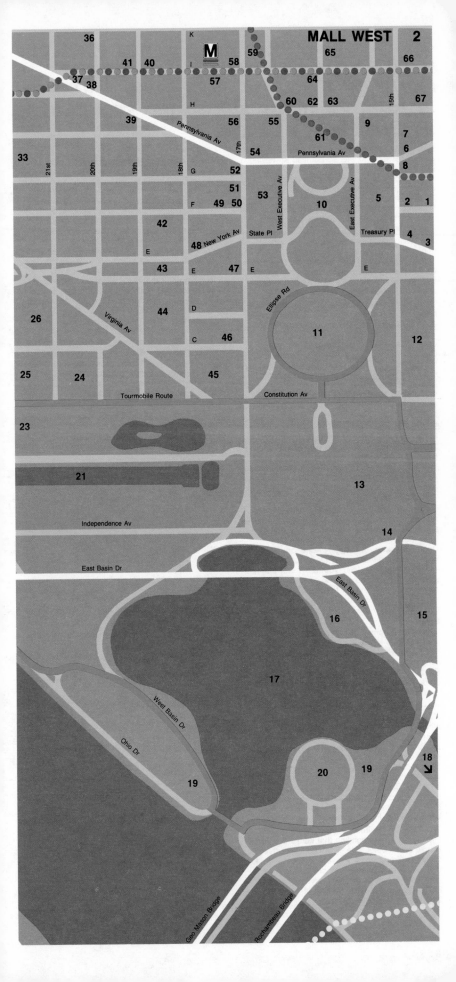

Before they painted it white, to cover the charring it received when the British burned it in 1814, the White House was known as the President's Palace.

That surely rankled its first presidential resident, **John Adams,** who was so horrified at moving into the unfinished, unheated shell of a building in the middle of nowhere that he refused to describe it to his as-yet-unarrived wife **Abigail,** for fear she wouldn't come to the new Washington at all. Instead, he circumspectly wrote her that *"You will form the best idea of it from inspection."*

The West Mall area was actually not very appealing to anyone in its early days. In fact, the *malarial effluvia* that was believed to come off the then-nearer Potomac River drove presidents and their families to the city's high ground every summer throughout the 19th century.

Gradually, of course, the nearby neighborhood began to grow. First came the still-standing **St. John's Church** across Lafayette Square. Those who worked with the executive branch of the government made their homes in the area. Capitol Hill, naturally, was where members of the legislative and judicial branches lived while they were in the capital. The 2 groups had some difficulty in socializing; getting from one area to the other in the city's first decades was an ordeal. There is speculation that placing the seat of government in a wilderness has had effects on the practice of politics and wielding of political power that are felt even today.

Though the members of the executive branch have long since moved to other neighborhoods, they have left their offices—and in some cases, their houses—behind. The most spectacular case is certainly **Lafayette Square,** in its heyday the very center of Washington.

"La Fayette Square was society," wrote **Henry Adams,** and he was right. Among the politically and socially powerful who made their homes there were **Andrew Jackson, Henry Clay, Daniel Webster,** and **Dolley Madison.** *"When you meet them in everyday life,"* wrote **President Tyler's** daughter-in-law, *"you forget that they are great men at all, and just find them the most charming companions in the world, talking the most delightful nonsense, especially Mr. Webster, who entertains me with the most charming gossip."*

Many of the homes of Lafayette Square still stand, thanks to the efforts of **President and Mrs. John F. Kennedy,** who suppressed a congressional order to build courthouses on the Square. The **Stephen Decatur House** is open to tours, though the **Blair House,** where foreign dignitaries stay, is not.

Webster's gossip, no doubt, surely included the still-told tale of how **Andrew Jackson** decided where the new **Treasury Building** should stand after the old one burned down. Jackson was crossing 15th Street listening to yet another report of Congress' agonizing over the decision. Having had enough, *Old Hickory* stuck his walking stick in the mud where he stood and ordered, *"Build it here."* They did, and, to the horror of later planners, interrupted the Capitol-to-White House vista, something the city has been trying to fix ever since.

The **Treasury Building** is open to the public, though the ornate building that flanks the White House on its other side, **The Old Executive Office Building,** isn't. **President Hoover** disliked that structure intensely and planned to have it converted to match the Treasury in all details. For better or worse, the coming of the Depression sidetracked him.

The city's most famous vista, from the **Capitol** to the **Washington Monument** to the **Lincoln Memorial,** could not have existed in Jackson's time. The ground on which the Lincoln Memorial stands was then river bottom, and even when it was reclaimed, House Speaker **Joe Cannon** promised that *"I'll never let a memorial to Abraham Lincoln be erected in that God-damned swamp."* For that matter, Washington's obelisk is not where it originally was supposed to be. Intended to be on an axis with the White House, engineers decided to move it a bit east; a happy decision as it turned out. That axis was completed in the 1930s when the **Jefferson Memorial** was built, and with the Washington Monument out of the way, the view between it and the White House was clear. **Franklin Roosevelt** asked that the White House trees be trimmed so that Jefferson might have a clear view of the president's home, and vice versa. It's been kept that way.

Visitors to the **Jefferson Memorial** are close to the **Bureau of Engraving and Printing,** where paper money is produced, and of course are right on top of the lovely Tidal Basin, where many a footsore visitor has been only too glad to while away an afternoon.

A comfortable view of the entire area can be had from the terrace of the elegant **Hotel Washington,** a favorite evening spot for Washingtonians.

L'Enfant's bill for the design of **The Federal City of Washington** totaled $95,000; after 8 years of silence, he finally accepted Congress' offer of $2,500.

When Pierre Charles L'Enfant died in 1825, the designer of Washington, DC, left an estate valued at a mere $46.

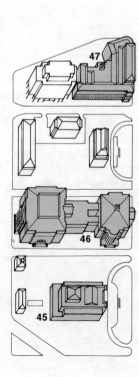

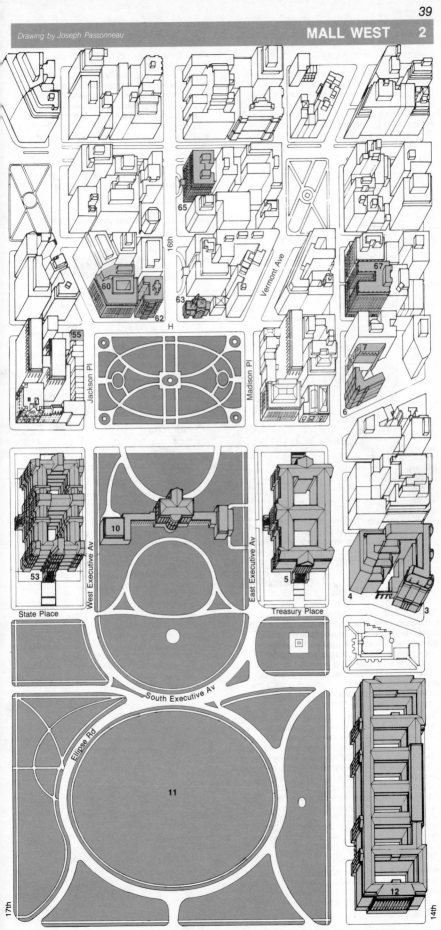

Drawing by Joseph Passonneau

1 **Garfinckel's** has been the most prestigious stop in the old F Street shopping corridor since 1938. Now the quality department store is spearheading the downtown retail renaissance with a multi-million dollar facelift. This is scheduled to coincide with the completion of developer **Oliver T. Carr's** controversial **Metropolitan Square**, the connecting shopping and office complex that has retained much—but not all—of the Beaux-Arts and historic facades of the landmarks along the half-block it occupies. The store caters to the carriage trade with high-fashion women's clothing and accessories; its men's shop offers tailored shirts in over 300 fabrics. *Open M-W & F 10am-6pm, Th 10am-8pm. Closed Su. 1401 F St. NW. 628-7730.*

2 **Old Ebbitt Grill.** ☆ ☆ $$ Though it's moved twice this century, the Old Ebbitt Grill maintains its reputation as a classic DC dining experience. You'll be served under Victorian gaslights in the company of a mounted walrus and a musk ox if you pay the Old Ebbitt Grill a visit. The Washington landmark, once again refurbished to reflect its original turn-of-the-century style, features an American cuisine menu that changes twice daily. Homemade pasta salads, skewers of flanksteak and perfectly grilled swordfish are but a few of the taste sensations; Old Ebbitt's fine mahogany-and-brass dining room is also famous for its rich desserts and old-fashioned ice cream made on the premises. *American. Open M-Th 7:30am-2am, F till 3am; Sa 10am-3am; Su 10am-2am. Reservations accepted. 1427 F St. NW. 347-4800.*

4 **Hotel Washington.** (1918, **Carrere** and **Hastings**) *Moderate/expensive.* Known as the *hotel with the view*, the Washington overlooks the White House and national monuments. Nearly every US president of the 20th century and thousands of national and international dignitaries have stayed here, attracted by the stately ambiance and extensive amenities. The Italian Rennaisance-inspired structure is the oldest operating hotel in the capital city. Part of its charm is the fine furnishings, including the original lobby's decor of brass, marble, Oriental rugs and other collector's items. *15th St. at Pennsylvania Ave. NW. Metrorail red line. 638-5900.*

Within the hotel are:

Two Continents Restaurant. Finest haute cuisine prepared by award-winning chef **Felix Veirans.** Breakfast and luncheon are served in the chic off-lobby location.

Western Plaza (See No. 39, District 1)

By Carlos Diniz

Its sister restaurant, **Two Continents in the Sky,** is open for dinner with a view during warm weather.

The Sky Terrace ($$) atop the grand old hotel is for clear, warm evenings and nights after the theater when gentle breezes flap canvas awnings and customers cradle a drink and stare into the panorama of the nation's capital from above. *Open daily noon-1am May-Sep. 347-4499.*

3 **Willard Hotel.** (1901, **Henry Hardenburg;** renovation 1984, **Vlastimil Koubek**) *Deluxe.* The classic Willard is more than 3-quarters of a century old, but don't despair. It is currently undergoing extensive refurbishment. When it reopens in May 1986, it is expected to be the most lavish and expensive hostelry in the capital. A sophisticated security system will protect the diplomats, heads of state and other dignitaries who will regularly stay here.

The first hotel on this site was built in 1819, and several have had this address, including the temporary home of **Julia Ward Howe**—she wrote *The Battle Hymn of the Republic* here. At the beginning of the 20th century, the then brand-new Willard was called *the home of presidents,* so often did it host foreign leaders visiting the White House. In 1923 **President Calvin Coolidge** lived here. *Peacock Alley,* the hotel's promenade, has been a focal point of Washington high society throughout the century. Hardenburg, who designed this fine Beaux-Arts corner, also created NYC's famous **Plaza Hotel.** *Metrorail red line. 1401 Pennsylvania Ave. NW. 293-1171.*

Within the hotel will be:

Willard Room. On a par with New York City's Palm Court, this restaurant will feature hot and cold buffets, after-theater drinks and desserts.

Crystal Room. Gourmet continental cuisine.

5 **Treasury Building.** (1836-1869, **Robert Mills** & **Thomas U. Walker**) After years of Congressional dilly-dallying, **Andrew Jackson** impatiently chose this site, even though it would block L'Enfant's intended view from the Capitol to the White House. Thus the oldest departmental office in DC turned out a grand Greek Revival obstacle. While the exterior surroundings are completely accessible, the interior is largely restricted to visitors. The lobby contains a cafeteria open to the public, and a stand with free brochures explaining the function of the Treasury. A small exhibit area, its entrance on East Executive Ave., features coins, medals and paper currency from 2 centuries. The building also houses a small theater which shows films describing various agencies within the Department. Only 10 percent of the Treasury's total work force is at this location; the Secretary of the Treasury's office is on the third floor. If you are brave, ask to see the famous spiral staircases. *1500 Pennsylvania Ave. NW. Metrorail red line. 566-2111.*

5 **Alexander Hamilton** balanced a national budget wrecked by war and established the Treasury, currency, the mint and a national bank, yet he was without a monument until 1923. The bronze portrait statue by **James Earle Fraser** is a masterpiece of naturalism, and young Mr. Hamilton cuts a very dashing figure. The statue's donor remains a secret. Rumors of the day spoke of a mysterious woman who always wore a veil. *Treasury Bldg., Treasury Pl. between E. Executive Ave. and 15th St. NW.*

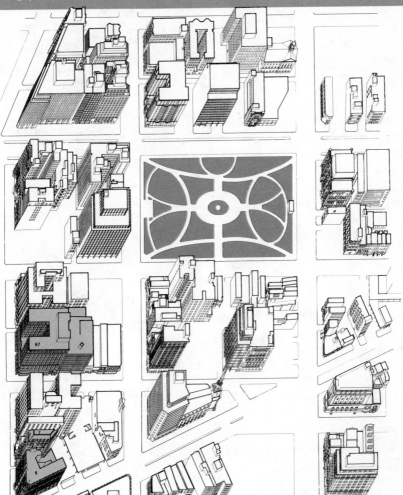

6 **National Savings & Trust Co.** (1880, **James Windrim**) The recently remodeled National Savings building is part of the Bankers' Classic group, which includes 3 other Roman temple structures: **American Security and Trust Co.** (1899, **York & Sawyer**) at 15th & Pennsylvania Ave. NW.; **Riggs National Bank** (1898, **York & Sawyer**), 1503 Pennsylvania Ave. NW.; and the **Union Trust Building** (1906, **Wood, Donn & Deming**), southwest corner of 15th & H Sts. NW. Windrim's design, which uses whimsical turrets and a strange mixture of Victorian ornamentation, is in direct juxtaposition to the other 3, which echo the Treasury building with their massive exterior columns. The intention was to give Washington's financial area a distinct and imposing face, a fashionable concept with bankers of that era. *15th & New York Ave. NW.*

7 **Folger Building & Playhouse Theater.** (1906, **Jules de Sibour**; theater, **Paul Pelz**) A most theatrical theater building, starring a 9-story tower capped with a majestic Beaux-Arts mansard roof. *715-725 15th St. NW.*

8 **Metropolitan Square.** (1983, **Vlastimil Koubek**) The new office/retail structure incorporates 3 old DC landmarks—the **Keith Theater/Albee Building,** the facade of the **National Metropolitan Bank,** and an expanded version of the historic **Old Ebbitt Grill**—into one modern complex. The adjoining Garfinckel's store, which can be entered from the Metropolitan Square lobby, adds its own energy to the block. *655 15th St. NW.*

Over 32 percent of Washingtonians are college-educated, the highest percentage of any American city.

9 **Dolley Madison House.** (1820) Now part of the Claims Court complex, this was the house where the widowed former first lady lived until her death in 1849. Power seekers and the social elite flocked to the area in the 1840s, so much so that the Lafayette Square house, its symbolic center, earned a reputation as the *real* lobby of the White House. Not currently open to the public. *H St. at Madison Pl. NW.*

Since 1973 the House of Representatives has been voting electronically. Forty-four terminals dot the floor of the House, usually attached to the backs of aisle seats. When representatives are called for a vote, they have 15 minutes to find the box and their voting card—it resembles a credit card—which they insert in the machine. They may vote *yea, nay* or *present.* Until the last 5 minutes, representatives may change their votes by plugging into another console.

Above the **Press Gallery** is a large electronic tote board with an alphabetical listing of all the representatives. Colored lights record how each voted. On the majority and minority leaders' desks, computers provide an instant breakdown of the vote according to party, state delegation, seniority, committee, whip zone, etc.

About 12 percent of the **US population** live in the Potomac Basin area.

Introductions/Theaters/Narrative black
Hotels purple
Museums/Architecture blue
Parks/Open spaces green
Restaurants/Nightlife red
Shops/Galleries violet

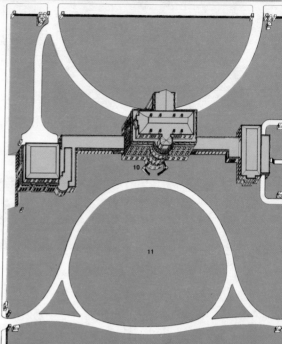

Drawing by Joseph Passonneau

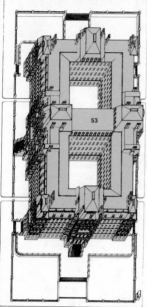

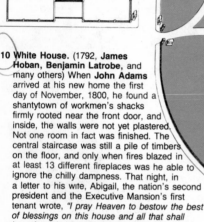

10 White House. (1792, **James Hoban, Benjamin Latrobe,** and many others) When **John Adams** arrived at his new home the first day of November, 1800, he found a shantytown of workmen's shacks firmly rooted near the front door, and inside, the walls were not yet plastered. Not one room in fact was finished. The central staircase was still a pile of timbers on the floor, and only when fires blazed in at least 13 different fireplaces was he able to ignore the chilly dampness. That night, in a letter to his wife, Abigail, the nation's second president and the Executive Mansion's first tenant wrote, *"I pray Heaven to bestow the best of blessings on this house and all that shall hereafter inhabit it. May none but honest and wise men ever rule under this roof."*

Since that less-than-auspicious first day, 39 families have called this house *Home.* The only US president not to list 1600 Pennsylvania Avenue as his home address was **George Washington,** who served his term in Philadelphia while the capital city was being built.

It was, in fact, George Washington who personally selected the site for the *President's Mansion* or the *President's Palace,* as it was more frequently referred to until **Theodore Roosevelt** dropped the imposing names and redubbed it *the White House.* When Washington staked out the site in 1791, the city was nothing more than an unpopulated wooded flatland, with one distinguishable rise in elevation which would later be known as **Capitol Hill.** One mile west of the hill—with a commanding vista of the Potomac and beyond that, Alexandria—the Executive Mansion would be built, Washington declared.

James Hoban, the original architect, was an Irishman, and despite many alterations the house remains as crisp, elegant and white as fine Irish linen. The Georgian country house he designed was first altered by **Thomas Jefferson,** who had lost the original design competition to Hoban but used his clout as third president to make up for it. During the War of 1812 the British decided to take remodeling into their own hands. They gutted the interior and burned a sizeable portion of the exterior for good measure. Hoban was enlisted to reconstruct the building after the fire. The building's Virginia sandstone was painted white to cover fire damage, and it is speculated that this is the origin for the moniker, *White*

House. Other alterations have included the front portico (1829); the wings (**McKim, Mead & White,** 1902); and modern amenities including running water (1833), gas (1848), bathrooms (1878) and electricity (1890). The house has been remodeled twice: in 1902, in conjunction with the wing additions, and in the late 1940s, after it was discovered to be too dangerous structurally to allow President **Harry Truman** to move in. The project took 3 years and required that the building be completely taken apart and reconstructed. It currently comprises 132 rooms.

Down through the years the mansion has witnessed one presidential wedding (**Grover Cleveland**), 5 First Family weddings, 11 births, 7 presidential funerals and at least 39 more minor redecorations— and numerous scandals.

Courtesy Bureau of Engraving & Printing

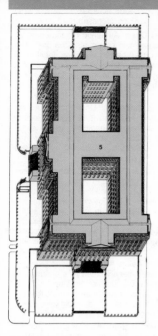

The White House tour takes you through 5 rooms on the mansion's first floor. The **East Room,** where **Abigail Adams** hung her laundry to dry and **Teddy Roosevelt's** children improved their roller skating, is today used for receptions, press conferences, concerts and dances. On the east wall is **Gilbert Stuart's** famous painting of George Washington, purportedly rescued by **Dolley Madison** with no time to spare when the British invaded the city in 1814. Seven presidents who died in office, including **Lincoln** and **Kennedy,** have lain in state in this room.

Connecting doors lead from the East Room, through the small reception room known as the **Green Room,** into the oval-shaped **Blue Room.** Grover Cleveland used this room as a wedding chapel in 1886 when he married **Frances Folsom,** and the White House Christmas tree usually stands here. Just off the Blue Room is **Mrs. Ronald Reagan's** favorite, the **Red Room,** where **Rutherford Hayes** secretly took the oath of office after the contested 1877 presidential race. The final tour stop is the **State Dining Room.** Be sure to note the inscription on the marble mantle, ordered put there by **Franklin Delano Roosevelt**—it's John Adams' White House prayer.

Admission to the White House is free, but tickets are required during summer. Tickets available at booths on the Ellipse south of the White House at 8am and are oftentimes all distributed by 9am. White House open Tu-Sa except Christmas and New Year's 10am-2pm Memorial Day-Labor Day; 10am-noon in the off-season. Be forewarned that especially during the summer months, the wait in line can be as long as 2 hours and the tour as short as 10 minutes. In the off-season, line up at the East Gate on E. Executive Ave. no later than 10 am. (People with handicaps need not wait in line. Go directly to the Northeast Gate on Pennsylvania Ave.) Signed tours for the hearing impaired are available Tu-Sa at 8am; call TDD 456-2216 to make advance arrangements. No tours are offered during state visits, so call ahead. The best advice: Contact your senator or congressperson far in advance of your visit (6 months is not too soon) and arrange for a VIP tour. This tour is offered earlier in the day than the regular tours (7:30-10am) and generally lasts about 30 minutes.

Special White House occasions: Each December, a candlelight tour of the White House dressed for Christmas is offered. In the spring and fall, an afternoon Garden Tour opens the usually off-limits White House grounds to the public. On Easter Monday from 10am-2pm, the traditional White House Easter Egg Roll takes place. Call or write for details. 1600 Pennsylvania Ave. NW. Metrorail red line. 456-1414.

Designed to serve not only as home but also as the office of the president, it was not uncommon for the 2 functions to get crossed. In 1902, the second floor was at last set aside for the exclusive use of the president's family, but as late as 1962 the First Family's meals were still being served on the non-private first floor since the second floor had no kitchen.

When **Jacqueline Kennedy,** wife of the 35th president, **John Kennedy,** arrived at the White House in 1961, she found the interior decor to be a mishmash of at least 34 different decorating tastes with very few historically accurate (or original) objects left intact. Deciding that *"everything in the White House must have a reason for being there,"* Mrs. Kennedy spearheaded an extensive restoration project aimed at bringing back to the White House the furnishings and possessions used during previous presidential administrations. Significant artifacts were scattered throughout the globe, but were available; early in the 20th century the descendant of a British soldier had graciously returned **James Madison's** medicine box, pilfered during the burning of the White House in 1814. Under Mrs. Kennedy's direction, people from all over the world pitched in on the project. Thanks in large part to the efforts of Jackie Kennedy and subsequent administrations, which have continued the collection, today's White House is as much a museum of priceless Americana as it is a home and an office.

The US president still remains one of the most sought-after public figures; he receives more than 20,000 letters daily.

1 MALL EAST

It's probably the biggest and best attended party the government throws, but you don't need a tuxedo. Since grass stains are almost inevitable, jeans and sneakers are just fine. It's the annual **Easter Egg Roll** on the White House Lawn, and all children under the age of 8 (and accompanied by an adult) are welcome. In 1983, 30,000 people frolicked on the grass while **Nancy Reagan** officiated and life-sized cartoon characters provided entertainment.

According to local legend, the kids of DC were big egg rollers over 100 years ago. Their favorite spot was the gently rolling slope of the Capitol lawn, which they destroyed on an annual basis. Luckily the wife of **President Hayes** was passing by when they were chased away in 1877. She took pity on the crying urchins and invited them to the White House. They've been coming back ever since.

Reports from President **Grover Cleveland's** day say that children swarmed the grounds, crowding around the White House basement door asking for drinks of water. Some of the kids even invaded the East Room where Cleveland was greeting the adult public. They had heard a rumor the president wanted to meet them, and though this was not the case, Cleveland obligingly shook many small grubby hands.

During World War II **Franklin Delano Roosevelt** canceled the egg roll. However, accounts of the last pre-cancellation event show how popular it had become with the public. Over 53,000 people braved scorching weather to be there. Ten were treated for heat exhaustion, 4 passed out, and 78 children lost their parents.

The egg roll remained on hiatus for 12 years, long after the war was over. The White House social secretary under Truman defended this gross humbuggery by calling the ceremony an *orgy of wasted eggs*.

Traditionally, the event is hosted by the First Lady, and it was **Mamie Eisenhower** who decided that happy times in the '50s warranted a comeback. After 12 years no one knew quite what to expect. Yards of storm fencing were put up to protect flower beds and the president's putting green. Restrooms and drinking fountains were hastily erected.

When the great day arrived, the lawn was mobbed. Kids threw more eggs than they rolled, and the Eisenhower children retreated rapidly to the White House. The president, who was holding his baby granddaughter, had to be rescued from an adoring throng by Secret Service agents. Even though the lawn was a matted mess of eggs, jelly beans and chocolate marshmallows, the event was acclaimed a huge success.

Nowadays, the government has more experience with these kinds of things and mopping up rarely takes more than an afternoon.

The latest change in the event came in 1981 with the Reagan administration. All participants were given wooden eggs with the White House insignia on them as a prize. In addition, the White House sends out thousands of eggs to politicians, sports and entertainment celebrities to be autographed and returned. These eggs are used in the **Easter Egg Hunt** which takes place off to the side of the White House, but concurrently with the egg roll.

All rolling now takes place in 8 well marked lanes, but real eggs and long handled spoons are still used. Twenty-five kids at a time are allowed into the enclosure used for the egg hunt.

The White House has also begun sending out eggs to respected American artists and foreign embassies for special decoration. Actually they get 2 eggs each—one for practice. The finished results, which are often quite wonderful, are exhibited in a display case on the lawn.

To attend, just show up at the *Southeast Gate to the White House between 10am and 2pm on Easter Monday. Some people line up as early as 7am.*

John Naisbitt
Author, *Megatrends*

The Bread Oven. Authentic French country restaurant. Bread and croissants—the best in the city—are baked on the premises. Ideal for breakfast meetings, this is also the best place for a non-egg breakfast in the city. Lunch and dinner are moderately priced and extravagantly delicious. *1220 19th St. NW. 466-4264.*

Radishes & Rainbows. Underground at the **Connecticut Connection,** this mall-type eatery features the freshest, healthiest salads and sandwiches in the US. Also frozen yogurt in 4 flavors. *1101 Connecticut Ave. NW. (Connecticut & L) 223-8880.*

The C&O Canal. Starts at the **Four Seasons Hotel** in Georgetown and winds almost 200 miles along the Potomac River to Cumberland, Maryland. The 8 to 11-foot-wide tow path is one of the great places to run in the world, partly because much of it overlooks the more beautiful bends in the Potomac. Also ideal for bicycling and just plain walking. Nicely populated on weekends. Contact the National Park Service.

Trocadero Asian Art. Washington's only Oriental art gallery, located in a beautiful, triangular glassed-in building on Dupont Circle. Talk with David or Kitty for an education in Oriental art. Modest prices for impressive pieces. *1501 Connecticut Ave. NW. 234-5656.*

Tea at the Four Seasons Hotel. The perfect break from Georgetown shopping: formal afternoon tea in a lush setting. *2800 Pennsylvania Ave. NW. 342-0444.*

East Wing of the National Gallery of Art. This **I.M. Pei** building is a piece of sculpture in itself, with a tremendous **Calder** mobile as its centerpiece. Revolving exhibits are beautifully staged, and the permanent **David Smith** room is a religious experience in a sacred space. *Constitution Ave. and 6th St. NW. 737-4215 for general information.*

The News Room. Best range and selection of out-of-town newspapers, city magazines, and special-interest magazines in town. Ice cream, quiche, or cappuccino are available while you browse. *1753 Connecticut Ave. NW. 332-1489.*

Dumbarton Oaks. Owned by trustees of Harvard University, this beautiful museum houses a fabulous pre-Colombian collection, and is surrounded by a variety of gardens that are breathtaking all year round. Picnic afterwards in adjacent Montrose Park. Museum is free; garden tours are $1. *1703 32nd St. NW. 338-8278.*

Yes! Bookstore. The East Coast's best bookstore for New Age religion, philosophy, and self-development. A bookstore with an intensely spiritual atmosphere and a far-reaching inventory. *1035 31st St. NW. 338-7874.*

The Phillips Collection. A private, eclectic collection of primarily American and French artists, Impressionists (including Renoir's *The Luncheon of the Boating Party*), Post-Impressionists, and Modernists. Favorites are **Edward Hopper, Arthur Dove, Paul Klee, de Stijl.** Exhibited in what was the Phillips home, this 1890s' house has been newly renovated and offers a lovely, intimate way to enjoy art. *1600 21st St. NW. 387-0961.*

Kramerbooks & Afterwards Cafe. Washington's #1 bookstore cafe. Singles scene; that's where I met my wife. Good luck! *1517 Connecticut Ave. NW. 387-1462.*

The Jefferson Memorial at Night. This tribute to America's architect and greatest citizen must be seen and experienced at night. It is located at the Tidal Basin; take a cab and have it wait.

---

11 Ellipse. The oval-shaped yard south of the White House is best known as the site of the National Christmas tree, which is lit by the president each December. Carolers and other holiday celebrants fill the area with pageantry throughout the holiday season. During the rest of the year vendors, chess players and strollers fill the park on sunny days.

2 Washington Area Convention & Visitors Association. This is a good place to start your visit to Washington, DC. The city's main clearing house for tourism information is in the WACVA's Department of Commerce center just east of the White House. Here you'll find desks filled with brochures offering all kinds of tips on everything from sightseeing to accommodations, to dining. WACVA, Traveler's Aid, National Park Service, White House Historical Association and International Visitors Information Service have staffs on hand to answer questions and offer advice. *Open M-Sa 9am-5pm, with special peak-season hours. (You can mail requests to 1575 Eye St., Suite 250.) Dept. of Commerce, 1400 Pennsylvania Ave. NW. Metrorail blue/orange lines. Phone information, 789-7000.*

Drawing by Joseph Passonneau

2 National Aquarium. In 1974, the oldest aquarium in the country celebrated its centennial. Eight years later, when it lost the federal funding necessary to maintain the 225-plus species of marine life, a private, non-profit group named the National Aquarium Society was formed to find other sources of support. With the help of grants and donations, the facility is still located in the depths of the Department of Commerce building. Green-lit tanks display 1,000 fresh and saltwater marine specimens, as well as rare giant Asian seaturtles. Cafeteria and small bookshop. Shark feeding every M, W, Sa at 2pm. *Admission charge. 14th St. at Constitution Ave. NW. 377-2825.*

13 Washington Monument. (1848-1885) Rising majestically from the center of the Mall, the Washington Monument's presence, both simple and grand, is felt over the entire city. At 555 feet and 5-1/8 inches, it is the tallest structure in the District and was the tallest in the world when it first opened to the public in 1886.

The 1836 Monument Committee, which launched a nationwide competition to select a landmark for the capital, favored **Robert Mills'** marble tower over **L'Enfant's** equestrian statue of Washington that was to stand on the current site of the Jefferson Pier. The original winning design had a richly decorated obelisk (stone tower) rising like a giant birthday candle from behind a circular Greek-style temple that would have held the tombs of Revolutionary War heroes. In front, there was to be a massive marble statue of Washington driving a *quadriga*—a Roman chariot pulled by 4 horses. Lack of money and public support for these frills have left us with this simple gleaming tower—the most recognizable symbol of Washington the city as well as Washington the man.

Courtesy
Bureau of Engraving & Printing

The White House enjoys triple protection: The uniformed division of the **Secret Service** guards the White House grounds; the **Park Police** of the National Park Service patrols the sidewalks around the White House; and Pennsylvania Avenue itself is covered by the **DC Metropolitan Police.**

Washington has the most historic places in the country: 158. In comparison, New York City has 111.

Funds for the monument initially came from private groups who solicited $1 from citizens across the nation. Construction on the tower proceeded for 7 years, until a single block of marble for the building was donated by the Pope. This infuriated the anti-papist Know-Nothing Party, which stole the Committee's records and sabotaged attempts to raise funds for the monument. Then the Civil War intervened, and the project was abandoned for almost 20 years. In 1876—after the war and the Centennial Exhibition—public interest was renewed and the project was turned over to the Army Corps of Engineers. They strengthened the foundation (although it still sinks ¼ inch every 30 years) and redesigned the monument, much improving the proportions of the original design. Four years later, the pyramidion was finally capped with a 9-inch tip made of solid aluminum (an exotic material at the time) and wired with 144 platinum lightning conductors. The $1 million tab was picked up by the government. Today, you can take a 70-second elevator up and down. The view from the top is magnificent. On the 4th of July the monument is the site of a splendid fireworks display. *Admission free. Open daily 9am-5pm, 8am-midnight during summer. Mall, south of the White House.*

14 Sylvan Theater. This outdoor theater with a huge lawn regularly presents delightful musicals, Shakespearean festivals and military bands, weather permitting. Thousands of people flock to the small stage during hot summer nights and claim the best picnic spots in front of the stage by spreading a picnic blanket, or setting up their own lawn chairs. *Admission free. Call 426-6700 for program information.*

When the **steam-operated elevator** first opened in the **Washington Monument** in the late 1800s, it was considered so unsafe that only men were allowed to ride in it. The more delicate women had to climb the 898 steps to the summit. Today there is an electric elevator and the trip takes only 70 seconds.

---

left to right: Stele of Hammurabi, Egypt; Obelisk at Axum, Egypt; Obelisk in India; Cleopatra's Needle, London; Stele at Axum, Egypt; Obelisk in Rome

Obelisks—tall, slender 4-sided monoliths that taper to a point or pyramid—were first used by the Egyptians. Pairs of the graceful geometric figures were used to adorn the doorways of temples; they were most often carved of red granite and honored **Ra,** the Egyptian sun god. Traditionally, obelisks were designed so that their height was 10 times the width of their flat bottom. The stone column was usually set on a circular base.

Several Egyptian obelisks have survived the ages, including those at the **Great Temple at Karnak** in Thebes. During the period of European colonialism, several of these Egyptian treasures were moved to Europe and the US. The obelisk at Paris' Place de la Concorde once stood at Luxor. Twin obelisks, both known as **Cleopatra's Needle,** have been separated; one now stands at London's Embankment, the other in New York City's Central Park.

Of course, the **Washington Monument** is obelisk-shaped and follows the Egyptian formula for an obelisk's height. But the fact that it isn't a single, solid stone—a monolith—keeps it from being a true obelisk.

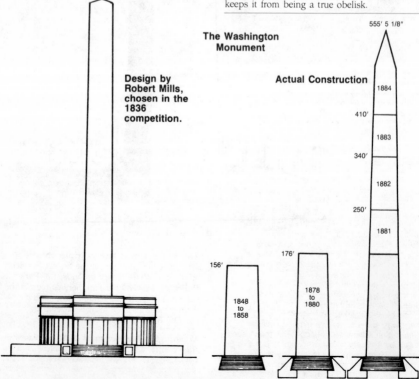

600'

Design by Robert Mills, chosen in the 1836 competition.

The Washington Monument

555' 5 1/8"

Actual Construction

1884

410'

1883

340'

1882

250'

1881

176'

1878 to 1880

156'

1848 to 1858

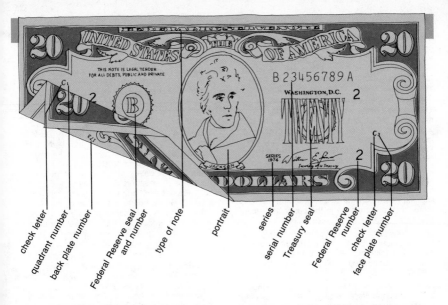

check letter — quadrant number — back plate number — Federal Reserve seal and number — type of note — portrait — series — serial number — Treasury seal — Federal Reserve number — check letter — face plate number

15 Bureau of Engraving and Printing. Once every fiscal year the Federal Reserve puts in an order at the Bureau of Engraving and Printing. The order is for paper money, so much of it, in fact, that the presses must roll 24 hours a day to print it. The Bureau estimates it will print 6 billion notes in 1984 at a face value of $60 billion. To put this all into perspective, if you were to have that much money in $1 bills and spend it at the reasonable rate of a $1 per second, it would take you almost 200 years to go broke. If instead of spending it you decided to lay out all those bills end-to-end, you could circle the equator at least 22 times.

The Bureau prints more than money: 40 billion postage stamps, treasury notes, military certificates, and invitations to the White House. In the past it's printed food stamps, and during the oil embargo of 1973, it had an order—never fulfilled—to print coupons for gas rationing.

Watching crisp sheets of money roll off the presses is great fun for kids and provides much fuel for fantasies of adults. The bureau offers a free 20-minute tour. **Enter through the main lobby** where some of the Bureau's products as well as part of a press plate, stamp sheets (4 times the size of the ones from the post office), and some first-rate examples of counterfeiters' nefarious art are displayed.

Continue to the gallery which is one story above the production floor and offers an excellent view of large sheets of money being printed, checked, overprinted with the treasury seal, cut, stacked and bundled for shipment. A recorded explanation of the sights plays over a PA system as you move along.

The tour ends in the **Visitors Center** where presidential portraits and commemorative coins are on display and for sale. You can also buy small bags of shredded money.

Admission free. Tours run M-F 8am-2pm. 14th and C Sts. SW. 447-9709/447-9916.

While coins are minted in several cities, all the paper currency in the country is made in Washington at the **Bureau of Engraving and Printing.** (You may have noticed the names of other cities on the Federal Reserve Seal, these are Federal Reserve Bank branches to which the money is shipped for distribution.) The Bureau is authorized to make $1, $2, $5, $10, $20, $50, $100, $500, $1,000, and $5,000 dollar bills, but in 1969 they stopped making anything over $100 because of lack of use. Some of the higher denomination bills may still be in the hands of collectors, but when they turn up at a bank they are pulled from circulation and destroyed.

About $20 billion worth of currency is printed each year, largely to replace bills that have worn out. The most common bill made is the $1 bill. Production of this bill alone takes up more than

half the Bureau's time, which is why they were so eager to re-issue the $2 bill in 1976. Unfortunately the new bill—along with the **Susan B. Anthony** dollar—was a resounding flop with the public and is no longer printed.

The value of the dollar you earn may be declining, but the quality of the paper it's printed on keeps improving. The stock (manufactured by a private firm under government contract) is 25 percent linen and 75 percent cotton. The longer fibers of this pulp give the paper exceptional strength. The paper is also shot through with miniscule fibers of blue and red silk to help thwart counterfeiters. In fact, making a similar paper is against federal law. The average life span of a $1 bill is 18 months—up almost 10 months from 1960. It costs 2.4 cents to make a note of any denomination. That's 24 bucks per 1,000 bills.

Money is still printed—as very few things are today—by an *intaglio* process. The design is cut deep into a *plate* and then, under great pressure, embossed on the paper. The process begins when a master engraver gouges out the design on a soft metal plate. After the plate has been cut and approved, it's case hardened by being dipped into a cyanide bath heated to 1,800 degrees. The plate is then taken to a transfer table where a small cylindrical steel roller is passed over it until the impression has been transferred. The master plate is returned to a vault and the new plate, called the *roller die*, is case hardened. The roller die is put on a step-and-repeat machine. The design, now raised, is pressed under great pressure on to a flat sheet of metal that will become the *press plate*. Once the design has been fixed on the plate and checked under a magnifying glass for mistakes, the process is repeated until the press plate holds the image of 32 bills. The new plate must be cleaned, trimmed, chrome-plated and curved to fit on the press before it's ready to print money. If you were allowed to look at a master plate, you would see how the minute amount of distortion that results from curving the image is accounted for in the original design.

In fact it's very rare that a new master plate must be engraved. The last time was in 1976 when the $2 bill was re-issued with design changes. The time before that was in 1960 when the words *In God We Trust* were added to the back of all notes.

After the now-cylindrical press plate has been inked and scraped—so that ink remains only in the indentations—80 tons of pressure is used to force the paper against it. The back of each bill is first printed with green ink (hence the moniker *greenback*). Twenty-four hours later the front is printed with black ink.

The average press plate is good for 300,000 sheets of bills. A good pressman will look at the fine line that borders all money; if he notices any

deterioration, the plate is pulled. It's stripped and replated, emerging strong enough for another 300,000 sheets. Old press plates are cut up and melted down. Contrary to what you may have seen at the movies, no counterfeiter has ever managed to steal one.

The printed sheets are moved to COPE machinery, which unfortunately has nothing to do with helping you cope with the rising cost of money. It stands for *Currency Overprinting and Processing Equipment*. This gizmo uses a different type of ink and the offset printing process to print the Treasury Seal, serial numbers, signatures and Federal Reserve Bank Seal on the bills. (They used to put sizing—like laundry starch—on the bills at this stage to make them crisp, but changes in the paper have made this unnecessary.)

In the final stage before shipping to appropriate Federal Reserve Banks, the COPE machinery cuts and stacks the bills in 100-note packages. These are assembled in 40-unit groups called bricks.

Later, banks around the country funnel money back to Federal Reserve Banks, where automatic counting machines sort the money, pull out worn bills, shred them and replace them with new ones.

Paper money design has changed very little since 1928, when the size of the notes was reduced. In 1935 the Great Seal, front and back, was added to the $1 bill and in 1960 the words *In God We Trust* were put on the back of all notes.

During World War II special money was printed that was easily differentiated from regular currency and could be declared void if it fell into enemy hands. American troops in North Africa and Sicily had bills whose Treasury Seal was printed in yellow. Another issue was printed for Hawaii and combat areas in the Pacific. The Treasury Seal and serial numbers were printed in brown, and the word Hawaii was overprinted on the face of the bill.

The old $2 bill was discontinued in 1963. When it was reissued in 1976, the picture of Monticello on the back was replaced with a reproduction of a painting by Trumbull of the signing of the Declaration of Independence. There wasn't room to reproduce the whole thing, so 6 of the signers were left out, greatly upsetting several state historical societies.

Before the Civil War, roughly one-third of all circulating paper money was bogus. Of course, having 1,600 separate state banks each designing and issuing their own notes only made the counterfeiter's life easier. The government responded by adopting a national currency in 1863. However, the new money was soon so widely counterfeited that the government created the Secret Service, whose special task was, and is, to fight enterprising crooks who stashed printing presses in their basements.

The fight continues and, according to the Treasury Department, super sophisticated commercial copying machines make the fight harder. In response to a perceived threat from a new line of color copiers due out at the end of the decade, the Treasury has set up a committee to recommend ways in which money can be made harder to copy.

One plan under consideration—to print each denomination in a different color—was rejected. Among the ideas still being considered are the addition of special threads to the paper which would be visible only under refracted light; background tinting of the bills with minute flecks of color; and optically variable printing, a method that gives a slight 3D effect and is very hard to duplicate.

No change will be made for several years until the Treasury decides to do so and new equipment is manufactured and tested. The new greenbacks, whatever their eventual color, will gradually be phased in, and outmoded currency slowly withdrawn, the same way gold and silver certificates have been phased out in the past.

16 Cherry Trees. Part of cherry blossom time's magic is that you never know exactly when it will arrive. Yet every spring—sometime between March 20th and April 17th—the trees bloom, lovers swoon and traffic around the Tidal Basin comes to a standstill.

Blossoms or no, each year the **Cherry Blossom Festival** begins with the ceremonial lighting of the Mall's **Japanese Lantern**. For a full week, pageants, parades, concerts and even a marathon run celebrate the return of the beloved blossoms. Festival planners have settled on the first week of April and nature usually obliges. About 2 weeks before the blooming, the meteorologists at National Capital Park Service make their predictions. You can write or phone them at **Ecological Services Library,** *1100 Ohio Dr. SW, Washington, DC 20242. 426-6796.*

The history of the trees is almost as colorful as their blossoms. Responding to a hint from **Mrs. William Taft,** the Japanese sent over a shipment of saplings in 1909. They were hardly uncrated before the Department of Agriculture declared them infested and had them destroyed. Apologies were tendered and accepted and in 1912, 3,000 more trees arrived in Washington. The hundreds planted around the Tidal Basin have become the most popular. The majority are *Akebono* trees with delicate white blossoms; scattered among them are *Yoshino* trees whose petals are pale pink.

The public was so taken with the trees that in the 1940s, when it was announced some would have to be moved to make way for the Jefferson Memorial, nature lovers chained themselves to tree trunks while the more militant occupied holes left by already uprooted trees. Later, after the Japanese bombing of Pearl Harbor, some of the trees were vandalized. In 1965, the US sent cuttings to Tokyo so the Japanese could replenish native stocks that had been weakened by war and pollution.

The best way to see the Tidal Basin blossoms is on foot. In fact, driving can be a miserable experience, with traffic stacked up and blocked-in drivers becoming irate. Park the car and use public transportation to reach the Mall area, then walk through the lovely, lively park, where the festive blossoms bring out vendors and street performers. Other places to see Japanese cherry trees are the Washington Monument grounds (3,000 trees), or East Potomac Park, where almost 2,000 pink, double-blossomed trees bloom 2 weeks later than their cousins at the Tidal Basin. *Take the 14th St. Bridge and head south on Ohio Drive to the park.* (You might also consider driving to **Kenwood,** just 6 miles northeast of downtown Washington. The town's quiet streets are lined for miles with tightly packed rows of pink and white blooming trees. *Take Exit 16 off the Capital Beltway, turn southeast on River Rd., left on Dorset, left on Highland. Or take Wisconsin Ave. from Downtown north to River Rd. Call Bethesda/Chevy Chase Chamber of Commerce for information, 301-652-4900.*

17 Tidal Basin. One of the Capital's most stunning outdoor areas, this park and breeze-swept lake are even more breathtaking when the 600 surrounding cherry trees are in bloom. An ideal place to picnic, jog, read; great views of the city, Jefferson Memorial, Washington Monument, and, soon to be built on 9 acres to the west, the FDR Memorial. On the east side are gardens of seasonal flowers—especially brilliant in spring, when the tulips bloom—and a concession stand that sells hotdogs and burgers and rents the little blue paddleboats that skim the lake. Near East Basin Dr. is the **Japanese Pagoda,** and near the **Kutz Memorial Bridge** the **Japanese Lantern** whose lighting signals the start of the Cherry Blossom Festival. The basin was created in 1897 to capture water from the Potomac and empty into the Washington Channel, possible because the river is an estuary here and rises with the tide. *Concession open daily Apr-Nov 11am-dusk; 488-9730. 15th St. at Ohio Dr. SW, East Potomac Park.*

9 Potomac Parks/Haines Point. These parks—East Potomac being the peninsula created by the Washington Channel, West Potomac being the area around the Tidal Basin and to the Lincoln Memorial—cover 700 acres at the west, Potomac River-end of the Mall. Scattered with monuments and some of the city's best views, pools and trees, they offer excellent recreational space. You can play golf at either of 2 public golf courses, ride bikes, paddle a boat, picnic, or just enjoy the Potomac sunshine. At Haines Point, the peninsula's southern tip, you'll find cool breezes, a respite from the city's bustle, and *The Awakening,* Seward Johnson's unusual 1980 aluminum sculpture that shows a figure rising out of the ground, as if just waking up. *South of Independence Ave., west of 14th St. SW. For information call 426-6700.*

The interior of the coffered dome (honeycomb-like recesses) is of Indiana limestone. The walls are of white Georgia marble and the floors of pink and grey Tennessee marble. Four entrances bring light and fresh air into the gracefully proportioned chamber. The landscaping around the memorial was done by **Frederick Law Olmsted, Jr.**

The interior is dominated by a 19-foot-high portrait statue of Jefferson—who stood 6 feet 2½ inches in life. He wears knee breeches, a waistcoat and fur-collared greatcoat given him by the Polish patriot **Thaddeus Kosciusko.** The sculpture is by **Rudolph Evans,** whose design was chosen over 100 other submissions. During dedication ceremonies, officiated by **Franklin Delano Roosevelt,** the sculpture was represented by a plaster model. It couldn't be cast in bronze until several years later when the war-time ban on domestic metal use was lifted.

10 Jefferson Memorial. (1943, **John Russell Pope**) The last great monument to be erected on the Mall is a fitting tribute to a man who was an accomplished architect as well as a powerful statesman.

Essentially an adaptation of the Roman Parthenon beloved by Jefferson, the memorial recalls Jefferson's own designs at his home Monticello and for the rotunda of the University of Virginia. The circular building is rimmed by 54 Ionic columns and is fronted, on the side facing the Mall, with a classical portico and a pediment supported by even more columns. Three other entrances bring light and fresh air into the gracefully proportioned chamber.

Like so much of the Mall, the Memorial site was under brackish water until the commencement of an 8-year-long dredging project. The land reclaimed wasn't strong enough to support the Memorial, whose every column weighs 45 tons, without a specially prepared foundation. Concrete-filled steel cylinders were driven 135 feet into the earth before being countersunk in bedrock.

Any local postcard stand will handily prove that the Jefferson Memorial is one of the most popular attractions in a city where you can hardly take 2 steps without tripping over something monumental in either bronze or marble. But it wasn't always so. At the time of its construction, the memorial was denounced as being too sweet and feminine. The columns caused it to be called a *"cage for Jefferson's statue,"* and the low, circular shape prompted one critic to rename the memorial *"Jefferson's muffin."*

Introductions/Theaters/Narrative black
Hotels purple
Museums/Architecture blue
Parks/Open spaces green
Restaurants/Nightlife red
Shops/Galleries violet

Open all night, though restrooms and display area, as well as external illumination, close at midnight. Rotunda is open and lighted through the night. Some parking available. East Potomac Park off 14th St. and East Basin Dr. SW.

21 Reflecting Pool. Dramatic wading pool captures reflections of both the Washington Monument and Lincoln Memorial on its glassy surface. The pool is 350 feet long by 180 feet wide; its depth is a uniform 3 feet. It has been the site of numerous celebrations and demonstrations, including the 1963 Civil Rights **March on Washington** which climaxed with **Martin Luther King, Jr.'s** *I Have A Dream* speech given to 250,000 crowded around, and in, the pool. (King stood on the steps of the Lincoln Memorial.) *West end of Mall, between the Lincoln Memorial and the Washington Monument.*

22 The Lincoln Memorial, so perfectly etched on Washington's landscape—not to mention the backs of the penny and $5 bill—was built only after much debate on its shape and location. Among the early proposals were an obelisk, a pyramid and—sponsored by car and real estate interests—a 72-mile-long memorial parkway between Gettysburg and Washington.

The site eventually chosen was a flea-ridden, soggy swamp that had to be drained and land-filled before construction could begin in 1914. Now a better choice seems unimaginable. The classically styled memorial anchors the east-west axis of the Mall. Lincoln gazes over the Reflecting Pool towards the Washington Monument and the Capitol. To the rear, a symbolic, imaginary line connects him with **Robert E. Lee's** home in **Arlington Cemetery.**

The **Capitol dome** is cast iron painted to look like marble. It must be repainted every 6 or 7 years, a job requiring 600 gallons of paint.

Architect **Henry Bacon** designed the building, which is essentially a Greek-style temple *("Coolly cribbed from the Parthenon"* one critic reported) with a Roman-style attic or roof. The entrance is on the broad side facing the Mall rather than on one of the narrow ends, as would have been typical in antiquity.

A colonnade of 36 Doric columns rims the building. Above them a frieze is inscribed with the names and admission dates of the 36 states in the Union at the time of Lincoln's death. (The date for Ohio is off by one year.) Higher up on the attic frieze are inscribed the names of the 48 states in the Union at the time of the memorial's dedication in 1922.

Daniel Chester French's statue, often called *the Brooding Lincoln*, commands the center of the memorial. French designed the statue but only supervised the carving; it took the **Piccarilli Brothers** 4 years and 28 blocks of white Georgia marble to execute it. The 16th president leans back in a monumental throne adorned with fasces, the Roman symbol of the authority of state. Much attention has been focused on the massive hands, which seem alive with emotion. Just before sculpting Lincoln, French had done a statue of **Albert Gallaudet,** famed teacher of the deaf. A close and perhaps imaginative examination of Lincoln's hands show one forming the sign of the letter A and the other signing the letter L.

From heel to head the statue measures 19 feet, but if Lincoln—our tallest president—were to stand, he would tower above the crowd at a height of 28 feet.

On the north and south walls of the memorial are murals 12 feet high and 600 feet long by **Jules Guerin.** One depicts the Angel of Truth liberating a slave. The other depicts allegorical figures of Truth and Justice.

When the memorial was dedicated in 1922, one of the speakers was **Dr. Robert Moton,** the black president of Tuskegee Institute. Ironically, upon his arrival, a Marine usher escorted him from the dais to the all-black section which was separated from the memorial and the rest of the audience by a roadway. Since that time the memorial has become a powerful symbol of the struggle for racial equality. In the '40s, the DAR refused to allow a performance by **Marian Anderson** at Constitution Hall. She sang her concert before more than 75,000 people from the steps of the Lincoln Memorial. Years later **Martin Luther King, Jr.,** made his *I Have A Dream* speech from the same steps.

The Memorial, a magnificent sight at all times, is most impressive at dawn and dusk. *It's open to the public 24 hours a day. A ranger is on duty from 8am-midnight. West end of Mall. 426-6841.*

Cave Under Lincoln. How odd to find a place of stillness under the teeming center of the nation's capital! Tour this vast stalactite- and stalagmite-filled cavern created by excavations for the monument and later by water dripping from the marble steps. A part of the diggings and substructure of the original (1914-22) building, the cave is a recent discovery. Columns over 45 feet high support the 900-ton statue. The National Park Service offers a free 1-hour guided tour. Wear hiking shoes and bring your own flashlight. Tour numbers limited, make reservations several weeks in advance. *Open Oct-Dec, Mar-Jul. M-F tours 8pm, Sa & Su 2pm and 8pm. West end of Mall. 426-6841.*

23 **Constitution Gardens.** Located between the Washington Monument and Lincoln Memorial, temporary Naval buildings from WWI stood here until after WWII. **Skidmore, Owings and Merrill** originally designed a lovely 50-acre park, but recession-era budget cuts marred the plan, and the result is considered disappointing by many. A 7½-acre lake with a landscaped island is surrounded by paths and bike trails. Over 5,000 trees create their own islands of shade. *17th to 23rd Sts. at Constitution Ave. NW.*

The **National Symphony** runs on a 52-week schedule; catch them at the **Kennedy Center,** or, during the summer season, at **Wolf Trap Farm Park.** Special free concerts held on the **Capitol's West Lawn** on Memorial Day, 4 July and Labor Day. *Call 785-8100 for schedule and program information.*

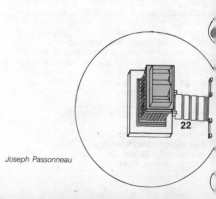

22

Joseph Passonneau

Vietnam Veterans Memorial. While not as controversial as the war it commemorates, *The Wall*, as it has come to be known, continues to be the focus of much disagreement. After a national competition in which there were 1,421 entries, the stark, handsome design of **Maya Ying Lin**, a 21-year-old Yale architecture senior, was chosen. She describes it as *"...a rift in the earth—a long polished black stone wall, emerging and receding into the earth. "* The jury described it as a place of quiet reflection and healing. There is no writing on the monument other than the names of the 58,007 Americans who perished in the Southeast Asian war. Names are inscribed in chronological order of death. On either side of the memorial are alphabetical directories to help find names (listed are name, panel number and line, counting from the top). An addition depicts 3 Vietnam-era servicemen. *At Constitution Gardens, west end of Mall.*

Cooper Lecky, Partnership

Federal Reserve. (1937, **Paul Cret**) Credit, dollar supply and that wispy notion of money's worth are regulated from the clean white marble structure, nicknamed *the Fed.* The agency sets discount rates, issues paper currency, and controls the backing of money with gold or government securities, and deals with any financial regulations that will affect national economics. If finance at the national level excites you, attend a meeting of the Fed, held nearly every Wednesday at 10am (you will find meetings announced in the *Federal Register).* Perhaps better thought of as *the Temple of the Dollar,* the Federal Reserve's handsome Art Deco home conveys this idea without resorting to the ostentation common in bank temple architecture. *Closed to the public. 20th St. at Constitution Ave. NW. 452-3000.*

5 National Academy of Sciences. Chartered under President Lincoln to provide an honorary society for scientists and an advisory panel for the government. As scientific knowledge exploded in the 20th century, a larger group, the **National Research Council,** was needed. Today the NRC, working in conjunction with the

Academy of Sciences and the **Academy of Engineering** and the **Institute of Medicine,** mobilizes thousands of scientists who work gratis on study committees when the government needs scientific information. Rather than do field work, these groups evaluate and synthesize all available and often contradictory information in a given field. In the past the NRC has reported on acid rain, toxic shock syndrome, the effects of diet on cancer, and ways in which the Secret Service might spot potential assassins.

The academy building was designed in 1924 by **Bertram G. Goodhue** in a delightfully understated Greek style. The grounds are pleasant and of particular interest is the **Einstein Memorial** in the southwest corner. The building is open to the public, yet seldom visited. Be sure to note the 6 window panels: They're 2 stories high and tell the story of scientific progress from the Greeks to the moderns. The **Great Hall** is also worth a peek. It's an ornate cruciform chamber with a 55-foot-

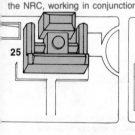
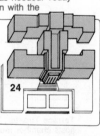
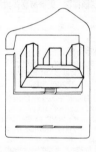

25

24

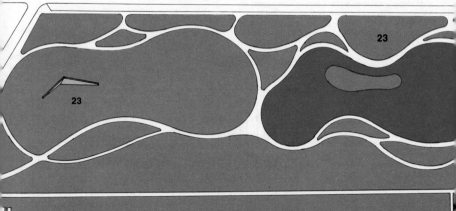

23

23

21

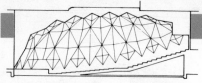

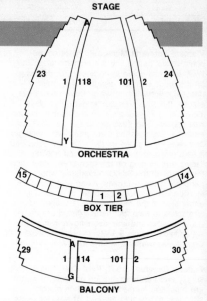

high central dome. In the hall a **Foucault Pendulum** illustrates the earth spinning on its axis. The pendulum, however, is often taken down for receptions so if you must see this astronomical demo, visit the Smithsonian Museum of American History, where a pendulum swings perpetually.

The academy auditorium (1970, **Harrison & Abramowitz;** project architect **Wallace K. Harrison;** acoustical design **Dr. Cyril Harris**) is one of the most acoustically perfect spaces in the city. The chamber walls are a huge curving shell covered with large diamond-shaped facets joined at the edges. Call the *Art-in-the-Academy Program* at 334-2439 for information on occasional free concerts. If you have a chance to attend one, it shouldn't be missed. *Admission free. Open M-Sa 9am-4pm. 2101 Constitution Ave. NW. 334-2000.*

26 State Department. Founded in 1789, this was the first of the 13 Cabinet departments to be created. Lobby exhibits detail the history of the agency, but the real attraction is the 8th floor's diplomatic reception rooms. These hold an ongoing display of some of America's finest antiques and artworks (1740-1825), cajoled from the country's top private collections and worth an estimated $25 million. You can get permission to see these lush rooms as well as the sweeping view only if you make reservations at least 4 to 6 weeks in advance. Write to the State Department's Visitors Office at 2201 C St. NW, Room 1493, FMAS/GS, Washington, DC 20520. *Admission free. 200 C St. NW. 632-3241.*

© Kennedy Center

27 Kennedy Center for the Performing Arts. When the Kennedy Center opened in 1971, Washington became a true focal point for the liveliest of national and international arts.

Overlooking the Potomac River, Edward Durell Stone's building also plays another major role: it stands as the only official monument to the slain president, memorialized in a 7-foot bronze bust (by sculptor Robert Berks) in the Grand Foyer. The interior space of the foyer is 6 stories high with more floor area than a football field, and is furnished with magnificent gifts from nations around the world. Cyril Harris did the top-quality acoustical design, and audiences sitting in one theater find it hard to believe that National Airport is just down the river and performances are underway in 2 other large theaters under the same roof. The Hall of States, a gallery containing the flags of each US state, and the Hall of Nations, displaying flags of every nation recognized by the US, help separate the 3 theaters spatially and acoustically, and provide good circulation from the building entrances on the east side to the theater doors on the west.

Concert Hall. The gold-white 2,750-seat theater, illuminated by Norwegian chandeliers, presents symphonies, choral groups, dance and other musical performances. Fantastic acoustics *(254-3776).*

Eisenhower Theater. Paneled with East Indian laurel. This theater seats 1,200 for evening and matinee performances *(254-3670).*

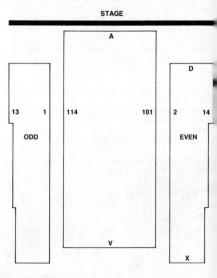

Terrace Theater. This smaller, 500-seat theater hosts chamber music, poetry readings and other events *(254-9895).*

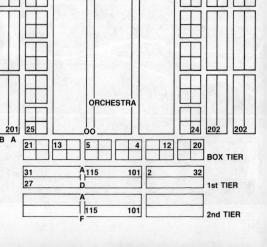

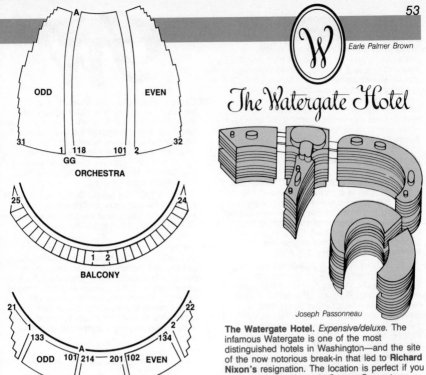

```
        A
  ODD        EVEN
31              32
   1  118  101  2
       GG
    ORCHESTRA

25              24
      1  2
     BALCONY

21              22
  1              2
  133         134
ODD 101 214—201 102 EVEN
       A
       G
    1ST TIER

17              18
  1              2
  135         136
ODD 101 216—201 102 EVEN
    2ND TIER
```

Opera House. Three tiers seat 2,300 before its golden Japanese silk stage curtain. Plays, ballet, opera and music *(254-9895)*.

Also at the Kennedy Center are:

Roof Terrace. ☆ ☆ ½ $$$ This opulent dining room boasts and intriguing menu of egg dishes, crepes and quiche. Dining here used to be a disappointing experience, but a recent upturn in quality seems to be a sincere promise for the future. *American. Open daily 11:30am-3pm, 5:30-half hour after last curtain. Reservations required. 833-8870.*

Curtain Call Cafe. $ Casual meals and scenery offered in a very busy cafe. The walls are lined with photos of previous Kennedy Center performers. Salads, sandwiches and entrees. *Continental. Open daily 11:30am-8:30pm. 833-8870.*

Encore Cafeteria. $ Serve yourself in this medium-priced crowded restaurant, which offers a great view of the Potomac and outdoor dining in the summer. *Cafeteria. Open daily 11am-8pm. 833-8870.*

The Hors D'Oeuvrerie. This lavish lounge, though often crowded, strives for a sedate atmosphere with its mirrored walls and plush red furnishings. For a drink and special hors d'oeuvres. *Open 5:30pm till half hour after final curtain. 833-8870.*

Also, the **American Film Institute Theater** screens films all year long *(785-4600)*. The Center also offers a variety of displays in the **Performing Arts Library,** free organ recitals and children's film classics in the AFI Theater.

During any theater intermission, feel free to wander up to the **Roof Terrace,** for the best evening view of Washington, the Mall and the river.

The Center is open 10am-11pm daily. Check with specific theaters for events, showtimes and ticket prices. Admission free. New Hampshire Ave. and Rock Creek Parkway. 254-3600.

Earle Palmer Brown

The Watergate Hotel

Joseph Passonneau

The Watergate Hotel. *Expensive/deluxe.* The infamous Watergate is one of the most distinguished hotels in Washington—and the site of the now notorious break-in that led to **Richard Nixon's** resignation. The location is perfect if you plan to visit the Kennedy Center, Georgetown, the White House or the State Department. Spacious luxury suites blend classic European and Oriental styles with contemporary decor. Added pluses: a complete shopping mall, exclusive health club, concierge service, 4 fine restaurants, and 3 lounges. The **Terrace Restaurant** serves breakfast and lunch; the **Wintergarden** serves continental cuisine for lunch, dinner and supper. The **Saddle Bar** lounge is renowned for its extensive collection of one-of-a-kind saddle blankets, and the **Potomac Lounge** is tops for tea, cocktails and piano music. *2650 Virginia Ave. NW. Metrorail blue/orange lines. 965-2300/800-424-2736/Telex: 904004.*

At the Watergate Hotel are:

Les Champs. The most prestigious address in Washington hosts one of the city's fanciest courtyard arcades of specialty shops and boutiques. The 30 boutiques of Les Champs round the exterior of the **Watergate 600 Office Building** and carry high-priced, high-fashion furs, crystal, antiques, imports, jewelry and probably the city's highest concentration of designer fashions. Among the shops are **Colette of Les Champs** for Italian and California designer sportswear and pret-a-porter; **Saint Laurent Rive Gauche** for Yves' seasonal designs; **Saks-Jandel** for top-dollar designer fashions; **Gucci I** and **Gucci II** for renowned men's and women's clothing, accessories and leather goods; **Arirang Imports** for small oriental gifts; and **Watergate Gifts** for ceramics, baskets, cards and original watercolors, plus a potpourri of other gift items. *Mall hours 10am-6pm. New Hampshire Ave. and F St. NW, across from the Kennedy Center. 298-4400.*

Jean-Louis at Watergate. ☆ ☆ ☆ $$$$ This tiny bastion of *nouvelle cuisine* is often mentioned as one of the most expensive—and one of the finest—restaurants in America. Jean-Louis' service, wine list and eminently imaginative cooking assure a top-flight dining experience. Menus offer a wide range of choices divided into 4 pricings. Cold first courses include terrines of foie gras, truffles, wild mushrooms; hot ones like scallops or lobster in special sauces tend to be more flavorful. Next come warm seafood salads and other herbed creations, then meat and fowl frequently prepared with exotic fruits and spices. The pastries are among the best in the country. *French. Open M-F noon-2pm, M-Sa 6:30-10pm. Closed Su and the month of Aug. Reservations required. Coat and tie requested. 2650 Virginia Ave. NW. 298-4488.*

28 Watergate Pastry. On the lower level of the Watergate apartment complex, a mall provides residents one-stop shopping and services, including valet, barber shop, a Safeway supermarket, optician and florist. This bakery is noted for its oven-baked delicacies, including a variety of mousse cakes, fresh and French pastries, and memorable wedding and birthday cakes with unusual fillings. There are also 25 flavors of homemade chocolate, including rum, almond, honey and orange. *Open M-F 8am-7pm, Sa 9am-7pm, Su 10am-5pm. 2534 Virginia Ave. NW. 298-4498.*

29 Howard Johnson's Motor Lodge. *Inexpensive.* A great bargain in a ritzy neighborhood. The hotel's 200 spacious rooms are functionally decorated and some have a balcony overlooking the Potomac. Dining in the **Lamplighter Room,** the coffee shop or the **Club Car** lounge. Free underground parking. *2601 Virginia Ave. NW. Metrorail blue/orange lines. 965-2700.*

30 Foggy Bottom Cafe. ☆ ☆ ☆ $$ Small and beautifully appointed, this trendy spot serves eclectic fare like sesame noodles, triple eggs benedict and steak tartare. The perfect spot for pre- or post-Kennedy Center dining. *Original American. Open M-F 7:30am-11:30pm, Sa & Su 8:30am-11:30pm. Reservations suggested. 924 25th St. NW (inside the River Inn). Metrorail blue/orange lines. 338-8707.*

31 The Intrigue Hotel. *Inexpensive/moderate.* One of the best buys in the neighborhood and a good place to bring families. The hotel restaurant is enjoyed by starwatchers as well as stars and government officials. Children under 12 stay free; pets are welcome. *824 New Hampshire Ave. NW. 337-6620.*

32 Guest Quarters Hotel. *Expensive.* Each of the 107 suites features a contemporary-style living room, dining area, spacious bedroom, large closets and a fully equipped kitchen. Standard amenities include room service with a light breakfast and hors d'oeuvres menu (no restaurant on the premises), valet/laundry, secretarial and telex services. The Guest Quarters also offers grocery delivery service, a best-seller lending library, babysitters, and dog-walking (traveling pets 25 pounds or less are allowed at a nominal fee). Self-service guest laundry, audio-visual equipment and temporary memberships to nearby health clubs have been included for business travelers. *801 New Hampshire Ave. NW. 861-6600/800-424-2900 Telex: 89-2346.*

During his career as a congressman and senator, **John F. Kennedy** lived in 5 different houses. All but one were in Georgetown:

1528 31st St. NW. This typically narrow Georgetown rowhouse was JFK's home when he was a bachelor freshman senator.

1400 34th St. NW. As the senator began to gain clout, he found it necessary to entertain lavishly and moved into this 4-story corner house. His sister, **Eunice,** usually served as hostess.

3271 P St. NW. This is where Jack Kennedy brought his new bride, **Jacqueline.**

3307 N St. NW. This was the last home the Kennedys occupied before moving to 1600 Pennsylvania Ave.

(For a while, the Kennedys also lived at **Hickory Hill,** off Chain Bridge Road near McLean, Virginia.)

The touring **Washington Civic Opera** makes 3 5-day pit stops at **Lisner Auditorium** during October, December and March; *call 676-6800 for schedule and program information.*

Washington Ballet Company graces the **Lisner Auditorium** with their classical and contemporary ballets a few days in October, December, January and April; *call 362-4644/362-3606 for information.*

33 George Washington University. The first president had hoped to establish a national university and so left his stock in the Potowmack Canal Co. (the precursor of the **Chesapeake & Ohio Canal**) as an endowment. But Congress could not agree on the Federal Government's role in such an institution, and the endowment was forfeited. Madison also pursued the issue, but with the same results.

Finally, in 1821, the Baptist Church raised funds to create the non-sectarian Columbian College; less than 100 years later this became George Washington U., the nation's first national university.

The University is the city's second largest landholder (after the Federal Government, of course), and therein lies its true prestige. Its present site is its third, and when the school settled here in 1912, it wisely engulfed many of the Foggy Bottom neighborhood's fine old homes, converting them into offices and dormitories. Now 20 full blocks of central DC are GWU-owned, making it a one-institution urban renewal force.

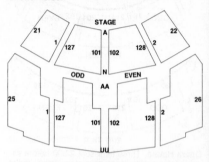

The 1,500-seat **Lisner Auditorium,** built as a classic modern structure in the '40s, is not only the home of the **Washington Civic Opera** and the **Washington Ballet,** but houses the **Dimock Gallery** in the lower lounges. Exhibitions of local, faculty and student artists change monthly. A permanent artwork to be seen at the auditorium is **Augustus Tack's** abstract mural, painted on the stage fire curtain. Most performances are by various independent production companies such as **Performing Arts Repertory Theatre Group, Philip Glass,** and **Twyla Tharp,** but occasionally the university presents concerts and other artistic events free of charge. The box office opens one hour before performances to offer last-minute tickets. Check local newspapers for individual listings. *21st and H Sts. NW. Lisner Auditorium, 676-6800. University located at 19th to 24th Sts. Pennsylvania to New Hampshire Aves. NW. For information, call 676-6000.*

34 West End Cafe. ☆ ☆ ☆ $$ Two spacious dining rooms, one decorated with Karsh celebrity portraits, the other outfitted with a bar and grand piano, make this a great place for romantic dinners or quiet luncheons. The food—entrees like steak bearnaise, chicken breast with apples in cream sauce, or lighter fare like eggs benedict and various salads—is moderately priced and carefully prepared. *American. Open M-F 7am-11:30pm; Sa 8-10:30am, 6pm-midnight; Su 8am-10pm. Reservations strongly suggested. 1 Washington Circle NW. 293-5390.*

35 Le Gaulois. ☆ ☆ ☆ $$ Inexpensive, first-rate cuisine ensures that this cluttered, 2-story dining room is always filled to capacity. Sample the cold fish appetizers, beef salads and quenelles, and then feast on numerous daily specials: pot au feu, roast duck with kiwi, lobster with beurre blanc, various veal dishes. *French. Open M-F 11:30am-2:30pm, 5:30-11pm; Sa 5:30pm-midnight. Closed Su. Reservations required well in advance. 2133 Pennsylvania Ave. NW. 466-3232.*

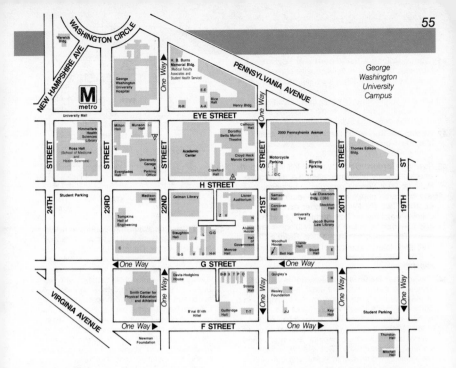

36 Crown Books. Book lover's browserie is chock-full of lush coffee table books at big discounts, odd but interesting publishers' overstocks, and the latest best sellers and popular paperbacks. Good selections of nonfiction, cookbooks and kids' books. Everything is less than list price. *Open M-F 9am-8pm, Sa & Su 10am-6pm. 2020 K St. NW. 659-2030.*

36 Prime Rib. ☆ ☆ $$$ The portions are large, the prime rib tops and the atmosphere very formal. Aside from the juicy 2-inch thick entree above, this restaurant whips up a superb rack of lamb and a special Crab Imperial. Soft sounds from the glass-topped grand piano provide the corresponding rarified atmosphere. *American. Reservations and jacket required. Open M-F noon-3pm; M-Th 6-11pm, F & Sa till 11:30pm. 2020 K St. NW. 466-8811.*

36 New York New York. ☆ ☆ $$ Swank dinner-n-dancing joint where dark colors and soft textures complement evening cocktails; well-prepared burgers, steaks and seafood; and popular dance music and videos. Also good for long lunches. *Open for lunch M-F 11am-5pm, dinner 5pm-midnight; dinner only on weekends; bar open M-Th till 1am, F & Sa till 2pm. 2020 K St. 293-2322.*

37 Arts Club. (1806, **Timothy Caldwell**) In 1916, the one-time residence of **James Monroe** became the permanent home for the Arts Club, a local association open to aficionados of 19th- and 20th-century art. The 55 rooms, spread over 2 floors and 2 buildings (the house next door was annexed to provide more space), present a fascinating spectrum of lesser-known artists and their work. While the exhibit upstairs is permanent, the lower level is a rotating gallery; exhibits change every 3 weeks and feature paintings by contemporary artists. The Club has received donations of period furniture to complement Caldwell's strong Georgian design. *Admission free. Open M, Tu & Th 9am-5pm; W 2-5pm; Sa & Su 1-5pm. 2017 I St. NW. 331-7282.*

38 Franz Bader Gallery. The oldest art gallery in the city, Bader gives contemporary European art an extensive representation. American paintings and prints, including the virtuoso graphics of **Peter Milton**, are shown as well. An annual highlight is an exhibition of new Eskimo carvings and prints from Canada. As a bonus, the gallery has the city's best arts bookstore. *Open Tu-Sa 10am-6pm. Closed Su & M. 2001 I St. NW. Metrorail blue/orange lines. 337-5440.*

The **Washington Monument** sways 0.125 of an inch in a 30-mile-per-hour wind.

39 Takesushi. ☆ ☆ $$ No tatami room and no Japanese beef stew—just fresh, tender fish served as sushi or sashimi the Tokyo way. Small, informal and very authentic; sample the bite-sized *ikura-uzura* (salmon roe with quail egg) or try the California *roru* cone-style. *Open M-F noon-2:30pm, M-Sa 5-10pm. 1010 20th St. 466-3798.*

39 Dominique's. ☆ ☆ $$$ Snazzy, fun, oftentimes outrageous. The seemingly endless menu lists everything from ostrich to rattlesnake, the champagne flows freely, the desserts are named after famous patrons (chocolate truffles for **Elizabeth Taylor**, a sherbet and raspberries concoction for **Farrah Fawcett**.) Hoopla notwithstanding, the simpler dishes are the best. Start with crab soup, move on to lamb stew, duck, quail or the fresh fish of the day. End with a crunchy almond amaretto souffle. *French. Open M-F 11:30am-2:30pm, 5:30pm-midnight; F & Sa till 1am. Closed Su. Reservations suggested. Coat and tie recommended. 1900 Pennsylvania Ave. NW. Metrorail blue/orange lines. 452-1126.*

40 Shezan. ☆ ☆ ☆ $$$ A glittery, wine-colored dining room, impeccable service and a menu of exquisitely prepared curries, grilled meats and rice dishes make this one of DC's finest Pakistani restaurants. The original of this 2-continent mini-empire is in Lahore, Pakistan; popular branches are in London and New York. *Pakistani. Open daily noon-2:30pm, 6-10pm. Reservations suggested. Coat and tie requested. 913 19th St. NW. Metrorail blue/orange lines. 659-5555.*

The statue of **Alexander Hamilton** in front of the south entrance of the Treasury building, proudly proclaims: *"He smote the rock of the national resources and abundant streams of revenue gushed forth."*

Introductions/Theaters/Narrative black
Hotels purple
Museums/Architecture blue
Parks/Open spaces green
Restaurants/Nightlife red
Shops/Galleries violet

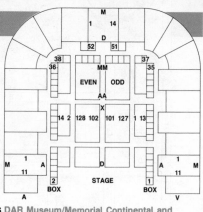

41 Charlie Chiang's Restaurant and Lounge. ☆ $
Sidewalk dining on a quiet, quaint corner of
downtown Washington. Linger all day over long
drinks, or try an ice-cold *Tsingtao* beer with fried
Chinese appetizers. *Chinese cafe. Open M-Th
11:30am-10:30pm, F & Sa till 11pm, Su till 10pm.
1919 I St. NW. 293-6000.*

42 Geological Survey of the US Government.
Maps and publications. *Open 8:15am-3:45pm.
19th & F Sts. NW. 343-8073.*

43 Rawlins Garden. Don't overlook this dainty park
where seasonal blossoms scent the air and the
National Park Service provides entertainment—
jazz concerts, puppetry, poetry—during warm
weather. Two shallow pools offer excellent
goldfish-watching on lazy spring days, when the
tulip-tree magnolia and water lily blooms are
fresh. The park's namesake was Grant's Chief of
Staff and, later, Secretary of War. *18th-20th Sts.
at E St. NW, just north of Dept. of Commerce.
426-6700.*

44 The Interior Department Museum is as multi-
faceted as the Department itself, encompassing
displays showing the history of the National Park
Service, Wildlife Preservation, Land
Management, Reclamation, Geological Survey,
Indian Affairs, etc. Indian crafts and artifacts, and
old documents such as original land grants and
surveys, are on display. There is an excellent
shop selling Indian crafts. *Admission free. Open
M-F 8am-4pm. 18th & C Sts. NW. Metrorail
blue/orange lines, I St. exit. 343-5016.*

45 Organization of American States. (1910, **Albert
Kinsey & Paul Cret**) Formerly the Pan American
Union, this coalition of the US and 26 Latin
American and Caribbean nations was formed in
1948. Its headquarters is one of the capital's
most striking buildings, the architectural style of
North and South America—with a little Italian
Renaissance as well—rendered in white
Georgian marble and black Andean granite.
Inside are the Hall of Heroes and Flags (as it
sounds, a collection of busts and banners), and
the Hall of the Americas, a grand room with
barrel-vaulted ceilings, columns, 3 Tiffany
chandeliers and parquet surfaces that hosts OAS
diplomatic soirees and recitals by artists from the
member nations. At the building's center are the
Aztec Gardens filled with exotic plants such as
guavas, banana trees, coffee trees, date plants,
breadfruit plants, rubber and cocoa trees. The
Peace Tree, planted by **President Taft** in 1910,
is fig and rubber grafted together, symbolic of the
cultural roots of the American continents. A
statue of the Aztec god of flowers, **Xochipilli,**
overlooks a blue-tiled fountain by **Gertrude
Vanderbilt Whitney.** Beyond, the **Museum of
Modern Art of Latin America** is a small but
excellent collection, and the only one of its kind
in the world. *(201 18th St. NW. 789-6016)* Off the
Tropical Patio, a small giftshop is filled with
vibrantly colored Latin American arts and crafts
(331-1010). The OAS is the oldest political
organization ﹞ith which the US has been
associated and hosts lectures and symposia on
improved trade and relations. Note the statue of
Queen Isabella I outside the building's entry, a
gift from Spain in 1966. Isabella rarely gets the
credit she deserves—for financing Columbus'
serendipitous expedition. *Admission free. Half-
hour tours available. Open M-F 9am-5pm. 17th
St. at Constitution Ave. NW. 789-3000.*

**46 DAR Museum/Memorial Continental and
Constitution Halls.** (1910, **Edward Pearce Casey**)
Members of the Daughters of the American
Revolution trace their lineages back to the
original colonies' fight for independence. The
4-story Memorial Continental Hall—an elaborate
Beaux-Arts affair marked by a vast porte-cochere
supported by enormous Ionic columns—
preserves that same period. Nearly 30 rooms
commemorate Colonial America and newer
states, including the **Tennessee Room,** with
White House furnishings from the Monroe
presidency; the **Oklahoma Room,** a crude
prairie farm kitchen; and the steamboat parlor in
the **Missouri Room.** Children and adults will
marvel at the antique toys and dolls in the **New
Hampshire Attic.** Children are encouraged to
play with hands-on replicas. An excellent
collection of Revolutionary War-era artifacts
includes silver by **Paul Revere.** Also at
Continental Hall is one of the nation's finest
genealogical archives (modest charge). Tours run
continuously. *Admission free. Open M-F
9am-4pm. 1776 D St. NW. 638-2661.*

Constitution Hall. (Seats 4,000) **John Russell
Pope** was a master of simple Roman forms, and
this building, with its clear circulation patterns
and acoustics that **Toscanini** found remarkable,
is among his best. It reigned for many years as
the city's major concert venue. Now supplanted
in popularity by the **Kennedy Center,** it still
attracts noted performers. *18th St. at D St. NW.
638-2661.*

DC Bests

**Marion Barry, Jr.
Mayor, Washington, DC**

**Our great sports teams:
Redskins, Bullets, Capitals,
Firebirds and Hoyas**

The new **Washington Convention Center** in the
middle of downtown, which opened last year on
budget and on schedule.

Our **new downtown,** particularly the new
developments of the Pennsylvania Avenue.

The **one-fifth of Washington that is all park.**

The **many flavors of Washington,** particularly
seafood and barbeque.

The **diversity of our people:** a multi-ethnic,
multi-racial, multi-national hometown.

Our **New Year's Eve celebration at the Old
Post Office** on Pennsylvania Avenue—an
evening of free entertainment and hometown
spirit.

The cleanest, most efficient and attractive
METRO system in the country.

Our **Potomac Riverfest** celebrating the
cleanliness and beauty of a great and lovely
river.

Our many **historical and livable neighborhoods**
all just minutes away from the heart of the
nation.

Canova Lions. Two lions—one asleep, the
other watchful—grace the entrance to the
Corcoran Gallery. They are bronze copies of
marble originals sculpted by **Antonio Canova**
in 1792 to commemorate **Pope Clement XIII.**
17th St. between New York Ave. and E St.

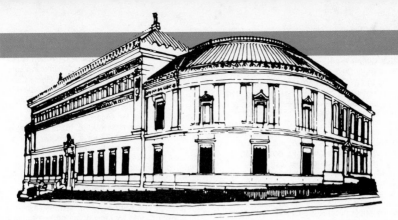

47 Corcoran Gallery. (1897, **Ernest Flagg;** Clark Wing 1927, **Charles Platt**) This collection of American artworks is one of the oldest in the country and is an excellent survey of native talent. Early portraiture, primitives, the Hudson River School, American Impressionists, Abstract Expressionists, Ashcan School, Pop and Minimalism—all are represented. In addition, 2 substantial bequests have given the Corcoran a small but impressive collection of European masters, including works by **Degas, Rubens, Rembrandt, Renoir, Millet.** Fine temporary shows of photography and works by Washington-area artists frequently fill the gallery.

The Corcoran is privately funded, something of a rarity in DC, where the Smithsonian-umbrella museums and galleries often dominate the art scene with their enormity. But this independence has allowed the museum a freedom not seen in many of the federally funded collections. In 1966 the Corcoran provided evidence of its success when it presented a 250-year, 700-painting survey of American art: nearly all the artworks were drawn from its permanent collection.

Banker and art collector **William Wilson Corcoran's** collection formed the basis for today's museum; indeed his favorite, the **Hiram Powers** sculpture *The Greek Slave* is here. For his works, Corcoran commissioned architect **James Renwick** to create a suitable home; that building is now called the Renwick Gallery (See page 58). These larger quarters are essentially Beaux-Arts, but American influences—particularly the long lines, and clean, massing characteristics of **Frank Lloyd Wright**—are also evident (it was Wright's favorite building in DC). White Georgia marble, verdigris roof and intricate grillwork add to the delicacy of the building, which the gallery moved into shortly after Corcoran's death.

The **Corcoran Art School** was founded along with the Gallery and Mr. Corcoran advised students to copy the works in his collection. Students and faculty exhibits are usually very good. Often in conjunction with exhibits, the gallery sponsors drama and dance performances and concerts in the **Frances & Armand Hammer Auditorium.** Gallery lectures are held each Wednesday at 12:30pm, and October through May you'll find chamber music being played on Sunday afternoons. The **Gallery Shop** sells books, posters, reprints and gifts. *Admission charge, Tu & W free. Open Tu-Su 10am-4:30pm, Th till 9pm. Free half-hour tour Tu & Th-Su 12:30pm (meet in Atrium). 17th St. at New York Ave. NW. 638-3211.*

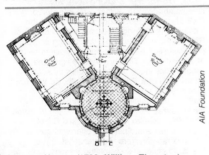

AIA Foundation

48 Octagon House. (1798, **William Thornton**) Originally built as a townhouse for **Colonel John Tayloe,** the Octagon has been the center of many official and private activities. The graceful mansion was spared the British fire that took the White House, and served as **James and Dolley Madison's** home during the fall and winter of 1814-15. It was here that Madison signed the **Treaty of Ghent,** establishing final peace with Great Britain. For several years the building changed hands and deteriorated. It was saved in 1899 when the American Institute of Architects took formal possession. Designed by the first architect of the Capitol, William Thornton, the Federal-style Octagon (really a hexagon!) is a successful solution to L'Enfant's site problem posed by radiating streets.

Because Thornton used the best building materials available, the fine restoration currently in evidence was possible. Original Chippendale and Federal-period furniture were placed in the light, high-ceiling rooms; the cornices of the original English Coade stone mantels were replaced with exact reproductions; and the rescued circular rent table was again placed in Madison's study, believed to be the location of the Treaty's signing. In 1949, the AIA moved its headquarters to a new, adjoining building. The allegedly haunted Octagon is now a registered National Historic Landmark owned by the AIA Foundation. *Admission charge. Open Tu-F 10am-4pm, Sa & Su 1-4pm. 1799 New York Ave. NW. 638-3105.*

49 Maison Blanche. ☆ ☆ ☆ $$$ Not far from the better known White House lies this luxurious, peaceful dining room, ideal for business luncheons and tete-a-tetes. **Chef Pierre Chambrin's** inventive preparation of filet mignon, duck, squab and seafood dishes makes for consistently surprising dining. The wine list is impressive but high-priced. A fixed-price menu is available upon request. *French. Open M-F 11:45am-2:30pm, M-Sa 6-11pm. Closed Su. Reservations suggested. Coat and tie requested. 1725 F St. NW. 842-0070.*

50 Winder Building. (1848) This building, the work of an unknown architect, represents 3 District firsts: the first cast-iron structure, the first central heating system, and the first speculative office building built privately but intended for use by the federal government. Notice how the windows grow smaller on the upper floors, a common 19th-century device for making a building appear taller. *Not open to the public. 604 17th St. SW.*

51 Crown Books. Stacks and racks of best sellers and publishers' overstocks at big discounts. If you like coffee table books, this is the place to shop for them. Also stock up on paperbacks, from current fiction to science, literary classics to cookbooks. *M-F 9am-8pm, Sa & Su 10am-6pm. 1710 G St. NW. 789-2277.*

52 Il Nuovo Sans Souci. ☆ ☆ ☆ $$$ Some of the best that Italian cooking has to offer. Try the delicate spinach tortellini, linguini with classic tiny clams or fresh salmon, *penne* coated with cream and chili sauce, saltimbocca alla romana (scaloppine with prosciutto) or shrimp Livornese in tomato sauce and capers. An exquisite, albeit expensive, night out. *Italian. Open M-F 11:30p-2:30pm, 6-10:30pm. Sa 6-10:30pm. 726 17th St. NW. 298-7424.*

53 Executive Office Building (Old State, War & Navy Building). Designed by **A.B. Mullet** and built between 1871 and 1888, this was the world's largest office building when finished. The inside is a fantasy of cast-iron posts, railings and cantilevered red stairways that connect 550 rooms along more than 2 miles of corridors; 900 Doric columns trim the outrageously mansarded, turreted and porched French Second Empire exterior. Regarded as a charming eccentricity reflecting the exuberance of post-Civil War America, at its completion the building was so hated that nobody wanted to pay the architect's fee. The north pediment contains a military monument that is particularly unrestrained. Not open to the public. *Pennsylvania Ave. & 17th St. NW.*

54 Renwick Gallery, National Museum of American Art. (1859, **James Renwick**) After taking several wrong turns and finally reopening in 1972, the nation's first art museum has now become one of its finest. Yet the Renwick isn't a museum in the traditional sense. It has no permanent collection, but rather hosts visiting exhibits and mounts special and always excellent shows. The forte here is American design, the fun/functional side of art. Past exhibits have included American pottery and porcelain, **Gustav Stickley** and Shaker furniture, American crafts and collection-portraits of the US through pop/commercial/industrial design that comprise everything from old neon signs to Coke machines, diner interiors to sunglasses. The other face of the Renwick is a time trip back to the presidency of U.S. Grant, when the building was designed to display the private art collection of banker **William Wilson Corcoran.** Two Second Empire-style rooms, all raspberry velvet and silk rope, were designed after the Tuileries in Paris and have been authentically restored to Gilded Age splendor. The Octagon Room was created to show off Corcoran's favorite treasure, **Hiram Powers'** nude sculpture *The Greek Slave.* When the museum opened, male and female visitors viewed it separately. The statue is gone, but the room's chandelier now satisfies the public's appetite for decadence. Though the building was commissioned in 1858, Corcoran's collection didn't move in for 2 decades; during the Civil War, the Quartermaster Corps was housed here. Shortly after installing his collection, Corcoran was forced to move it to larger quarters (See Corcoran Gallery). Various agencies used the building for offices until, in the late 1950s, it was threatened with demolition. The Kennedy Administration lobbied to salvage it, and **Lyndon Johnson** presented it to the Smithsonian, who directed the elaborate, painstaking and excellent restoration. The Renwick is officially part of the National Museum of American Art under the Smithsonian umbrella. Two of its 9 galleries are devoted to design by foreign artists. In conjunction with theme exhibits, there are often lectures, films, concerts, dance performances, etc. Short films on art, design and craftsmanship, as well as social and cultural subjects, are scheduled twice monthly, on Thursdays, during lunch hours. The gift shop has an excellent selection, often enhanced by the handicrafts of the artists whose works are currently on display in the galleries. *Admission free. Open daily 10am-5:30pm, till 9pm in summer. Tours by appt. 10am, 11am, 1pm, call 357-3095. Pennsylvania Ave. at 17th St. NW. 357-1300.*

54 Blair House (The Blair-Lee Houses). (1824; restored in 1931, **Waldron Faulkner**) These fine old homes are now owned by the government and used to house visiting dignitaries. Not open to the public. *1650 Pennsylvania Ave. NW.*

American Red Cross. Clara Barton organized the US branch of this international service organization in 1881. The centerpiece of its 3-building headquarters is the **marble palace** (1917, **Trowbridge & Livingston**), which commemorates the women who ministered to Civil War wounded. Historical exhibits fill the lobbies of all 3 floors; included are a century of Red Cross uniforms and a fascinating collection of recruitment and public service posters. A trio of stained-glass **Tiffany** windows lights the second floor lobby, and sculptures by such artists as **Hiram Powers** and **Felix de Weldon** decorate the buildings and grounds. To the south of the building, a small garden memorializes Red Cross workers killed in action. From this complex, over 3,000 Red Cross chapters are coordinated to offer vital community services ranging from disaster relief and blood banks, to children's swimming lessons. *Open M-F 9am-4pm. 17th St., D-E Sts. 737-8300.*

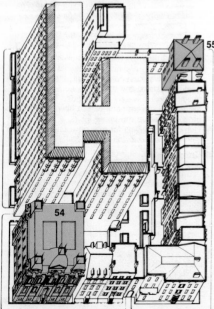

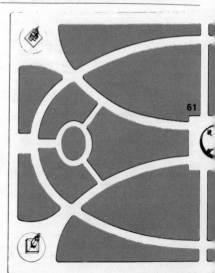

59

Director's Bests

Lloyd E. Herman
Director, Renwick Gallery

There is a very special feeling I sometimes have, sitting in my first-floor office in this high-ceiling building that was built in 1859 as the city's first art gallery. Just about 6 feet on the other side of my office wall is the presidential guest house, **Blair House**, where heads of foreign nations and other dignitaries come to stay on official visits to our nation's capital. Though of course I can't hear what transpires behind those walls, part of Washington's uniqueness as a world capital is the presence of world leaders. Their closeness to my very desk seems almost eerie sometimes. The police always barricade the sidewalk in front of Blair House all of the way to our front steps when a state visitor is in residence there, and we can always judge a foreign leader's popularity (and sometimes his lack of popularity) by the number of citizens who crowd our front steps to see the celebrated policy-maker coming or going from house to house to limousine. **Golda Meir** was by far the most popular; I could hardly get into and out of the Gallery when she stayed next door. But when the **Shah of Iran** made his last visit to Washington we had to close our front doors and barricade the entire sidewalk, the protestors were so threatening. Inside my quiet office—though I can see nothing but treetops and the only other French Second Empire building in Washington across the street—the hush is sometimes broken by cheering crowds, or angry marchers to the White House, or the shouted commands of police through their bullhorns. It makes me know that I am in Washington, near the heart of the action!

Though the Renwick Gallery is a relatively small building as Smithsonian museums go, its namesake, architect **James Renwick**, understood the illusions of grandeur. He created tall doorways leading to high-ceilinged galleries, and even made the wainscot extra high to dwarf the human presence. Yet, even with these visual tricks, few visitors are prepared for the experience when they climb our grand staircase and behold the opulent room we call the **Grand Salon**—tassled and draped, and hung with tiers of paintings to resemble a grand drawing room of the 1870s. Once the main painting gallery when the building opened as the **Corcoran Gallery of Art**, it is one of the most spectacular 19th-century period rooms in America. I have seen harried executives hiding out in its quiet on a midweek midafternoon with their business papers to escape phone calls or office callers. But it is at its best when our resident chamber music group fills the air with their melodies from the past. The sight and sound combine to make one almost wish to have lived before the automobile and central air conditioning! It is a mood to treasure.

55 Decatur House. (1818, **Benjamin Latrobe**) **Commodore Stephen Decatur,** brave and reckless hero of the War of 1812, built this house, many say with proceeds from government-sanctioned privateering. Its simple exterior and formal interiors—especially the splendid second-floor ballroom—represent the best of the Late Federal style. *Open Tu-F 10am-2pm, weekends and holidays noon-4pm. Admission charge. 748 Jackson Place NW (at Lafayette Square).*

56 Sidney Kramer Books. This branch of the 3-store Kramer group features economics and social sciences. *Open daily 9am-6pm. 1722 H St. NW. 298-8010.*

57 Map Store. Maps of every area in the world, plus good guide and travel books. *Open M-F 9am-5:30pm. 1636 I St. NW. 628-2608.*

58 Barr Building. (1930, **Stanley Simmons**) Although the facade of this office building is encrusted with English High Gothic decorations, they don't conceal the emerging modern structural form. Its more utilitarian neighbors are a striking contrast. *Not open to the public. 910 17th St. NW.*

59 Admiral David G. Farragut. Civil War hero and the first admiral in the US Navy, it was Farragut who said, *"Damn the torpedoes, full speed ahead!"* Sculpted by **Vinnie Ream Hoxie** in 1881 and cast from the metal propeller of the *USS Hartford*, Farragut's flagship. *Farragut Sq., K St. between 16th and 17th Sts. NW.*

Bachelor's haven. DC ranks second in singles population in the US, and over 51 percent are female.

Drawings by Joseph Passonneau

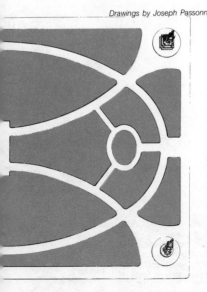

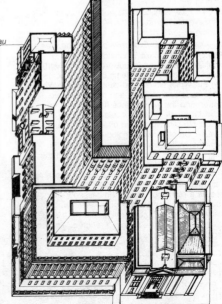

60 US Chamber of Commerce Building. *(1925, Cass Gilbert)* Another of DC's innumerable Roman temples, this one trimmed with a wall of Ionic columns to harmonize with the nearby Treasury Building. *1615 H St. NW. 659-6000.*

61 Lafayette Square. Designed by **L'Enfant** as part of *President's Park*, Thomas Jefferson made this area public land. It was here that laborers camped and bricks were dried during White House construction. First called *Jackson Square*, it was renamed for Revolutionary War hero **Major General Marquis de Lafayette** at a reception held during his last US visit. Lafayette's statue is at the park's southeast corner. He is shown standing before the French people asking them to support the American Revolution. As a fiery 19-year-old, Lafayette traveled to America, where he became a close friend of George Washington. At Yorktown, Virginia, he successfully led colonial troops against the British.

Andrew Jackson, however, still towers at the park's center. He is shown riding a spirited horse as he reviews troops before the Battle of New Orleans. The first equestrian statue cast in the US, it was sculpted in 1853 by **Clark Mills.** Around its base are 4 Spanish cannons captured by Jackson at Pensacola, Florida. **Major General Comte Jean de Rochambeau,** another Frenchman who distinguished himself in the US Revolutionary War is at the park's southwest corner. **Brigadier General Thaddeus Kosciuszko,** Polish-born hero of Saratoga, is at the northeast corner. **Baron Von Steuben,** Prussian native and leader at Valley Forge, is at the park's northwest corner.

During the socially uneasy 1960s, the park was often the scene of demonstrations. Today it is filled with chess players and brown baggers catching the lunchtime sun. During summer, the National Park Service hosts noontime concerts. *Pennsylvania Ave. to H St. NW, Jackson Pl. to Madison Pl., just north of White House.*

62 Hay-Adams Hotel. *Expensive/deluxe.* The *creme de la creme* of deluxe Washington hotels. Exquisitely decorated in Edwardian and Georgian styles, the 8-story Hay-Adams is directly across from the White House and caters to many White House guests, dignitaries and heads of state from around the world. Since its purchase by **David Murdock** in 1983, it has undergone fashionable renovation and offers high-security services. Other services include courtesy limousine, valet service, and a choice of *The Washington Post,* the *New York Times,* and the *Wall Street Journal* delivered at your door. A 24-hour maid and butler service is also available. Until 1925, the property consisted of 2 mansions used as a residence for the Ambassador of Brazil. The *Adams Dining Room* serves English cuisine on Ching Dynasty china; the *John Hay Room* specializes in delicious French cuisine and a special champagne brunch featuring salmon quiche. *800 16th St. NW. 638-6600.*

Federal workers make up 36 percent of DC's work force, with service and trade industries also contributing highly. Tourism, DC's second largest industry, brings in over $1 billion every year, and generates about 45,000 jobs.

63 St. John's Church & Parish House. (1816, **Benjamin Latrobe;** 1883 remodeling, **James Renwick)** Called *the Church of Presidents,* since *Pew 54* has been occupied (at least once) by every man to hold that office since the building was built. It was also the architect's own church: a simple Greek Cross plan that did not include the portico, extended nave or steeple. Renwick enlarged the seating and added the Palladian windows. The nearby Parish House is a French Second Empire opus that lost no elegance in its scaled-down form. *Sunday services (Episcopal) at 8, 9, & 11am. 1525 H St. NW. 347-8766.*

64 Tuckerman House. (1886, **Hornblower & Marshall)** An odd blending of Richardsonian Romanesque and Classical influences. Its resemblance to Richardson's now-gone Hay and Adams houses that stood nearby has led to speculation that he may have been personally involved with this design. *1600 I St. NW.*

65 The Sheraton Carlton. *Moderate/expensive.* This magnificent reproduction of a Renaissance palace, located 2 blocks from the White House, still glistens—especially after a recent facelift. Within its rich stone walls, elaborately carved ceilings and Palladian windows, you will find redecorated rooms and service fit for a king—or queen. Have afternoon tea in the Lobby Court or try a delicious champagne Sunday brunch in the Crystal Room. Complimentary valet parking. *923 16th St. NW. 638-2626/800-325-3535.*

Within the hotel is:

Sheraton Carlton Wine Bar. Connoisseur wines, fruit 'n' cheese snacks and the sky—whether clear, blue or sprinkled with stars—make this one of DC's most romantic outdoor bistros.

66 Val de Loire ☆ $$/$$$ A touch of nouvelle cuisine awaits you at this softly-lit restaurant. Chef-owner **Christian Boucheron** tempts you with specialties of truffles, salmon and crabmeat in *beurre blanc* sauce, venison in wine and white chocolate mousse. *French M-F 11:30am-2:30pm, M-Sa 5:30pm-midnight. Closed Su. 915 15th St. NW. 737-4445.*

67 Southern Building. (1912, **Daniel Burnham)** Here Burnham's typical flamboyance is restrained to a large degree; the clean lines, carefully chosen materials and balanced proportions (designed to make it blend gracefully with its neighbors) show great discipline. But it may have been too much for him: Look up at the florid cornice! Architect **Moshe Safdie** restored this commercial office building according to its original specifications, since Burnham settled for fewer floors than planned. *1425 H St. NW.*

Introductions/Theaters/Narrative black
Hotels purple
Museums/Architecture blue
Parks/Open spaces green
Restaurants/Nightlife red
Shops/Galleries violet

Pennsylvania Avenue Walking Tour.

During the US's post World War II urban exodus, many center cities became neglected and many of the nation's best-loved main streets fell into disrepair. But now that we are rediscovering our city's vital centers, those same streets are finding new life.

Pennsylvania Avenue, the broad *Main Street of the US,* has just such a history. The 1.3-mile-long connection between the **Capitol** and the **White House** has seen the back-and-forth parades of victory, anger and tragedy that read like mercury rising and falling on a thermometer— a measure of the nation's political temperature. Seas of women have marched here seeking the right to vote and equality under the law; blacks have marched here demanding racial equality—and the Ku Klux Klan has gathered here in an effort to deny equality. After WWII, General **Dwight Eisenhower** paraded victorious American forces down the street. Less than 20 years later, a riderless horse lead **John Kennedy's** funeral cortege through the capital as Washingtonians and the nation said their final farewell.

Meanwhile, the central city's shops and offices were moving to new suburban centers, and Pennsylvania Avenue was left with dingy storefronts and struggling businesses.

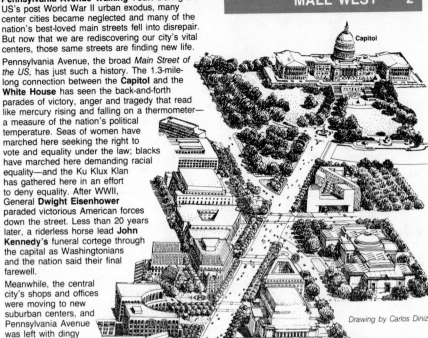

Drawing by Carlos Diniz

1 Treasury Building
2 Sherman Park
3 Washington Hotel
4 Willard Hotel

5 National Press Club
6 National Place/National Center
7 J.W. Marriott
8 American Cities Building
9 1201 Pennsylvania Avenue
10 Pavilion at The Old Post Office
11 J. Edgar Hoover Building
12 Evening Star Building
13 1001 Pennsylvania Avenue
14 Sears World Trade Building
15 Gallery Row
16 717 D Street
17 Canadian Chancery
18 Western Plaza
19 Pershing Park
20 John Marshall Park
21 Meade Plaza

But no longer: Today *The Avenue* is going through one of the US's most exciting downtown renovations, a loving preservation of its beautiful old structures and tasteful addition of new complexes that complement their older neighbors. The facelift along *The Avenue* includes pedestrian-wooing features like parks, shade trees, brick sidewalks, kiosks and benches. A total of 22 blocks are included in the redevelopment.

Two **Metro stops**—one at the **Pavilion at the Old Post Office** and another at 7th Street near **Market Square**—also make *The Avenue* convenient for visitors, including suburban shoppers who are rediscovering Downtown, the multitude of government and central city workers whose offices are nearby, and visitors from around the country and the world who come to see DC's many historic attractions.

Tickets:

Capital Centre. *1 Harry S. Truman Drive, Landover, Maryland. M-F 10am-5:30pm. 350-3400.*

Friends of Kennedy Center. *Hall of States. M-F 10am-9pm. 254-3774.*

Ticketron. *1101 17th St. NW. M-F 10am-6pm. Also locations in Sears stores, Woodward & Lothrop stores and at University of Maryland. 659-2601.*

TicketPlace. *F St. Plaza, between 12th and 13th, NW. Half-price tickets available. M noon-2pm, Tu-Sa 11am-5:30pm. 842-5387.*

WGMS. 570am, 103.5fm. *Broadcasts ticket information, 468-1800.*

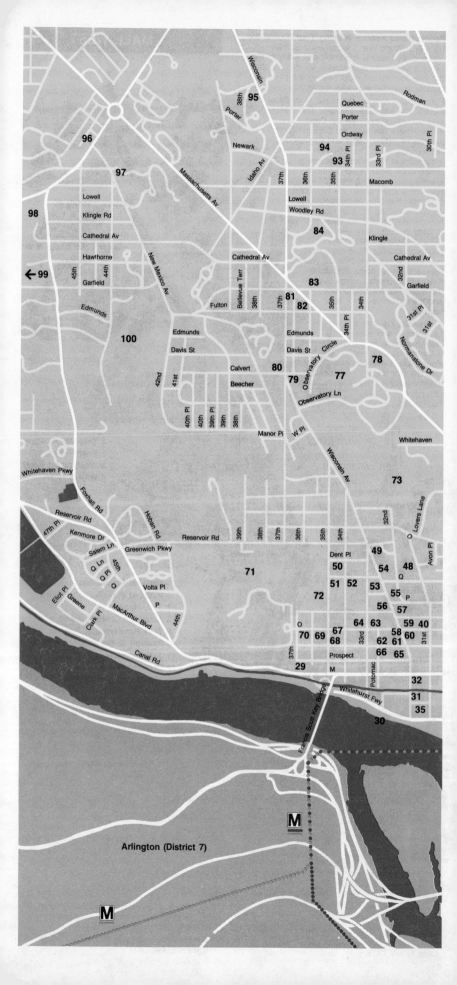

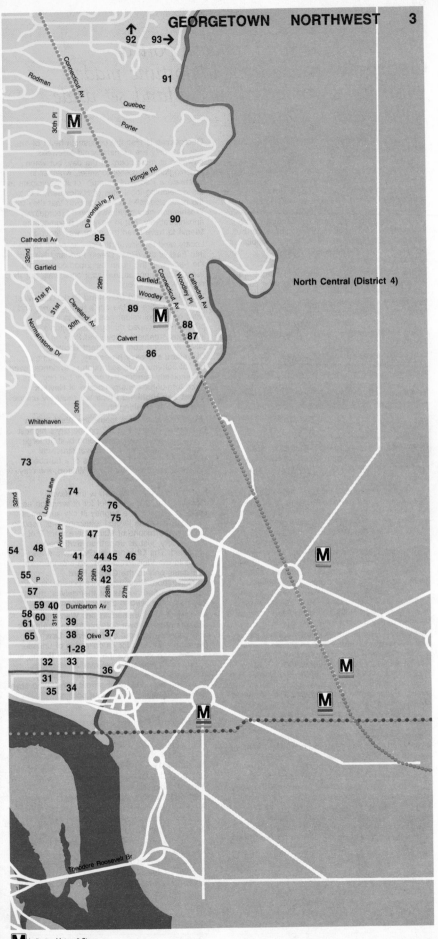

↑
92   93→

91

Rodman

30th Pl

Connecticut Av

Quebec

Porter

M

Klingle Rd

Devonshire Pl

85

90

Cathedral Av

32nd

Garfield

31st Pl

31st

Cleveland Av

30th

29th

Normanstone Dr

Garfield

Woodley

Connecticut Av

Woodley Pl

Cathedral Av

North Central (District 4)

89

M

88
87

Calvert

86

30th

Whitehaven

73

32nd

Lovers Lane

74

76
75

Avon Pl

47

54

48

Q

41

44 45

46

30th

29th

43

42

28th

27th

55

P

57

59 40   Dumbarton Av

58
60

31st

39

61

65

38   Olive 37

1-28

32   33

31

35   34

36

M

M

M

M

M

Theodore Roosevelt Br

M *Indicates Metrorail Stops*

The little Maryland tobacco port of **Georgetown** thought its fortune made when it was included in the land set aside for a Federal District.

Business was expected to come flooding in, real estate values to soar. What happened was very different. Not only did Georgetowners fail to grow rich, they discovered they had lost the right to vote for the president who was to live among them and no longer had a Congressman. A century later, in the 1890s, they were to lose their city as well, as Washington swallowed Georgetown whole. Perhaps it was spite or the assertion of a strong spirit of independence, but during the Civil War, when DC was the capital of the Union, Georgetown was a hotbed of secessionism.

By the early 20th century much of Georgetown, like much of the rest of DC, had become poor and run-down. Still it managed to nurture the talents of young **Duke Ellington** who grew up here. The neighborhood's appeal to the well-to-do began with a massive DC population growth during the '40s and its *discovery* by members of the New Deal.

Despite changing demographics, the neighborhood has never lost the sense of its separate identity. The area is officially known as **West Washington,** but everyone thinks of it still as Georgetown, and its people continue to refer to themselves as Georgetowners, even down to occasionally giving their address as *Georgetown, D.C.*

And they have kept their distance in other ways as well. They wanted nothing to do with the subway, so it doesn't stop here. They wanted nothing to do with the city's new lottery, and no tickets are sold here.

Georgetown's independence has finally paid off—but it may be a mixed blessing. Business has indeed come flooding in. Today the area is home to numerous chic restaurants and boutiques, and has become the shopping heart of the city to such a degree that shopping malls, such as the elegant **Georgetown Park** are being squeezed between the existing 18th- and 19th-century buildings. Of course, real estate values finally did soar, to put it mildly. The tiny homes originally built by Irish navvies—laborers on the Chesapeake & Ohio Canal—who wanted to be near the Fathers of Jesuit **Georgetown University** now cost as much as $250,000.

Georgetown's homes, of course, were not all built by navvies. **Tudor Place,** a private home, has been in the same family for 2 centuries, and has hosted such notables as **Martha Washington, General Lafayette,** and **Robert E. Lee. Dumbarton Oaks** is now open to the public, as are its famous **gardens.** The **Kennedy** house, where **JFK** lived when he was a Senator, is still a private home, but many people seek it out.

The tree-lined **C&O Canal,** one of the city's favorite spots for bicycling and canoeing (both may be rented at **Fletcher's Boat House,** 3 miles upriver), or just strolling, is a failed 19th-century effort to bring inland commerce to the city's ports (Baltimore started its railroad the same year Washington started its canal; a textbook case of the wrong technology at the wrong time). Locals thank **Justice William O. Douglas** for its survival; in the blacktop-happy '50s, it was going to be turned into a 4-lane highway.

Georgetown is also the pedestrian heart of the city. Not only are its narrow old sidewalks crowded at most hours of the day, but when Washingtonians gather together, whether to celebrate a Redskins triumph, or to participate in the developing local rites of **Halloween,** it is to the brick sidewalks of Georgetown that they take. Washington may have swallowed Georgetown administratively, but in daily life, it sometimes seems to have been the other way around.

Locals tend to think of the city as being divided into *East of the (Rock Creek) Park* and *West of the Park,* with the ritzier neighborhoods to the West. This is not as true as it once was, but the notion is hanging on.

Woodley Park and **Cleveland Park,** both West of the Park, are on the city's high ground, and were once cool wilderness areas to which presidents escaped during Washington's infamous summers. Cleveland Park, in fact, takes its name from **President Grover Cleveland's breezy hideaway.** This summer retreat community is still much in evidence, even if completely surrounded now by the city. The huge turn-of-the-century houses of **Newark Street** and **Highland Place** are relatively unique survivors for Washington.

Up the hill from them looms the **Washington Cathedral,** begun in 1907 on the city's highest point. Still unfinished, it is being built, in large measure, according to medieval structural principles. It holds the remains of a number of notables, including **Woodrow Wilson,** the only president buried in the city.

Nearby on a hill of its own is the **Naval Observatory,** not as useful for observation as it once was now that a brightly lit city surrounds it. In darker days, its largest telescope was used to discover the moons of Mars; there were 2 of them, oddly, just as **Jonathan Swift** had predicted. The Observatory grounds are also home to the **Vice President,** an arrangement that dates only to the **Gerald Ford** administration. Previously, vice presidents were expected to find homes for themselves, though they generally lived in the vicinity anyway.

At the foot of all these hills lies Washington's **National Zoo,** known not only for its beauty—it was originally laid out by **Frederick Law Olmsted**—but also for its collection of unusual animals. The stars are the rare **white tigers,** and the **pandas,** who are local media celebrities. During mating season the pandas regularly crowd the president off the front page. Who says Washington thinks only about politics?

Washington Performing Arts Society is the city's largest non-profit arts organization. Supported by 7,000 members, the Society brings more than 400 performers per year to the **Kennedy Center,** its largest co-sponsor, as well as to the **Lisner Auditorium** and the **Warner Theatre.** The year-round events include the **International Orchestra Series** featuring the *St. Louis Symphony Orchestra,* the *Israel Philharmonics* and the *Prague Symphony Orchestra;* **Star Recitals** by well-known opera singers and symphony soloists, and **Dance America,** a modern dance series showcasing groups like **Alvin Ailey** and the **Dance Theatre of Harlem.** Premium seats are split between the Society's box office and the Kennedy Center; the remainder go to Ticketron and smaller ticket agencies. *Box Office open M-F 9am-5pm. 1330 G St. NW.* 393-4433.

In 1861, France sent a gift stone from the tomb of **Napoleon Bonaparte** to the Washington Monument. The stone, reported to have arrived at the Brooklyn Navy Yard that same year, is still missing.

Drawing by Carlos Diniz

The Four Seasons Hotel. *Expensive/deluxe.* This refined, glittering facility is a favorite of Hollywood stars and entertainers visiting the capital. Ask for a room overlooking the historic C & O Canal or Rock Creek Park. Overflowing with luxury and personal service from a multilingual staff, the 208-room Four Seasons offers guests such amenities as 24-hour room service, same-day valet, one-hour pressing, complimentary shoeshine, twice-daily maid service and valet parking (an extra plus in hard-to-park Georgetown). Visit the lush **Garden Terrace** for tea and pastries; the **Plaza Cafe** is an open-air courtyard restaurant. *2800 Pennsylvania Ave. NW. 342-0444/Telex: 904008.*

Within the hotel is:

Aux Beaux Champs. ☆ ☆ ☆ $$$ Settle into a plush velvet chair in this hushed, ultra-posh dining room and sup on foie gras, caviar, lobster, wild game and other delicacies. Superb wine list. High tea served every afternoon in the hotel lobby overlooking Rock Creek Park. *Continental. Open M-F 7am-11pm, Sa & Su 8am-11pm. Reservations required. Coat and tie recommended. 342-0810.*

Enriqueta's. ☆ ☆ $$ Expect quality tacos and enchiladas at this small, unpretentious Mexican spot, but branch out to sample mussels in fiery ranchero sauce, pork-stuffed peppers with fruit sauce, and the indescribable chicken mole. *Mexican. Open M-Th 11:30am-10pm, F & Sa till 11pm, Su 5-10pm. Reservations suggested. 2811 M St. NW. 338-7772.*

3 **Geppetto's.** ☆ $ There's always a line snaking out the door of this noisy, marionette-filled pizza place. Fill up on hearty soups and salads and Geppetto's popular Sicilian-style deep-dish pizza. *Italian. Open M-Th noon-11:30pm, F & Sa till 1:30am; Su 4-11:30pm. No reservations. 2917 M St. NW. 296-0887.*

4 **Viet Huong.** ☆ ☆ $ Storefront restaurant whose specialties include caramel pork and *golden coins,* a dish of skewered meats and pineapple. Soups are delicious, but the spring rolls are often disappointing. *Vietnamese. Open M-F noon-10:30pm, Sa & Su till 1:30am. Reservations suggested. 2928 M St. NW. 337-5588.*

5 **Vietnam Georgetown.** ☆ ☆ $ Small (but with garden seating in seasonal weather) and reasonably priced. Crisp rolls are a treat, as is the Vietnamese crepe. Portions are small, and some dishes tend to be overly sweetened with caramel or cinnamon. *Vietnamese. Open daily 11am-11pm. Reservations accepted. No credit cards. 2934 M St. NW. 337-4536.*

6 **3000 Block of M Street.** (1800; restored 1955 by **Howe, Foster & Snyder**) A fine row of Revolutionary War-era shops and homes is highlighted by the restored pair at *3001-3009 M Sts.*

7 **Georgetown Marbury House.** *Moderate/deluxe.* This 164-room deluxe hotel offers guests a dozen floor plans, including a spacious duplex suite. An 18th-century facade and quaint decor keep the flavor of Olde Georgetown alive. Visit the sidewalk cafe during the spring, summer and early fall, and enjoy your favorite beverages and pastries. An added treat: Georgetown's only outdoor non-residential swimming pool. *3000 M St. NW. 223-2959/800-368-5922.*

8 **Loughboro-Patterson House.** (1806; 1964 restoration, **Macomber & Peter**) An authentic Federal-period restoration made more interesting by a single delicate dormer in the roofline. *3039-3041 M St. NW.*

The Junior League Shop, located in the old **Nathan Loughboro** house, is first-rate for second-hand designer and classic clothing. You'll find top-name women's clothing tossed aside—often after a couple nights out—by Washington's hoity-toity. Great buys on kids' clothing, too. Profits go to a good cause and finds can be phenomenal. *Open M-F 9:30am-3pm, Tu & Th evenings 6:30pm-9pm, Sa 10am-3:45pm. 3037 M St. NW. 337-6120.*

9 **Old Stone House.** (1766) The oldest surviving structure in DC predates the Revolution. It is thought to have been built by cabinetmaker **Christopher Layhman.** The 5 rooms of the simple 2-story house now contain exhibits and crafts demonstrations. *Open W-Sa 9am-5pm. 3051 M St. NW. 426-6851.*

9 **Fendrick Gallery.** Washington's trendiest art gallery, located in the heart of Georgetown, shows all the latest in American painting, sculpture and graphics. This is the place to view craft objects turned fine art, such as **Albert Paley's** decorative ironwork and **Wendell Castle's** elaborate furniture. *Open M-Sa 10am-4pm. Closed Su. 3059 M St. NW. 338-4544.*

10 **Apana.** ☆ ☆ $$$ This quiet, dimly lit gem of a dining room serves Indian food adapted to American tastes. Start with *samosas* (triangular meat- and vegetable-filled pastries), then choose from such dishes as brandied sirloin steak cubes, trout with almonds, cornish hen with coriander, or shrimp with coconut. Custom spicing available for some dishes. *Indian. Open Su-Th 6-11pm, F & Sa till midnight. Reservations suggested. Coat and tie recommended. 3066 M St. NW. 965-3040.*

11 **The Kite Site** conjures up every kind of kite imaginable, from simple Franklin models to multi-surfaced Eastern dragons. Perhaps the best collection of boomerangs on the East Coast. *3101 M St. NW. 965-4230.*

12 **The Irish Corner.** One-stop shopping for all apparel from Eire, including handknitted sweaters, scarves, shawls and caps. *3122 M St. NW. 338-1338.*

12 **Mr. Smith's.** Fresh fruit daiquiris are the specialty of this colorful, brick-walled, garden cafe. Good burgers and sandwiches, spicy chili. *Open M-F 11am-1pm, Sa & Su till 2pm. 3104 M St. NW. 333-3104.*

13 **Urban Outfitters** is one of Georgetown's newest attractions, carrying clothes, kitchenry and kitsch for surviving modern city life. *M-Th 11am-11pm, F & Sa 11am-midnight, Su noon-10pm. 3111 M St. NW. 342-1012.*

13 **Crown Books.** Books and magazines at substantial discounts. You'll find best sellers and pretty picture books, but the publishers' remainders at bargain prices are a book lover's dream-come-true. *3131 M St. 333-4493.*

The **oldest operating elevator,** installed by Otis in 1854, is still operating in its shaft on *637 Indiana Avenue NW.* It passes inspections every 6 months, having been trouble-free for more than 130 years.

14 Nathan's. ☆ ☆ $$ An important Georgetown pit stop, where the bar's inventory of spirits surpasses 500. Nathan's is a favorite drinking ground for Washington's intelligentsia and professionals who have arrived. The restaurant is equally noteworthy: Lunchtime, the Italian cuisine gives way to good and simple American fare; dinner is a reliable performance of hand-made pasta, fresh seafood and veal. Nathan's has also created a brunch reputation among local trendsetters, so plan a visit and enjoy eggs in 10 different varieties of Benedict. *Open M-W 11am-3pm, 6-11pm; Th-F 11am-3pm, 6pm-midnight; Sa 9am-3pm, 6pm-midnight; Su 9am-3pm, 6-11pm. 3150 M St. NW 338-2000.*

15 American Cafe. ☆ ☆ $$ The quintessential Georgetown hangout—small and crowded, but very chic. Its sister restaurant is at 227 Massachusetts Ave. NE (see Dist. 1) *American. Open Su-Th 11am-3am, F & Sa till 4am. Reservations suggested for large groups. 1211 Wisconsin Ave. NW (near M St. NW). 737-5153.*

16 Annie's. The local hangout for collegiate video-preppies. A small dance floor next to an oak bar provides room for trying out tactical moves—political and otherwise. Happy hour from 5-9pm and Tuesday ladies' nights ensure some jampacked evenings. During football season—especially the Superbowl—Annie's becomes Georgetown's official headquarters for serious beerbusting. *Open M-F 5pm-2am, Sa & Su 3pm-3am. 3204 M St. (Wisconsin Ave. and M St.). 333-6767.*

17 Charlie's Georgetown. ☆ ☆ ☆ $$$ When famed jazz guitarist **Charlie Byrd**, known for his magical blend of classical, jazz and Brazilian sounds on nylon strings, opened this jazz club, it added another dimension to the city's music scene. Modern, spacious and a little more plush than many jazz aficionados prefer, Charlie's packs 'em in. The entrance opens into the **Riverfront Piano Bar** where soft jazz on a baby grand and the Rosslyn skyline across the Potomac attract a polished and professional clientele. The formal dining room in the back also offers shows (8:30pm & 10:30pm) where Byrd and guests such as **Herbie Mann**, the **Modern Jazz Quartet** and **Bobbie Short** perform nightly. *Open M-Th 5pm-2am, F 5pm-3am, Sa 6pm-3am, Su 6pm-2am. 3223 K St. NW. 726-3567.*

18 J Paul's. ☆ ☆ $ This year-round watering hole for upscale Baby Boom politicos seems to divide its clientele into 2 groups—the huge antique bar for the career-hungry, and the casually chic back-room restaurant for those who find satisfaction in well-prepared American fare such as steak and seafood. Although originally built as a saloon, the large bay windows, dark marble table tops and high ceilings give J. Paul's an air of elegance. A place for mingling, good food, music and laughter, and casual staring. *American. Open M-Sa 11:30am-2am, Su Brunch 10:30am. 3218 M St. NW. 3333-3450.*

19 Laura Ashley. For that English country look that's heavy on florals and the pocketbook, from women's clothing to wallpaper. *Open M-W & Sa 10am-6pm, Th till 8pm, Su noon-5pm. 3213 M St. NW. 338-5481.*

20 Georgetown Park. By any standards, this $100 million shopping complex with more than 100 trend-setting stores, boutiques and shops impresses—even the non-shopper. Billed as *The World's First Shopping Park,* it is the only such commercial venture that overlaps a National Park—the historic C&O Canal that has supported Georgetown trade since 1831. Certainly, it was the first DC shopping mall to capture the imagination of well-heeled shoppers and reverse the retail traffic pattern back into West Washington. And it may be the first shopping mall anywhere to be included on group tour itineraries.

Built in 1981 behind the preserved and reconstructed century-old facades at the heart of commercial Georgetown, the mall boasts a magnificent Victorian interior. Its 3 levels of brass-and-iron railed mezzanine shopping encircles a grand atrium with a central fountain and indoor garden that flourishes under the block-long skylight roof. All details, from the brass-and-glass elevators to regular performances of classical music by local musicians, give Georgetown Park an aura of sophistication. The prices do too. This is not a bargain-hunter's paradise. Sale signs are rare, usually small and unobtrusive. Buzz-words like European-tailored, chic and unique aren't exaggerations here. This is snob shopping at its best.

Among the internationally flavored shops and stores, for instance, is the first East Coast branch of **Abercrombie & Fitch** (965-6500), the fun, excessive sporting emporium that fled NYC for Texas and California a few years back, with merchandise ranging from complete safari outfits to dwarf billiard tables. An elegant branch of **Garfinckel's** (628-8107) that caters mainly to women is the largest store among the mall's many small and tony boutiques, such as the preppie **Davison's of Bermuda** (338-4998) and **Cache** (342-0146), a high-fashion women's shop from Miami. Contemporary home furnishings and craftwork are featured at the 35,000-square-foot Brit import **Conran's** (298-8300) and at **Scan** (333-5015). For fine toys, there's **FAO Schwarz** (342-2285), and **Chesapeake Knife and Tool Co.** (338-5700) carries an international selection of quality cutlery, hunting and collectors' knives and accessories. **Senor David** (337-5621) handles Italian men's wear, **Narragansett** (342-2275) goes for the traditional and classic in men's and women's clothing, and **Britches of Georgetown** is the popular man-tailored shop for women. **Godiva Chocolatier** (342-2232) for

---

GEORGETOWN PARK™

calories (fine chocolate); **Waldenbooks'** *(333-8033)* plethora of paperback bestsellers and fine art, literature and history books at big discounts; and **Uno** *(342-2300)* for one-of-a-kind handcrafted gold and silver jewelry have all found their upper-crust niche at Georgetown Park. Underground parking at reduced rate with shop validation sticker. *Store hours M-Sa 10am-9pm, Su noon-6pm. 3222 M St. NW; entrances on Wisconsin Ave. and M St. 342-8190.*

20 Place Vendome. ☆ ☆ $$ Located at the liveliest intersection in town, this is the place to go for a light snack, dessert, hearty meal or late supper. Chocolate desserts and hazelnut mousse are a must. Avoid dishes with nouvelle pretentions. *French. Open Su-Th 11:30am-midnight, F & Sa till 2am. Reservations suggested. 3200 Wisconsin Ave. NW (M St. NW). 333-6444.*

21 Clyde's. ☆ $$ During the disco '70s, this pub/fern bar was one of the East Coast's most crowded singles meeting places—a legend in its own time. Capitol Hill and business executives— of both sexes—still come to see who else is here. The **Omelet Room** is favored for breakfast and brunch, the leafy atrium for cocktails. *Pub/grill. Open M-Th 11am-2am, F till 3am; Sa 10am-3am; Su 9am-4pm. Omelet Room opens at 7:30am M-F, 9am weekends. Reservations weekdays only. 3236 M St. NW. 333-0294.*

22 Georgetown Leather Design, at its original location (it has expanded into the suburban malls), carries high-quality handmade leather and suede goods, including blazers, coats, boots and belts for men and women. *Open Su-W & F 10am-6pm, Th & Sa 10am-8pm. 3265 M St. NW. 333-9333.*

23 El Caribe Georgetown. ☆ ☆ ☆ $$ A bit ritzier and slightly more expensive than its Adams-Morgan counterpart, this El Caribe offers the best of Central and South American specialties in a friendly, bustling atmosphere. Begin with the fried squid, gazpacho or tiny meat pies called empanaditas. Main dishes include chicken and Spanish sausage, *paella,* 2 types of seafood stew, and tongue in chili sauce. Rice and black beans abound. *Central/South American. Open Su-Th 11:30am-11:30pm, F & Sa till midnight. Reservations suggested. 3288 M St. NW. 338-3121.*

24 Las Pampas. ☆ ☆ $$ White tablecloths, gracious service and succulent grilled meats and poultry in a cozy Argentinean spot. *Argentinean. Open Su-Th 11am-midnight, F & Sa till 2am. Reservations suggested. 3291 M St. NW. 333-5151.*

25 Tandoor. ☆ ☆ ☆ $$ You can watch the cooks grilling tandoori chicken, beef, lamb and seafood through a window in the downstairs dining room. Curries spiced according to preference. Excellent breads. *Indian. Open M-F noon-2:30pm, 5:30-11pm; Sa 5:30pm-midnight; Su 5-10:30pm. Reservations suggested. 3316 M St. NW. 333-3376.*

26 Madurai. ☆ ☆ ☆ $ This cozy, informal place offers superb Southern Indian cooking at low cost. Try the lentil soup, assorted vegetable curries with homemade *panir* (spongy, wonderful cheese), crispy *masala dosai* (long, thin crepes filled with curried veggies). All-you-can-eat Sunday lunch and dinner. *Indian vegetarian. Open M-Sa noon-2:30pm, 5-10pm; Su noon-4pm, 5-10pm. No reservations. 3318 M St. NW. 333-0997.*

Washington is the country's 5th most suburban city, with over 79.6 percent suburban, or more than 379 suburbanites per every 100 central city residents.

27 Bamiyan. ☆ ☆ $ This unassuming place will convince you of the glories of Afghanistan's unique cuisine. Enjoy juicy shish kebabs of lamb, chicken and beef; wonderful scallion dumplings in minted meat sauce; and curried stews. But the real treat is the *goshefeel* (elephant ear) pastry—a giant fried pastry sprinkled with sugar and pistachio crumbles, every bit as delicious as it sounds. *Afghani. Open M-Sa 5:30-11pm. Reservations suggested. 3320 M St. NW. 338-1896.*

28 Eagle Wine & Cheese has catered to Georgetown crowds for years with discount prices on imported beers, wines and liquors— and a vast selection of cheeses of the world. Expertise on-staff plus wine and cheese tastings make it all the more popular. *Open M & Tu 9:30am-6pm, W-Sa 9:30am-8pm. 3345 M St. NW. 333-6655.*

29 The Exorcist was filmed at 3600 Prospect Street. The red brick building, owned by Georgetown University, was modified for the story, but you can see the steep steps where the title character met his fate.

30 Georgetown Waterfront. Once tall ships docked here with goods from the industrial North, agricultural South, or exotic lands. Plans to recapture this romantic era are in early stages.

31 Grace Episcopal Church. (1866) Early Gothic Revival stone church was established as a mission to the boatmen on the Chesapeake & Ohio Canal. *1041 Wisconsin Ave. (7th St.)*

32 Bowl & Board specializes in handcrafted and imported wooden items, from butcher blocks and salad bowls to utensils and train whistles. *Open M-Th 11am-7pm, F & Su 10am-8pm. 1066 Wisconsin Ave. NW. 338-5919.*

32 Blues Alley. This intimate night spot is filled with jazz fans who come to hear big stars like **Dizzy Gillespie** and **Woody Herman.**

To complement the music, Blues Alley serves regional New Orleans-style dishes, medium-priced seafood and steaks. Dinner guests are given preferential seating during the shows *(9pm & 11pm;* sometimes a third performance is added at *12:45am on weekends).* It's possible to enjoy the music and the candlelit ambiance without eating, but there is a cover charge. In either case, reservations are a must. (In 1982, Washington's oldest and most prominent jazz club officially donated its name to the very street it stands on.) *Open daily 7pm-2am. Blues Alley off Wisconsin Ave. NW. 337-4141.*

33 Tout Va Bien. ☆ ☆ ☆ $$ A small, posh cafe serving reasonably priced nouvelle fare: duck with raspberry sauce, chicken galantine, baby salmon, fruit tarts made to order. *French. Open M-Th 11:30am-11pm, F & Sa till 11:30pm, Su 5:30-10:30pm. Reservations suggested. 1063 31st St. NW. 965-1212.*

33 La Ruche. ☆ ☆ ☆ $$ This serene and cozy cafe is renowned for its fresh fruit tarts, chocolate mousse and luscious cakes. But don't forget the huge, inventive salads, rich slices of quiche and zucchini pie, and low-priced daily specials like mussels, chicken breast with apples, and trout almondine. Outdoor dining in warm weather. *French. Open M-F 11:30am-midnight, Sa & Su till 1am. No reservations. 1039 31st St. NW (M St. NW). 955-5940.*

33 Yes! Inc. The nation's largest New Age book and networking store stocks subjects from holistic medicine, nutrition and mysticism to healing, and East-West philosophy. The recordings section is great for peculiar but choice items: Eastern meditative music, natural sounds from the African jungle, medieval hymns or Celtic tunes. *Open 7 days 10am-7pm, Th till 9pm. 1035 31st St NW. 338-6969.*

Introductions/Theaters/Narrative black
Hotels purple
Museums/Architecture blue
Parks/Open spaces green
Restaurants/Nightlife red
Shops/Galleries violet

34 Foundry Mall is small, out-of-the-way and nicely situated next to the canal where each summer free jazz and bluegrass concerts attract crowds. Among the shops along its indoor walkways is **The Angler,** a first-class store for fishermen (333-1156). *Thomas Jefferson St. between M and K Sts. NW.*

35 The Bayou attracts an 18 to 40 crowd with diverse, nationally known performers from the jazz, fusion and blues arenas. The casual split-level nightclub seats 500 and is concert-oriented; drinks, sandwiches and pizza are served in simple brick and wood surroundings. During intermissions, a large screen features Top 40 videos. DJs spin post-show dance tunes until closing time. Tickets at box office or Ticketron outlets. *Open Su-Th 8pm-2am, F & Sa 8pm-3am. 3135 K St. NW. 333-2897.*

36 Chesapeake & Ohio Canal. This is one of the last and best preserved of the great system of canals that helped move goods westward in the late 18th and early 19th centuries. An engineering marvel, the canal employs 74 locks and the 3,100-foot **Paw Taw Tunnel** carved through the stone mountains of western Maryland. The C&O extends 184½ miles from Georgetown to Cumberland, Maryland, where the Allegheny Mountains interrupted its intended meeting with the Ohio River. **George Washington** had envisioned such a canal, and invested $10,000 in the Potowmack Canal Company—those stocks were eventually left to endow **George Washington University**—and supervised much of the work on this early canal, precursor of the C&O. **John Quincy Adams** broke ground for the larger canal on July 4, 1828, and for several decades mule-drawn canal clippers carried lumber, coal, whiskey and grain from the West at about 4 miles per hour. By the end of the 19th century the Baltimore & Ohio Railroad had stolen most of the canal's customers; by 1924 the C&O was obsolete.

The best preserved portion of the C&O is a 22-mile stretch from Georgetown to Seneca, Maryland, but you can hike or bike the old **Towpath** for the entire length of the canal. The NPS sponsors some guided hikes and maintains campsites. The timberland that nestles along the waterway and its rich wildlife make the spot perfect for such activities, as well as rock climbing (by permit) on its rugged overhangs, canoeing and boating, and ice skating in winter. There are even some old gold mines, battlesites and cabins along the route.

Catch the mule-drawn **Canal Clipper** at the dock, 30th & M Streets in Georgetown (there's a charge for the ride, call 299-2026 for information) or at the famous old **Great Falls Tavern** in Great Falls, Maryland (see Beltway, call *301-299-3613/299-3614* for information).

Canoes and boats can be rented at **Fletcher's Boat House,** *4940 Canal Rd. NW.* (244-0461), just 3 miles north of Georgetown; **Jack's Boats** (337-9642) at *3500 K St. NW;* or **Swain's Lock,** *on River Rd. just north of Potomac, Maryland. For information call C&O district headquarters at 301-484-3475.*

37 Decatur House. (1813, **John Stull Williams**) After Commodore **Stephen Decatur,** the dashing naval hero of the War of 1812, was killed in a duel, his widow moved to this stately Federal-style home, *Private residence. 2812 N St. NW.*

38 John Laird Mansion (Laird/Dunlop House). (1799, **William Lovering**) Originally the home of tobacco merchant **John Laird. Robert Todd Lincoln,** son of the president, also once owned the Federal period mansion. *Private residence. 3014 N St. NW.*

39 Washington Post Office, Georgetown Branch. (1857, **Ammi B. Young**) A timelessly simple composition of heavy, plain stone walls; acclaimed as one of the best Italianate Federal buildings ever built. *1221 31st St. NW.*

Ninety-six percent of the river-front property in Washington, DC, is owned by the government.

40 Booked Up. Novelist **Larry McMurtry's** antiquarian book shop's tall and endless shelves hold mostly first editions and rare out-of-print books. Open by appointment. *1209 31st St. NW. 965-3244.*

40 Christ Episcopal Church. (1817, **Henry Laws**) A scaled-down Gothic cathedral with an unusual gabled tower. Although it's too small to be really awe-inspiring, it fits neatly into the neighborhood. **Francis Scott Key** was a member of the congregation. *Services Su 8am, 9:15am & 11am. O & 31st Sts. NW. 333-6677.*

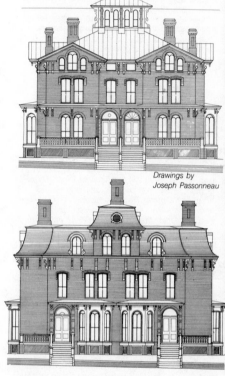

Drawings by
Joseph Passonneau

41 Cookes Row. (1868, **Starkweather & Plowman**) Although Georgetown is perhaps best known for its Federal-style buildings, this group of mid-Victorian charmers offers a welcome twist on the row house theme. The 4 duplexes contain twice as many residences, each with a side yard and over 4,000 square feet of space. The exterior details—bay windows, dormers, porches—give each building its own character (2 are in the French Mansard style; the other pair is vaguely Germanic). But inside, they are not nearly as individual as they look: all 4 have the same floor plan. *Private residences. 3009-3029 Q St.*

42 Reuben Daw's Fence. (1860s) This fence, made of musket barrels from the 1848 Mexican-American War, encloses 3 houses on P St. and a pair on 28th St. *2803 P St.*

43 Miller House. (1840, **Benjamin Miller**) A New England clapboard house set down in the midst of the city's original neighborhood. The portico is an early hint of the Greek Revival styles that gained popularity soon after. *Private residence. 1524 28th St.*

44 Mackall Square. (1820, **Benjamin Mackall**) A typical Georgian home, though the square porch affixed to the front is a bit gaudy by comparison to the rest of the house. *Private residence. 1633 29th St. NW.*

45 Evermay. (1792) This was considered the most elegant house in the city even back when opulence was the norm. Now occupied by DuPont heirs, it has been restored to its former extravagance, and features a garden of such Southern favorites as azaleas, magnolias and boxwood. *Private residence. 1623 28th St. NW.*

46 Dumbarton House. (1750) Known until 1932 as Bellevue, this is a very typical mid 18th-century Georgian home complete with oval rooms, ornate mantles and breezy hallways. **Benjamin Latrobe** remodeled the house in 1805, installing the rear bays. Now owned by the **Society of Colonial Dames,** who have maintained the Federal furnishings, including Hepplewhite and Sheraton pieces, and fine collections of silver and china. Worth a visit. *Admission free, contributions accepted. Open M-Sa 9am-noon. Closed Jul-Aug. 2715 Q St. NW. 337-2288.*

47 Beall House. (1784) **George Washington's** great-nephew, **Colonel George Corbin Washington,** and his bride, **Elizabeth Beall,** were given this house as a wedding gift by her father. The original Georgian structure has been much altered. *Private residence. 30th and R Sts. NW*

48 Tudor Place. (1794, **Dr. William Thornton;** wings added 1805-1816) **Martha Washington's** granddaughter, **Martha Parke Custis,** and her husband, **Thomas Peter,** were the original occupants of this house; their heirs still live here. A vast expanse of greensward in front and impressive gardens in the rear help fill one of the largest lots in Georgetown. *Private residence. 1644 31st St.*

49 Japan Inn. ☆ ☆ $$$ Sit at a communal table in the *Teppan-Yaki Room* and have your steak, chicken or shrimp cooked on stainless steel grills right before your eyes. If you want a more private experience, reserve a tatami room upstairs; you'll sit at a low table and sup on sukiyaki and *shabu shabu* prepared by a kimonoed waitress. Or have a full dinner of sashimi, sushi or tempura. *Japanese. Open M-Th noon-2pm, 6-10pm; F & Sa 6-10pm. Closed Su. Reservations suggested. Coat and tie recommended. 1715 Wisconsin Ave. NW (R St. NW). 337-3400.*

50 Mackall-Worthington House. (1820, **Leonard Mackall**) A large Federal-home that was once the focal point of the neighborhood it occupies. The incongruous mansard roof was added later. *Private residence. 1686 34th St. NW.*

51 Volta Bureau. (1893, **Peabody & Stearns**) A strange amalgam of early Greek Temple and office building, it is home to the **American Association for the Teaching of Speech to the Deaf. Alexander Graham Bell** funded the building with money he received from his invention of the telephone, and within the building is a small monument to him. *1537 35th St. NW.*

52 Pomander Walk. (1885) Renovation in the 1950s changed this from a blighted alley to a charming and fashionable set of small homes. *Private residences. Volta Pl. between 33rd & 34th Sts. NW.*

53 Volta Place Gallery. Washington's sole gallery specializing in authentic traditional African tribal art. Ritual, utilitarian and decorative works are featured. Exhibitions often focus on specific regions of Africa or on selected art forms such as ancestor statues. *Open Tu-Sa noon-6. Closed Su & M. 1531 33rd St. NW. 342-2003.*

54 Audubon Book Shop. Inconspicuous amid its flashier neighbors, this is the city's best collection of bird and nature books, plus other avian gifts and accessories. *Open Tu-Sa 10am-7pm. Closed Su & M. 1621 Wisconsin Ave. NW. 337-6062.*

55 Adams Davidson Gallery. Nineteenth-century American oils, watercolors and drawings are the specialty of this gallery. The place to view Hudson River School landscapes from the 1850-75 period by such masters as **Thomas Cole** and **Frederick Church.** *Open Tu-F 10am-5pm, Sa noon-6pm. Closed Su & M. 3233 P St. NW. 628-0257.*

55 Peter Mack Brown. This veteran antiques dealer is well regarded for his 18th-century French and Continental furniture. Silver, bronzes, porcelains and fine English and American furniture are other specialties of the shop. *Open 11am-4:30pm. Closed Su. 1525 Wisconsin Ave. NW. 338-8484.*

M

Bamiyan
Madurai
Tandoor

Eagle Wine & Cheese

33rd

El Caribe

Las Pampas
Georgetown Leather Design

Potomac

Georgetown Park

J. Paul's
Annie's

Georgetown Park
Clyde's
Laura Ashley
Place Vendome

Wisconsin

American Cafe
Nathan's
Irish Corner
Mr. Smith's

Urban Outfitters
Crown Books
Kite Site

31st

Apana
Fendrik Gallery
Old Stone House

Jefferson

Junior League Shop
Loughboro-Patterson House

Marbury House

Historic Georgetown Block

30th

Viet-Huong Cafe
Geppetto's
Marbury House

Vietnam Georgetown

29th

Four Seasons Hotel

Enriqueta's

28th

Pennsylvania

56 Cafe de Ipanema. ☆ $$ It takes an adventurous palate to appreciate Brazilian cooking. *Feijoada—* the national specialty of fresh and cured meats, sausage, black beans, greens and onions in a pungent sauce—is available every Wednesday, Saturday and Sunday. *Brazilian. Open M-Th 11am-11pm, F & Sa till 3am, Su till midnight. Reservations suggested. 1524 Wisconsin Ave. NW (P St. NW). 965-6330.*

57 Commander Salamander. Lots of funk and punk, with heavy emphasis on multi-colored leopard designs, rhinestone sunglasses and the latest in hairspray colors. New Wave trinkets, jewelry and thumpin' music draw a clientele worth seeing. *Open M-W 10am-7pm, Th 10am-10pm, F & Sa 10am-midnight, Su noon-7pm. 1420 Wisconsin Ave. NW. 333-9599.*

57 Little Caledonia is one of those off-the-beaten-track collections of shops in the middle of Georgetown. Prime browsing territory for objets d'art, china, cookware, fabrics, gifts and other quaint merchandise. *Open M-Sa 10am-6pm. 1419 Wisconsin Ave. NW. 333-4700.*

58 Au Pied de Cochon. ☆ $ This bustling, affable 'round-the-clock bistro serves immense portions of hearty French fare: omelets, quiches, crepes, pigs feet, ratatouille. The black bean soup is great, but when available, the best buy is lobster. During nice weather, the outdoor cafe is perfect for meeting friends; during cold months it becomes an enclosed greenhouse where you can keep warm with mugs of coffee and watch the rain or snow. *French. Open 24 hrs., except M (closed 1am-11:30am). No reservations. 1335 Wisconsin Ave. NW (Dumbarton St. NW). 333-5440.*

59 Aux Fruits de Mer. ☆ ☆ $ An illuminated window aquarium decorates the exterior of this informal, inexpensive seafood establishment. Order from a large selection of fresh fish, broiled lobster stuffed with crabmeat, frog legs and bouillabaisse, all served with cole slaw and mounds of fries. *Seafood. Open Su-Th 11:30am-2am, F & Sa till 3am. No reservations. 1329 Wisconsin Ave. NW (Dumbarton St. NW). 965-2377.*

59 Early American Shop. For 36 years, the established purveyor of period American country and high-style antiques, buying and selling along the entire Eastern seaboard. *Open M-Sa 11am-6pm or call for an appointment. 1319 Wisconsin Ave. NW. 333-5843.*

59 The Georgetown Inn (expensive) has every bit of the charm, elegance and village ambiance that this community is noted for. You become an honored guest in the 18th-century mansion. Located in the heart of this bustling mid-city village, where sidewalk cafes and small boutiques abound. Exquisitely restored and refurnished throughout. Free parking. *1310 Wisconsin Ave. NW. 333-8900/800-424-2929.*

Within the hotel is:

Les Ambassadeurs. ☆ ☆ $$ Leather banquettes, crystal chandeliers, suave service and fashionable, mostly high-quality food can be had for a relative song. Nice champagne brunch on Su. *French. Open M-Sa noon-11pm; Su 11am-3pm, 6-11pm. Reservations suggested. 1310 Wisconsin Ave. NW. 333-8900.*

Maison des Crepes. ☆ $ Buckwheat crepes filled with hot and cold vegetables, meats, cheeses and fruit, plus other French dishes served in a homey, country-style setting. *French. Open M-Th 11:30am-11:30pm, F & Sa till 1am; Su 11am-11:30pm. Reservations accepted for large groups only. 1303 Wisconsin Ave. NW (N St. NW). 337-1723.*

Building the C&O Canal was serious business. Any slaves or hired whites who ran away from duty were sentenced to have their heads and eyebrows shaved immediately upon arrest.

60 Britches of Georgetown is the uncontested headquarters for young urban professionals seeking a distinctively trendy and prepped look. And for active outdoorsmen who want that well-turned-out look, **Britches Great Outdoors** is only 2 blocks up Wisconsin Ave. (at 1357). *Open 7 days, 10am-6pm, Th till 8pm. 1247 Wisconsin Ave. NW. 338-3330.*

60 The Book Annex/Record & Tape Ltd. Possibly the best stocked and certainly the most popular book and record store in town. Its staff is knowledgeable and will special order books not in stock. The classical recording section is tops. Famous authors appear now and then to autograph their latest offerings. *Open M-Sa 10am-10pm, Su noon-6pm. 1239 Wisconsin Ave. NW. 338-9544.*

60 Mr. Henry's One of the area's more reasonably priced bars, Georgetown residents of mixed ages and persuasions come to relax here. The menu lists mainly sandwiches; special summer or winter drinks are available with the changing seasons. Friday nights, pianist **Kim Jordan** plays nostalgic evergreens. Sunday mornings, the regulars turn up for a buffet-style brunch, served on the outside deck during summertime. The decor, with dark wood walls, checkered tablecloths and bentwood chairs, contributes to the casual mood of this neighborhood pub. *Open daily 11:30am-2am. 1225 Wisconsin Ave. NW. 882-7610.*

60 Alexander Julian Shop. Features the exciting and colorful pastel designs in men's clothing by Alexander Julian. *Open M-Sa 10am-5pm, Th till 8pm, Su noon-5pm. 1242 Wisconsin Ave. NW. 333-1988.*

61 French Bread Factory is a chic hole-in-the-wall (all very modern though) where fresh almond, ham 'n cheese and fruit croissants and pastries are sold along with the morning *Post. Open daily, F & Sa till midnight. 3222 N St. NW. 338-7776.*

61 Martin's Tavern. ☆ ☆ $$ The oldest tavern in Georgetown—warm, classy and quieter than most other Irish pubs. Tiffany lamps and the gold framed paintings give the place a clubby feeling. The conservative clientele comes for the Virginia crabcakes or the excellent Irish lamb stew. *Irish/American. Open daily 8am-midnight; breakfast 8am-3pm. 1264 Wisconsin Ave. NW. 333-7370.*

62 Smith Row. (1815, **Walter & Clement Smith**) Six Federal houses, side by side and identical except for the most subtle variations in color and form. *3255-3263 N St. NW.*

63 St. John's Episcopal Church. (1809, **Dr. William Thornton;** renovation 1870, **Starkweather & Plowman**) The second oldest Episcopal Church in the District. Like Thornton's design for the Capitol, this Georgian edifice was drastically altered in later years. *Open M-F 9am-4:30pm. Services Su 8am, 9am & 11am. Potomac & O Sts. NW. 338-1796.*

63 Cynthia Fehr Antiques. This townhouse gallery on a cobblestone street features 18th- and 19th-century furniture, English and American paintings of the same period, Staffordshire ware, Chinese porcelains and other objets d'art. *Open M-Sa 11am-5pm. Closed Su. 3214 O St. NW. 338-5090.*

64 Cox's Row. (1805) Often acclaimed as the finest series of Federal row houses in Georgetown. Some of the middle houses were remodeled during the Victorian era; the end houses are as built. *Private residences. 3331-3339 N St. NW.*

65 Morton's of Chicago. ☆ $$$ A favorite of Capitol Hill regulars and other power brokers, this macho steakhouse makes a show of parading their raw beef, chicken, even onions before you in order to demonstrate quality and freshness. *Steakhouse. Open M-Sa 5:30-11pm. Closed Su. Reservations required. Coat and tie recommended. 3251 Prospect St. NW (Wisconsin Ave.). 342-6258.*

66 Booeymonger Restaurant and Delicatessen. ☆ $ This small, '60s-ish cafe and carry-out assembles huge, specialty sandwiches. *Cafe/carry-out. Open M-F 8am-midnight, Sa & Su 9am-midnight. No reservations or credit cards. 3265 Prospect St. NW (34th St. NW). 333-4810.*

7 Quality Hill. (1798, **John Thomas Mason**) The entire neighborhood may have once been called *Quality Hill*, after its many fine homes; somehow, this house inherited the nickname. *Private residence. 3425 Prospect St. NW.*

8 Stoddert House. (1787) A large, rangy and ornate Federal townhouse, owner and architect **Benjamin Stoddert** called it *Halcyon House*. Although the north facade has been completely redesigned, the south side, like the interiors and garden, remain as they were 2 centuries ago. *Private residence. 3400 Propect Ave. NW.*

9 Prospect House. (1788, **James M. Lingan**) The view of the Potomac commanded from this sharply detailed Federal house is the basis for the name. *Private residence. 3508 Prospect St. NW.*

0 1789. ☆ ☆ $$$ Located in an 18th-century house, this dining room boasts fireplaces, early American furnishings and etchings, and an extensive menu featuring imaginative dishes like chicken breast with pecans and morels, salmon with 2 caviars, and oysters in puff pastry. Intriguing but overpriced wine list. *French. Open M-Th 6pm-1am, F & Sa till 2am. Closed Su. Reservations required. Coat and tie recommended. 1226 36th St. NW (Prospect St. NW). 965-1789.*

70 F. Scott's. The music of Broadway and the Big Band era, art deco flourishes, and movers and movers in politics and the arts fill this ultra-chic bar. *1232 36th St. NW. 965-1789.*

0 Georgetown University Shop (at 2 locations, in Georgetown and at the Chevy Chase Center) was preppy before preppy was cool, and has a reputation for quality menswear and classic sportswear for women. *1248 36th St. NW in Georgetown (337-8100) and at Wisconsin and Western Aves. NW (337-8100). 656-4004.*

GEORGETOWN UNIVERSITY

71 Georgetown University. The country's oldest Roman Catholic university is a pleasant place to walk along shady, cobblestoned streets. Founded by **John Carroll** in 1789, the school has always been open to *"students of every religious profession"* and today includes those from 91 countries.

Old North Building was the original structure, finished in 1792. The fortress-like **Healy Building** (1879, **Smithmeyer & Pelz**) is a grim German Gothic affair topped with an amazing spire. (When you're across the river in Arlington, note the best view of the school's famous spires.)

The building was named for **Reverend Patrick Healy, SJ**, the country's first black man to earn a PhD. (The university's current president is the Reverend Healy's grandson.) GU's highly regarded School of Medicine sponsors a 535-bed hospital. Other colleges include schools of arts and sciences, nursing, dentistry and language, as well as the country's most applied-to law school. The university's location in the national capital is one reason it includes the country's first and largest foreign service program.

Campus tours can be arranged by telephone or at the **Visitors Center** on the first floor of the Healy Building, *open M-F 8am-6pm, Sa 9am-5pm. Main entrance, 37th & O Sts. 625-4866.*

72 Convent of the Visitation. (1820-1872) The convent's 3 buildings—an 1820 Federal-style chapel, a Gothic monastery (1832-1857), and an ornate Victorian school building dating from 1872—represent a merry pastiche of 19th-century taste. *35th & P Sts. NW.*

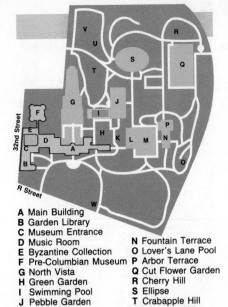

A Main Building
B Garden Library
C Museum Entrance
D Music Room
E Byzantine Collection
F Pre-Columbian Museum
G North Vista
H Green Garden
I Swimming Pool
J Pebble Garden
K Beech Terrace
L Urn Terrace
M Rose Garden
N Fountain Terrace
O Lover's Lane Pool
P Arbor Terrace
Q Cut Flower Garden
R Cherry Hill
S Ellipse
T Crabapple Hill
U Forsythia Hill
V Fairview Hill
W Garden Entrance

73 Dumbarton Oaks. (House, 1800) This lovingly preserved 19th-century estate is one of the capital's very special places, famous both for the lavish mansion where groundwork for the United Nations charter was laid, and for its exquisite gardens. Originally part of the Port of Georgetown land grant made by **Queen Anne** in 1702, the house was built 100 years later. In the 1920s the ramshackle estate was bought by former Ambassador to Argentina **Robert Woods Bliss**, and he and his wife began creating the present museum and garden. A small pre-Columbian museum (1963, **Philip Johnson**), a grouping of 9 domed glass cylinders, houses excellent collections of works by Byzantine and pre-Columbian artisans, including jewelry and metalwork. The restored home is a collection of European art and architectural treasures. In the music room, the Blisses entertained—and were entertained by—such noted friends as pianist **Jan Paderewski** and composer **Igor Stravinsky**, who wrote his *Concerto in E Flat*, the *Dumbarton Oaks Concerto*, to commemorate the couple's 30th anniversary. El Greco's *The Visitation* hangs in the room. Concerts are still held here; *call 342-3200 for information.*

Several libraries house books reserved for scholars, although the **Rare Books Room** is sometimes open for viewing. The estate has over 100,000 books on Byzantium and pre-Columbian art and on landscape gardening. The 16 acres of gardens designed by **Beatrix Farrand** and Mrs. Bliss are a wonderland of manicured walkways and thematic culs-de-sac. One of the favorite garden spots is the **Pebble Garden Fountain**, an expanse of intricately patterned pebble mosaics which, in spring and summer, are flooded with a thin layer of water. A graceful Italianate fountain features a pair of putti romping on seahorses while water springs forth from the hands of a third.

Admission free. R St. at 31st St. NW. The Dumbarton Collections open Tu-Su 2-5pm. 32nd St. NW. one block west of Wisconsin Ave. (Park on R, S, or 36th St.) Call 338-8278/Tour information: 342-3290.

Dumbarton Oaks Park is 27 acres of natural woodlands noted for its profusion of spring wildflowers. The fact that it's only accessible by foot, via **Lovers Lane** off R and 31st Streets, helps keep it unspoiled. *Dumbarton Gardens opens daily, weather permitting, Apr-Oct 2-6pm. Admission charge, Nov-Mar 2-5pm. 338-8278.*

"It is our national capital. It belongs to us, and whether it is mean or majestic, whether arrayed in glory or covered with shame, we cannot but share its character and its destiny." **Frederick Douglass**

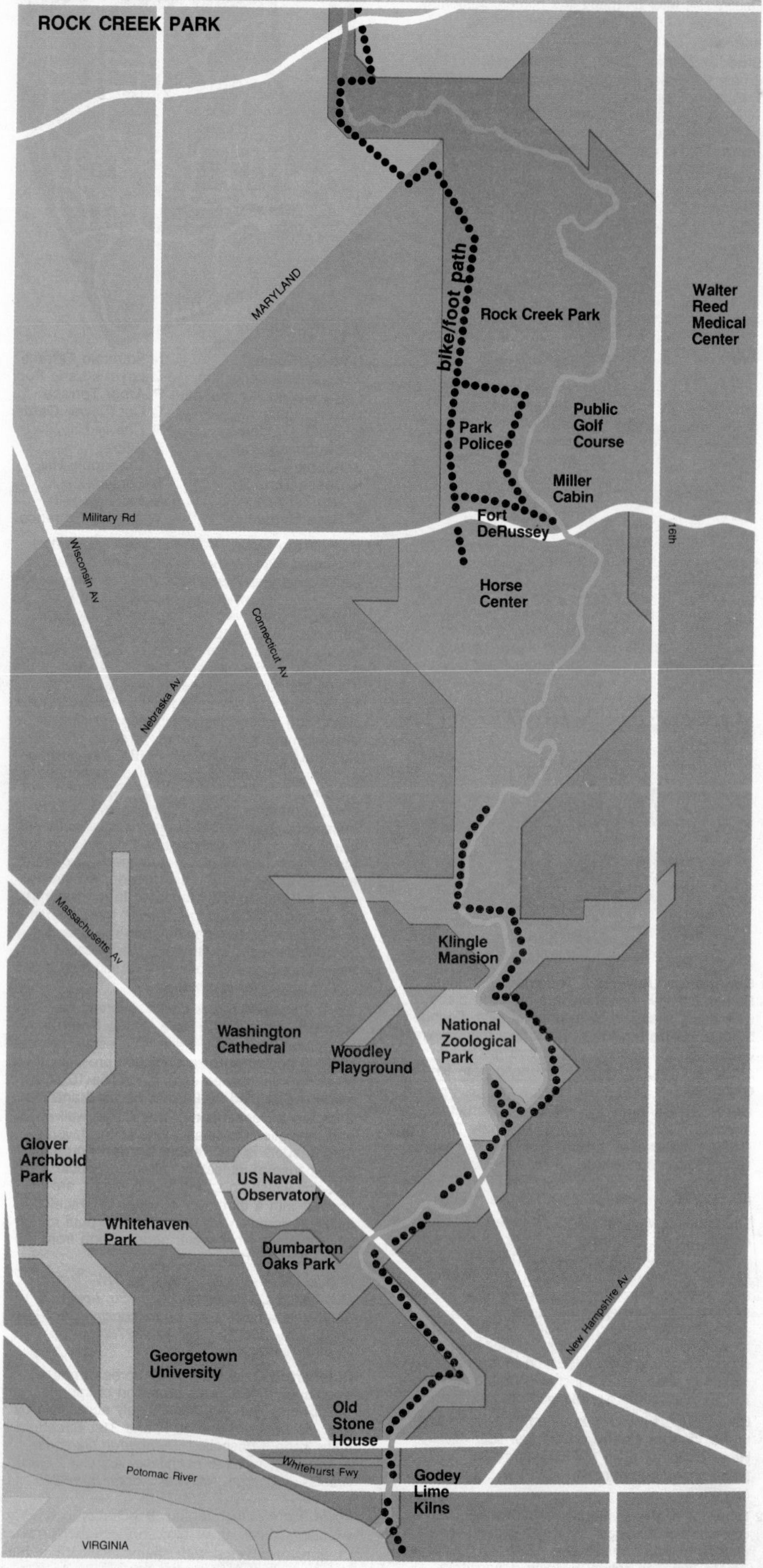

ROCK CREEK PARK

MARYLAND

Rock Creek Park

Walter Reed Medical Center

bike/foot path

Park Police

Public Golf Course

Miller Cabin

Fort DeRussey

Military Rd

Horse Center

Wisconsin Av

Connecticut Av

Nebraska Av

16th

Klingle Mansion

Massachusetts Av

Washington Cathedral

Woodley Playground

National Zoological Park

Glover Archbold Park

US Naval Observatory

Whitehaven Park

Dumbarton Oaks Park

New Hampshire Av

Georgetown University

Old Stone House

Godey Lime Kilns

Potomac River

Whitehurst Fwy

VIRGINIA

Montrose Park. Small, quiet woodland park with tennis courts, playground, picnicking, walking trails. **Lovers Lane,** a cobblestoned walking path, forms the western border, separating Montrose and Dumbarton Oaks parks. *R St. at 31st St. NW. 426-6834.*

Oak Hill Cemetery. Given to the city by **William Wilson Corcoran,** such notables as **John Howard Paine** (author of *Home, Sweet Home*), statesmen **Edwin M. Stanton, James G. Blaine** and **Dean Acheson,** and socialite **Peggy O'Neil** are buried here. The **Gatehouse** (1839, de la Roche) and small, simple Gothic Revival chapel (1850, **James Renwick**) are architecturally noteworthy. *North end of 28th & 29th Sts. NW.*

Rock Creek Park. In 1890, **President Benjamin Harrison** signed Congress' million dollar endowment of Rock Creek Park, mandating the preservation of this rugged 1,700-acre stretch, once home of the Algonquin Indians. Over the centuries it has nurtured bear, elk and even bison; early settlers tapped the creek's swift waters to power their grist mills and saw mills; later the woodlands allowed a moment of escape for such harried leaders as **John Quincy Adams** and **Teddy Roosevelt.** The park still stubbornly maintains its sense of ruggedness as it winds for 4 miles along Rock Creek. Wildlife and wildflowers are abundant here; you can still see the occasional deer and perhaps even a fox. Birders haunt the place, their field glasses searching for thrush, chickadees and ducks. **Fort DeRussy,** one of the capital's chain of defenses against the Confederate Army, is still in evidence. If all this seems too idyllic, it is. Rock Creek's waters are sour with pollution and many of the fish have died. Fishing, swimming and wading are prohibited. The park has many lovely picnic spots with tables and shelters, but reservations must be made Mar-Oct; call *673-7646.*

Rock Creek Park's bike/jogging path begins in West Potomac Park just below the **Kennedy Center** and winds along the creek and beside park roads. Sites near the route include the **Watergate** and the **National Zoo,** where the hilly terrain is an especially pleasant challenge for running enthusiasts. The path ends just north of the **Old Pierce Mill** at the city's outskirts, a 9-mile trek from the West Mall. *Park information, 426-6834.*

Rock Creek Nature Center is the place to orient yourself to the park. This National Park Service is especially great for kids, who can view wild animal exhibits or watch the workings of a beehive behind glass. There are nature films, planetarium shows and guided hikes. **Rock Creek Horse Center,** nearby, has trail ponies for exploring the park the way early adventurers did. *Open Tu-F 9:30am-5pm, Sa & Su noon-6pm; Dec-Apr Sa & Su noon-5pm. Special programs Sa & Su 2pm. Guided hikes Sa & Su 3pm. 5200 Glover Rd. south of Military Rd. at Oregon Ave. NW. 426-6829.*

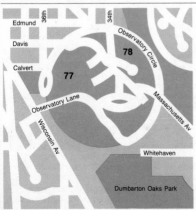

Naval Observatory. The observatory hopes to limit visitors to advanced students of celestial mechanics. If you fit into that category, you have 2 opportunities to see the big 'scope: at the building, exhibits and telescopes tour *(M-F 2pm),* or during the monthly full moon viewing.

Reservations are required well in advance for both. The 111-year-old, 26-inch refractor was used in the 1877 discovery of the Martian moons; the complex's main hall is named for **Dr. Asaph Hall,** who made that discovery. Originally the *Depot of Charts and Instruments,* this service was located in Foggy Bottom and was charged with keeping navigational charts; its first astronomical involvement was for the testing of ship chronometers. The circle which encloses the present site was not part of L'Enfant's plan, but was created to protect the station's delicate instruments from the rumblings of encroaching city traffic. The **Master Clock of the United States,** the world's most accurate timepiece, is kept here. *34th St. at Massachusetts Ave. NW. 254-4569.*

78 Vice President's House. In the early 1970s, Congress decided that too much money was being spent on security measures for the homes of US vice presidents. Over the protests of the Navy, in 1975 it co-opted this house, which for decades had been home to naval admirals. Despite the fact that it is located on a navy post, which makes it easy to defend, the large, sunny Victorian home with acres of lawn doesn't seem like a fortress at all. Not open to the public. *Observatory grounds.*

79 Sushi-Ko. ☆ ☆ $$$ DC's first sushi bar is still one of its best. Expert chefs prepare a vast range of raw and cooked fish and seafood, as well as tempura and a few broiled dishes. *Japanese/sushi bar. Open Tu-F noon-2:30pm, 6-10:30pm; Sa 5-10:30pm; Su 5-9pm. Reservations accepted. 2309 Wisconsin Ave. NW (Calvert St. NW). 333-4187.*

80 Germaine's. ☆ ☆ ☆ $$$ A pristine, modern dining room featuring pan-Asian cuisine including Vietnamese, Thai, Korean, Chinese and Indonesian. Order from a wide offering of appetizers: sates (skewered meats with peanut sauce), scallop salad, dumplings, Korean beef. Superb seafood dishes. Charming Germaine will no doubt visit you during your meal and make sure all is well. *Pan-Asian. Open M-F noon-2:30pm, Su-Th 6-10pm, F & Sa 6-11pm. Reservations suggested. Coat and tie recommended. 2400 Wisconsin Ave. NW (Calvert St. NW). 965-1185.*

81 The Wellington Hotel. *Inexpensive.* Considered the best buy in ultra-fashionable upper Georgetown, the Wellington caters to British Embassy clientele. Rooms are modern but have traditional European touches for unexpected state-side elegance. Restaurant on premises, but you can also book a room with a kitchenette. *Valet service. 2505 Wisconsin Ave. NW. 337-7400/800-368-5696.*

82 La Fleur. ☆ ☆ $$ Both the food and atmosphere are soft, cool and colorful in DC's most pleasing outdoor eatery. Soft cushions, a tent-top and bubbling fountain serves the setting for good dining on summer salads, seafood dishes and other light fare. *American. Open daily noon-3pm, 6-11pm; Sa & Su champagne brunch. 3700 Massachusetts Ave. NW. 342-0224.*

83 Santa Sophia Greek Orthodox Church. (1956, **Archie Protopappas**) The largest Greek Orthodox congregation in the country meets in this magnificent Byzantine-inspired building. The mosaic work is unparalleled and definitely worth seeing. *Visits by appointment. Services Su 10am. Massachusetts Ave. at 36th St. NW. 333-4730.*

Teddy Roosevelt's favorite pastimes in Washington were strenuous walks, *"perhaps down Rock Creek, which was then as wild as a stream in the White Mountains."*

Introductions/Theaters/Narrative black
Hotels purple
Museums/Architecture blue
Parks/Open spaces green
Restaurants/Nightlife red
Shops/Galleries violet

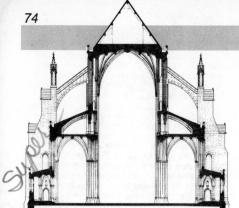

Courtesy Washington Cathedral

84 Washington National Cathedral. (Begun 1907, **Vaughn & Bodley**) High on Mount Saint Alban Hill, the limestone towers of this Gothic cathedral rise above the treetops of the city of Washington. For most of this century it has been growing slowly in size and splendor. It's hoped that the current phase of construction will be completed by the end of the decade.

The work began nearly 100 years ago when, in 1893, the Protestant Episcopal Cathedral Foundation was created by an act of Congress, and **Henry Yates Statterlee,** first Bishop of Washington, began securing the land and raising funds—a duty that would last a lifetime. Two architects were hired, **Dr. George Bodley** of Britain, and **Henry Vaughn,** an American. Though they had to exchange drawings across the Atlantic, the design—for what would become the sixth largest cathedral in the world—was completed in only 13 months. No less important was the hiring of the **George A. Fuller Company** as chief contractors, which they remained until 1980. Over the years the company maintained a staff of technicians able to build with limestone in the Gothic style of the 14th century.

In 1907 **Teddy Roosevelt** officiated at ground breaking ceremonies for the Cathedral. For the occasion he used the same silver trowel **George Washington** used when laying the cornerstone of the US Capitol.

Architect **Philip Frohman,** took over the project in 1919, refining the design and supervising every facet of construction. During 40 years of service he never tired of the project. He could be seen climbing the scaffolding into his 70s.

If America were to have an official national cathedral, this would certainly be the one. No federal money was used in its creation, but citizens from every part of the country have contributed funds. Over the years it has been the site for the burial services of presidents **Wilson** and **Eisenhower** and generals **MacArthur** and **Bradley.** Services for US servicemen killed in Vietnam were held here, as were prayer meetings for the Iranian hostages, and a memorial service for **Anwar Sadat.**

Though the Cathedral is the seat of the Washington Episcopal diocese, it has maintained the ecumenical stance of its founders. It has no standing congregation, but opens its doors to worshipers of all denominations.

The church is built in the shape of a cross, with twin towers in the (still under construction) west and a **Gloria in Excelsis Tower** in the center. Ninety-six angels, each with a different face, are carved in a frieze around the tower, which holds a 10-bell peal and a 53-bell carillon.

As you tour the Cathedral, remember that in Gothic architecture structure and symbol merge into one. The design must communicate as much as the hymnals, but often without words, so look closely for the narratives and references in the intricate carvings and luminous windows.

Enter the Cathedral at the **North or South Transept,** or through the doors at the west end. Entering from the west you will find yourself in the **Narthex** (an enclosed porch). Laid into the mosaic floor are seals of the 50 states.

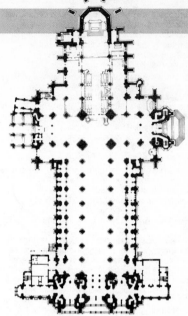

In the **Nave** above the **Warren Bay** is the **Space Window.** It commemorates the scientists and astronauts of **Apollo XI.** An actual piece of moon rock retrieved on that mission is embedded in the glass! Further down is **Wilson Bay** containing the tomb of the only president buried in the District of Columbia. Carvings symbolize aspects of **Woodrow Wilson's** life. A crusader's sword on the sarcophagus symbolizes his quest for peace through the League of Nations. Look for a thistle (Scottish heritage) and the seal of Princeton University (Wilson was once its president).

A few steps toward the center of the Cathedral should place you in the **Crossing,** a truly magnificent space where the transepts bisect the nave. Four massive stone piers soar 98 feet up to meet the vaulted ceiling. The pulpit is made of stones from **Canterbury Cathedral** and it was here that **Martin Luther King, Jr.,** delivered his last sermon before his assassination in Memphis, Tennessee.

The charming **Children's Chapel** shouldn't be missed. Everything is scaled down and designed to delight the child. The windows tell the stories of **Samuel** and **David** as boys, and the kneelers are embroidered with all manner of animals—pets as well as wild beasts. The ceiling—the only fan vaulting in the Cathedral—is as delicate as a christening gown's lace.

The altar panel in the **Holy Spirit Chapel** was painted on wood by **N.C. Wyeth,** father of **Andrew Wyeth.** Golden-haloed angels sing the praises of God on a piercing field of blue.

If you've been walking along the aisles, now might be a good time to step more toward the center and admire the nave. Part of the genius of Gothic architecture was the flying buttress, which by transferring the weight of the roof off the walls and outside the building, allowed the walls to be opened up with stained glass windows. As you walk down the nave, scores of windows on either side depict biblical themes as well as great artists who have glorified God in their works, such as **Dante, Milton, Bach** and **Sir Christopher Wren.** Turn toward the western end of the Cathedral for the dazzling **West Rose Window** designed by **Rowan LeCompte.** It is a fiery wheel (25 feet, 11 inches in diameter) that burns with kaleidoscope color, particularly as it catches the last rays of a setting sun.

On the lower floor, or **Crypt,** you will find 4 more chapels, burial vaults, a **gift shop/book store** (with excellent Cathedral guides) a **visitors' center** and a **brass rubbing center.**

Fifty out of every 1,000 Washingtonians are lawyers—the highest per capita ratio in the nation.

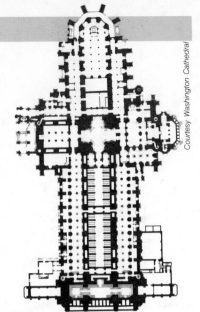

Courtesy Washington Cathedral

Before leaving the Cathedral, you might want to go up to the **Pilgrim's Observation Gallery**, which can be reached by an elevator in the west end of the main level. Located in the twin towers, the 70 windows of the gallery provide a panoramic view of Washington, Maryland and Virginia, as well as a bird's eye view of some of the Cathedral's exterior carvings.

The Cathedral's **Close** (grounds) is a 57-acre plot that includes 5 schools, a preachers' college, and some delightful gardens. A stroll here can be a restful way to end the afternoon.

Leave the Cathedral from the **South Transept** or **West Doors** and go to the **Herb Cottage**, where sachets, herbs, honey and gourmet herb vinegars are for sale. Outside, a small herb garden is redolent with the scent of rosemary and mint.

Continue south to the **Bishop's Garden:** Pass through a Norman arch and enter one of the city's loveliest garden spaces. Actually a series of several gardens, it includes a rose garden, a medieval herb garden, boxwood, magnolia, and the **Shadow House**, a small stone medieval summer cottage that's cool in the summer and dry in the rain—a perfect spot to relax.

A bit further down the hill is the statue of Lieutenant General **George Washington**, a heavily gilded bronze of young Washington astride a graceful well-muscled horse— according to rumor, the spitting image of the famous racehorse **Man O' War.** In the style of the ancient Egyptians, the horse's eyes are made of glass (1959, **Herbert Hazeltine**).

You might also take a walk on the **Woodland Path**, maintained by local garden clubs. It starts at a Japanese footbridge and makes its way up a wooded hill planted with wildflowers.

The **Cathedral Greenhouse** southeast of the church raises rare herbs. A catalog of those on sale is available on request.

Bounded by Massachusetts Ave., Wisconsin Ave., Woodley Rd., and 34th St. NW. Served by most of the Massachusetts and Wisconsin Ave. buses. Tours are free and take about 40 minutes. They leave continuously from the west entrance between 10am and 3:15pm. Or you can take your own tour until 4:30pm. Services are held M-F at 7:30am, noon and 4pm. Sunday services are held at 8, 9, 10, 11am and 4pm. Pilgrim Observation Gallery is open M-Sa 10:15am-4pm and Su 12:30-3:15pm. Dec-Feb the Gallery is only open weekends.

The carillon is played every Saturday afternoon at 4:30pm, and organ recitals follow afternoon prayers on Sunday. For more information on the many performances and concerts at the Cathedral *call 537-6200.*

85 **Woodley House/Maret School.** (1800, **Philip Barton Key**) The bold massing of this Georgian house is echoed in the inviting Ionic portico, but obscured by the new classroom building out front. Four 19th-century presidents used this as a summer home. *Private grounds. 3000 Cathedral Ave. NW.*

The SHOREHAM

86 **Shoreham Hotel.** (1929, **Harry Bralove**) *Expensive.* There is not a more luxurious hotel overlooking the beautiful woods of Washington's Rock Creek Park. The historic and elegant Shoreham has hosted many presidential inaugurations. **President Truman** held his private poker games in room D-406. The hotel's ambiance has attracted such luminaries as **Clark Gable, Rudy Valle, Marilyn Monroe** and **Gary Cooper.** The **New Leaf** restaurant serves Continental and American cuisine. The **Marquee Lounge** offers big band sounds in an Art Deco setting. Try the elegant Sunday brunch featuring champagne and piano music in the **Garden Court.** One block from the Metro Station, with easy connections to all points of interest in Washington. *2500 Calvert St. NW. 234-0700/Telex: 710-822-0142.*

87 **Moghul Mahal.** ☆☆ $$ Juicy, grilled lamb and chicken and other refined Indian dishes in a dramatic setting. Indian. *Open M-F 11am-10:30pm, Sa & Su 5:30-10:30pm. Reservations accepted. 2623 Connecticut Ave. NW (Calvert St. NW). 483-1115.*

88 **The Baron Gourmet Delly.** ☆ $ Very crowded and noisy, this is one of DC's few delis that actually serves up a decent corned beef sandwich and bowl of matzo ball soup. *Deli. Open daily 7am-9pm. No reservations. 2643 Connecticut Ave. NW (Calvert St. NW). 332-3555.*

89 **Sheraton Washington Hotel.** *Moderate/ expensive.* Almost a city in itself, this power-center hotel's 1,505 rooms are usually filled with in-town businessmen taking advantage of the exhibit, meeting, banquet and ball rooms. Escapes from the work-a-day world include game room, huge swimming pool (open May to September), beauty and barber shops and lounges. Culinary delights in 4 restaurants range from the pies, cookies and European pastries at **Wolfgang's Pastry Shop,** to American-style fine dining at **Americus.** Gift shop/news stand, concierge service, post office and copy center. *2660 Woodley Rd. NW. 328-2000/Telex: 892630.*

90 **The National Zoological Park**, also called the *Washington Zoo*, sprawls over 176 acres, allowing plenty of room for its 2,900 animals.

Established in 1890 under the direction of the **Smithsonian Institution**, the zoo moved its early pens from the Washington Mall to Rock Creek when **Samuel Pierpont Langley,** the Smithsonian's third secretary, persuaded Congress to provide the new zoo site to protect the American Bison from extinction.

When you enter the zoo, follow a broad *red stripe* along the main trail, called **Olmsted Walk.** You'll be guided by large totem poles which mark 6 animal area trails: the *orange* **Lion Trail,** *brown* **Elephant Trail,** *black* **Zebra Trail,** *green* **Crowned Crane Trail,** *blue* **Polar Bear Trail** and the *yellow* **Raccoon Trail.** Along Lion Trail you'll find the **William M. Mann Lion-Tiger Exhibit,** named for the zoo's director from 1925 to 1958. A circular walkway overlooks 3 large outdoor yards for a close-up view of the great cats. The area features full-maned Atlas lions, rare blue-eyed white tigers, plus leopards and cheetahs. All the zoo's tigers are descendants of **Mohini,** a white tiger brought from India in 1960.

Courtesy National Zoological Park and Lance Wyman/Bill Cannan.

Connecticut Av Entrance

Harvard St Entrance

At least 30 species call the **Monkey House** home, including the small black gibbons with their white fluffy cheeks, the Madagascar lemurs and the lion-tailed macaques from India.

In the **Reptile House**, a compound heating system warms some of the collection's 2,500 species of amphibians and 7,000 species of reptiles, from the tiniest of snakes to the venomous king cobras, giant pythons and anacondas.

Designed in 1931 by **Albert Harris**, the building is an Italian-Romanesque styled structure. Its stone corbels are carved with intricate reptilian heads and its columns rest on carved stone turtles.

Outside the Reptile House, 500-pound Aldabra tortoises wander in the summer months. Crocodiles bathe in crocodile pools—indoors in winter, outdoors in summer. Also watch for the tortoises of Gala, giant Komodo dragon lizards and alligators.

The **Great Ape House** gives you and the apes a perfect look at one another. Four-hundred pound lowland gorillas watch you from indoors and out. The building, especially designed for apes, features sculptured steel-frame trees.

All of the zoo's orangutans were born here in captivity. Their housing is carefully constructed, as orangutans like to unbolt and take things apart.

The **Small Mammal House's** exotic creatures include meercats, who live in rock crevices; golden lion tamarins, small blond monkey-like creatures; the fox-like fennec; and tiny elephant shrews. Take a look at hardier animals exhibited outdoors behind the **Mammal House.**

The **Elephant House** guides you to elephants, hippos, rhinoceroses and giraffe. Favorites include the versatile-trunked Asiatic elephant and the African elephant with its large ears.

In 1972, the People's Republic of China donated 2 giant black-and-white pandas, **Ling-Ling** *(Cute Little Girl)* and **Hsing-Hsing** *(Bright Star)* to the National Zoo. A moon gate—a round open-work enclosure, separates their yards, but still allows them to sit next to and see each other. Up in

the trees along Zebra Trail, lesser pandas spy on unsuspecting viewers. The small, impish animals have chestnut and white markings.

Along Zebra Trail roam kangaroos, antelopes, zebra and deer. The **Bird House** on **Crowned Crane Trail** has 190 species in its **Indoor Flight Room** and **Great Flight Exhibit,** from huge Andrean condors to the smallest humming birds. Penguins slosh around in a room specially refrigerated to simulate home.

Polar Bear Trail takes you by river otters, gray seals and the giant polar bears. **Raccoon Trail** divides bears from other American animals. Housed here is the second **Smokey Bear,** the model for firefighters' Smokey The Bear. His legend began in 1950, when a small, badly-burned black bear cub was rescued and brought to the zoo.

Zoo centers treat visitors to Zoology lessons at **Zoolab** in the Education Building and **Birdlab** in the Bird House. The zoo offers daily free films, slide shows and wildlife films in the Education Building auditorium.

The zoo also runs a 3,100-acre preserve near Front Royal, Virginia, for the study of endangered species.

Open daily, except Christmas, 8am-8pm. Buildings open 10am-6pm summer, 10am-4:30pm winter. Gifts are available at the Panda Gift Shop, the Mane Gift Shop and the Seal Shop. Accessible by wheelchair. 3000 Connecticut Ave. NW. Call 673-4800 for zoo information.

91 Pierce Mill. (1810) This old mill is still grinding wheat and corn, powered by the waters of Rock Creek, just like it did in the 1820s. You can even purchase the old-fashioned meal—for biscuits just like Grandma used to make, literally! It's a treat to watch the hypnotic roll of the machinery of this WPA-restored landmark. *Admission free. Open W-Su 9am-5pm. Tilden St. At Beach Dr. Rock Creek Park. 426-6908.*

92 Hillwood. There are at least 4 good reasons to visit the estate of the late **Marjorie Merriweather Post**, cereal heiress and longtime cornerstone of DC—and American—social standards. The house, a 40-room Georgian mansion of red brick, dates from the 1920s, when it was a showpiece of Gatsbyan formality. The house was purchased by Post in 1955, and under her direction Hillwood surpassed its earlier opulence; the heiress' staff included a chef, butler, footman and resident curator. The latter is a clue to the estate's second raison d'etre; it is every bit a museum, displaying an excellent, eccentric collection of French and Imperial Russian art. Included are gilded icons and religious

"Fellow Citizens! God reigns, and the Government at Washington still lives!"

James A. Garfield, *speech on assassination of Lincoln, April 1865.*

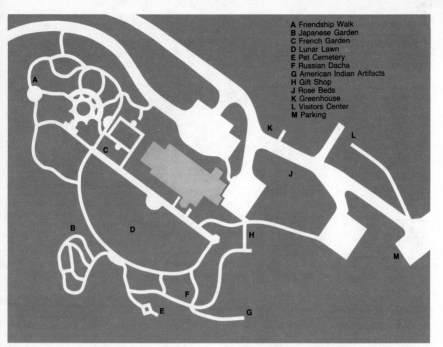

vestments, fine portraiture and folkart, Fabergé eggs, gold and silver craftsmanship, and fine porcelain, including the royal service of **Catherine the Great** (Marjorie Merriweather Post had traveled with one of her husbands, the first Ambassador to Russia, following the Revolution). Fine French furniture and tapestries fill the house.

Outside, on the 25-acre estate, are formal Japanese and French gardens, a one-room Russian summer house, and a **Rose Garden. Perry Wheeler** created the gardens—it was he who designed that more famous Rose Garden at the White House—which exhibit over 3,500 varieties of flora. Within the greenhouse alone are over 5,000 kinds of orchids. Finally, to the southeast, over the treetops of Rock Creek Park, is a stunning view of the Washington Monument. *Admission charge. Tour lasts 2 hours (no children under 12) and reservations must be made several weeks in advance; tours M, W-Sa 9am, 10:30am, noon, 1:30pm. 4155 Linnean Ave. NW. 686-5807.*

Rosedale. (1793) A genteel and breezy clapboard house, built as a country home before the city grew out to surround it. *Private residence. 3501 Newark St. NW.*

Winthrop Faulkner Houses. (1964, Winthrop Faulkner) Three mid-20th-century houses that fit into their surroundings by using the vernacular of their older neighbors very effectively. *Private residence. 3500 block of Ordway St. NW.*

Friends' School Administration Building (The Highlands). Built as a country home before this stone Georgian house features unorthodox but handsome square columns that were not part of the original design. *Private grounds. 3825 Wisconsin Ave. NW.*

American University. One of the area's leading educational and cultural forces, Methodist-affiliated AU was incorporated in 1893 by an Act of Congress. **Hurst Hall,** the oldest building on the school's 77-acre campus, dates to 1896. The public is welcome at many of the university's activities, including movies at the **Wechsler Theater** (483-5825), lectures at **Gaston Hall** (532-5972), and concerts in the **New Lecture Hall** (483-5825), where the **Opera Theater of Washington** makes its home. *Guided campus tours, 686-2000 by appointment. Massachusetts and Nebraska Aves. NW. 686-2288.*

Getting into the fitness craze, giant pandas **Ling-Ling** and **Hsing-Hsing** will have a special gym and *panda furniture* built for them at the National Zoo.

97 Hull Gallery. This gallery shows American art exclusively, and is well-known for its rediscovered prints, watercolors, and drawings by talented but relatively unknown late 19th- and early 20th-century artists such as **Martin Lewis.** *Open M-Sa 9:30am-5pm, closed Su. 3301 New Mexico Ave. NW (Foxhall Square), 2 blocks south of Nebraska. 362-0507.*

97 Sutton Place Gourmet is a comprehensive, one-stop gourmet food store that has prime meats (the aged filets are unmatched), freshly baked pastries and breads, produce from around the world, cheeses, wines, fresh seafood and prepared entrees ready to take home and serve. *Open M-Sa 10am-8pm, Su 10am-6pm. 3201 New Mexico Ave. NW (Foxhall Square). 363-5800.*

97 Jackie Chalkey Fine Crafts has a dual personality—part fine handcraft shop, part high-fashion store—carrying signed porcelains, earthenware, metal collage jewelry and exquisite knitwear, all priced as art. Sweaters can sell for over a thousand dollars! *Open M-Sa 10am-6pm. 3301 New Mexico Ave. NW (Foxhall Square). 686-8884.*

98 Battery-Kimble Park. Lots of nature and history fill this compact little greenspace, a garden of blooming flowers in spring and fiery leaves in autumn. A walking and cycling path winds through the park. A small cannon battery, part of the capital's chain of Civil War defenses, is preserved by the National Park Service. *Nebraska Ave. at Foxhall Rd. 767-7011.*

99 Hilda's. ☆ ☆ $$$ A true Renaissance woman, Hilda designed her gallery-like restaurant, built the mosaic and wood tables, painted the exotic canvases on the walls, and now oversees both the kitchen and the dining room. Choose carefully from the high-priced menu of light fare (quiches, sandwiches, fish salads, pates) and international entrees. Outstanding homemade pastries. Live jazz. The covered outdoor patio is perfect for a rendezvous—even on a rainy day. *Continental. Open M-F 11am-10:30pm, Sa 6-10:30pm. Reservations required on weekends. 5125 MacArthur Blvd. NW (Arizona Ave. NW). 244-9191.*

100 Glover-Archbold Parkway. When you tire of the bustle and cold monumental marble of the capital, this is the most perfect escape: a deliciously unkempt 100 acres where you'll be just another member of the wildlife that finds sanctuary here. Paths wind through the park, crossing Foundry Branch creek. A good place for birdwatching and picnicking. *Wisconsin Ave. west to Reservoir Rd. 426-6834.*

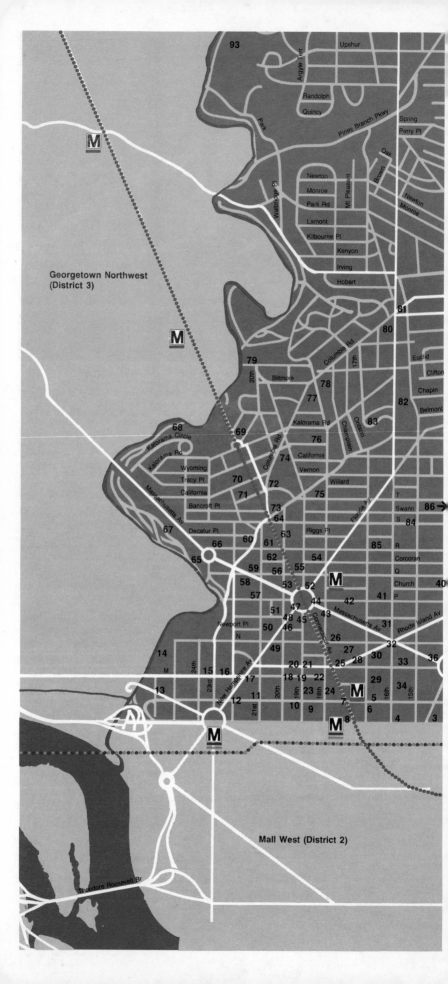

Mall East (District 1)

M Indicates Metrorail Stops

Washington is the *international city and the center of its diplomatic life is* Embassy Row *along* Massachusetts Avenue, NW.

Here the street is lined for block after block with embassies from nations large and small, friendly and otherwise. A different flag hangs in front of almost every building.

Many of the embassies have taken the homes of 19th-century Washington financiers who had come here because society was—and remains—relatively fluid; new arrivals in the transient city were not viewed with the arms-length suspicion they might have encountered elsewhere. To participate adequately in Washington's social season—the city was then known as a winter Newport—the nation's industrial millionaires built their mansions in the fashionable area along Massachusetts Avenue.

Embassy Row passes through **Dupont Circle**, which is the center of non-Federal Washington. In its early days it was also surrounded by mansions and a number of them still survive, including the **Cissy Patterson House**, the **Blaine House**, and the **Christian Heurich House**, home of Washington's great brewer and today headquarters of the **Columbia Historical Society.**

Today the Dupont Circle area has become a kind of Greenwich Village and includes young couples who arrived with gentrification, holdovers from the counter-culturalists who flocked to the area in the '60s and '70s, and a significant gay community. Its streets, mostly lined with late 19th-century homes, are often crowded with pedestrians and the area's office workers. Among its many unusual stores and shops along Connecticut Avenue is **Kramerbooks and Afterwords,** a combination bookstore-cafe and a Washington innovation that's spreading through the country.

The artery that cuts directly through Washington's north-central area is 16th Street, unusual because there is virtually no commercial activity along its great length. The street is home to an amazing variety of churches, from mainstream denominations to more exotic groups and cults. A few blocks away, 18th Street near Columbia Road has only recently blossomed with smart cafes, and a bouquet of antique and junque shops. The street has become a mini-attraction of its own.

Much of the street's character is the doing of the remarkable **Mrs. John Henderson,** who built herself a now-gone castle along it, directed the development of **Meridian Hill Park,** and had a number of impressive buildings put up in order to attract embassies. Many of these are still standing, including the **Pink Palace** that serves as headquarters of the **Inter-American Defense Board,** and the embassies of **Poland** and **Spain.** In 1912, Mrs. Henderson even had the street renamed **Avenue of the Presidents**—but the appellation lasted only a year. Today the area has fallen on hard times and visitors are advised to be cautious, especially of secluded areas such as the once-lovely parks.

Just off 16th Street are a pair of neighborhoods where the city's black upper-class has gathered: the **Gold Coast** and the newer **Platinum Coast.** Years ago, the city's black professionals lived in **Le Droit Park,** near **Howard University,** and that area has retained much of its architectural distinction.

Rock Creek Park borders this district, winding all the way from the Potomac River into Maryland. Washingtonians jog, bicycle, and drive through it in large numbers every day, picnic there on weekends, and yet leave it serene. Among its attractions are old **Pierce Mill,** and the nearby **Art Barn.** An old log cabin that once belonged to hermit-poet **Joaquin Miller** is there as well. But the relief in the landscape that the rocky stream and profusion of trees offers is, for most residents, attraction enough.

1   **Marrakesh.** ☆ ☆ $$$ Lovingly prepared and presented Moroccan cuisine in a dining room straight out of the Arabian Nights. There is no menu; the diner makes few choices, waiting for the meal to appear course by course: cold vegetable platters, followed by *b'stilla* (a sweet chicken pie), poultry and lamb, couscous, fruits and nuts, pastries and beverages. A meal fit for a sultan. *Moroccan. Open daily 6-11pm. Reservations required. 617 New York Ave. NW (6th St. NW).* 393-9393.

2   **The Henley Park.** *Moderate/expensive.* Fashioned after England's fine hostelries, this elegant refurbished apartment building seems truly royal. Convenient midtown business district location is near the Convention Center. Catch a refreshing afternoon tea *(4-6pm)* in the **Wilkes Room** off the hotel's parlor. *926 Massachusetts Ave. NW.* 638-5200/800-368-5877.

3   **Sholl's.** ☆ ☆ ☆ $ Either of Sholl's K Street cafeterias offers quality and freshness at bargain prices. Tourists, locals and business types load their trays with homemade biscuits, grits, roast turkey and dressings, ham, roast beef, seasonal fruits and salads, and fruit pies. No better value in the city. *American. Open M-Sa 7am-8pm. Closed Su. No reservations. No credit cards. 1433 K St. NW.* 783-4133. *(Also at 1990 K St. NW.* 296-3065.)

4   **The Capital Hilton.** *Moderate/expensive.* If you like a lot of high-powered excitement, this is the place to stay. Located near Washington's bustling business district, the Capital Hilton has been extensively refurbished since it was called the **Statler Hilton.** It now has several fine restaurants, plus gift, flower and candy shops in the lobby. Guest rooms and suites have contemporary decor. Ask for a corner room for more windows and a doubly nice view. *16th and K Sts. NW.* 393-1000/Telex: 710-822-9068.

Within the hotel is:

Twigs. ☆ $$ All wicker and sunlight, this is a serene place for Sunday brunch or a special luncheon. *American. Open daily 7am-10:30pm. Reservations recommended.* 393-1000 (ext. 1621).

5   **Hubbard Memorial Library.** (1902, **Hornblower & Marshall**) A simple, massive Italianate library building with enormous Romanesque windows lighting the second story. *1146 16th St. NW.*

6   **International Union of Operating Engineers.** (1957, **Holabird, Root & Burgee**) Still the most handsome International-style office building in Washington, the IUOE headquarters took its inspiration from New York's landmark **Lever House.** Aqua glass, stainless steel and a variety of white, black and green marbles form the building's elegant surfaces. *1125 17th St. NW.*

Connecticut
Connection

7   **Connecticut Connection,** located at the **Farragut North Metro station,** was among the first of a new breed of lunch crowd malls built around downtown Metrorail stops. With a couple of dozen shops and restaurants in 2 underground levels that are reminiscent of Montreal's subway shopping, it serves Washington's *central business district* with specialty shopping. Stores include **Crabtree and Evelyn** *(659-0099),* an international soap-toiletries-herbs-spice shop; **Arthur Adler** *(628-0131)* for conservative, classic tailoring for men; and **Theodore Nye Jewelers** *(223-2012)* for custom designs and the area's largest rep of the Rolex Oyster watch. *Open M-Sa 10am-6pm. 1101 Connecticut Ave. NW.* 783-1101.

The Mayflower Hotel. (1924, **Warren & Wetmore**) *Expensive/deluxe.* One of the most luxurious and historic hotels in DC, the yellow brick and limestone Beaux-Arts building houses a 475-foot-long lobby accented with Italian marble, brilliant chandeliers and ornate ceilings. Ask for a renovated room with furnishings by **Henredon.** The ornate Grand Ballroom is one of the last in the world; its Wedgwood-like bas-reliefs, terraces and balconies are topped by a 21-foot ceiling. This centrally located, 721-room hotel has been serving Washington's most glittering clientele with elegance and style for the last half century. *1127 Connecticut Ave. NW. 347-3000/Telex: 89-2324.*

Duke Zeibert's. ☆ ☆ $$$ Seems like yesterday that Duke Zeibert, legendary DC restaurateur, retired from his New York-style eatery—but now he's back and eager to please. This is a new, spritzed-up location; the deli staples—calf's liver, brisket, chicken- and beef-in-the-pot—are as good as ever. There are also American-style offerings such as steaks, soft-shell crab, crab cakes, lobster and other seafood. Save room for one of the mammoth desserts. *American. Open M-Sa 11:30am-11:30pm, Su 5-10pm. Reservations suggested for dinner. 1050 Connecticut Ave. NW (L St. NW). 466-3730.*

Le Pavillon. ☆ ☆ ☆ ☆ $$$$ A singular dining experience. Owner-chef **Yannick Cam** and his wife, **Janet,** have created a restaurant of austere beauty and constant culinary surprise. The *nouvelle cuisine* menu changes daily; meals consist of many small, contrasting courses—fish, meat, vegetables, seafood, superb desserts—thrilling to both the eye and the palate. Be prepared to pay for such artistry. *French. Open M-F 11:45am-1:30pm, M-Sa 6:45-9:30pm. Closed Su. Reservations required. Coat and tie recommended. 1050 Connecticut Ave. NW (L St. NW). 833-3846.*

Mel Krupin's. ☆ ☆ ☆ $$$$ As much an arena as a restaurant, where journalists, sports figures, politicians and lawyers sup on huge portions of chopped liver, matzoh ball soup, crab cakes, herring, boiled beef and other plain but filling fare in the well-oiled comfort of this clubby, macho dining room. *American. Open M-F 11:30am-11pm, Sa noon-11pm. Dinner reservations accepted. 1120 Connecticut Ave. NW (L St. NW). 331-7000.*

Brooks Brothers. Setting the tone of the lower Connecticut Avenue area where there are more lawyers per square foot than anywhere else in America, this classic, traditional menswear store keeps a hefty stock of 3-piece blue pin-striped suits. *Open M-Sa 10am-6pm. 1840 L St. NW. 659-4650.*

10 T.H. Mandy is the best downtown discount stores for women's sportswear, carrying designs by **Sasson, Kasper, John Meyer** and others. Prices are cut by up to 50 percent, the selection is good, and the service is attentive and friendly. *Open M-Sa 10am-6pm, Th till 8pm. 1118 19th St. NW. 659-0024.*

10 Luigi's. ☆ ☆ $$ Candlelit, crowded and casual, this is one of the most reasonable and reliable Italian restaurants in DC. The pizza is crusty, the pasta available with a variety of sauces, the house wine good and cheap. *Italian. Open daily 11:30am-2am. Reservations accepted. 1132 19th St. NW (L St. NW). 331-7574.*

11 Richard's Pier 20. ☆ ☆ $$ Fresh seafood in a plush, inviting setting. Order the simpler dishes—raw oysters or oysters Rockefeller, grilled fish, seafood salad, crab cakes—and try the excellent salads and vegetables. *Seafood. Open M-F noon-2:30pm, 6-10:30pm; Sa 6-11pm. Closed Su. Reservations suggested. Coat and tie recommended. 1120 20th St. NW (L St. NW). 775-8821.*

12 Ramada Renaissance Hotel. *Moderate/expensive.* Located in the fashionable West End of Washington, this 350-room convention hotel is ideal for executive meetings with its 8 conference rooms and audio visual center. Rooms have a work desk—a detail underlining the Renaissance's attention to the business traveler. Ask about the **Renaissance Club** which includes complimentary breakfast, afternoon tea and cocktails, concierge service and free newspaper. Foreign currency exchange service, government and corporate rates are available. *1143 New Hampshire Ave. NW (at 22nd and M Sts.). 775-0800/Telex: 710-822-9202.*

13 One Step Down. Hot jazz sounds emanate from this dark and smoky little hangout. The line-up of local musicians attracts fans of all ages. Shows 10pm, 11:30pm and 1am on Fridays and Saturdays; all-day jam sessions on Sundays. During the week a jazz jukebox substitutes, playing everything from vintage Dixieland to fusion. Limited menu offers sandwiches, pizza, etc. *Cover charge. Open M-Th & Su 10am-2am, F & Sa 10am-3am. 2517 Pennsylvania Ave. NW. 331-8863.*

14 Rock Creek Park. Jogging and bike paths wind along this old mill stream. (See District 3, page 73 for more information.)

15 Bread and Chocolate Tearoom. ☆ ☆ $ Tearoom featuring quiches and other egg dishes, soups, flaky croissants and rich cakes and pastries. Take-out, too. *Cafe/bakery. Open M-Th 7:30am-6pm, F & Sa till 6:30pm; Su 8am-5pm. No reservations. 2301 M St. NW (entrance on 23rd St. NW). 833-8360.*

16 Blackie's House of Beef ($$) has been serving large portions of beef, potatoes and other hearty fare to families and out-of-town groups for decades. *American/steakhouse. Open M-Sa 11am-10:30pm; Su 4-10:30pm. Reservations suggested. 22nd and M Sts. NW. 333-1100.*

17 Crown Books. Best sellers and general interest books at a substantial discount. Excellent selection of coffee table books at big savings. Several DC-area branches. *Open M-Sa 9am-8pm, Su 11am-5pm. 1200 New Hampshire Ave. NW. 822-8331.*

Occasional press conferences at the White House take place in **The Roosevelt Room,** formerly named the *Fish Room.* An aquarium and mementoes from Roosevelt's fishing trips gave the room its somewhat playful name. His administration went even further by calling it *the morgue* because of the many people who sat in there waiting for the president. **John F. Kennedy** continued the fish theme by mounting a sailfish on the wall; the motif was ended by **Richard Nixon,** who refurnished and renamed the room after one of his greatest predecessors.

About 12 percent of the **US population live in the Potomac Basin area.**

Introductions/Theaters/Narrative black
Hotels purple
Museums/Architecture blue
Parks/Open spaces green
Restaurants/Nightlife red
Shops/Galleries violet

18 The Bread Oven. ☆☆ $ The original and best of these reasonable restaurant/bakeries is a spacious, basket-filled room featuring serve-yourself breakfasts of flaky croissants, brioches and coffees; the best French bread in town; and a rotating lunch and dinner menu of well-prepared terrines and pates, chicken dishes, bouillabaisse, duck, calf's liver and other bistro fare. *French. Open M-F 7:30am-10pm, Sa & Su 8am-10pm. Reservations required for 5 or more.* 1220 19th St. NW (N St. NW). 466-4264.

18 Sichuan Garden. ☆☆☆ $$$ Black lacquered furnishings, polished service and superb Chinese cuisine. Start with sweet-sour soup or dumplings, then order squid, scallops, shrimp, duck, or a host of other delicately prepared main courses. *Chinese. Open daily 11am-3pm, 5:30-11pm. Reservations suggested. Coat and tie recommended.* 1220 19th St. NW (Jefferson St. NW). 296-4550.

19 The Palm. ☆☆ $$$ Large portions of well-prepared hungry man fare—prime ribs, steak, potatoes, cheesecake—in a ferny setting. *American. Open M-F 11:45am-10:30pm, Sa 6-10:30pm. Closed Su. Reservations required. Coat and tie recommended.* 1225 19th St. NW (N St. NW). 293-9091.

19 Numbers. Washington's version of **Studio 54** or any other renowned glitter palace. The trendy clientele, the music and the flashing lights are almost generic; international young professional types gyrate on the dance floor to the tunes of prime Top 40 disco. Above them, a pair of 10-foot video screens projects the latest in music videos. Numbers' sound system is quite elaborate, and the customary speakers in every nook and cranny are guaranteed to drown any small talk.

Numbers packs in over 1,000 guests on the weekends. Weekday attractions include fashion shows from local boutiques, and *Ladies' Night* with free admission for women. *Cover charge. Open Tu-Su 9pm-3am.* 1330 19th St. NW. 463-8888.

20 Columbia Society/Heurich Mansion. (1880, **J. G. Myers**) Once a poor German immigrant, the wealthy 19th-century beer magnate **Christian Heurich** was one who spared no expense. His legacy to Washington, a 31-room turreted Romanesque Revival mansion, gives an accurate picture of life at the turn of the century. Many of the opulent interiors are intact, and the building houses Washington DC's local historical association, the **Columbia Historical Society.** The society maintains a wonderful collection of books, clippings, detailed journals, photos and artifacts focusing on the social mores of the city. *Admission free (donations welcome). Small daily charge for study of any materials. Open F & Sa 9:30am-4pm. Guided tours every 45 minutes, F & Sa noon-4pm.* 1307 New Hampshire Ave. NW. 785-2068.

21 Claire Dratch. An exceptional fashion salon for women, featuring such designers as **Perry Ellis**, **Albert Nipon** and **Anne Klein.** *Open M-Sa 10am-6pm, Th till 7pm.* 1224 Connecticut Ave. NW. 466-6500.

22 Cantina d'Italia. ☆☆☆☆ $$$$ Settle yourself in one of a series of crowded, stuccoed dining rooms, wait for the captain to interpret the confusing, constantly changing menu, and then begin a meal of unparalleled Northern Italian cuisine: first courses of fresh pasta with sauces of basil, cheese, snails, sausage, veal and spinach; wonderful seafood salad or a plate of tomatoes with mozzarella and basil; enormous main courses of risotto, sausages sauteed with grapes, rabbit, and duck with raisins, sausage and marsala; and superb espresso cheesecake. Pricy but elaborate wine list. *Italian. Open M-F noon-2:30pm, 6-10:30pm. Closed Sa & Su. Reservations required. Coat and tie recommended.* 1214-A 18th St. NW (N St. NW). 659-1830.

22 The Astor. ☆ $ Low-priced Greek food—tarama salad, squid, good soups, baked eggplant with onion and tomato sauce—or plain American fare for the less-adventurous palate. Belly dancing and more costly dishes in the second-floor rear dining room. *Greek. Open Su-Th 11am-1am, F & Sa 11am-2am. Reservations accepted.* 1813 M St. NW. 331-7994.

23 Gary's. ☆ $$$ With its mahogany chairs, curved banquettes and abundance of silk and velvet, Gary's is definitely one of DC's more elegant spots for a steak dinner. Order the straightforward fare—swordfish, tuna steak, lamb chops, lobster and the various cuts of beef—or take your chances with the exotic dishes. *American. Open M-F 11am-11:15pm, Sa 6-11:15pm. Closed Su. Reservations suggested. Coat and tie recommended.* 1800 M St. NW. 463-6470.

24 Le Lion d'Or. ☆☆☆☆ $$$ The oldest of this city's fine French restaurants, Le Lion is known for its simple but masterful preparation of specialties like duck sausage with port, poached scallops, roast pigeon with garlic cloves, crab in *remoulade*, squab with wild mushrooms and other delicacies. Service is impeccable, the dining room plush, and this is a place to be seen as well as served. *French. Open M-F noon-2pm, 6-10pm; Sa 6-10pm. Closed Su. Reservations required. Coat and tie required.* 1150 Connecticut Ave. NW (entrance at 18th and M St. NW). 296-7972.

25 Joe & Mo's. ☆☆☆ $$/$$$ Known for its tasty roast beef and steaks and hearty home-baked breads, Joe & Mo's provides great service at a reasonable price. For the meat-and-potatoes crowd who also want to be seen. *American. Open M-F 11:30am-10:45pm, Sa 6:30-10:45pm. Closed Su. Reservations required.* 1211 Connecticut Ave. NW. 659-1211.

25 Longfellow Building. (1940, **William Lescaze**) The first Modern glass box in DC, its historical claim to fame is that it was among the very first buildings anywhere to articulate office space and service area as separate design elements. 1741 Rhode Island Ave. NW.

25 St. Matthew's Cathedral. (1899, **Heins & LaFarge**) John F. Kennedy worshiped in this church and his funeral mass was said here; an inscription marks the spot. The dome, reminiscent of the *Cathedral of Santa Maria del Fiore* in Florence, and simple brick geometries of the exterior give no hint of the florid interior's fine mosaic work. *Open daily, call for times of Su mass.* 1725 Rhode Island Ave. NW. 347-3215.

26 The Gralyn Inn. *Moderate.* This cozy English country-style inn, formerly the home of the Persian embassy, is decorated with antique furnishings, and its lounge has a fireplace with an imposing portrait of **George Washington.** Known as a *British hotel* since 1941, the Gralyn primarily served an English clientele during World War II; the NATO Group has stayed here for over 20 years. The Inn has had a single owner, **Mrs. Hamilton Morrison**, since it was built by combining 2 mansions in 1939. Twenty apartments and 34 rooms available, some with private bath. Cherrywood paneled *Room 11* is a special treat. Breakfast is the only meal served. Garden dining in the summer. *Daily rates only.* 1745 N St. NW. 785-1515.

26 Tabard Inn. *Moderate.* A heaven for Anglophiles, this Olde World inn has only 39 rooms. Guests congregate in a large first-floor parlor and cocktail lounge. Many rooms have fireplaces, and at least one second floor room has an upright piano. Rooms are warm and comfortable, with a family-like atmosphere: Most of the staff have been with the inn for many years. Breakfast included in room price. 1739 N St. NW. 785-1277.

The average **year-round** temperature for the Potomac Basin is 54 degrees.

Introductions/Theaters/Narrative black
Hotels purple
Museums/Architecture blue
Parks/Open spaces green
Restaurants/Nightlife red
Shops/Galleries violet

Within the hotel is:

Tabard Inn Restaurant. ☆ ☆ $$ A casual, bustling dining room hung with folk art and featuring a menu of healthy, inventive dishes: lavish salads, fresh fish with crisp vegetable garnishes, burgers covered with Stilton cheese or salsa verde, fresh pasta. Homemade desserts. Garden dining in warm weather. *Original American. Open M-W 7am-10:30pm, Th-Sa 7am-11pm, Su 8am-10pm. Reservations suggested at dinner. 833-2668.*

6 Canterbury. *Expensive.* A unique re-creation of 18th-century elegance, mixed with the comfort and luxury of European lodgings. Elegant suites consist of a sitting area, dressing room and wet-bar; complimentary Continental breakfast and newspaper daily. Ask about the *Suite and Luxurious Weekend Package. Off Connecticut Ave. near Dupont Circle at 1733 N St. NW. 393-3000/800-424-2950.*

Within the hotel is:

Chaucers. ☆ ☆ $$ Sit in the elegant, cheery basement dining room, or the skylit courtyard, and enjoy well-prepared specialties including seafood dishes like gingery red snapper or shrimp in pernod and butter. *Original American. Open M-F 7am-11pm, Sa & Su 8am-11pm. Reservations suggested. 296-0665.*

27 Iron Gate Inn. ☆ ☆ $$ Old World atmosphere augmented by one of the prettiest garden restaurants in town. Solid Middle Eastern cooking: *hummus, baba ghanouj* with baskets of warm pita, good stuffed grape leaves, lamb dishes, *baklava. Middle Eastern. Open daily 11:30am-10:30pm. Reservations suggested for dinner. 1734 N St. NW (Connecticut Ave.). 737-1370.*

28 Sumner School. (1872, **Adolph Cluss**) This neglected but historic red brick schoolhouse once had a clock tower rising above its elegant roofline. It was the first school for black children established in the District. *17th & M Sts. NW.*

29 National Geographic Society/Explorers Hall. (1964, **Edward Durell Stone**) The National Geographic Society has been funding worldwide exploration and publishing its perennially optimistic monthly travelogue since 1888. Its format and high quality have remained virtually unchanged in all that time, though its subscriber base has grown from 1,000 to a hefty 11 million.

This modern structure is the Society's headquarters. The first of Stone's many Washington buildings, it may also be his best: a monument to balance and restraint. On its ground floor it houses **Explorers Hall**, a free, low-key museum that can easily be experienced in an hour's time. Most exhibits relate to Society-funded studies. An exhibit on prehistoric man includes a walk through a cave facsimile. Dioramas illustrate the lives of Southwest American cliff dwellers. There is a huge ancient Olmec stone head, one of the sleds Admiral **Robert Peary** used to reach the North Pole, and a piece of moon rock retrieved by Apollo 12. Probably the best-known object in the hall is the giant freestanding globe which has become the symbol of the Society—it's 11 feet tall and 34 feet in circumference at the equator.

You will also find frequently changing exhibits of photography and a small theater showing films on Society-related projects. The publication desk has an excellent collection of National Geographic maps, atlases and lavish photography books. *Admission free. Open M-F 9am-6pm, Sa & Su 9am-5pm. 17th & M Sts. NW. For information call 857-7588; for group globe demonstration, call 857-7689.*

30 B'nai B'rith Klutznick Museum. Twenty centuries of history, with emphasis on early Jewish American settlements, are represented by more than 500 objects, making the permanent collection one of the largest in the United States. Artifacts such as 1,000-year-old coins and 16th-century Torah wrapper help to introduce visitors to Jewish history. Subjects from archaeology to modern art are covered in a series of annual exhibitions. Free films are scheduled year-round and nationally known columnists and speakers hold lectures on a weekly basis. **Women Four Freedoms Library** gives an extensive 7,000-volume overview of liberal and socialist texts. Next to the museum's giftshop is the **National Jewish Visitors Center,** providing hospitality services and information on Jewish sights and events in Washington. Group and multi-lingual tours arranged in advance by calling *857-6583. Admission free. (Tax deductible donations welcome.) Open Su-F 10am-5pm except Jewish holidays. 1640 Rhode Island Ave. NW.*

30 The Gramercy Hotel. *Moderate/expensive.* Located on the edge of **Embassy Row,** the refurbished lobby is spacious and sophisticated: Clocks in the lobby give time from around the world. Rooms have been redone as well. All registered guests receive a complimentary membership to the **Gramercy Swim Club.** Enjoy special weekend packages and sightseeing tours. *1616 Rhode Island Ave. NW. 800-368-5957/347-9550.*

30 National Rifle Association Firearms Museum. Displays of antique and modern weapons, films on wilderness survival and firearms safety, and an introduction to the NRA's many programs are available here. *Admission free. 1600 Rhode Island Ave. NW. 828-6253/828-6194.*

31 First Baptist Church. (1955, **Harold E. Wagoner**) The massing of this Neo-Gothic church, reminiscent of **Frank Lloyd Wright,** leads the eye upward to a steeple that isn't there. *16th St. at O St. NW.*

31 Forest Industries Building. (1961, **Keyes, Lethbridge & Condon**) The scale and crispness of this concrete building make it quite welcoming; the open entrance court makes it appear taller while observing the city's height restriction. *1619 Massachusetts Ave. NW.*

32 Best Western Executive House Hotel. *Inexpensive.* This standard Best Western hotel is clean and modern, a convenient and accommodating West End hostelry. Pool and sundeck area. *1515 Rhode Island Ave. NW. 232-7000/800-424-2461.*

33 The Madison Hotel. *Expensive/deluxe.* This *tres chic* hotel has the spirit of a truly fine French auberge. Geared for those who want full service combined with privacy. If you are an art lover, you will enjoy museum and art pieces on display throughout the hotel. The elegant lobby is filled with exquisite **Louis XVI** commodes, marquetry writing tables and antique gold leaf girandole mirrors. Ask for a room on the M Street side for best views. Private bars in rooms are always well-stocked. *1507 M St. NW. 862-1600/Telex: 710 822-0145.*

Within the hotel is:

Montpelier Room. ☆ ☆ $$$$ An opulent dining room of blue and gold, adorned with magnificent china and roses, and run by a discreet and efficient staff. The menu of extremely expensive, traditional continental dishes contains no imaginative fare but all are very well-prepared. *Continental. Open daily 6am-midnight. Reservations suggested. Coat and tie required. 862-1712.*

Immediately after the attack on Pearl Harbor, anti-aircraft guns were set up to protect the capital. One such gun, mounted on the roof of the Department of the Interior building, accidentally went off and hit a panel of the Lincoln Memorial in several places. Although the holes that riddled Maryland's state seal have been patched, the marks are still visible at a closer look.

34 Metropolitan AME Church. (1854-1881, **Samuel T. Morsell**) Members of the congregation once hid slaves escaping on the *Underground Railroad* behind this broad Victorian Gothic facade; the influential black congregation has been active in the civil rights struggle ever since. This is the national headquarters of the African Methodist Episcopal Church. Funeral services for **Frederick Douglass** were held here. Of architectural interest are the 2-foot-thick brick bearing walls on the first floor, which support the vast second-story sanctuary. *1518 M St. NW.*

35 Vista International. *Expensive.* A new luxury hotel on the edge of exciting Georgetown, which features 6 suites with whirlpools by world-renowned fashion designer **Hubert de Givenchy.** Two executive floors have a club-like lounge. Another plus is the **American Harvest Restaurant** which specializes in native American dishes such as wild game, cranberries, and pumpkin. After dinner, discover the **Tower Lounge** where rare ports and cognacs are served by the glass. *1400 M St. NW. 429-1700.*

35 Major General George H. Thomas. One of the city's more striking equestrian statues. Thomas, aka *the Rock of Chickamauga*, holds his horse firmly in check as he surveys the battlefield. Sculpted in 1879 by **John Quincy Adams Ward.** *Thomas Circle, Massachusetts Ave. at 14th St. NW.*

36 Luther Place Memorial Church. (1870, **Judson York**; addition 1952, **L.M. Leisenring**) This Civil War-era church, built in thanksgiving for the fighting's end, is a soaring Neo-Gothic structure of red sandstone that provides a fitting balance to the National City Christian Church across the street. *Open M-F 9am-5pm, Su services 8:30am & 11am. 1226 Vermont Ave. NW. 667-1377.*

37 National City Christian Church. (1930, **John Russell Pope**; addition 1952, **Leon Chatelain, Jr.**) The bigger-than-life scale of this Colonial-style church is heightened by its position on a small knoll. This perch, coupled with the **Inigo Jones**-inspired steeple, makes it the highest building in town. Presidents **Garfield** and **Lyndon Johnson** worshiped here. *Services (Disciples of Christ) Su 11am. 14th St. & Massachusetts Ave. NW.*

38 Church of the Ascension of St. Agnes. (1875) A High Victorian Gothic composition that befits a High Church congregation known for its musical tradition. The interior includes cast-iron columns, walnut pews, a vigorous gold and silver leaf mural, and more recent abstract windows in the nave. *Massachusetts Ave. & 12th St. NW.*

39 Logan Circle. The elegant mansions encircling this park stand in various states of repair; several of the best are now embassies, while many are simply uninhabitable. *13th St. & Vermont Ave. NW.*

40 Studio Theatre. Stage Productions. *1401 Church St. NW. 483-9779.*

41 Foundry United Methodist Church. (1904, **Appleton P. Clark**) Rusticated gray granite is formed into the fan vaults characteristic of High Gothic Revival; the low-dome contributes to its renowned acoustical qualities. Its name honors Georgetown foundry owner **Henry Foxhall,** who founded the church. *Services Su 9:30am & 11am. 1500 16th St. NW. 332-4010.*

42 New Playwrights' Theatre. Testing ground for works-in-progress as well as full productions of new plays. *1742 Church St. NW at Dupont Circle. 232-1122.*

43 National Trust for Historic Preservation (McCormick Apartments). (1917, **Jules Henri de Sibour**) The McCormick building was once the most opulent apartment house in the District, with only one 11,000-square-foot apartment per each of its 6 floors. Such notables as **Andrew Mellon** lived here. It is the best of de Sibour's many DC works (which include the nearby **Canadian Chancery**), bringing a Parisian flair to the neighborhood. *1785 Massachusetts Ave. NW.*

The Baltimore and Ohio Railroad line was finished on Christmas Eve in 1852.

44 Washington Club (Patterson House). (1902, **Stanford White**) Another oddly shaped building adapted to L'Enfant's oddly shaped lots. In this case, the gleaming white Italian palazzo was built for the publisher of the *Washington Times Herald.* It now houses a women's club. *15 Dupont Circle NW.*

KRAMERBOOKS &afterwords *A cafe*

45 Kramerbooks and Afterwords, a Cafe. ☆ $ Building a cafe at the rear of a bookstore isn't a new idea—but a browsing crowd of bookworms, artists and neighborhood gadflies confirms it's a good one. This Dupont Circle institution specializes in popular hardcovers and paperbacks, a little quiche and a split of wine. During the late hours, it's a popular meeting spot for gays. *Open M-F 8am-1am, Sa 10am-3am, Su 10am-1am, 1347 Connecticut Ave. NW. 293-2072.*

45 Bacchus. ☆ ☆ $ Sit at a tile table in one of 2 small, pretty dining rooms, and make a meal out of Bacchus' great Middle Eastern appetizers: *hummus, baba ghanouj,* stuffed grape leaves, homemade sausage, *tabuli.* Or order from a list of filling lamb and chicken entrees. The wine list is interesting and reasonable. *Lebanese. Open M-F noon-10:30pm, Sa 6-10:30pm. Closed Su. Reservations suggested. 1827 Jefferson Pl. NW (19th St. NW). 785-0734.*

45 Euram Building. (1971, **Hartman-Cox**) One of Washington's architectural stars. Eight stories of brick, glass and pre-stressed concrete surround a vivid inner courtyard; the bold geometries and sleek style betray its Italian ownership. *21 Dupont Circle NW.*

46 Dupont Garden. ☆ ☆ $$ Reasonable, predictable Cantonese menu. *Dim sum* at weekend brunch. Delicious chocolate-covered fried ice cream for dessert. *Cantonese. Open daily 11:30am-10:30pm. Reservations suggested. 1333 New Hampshire Ave. NW at Dupont Circle. 296-6500.*

47 Dupont Fountain. There was once a bronze statue here of Civil War admiral Samuel Francis Dupont. Happily, the Dupont family whisked it away to Delaware, replacing it with this graceful marble fountain (1921, **Daniel Chester French**). Below the basin are figures representing the wind, the sea and the stars. *Dupont Circle, Connecticut Ave. between 19th & P Sts. NW.*

48 The Hampshire Hotel. *Moderate/expensive.* Not as lavishly decorated as others in the neighborhood, but this Best Western hotel has comfortable accommodations. Suites are spacious with a stocked wet bar and a sitting room area. Warm and responsive staff. Restaurant and bar. Located within walking distance of Georgetown's shops and restaurants. *1310 New Hampshire Ave. NW. 296-7600/800-368-5691.*

49 Embassy Square Hotel. *Inexpensive/moderate.* Recently purchased by the Quality Inn chain, this hotel has a certain charm way surpassing its sister hotels. An air of Washington elegance is apparent in the lobby's oil portraits, fine woods and high ceilings. Also unusual are the suites: Choose from 4 different styles. Ask for one overlooking the courtyard or *Room 117,* the nicest in the house. Other pluses: convenient location, multi-lingual staff, sauna room, underground parking, and a country-estate style restaurant and bar. Ask about weekend specials. *2000 N St. NW. 659-9000/Telex: 440323 BHOB UI.*

Introductions/Theaters/Narrative black
Hotels purple
Museums/Architecture blue
Parks/Open spaces green
Restaurants/Nightlife red
Shops/Galleries violet

50 Marston Luce Gallery. Specializes in 19th-century American folk art—weather vanes, furniture, decoys, carvings, signs, paintings. A specialty is Pennsylvania majolica ware, brightly painted lead-glazed earthenware, which is having a resurgence in interest among collectors. *Open M-Sa 11am-6pm. Closed Su. 1314 21st St. NW. 775-9460.*

51 Second Story Books is the District's leading group of used-book stores. Three separate shops feature floor-to-ceiling shelves of old, used, rare and out-of-print books—all at reasonable prices. Free search service and appraisals. *Open 7 days, 10am-10pm. 2000 P St. NW at Dupont Circle. 659-8884. (Also at 3236 P St. NW, Georgetown (338-6860), and 816 N. Fairfax St., Alexandria, VA, 548-4373.)*

51 Torremolinos. ☆☆ $$ This small, dimly lit Spanish eatery doesn't skimp on either the garlic or olive oil. Seafood is a winner, from the softshell crabs (in season) to the grilled fish, to the seafood stew. Other recommended dishes include veal with olives, chicken in a brown, garlicky sauce, and tripe and sausage stew. *Spanish. Open M-F 11:30am-2:30pm, 6-10:30pm; Sa 6-10:30pm. Closed Su. Reservations suggested on weekends. 2014 P St. NW. 659-4382.*

51 Blaine Mansion. (1881, **John Fraser**) A Victorian fortress that was once the home of 3-time presidential hopeful **James Blaine**. *2000 Massachusetts Ave. NW.*

52 Dupont Plaza Hotel. *Moderate.* This hotel is surrounded by 3-story Victorian row homes, foreign embassies, bookstores, boutiques, and quaint cafes which contribute to its charming bohemian village atmosphere. Attractive rooms have wet bars and refrigerators; suites overlook the park. **Stephanie's Lounge and Restaurant** features Continental and Viennese-style cuisine. You'll enjoy Dupont Circle Park across the street, especially in summer when it's a gathering place for artists and strollers who play chess, perform, catch a suntan, or just talk. *1500 New Hampshire Ave. NW. 483-6000.*

53 Cafe Splendide. ☆☆ $ A cheery, intimate tearoom setting, friendly service, and large portions of Austrian food—seasoned hamburgers with green pepper and bacon, brochette of beef and pork tenderloin, chicken breast *zingara*, interesting salads, homemade strudel and other pastries—make this one of the least pretentious eateries in the neighborhood. *Austrian. Open daily 9am-11:30pm. Reservations suggested. 1521 Connecticut Ave. NW (Q St. NW). 328-1503.*

54 Belmont House (Eastern Star Temple). (1908, **Sanson, Trumbauer**) Architect **Ernest Sanson** was imported from France specifically for this project (American **Horace Trumbauer** was the project manager), and the resultant building fairly drips with Gallic romanticism. The shape was mandated by the wedge-shaped lot; the opulent interiors, complete with **Louis Tiffany** glass, brought the total construction cost to $1.5 million. Much of the original owner's art collection remains in the house, though it was sold (actually given—the price was a paltry $100,000) to the Order of the Eastern Star in 1937. *1618 New Hampshire Ave. NW.*

55 Kathleen Ewing Gallery. Specializing in 19th-century vintage and 20th-century masterwork images, this photography gallery holds monthly exhibitions and represents 30 US and European photographers. *Open W-Sa noon-6pm. Closed Su-Tu. 1609 Connecticut Ave. NW. 328-0955.*

55 The News Room. In a town of diplomats, politicians and media junkies, this shop's comprehensive collection of out-of-town and foreign newspapers and magazines is a necessity. *Open Su-W 8am-9pm, Th-Sa 8am-midnight. 1753 Connecticut Ave. NW. 332-1489.*

The room that served as **Lincoln's death chamber** in the Petersen House, also lodged the president's assassin—actor **John Wilkes Booth** once rented the very same bedroom and slept in the same bed before committing his ghastly deed a few weeks later.

56 Vincenzo. ☆☆☆ $$$$ Within these chic, austere interiors, seafood is prepared with a knowing Italian flair. Start with antipasto: bean and pepper salads, sardines or stuffed whole artichokes, and good ham. Then move on to pasta prepared with diverse sauces of seafood, and main courses like grilled whole fish or *fritto misto*. Interesting wine list. *Italian/seafood. Open M-F noon-2pm, 6-10pm; Sa 6-10pm. Closed Su. Reservations suggested. Coat and tie recommended. 1606 20th St. NW (Q St. NW). 667-0047.*

56 Cherishibles. Eighteenth- and 19th-century American folk art is the specialty of this shop, with particular emphasis being given to quilts. Weather vanes, decoys, whirligigs, and hand-carved wooden architectural collectables are also customary items. *Open M-Sa 11am-6pm Closed Su. 1608 20th St. NW. 785-4087.*

57 Backstage Books. Books, scripts, sheet music and publications inspired by the performing arts. Also stocks dancewear, stage make-up and record albums. *Open M-Sa 10am-6pm. 2101 P St. NW. 775-1488.*

57 Gallery K. European and American contemporary paintings, sculptures and drawings as well as American folk and Indian art are shown. Up-and-coming young Washington area artists such as **Jody Mussoff** and **Fred Folsom** are often featured. *Open Tu-Sa 11am-6pm. Closed Su & M. 2032 P St. NW. 223-6955.*

57 The Georgetown Hotel. *Moderate/expensive.* Located in one of Washington's most prestigious areas between the White House and Embassy Row. Suites are large with separate living area and full kitchen. **Herb's** restaurant, called *Algonquin South* by *The Washington Post*, is known for its eclectic American cuisine and lively late-night atmosphere. Amenities package at the hotel includes seasonal outdoor pool, sauna and exercise room, beauty salon, gift shop, valet and concierge services, complimentary in-room coffee/tea services, and free HBO. *2121 P St. NW. 293-3100/800-424-2884/Telex: 140952 GTNHOT.*

Within the hotel is:

Herb's. ☆ $$ With its red booths and walls festooned with pictures of and by local artists and performers, Herb's fancies itself the Sardi's of Washington. Friendly waiters serve you great looking but unevenly prepared specials of fish, pasta and other dishes. Sandwiches and omelettes are large and tasty, desserts rich and plentiful. *American. Open daily 8am-2am. Reservations accepted. 2121 P St. NW. 333-4372.*

58 The Ritz Carlton. *Expensive.* Everything here is so elegant, including the fact that the RC's refinement is whispered, not shouted. The 180 rooms and suites are graced with niceties such as handcarved mahogany headboards and bedspreads in embroidered English chintz. Laundry and valet, concierge and night butler available. The **Fairfax Bar** (with woodburning fireplaces) has the atmosphere of a private club. *2100 Massachusetts Ave. NW. 835-2100/800-424-8008/Telex: TWX7108229228.*

Within the hotel is:

Jockey Club. ☆☆ $$$ Clubby elegance and a staff schooled in the grand old manner. Continental menu with subtle French hints; the soft-shell crabs are prize-winners. *Continental/French. Open daily 7-10am; M-F noon-2:30pm, 6-11pm; Sa & Su brunch noon-2:30pm. Jacket required, reservations suggested.*

58 Anderson House/Society of the Cincinnati. (1900, **Little & Brown**) In 1783, a group of Revolutionary War officers facing demobilization proposed this elite fraternal organization to preserve their select camaraderie. At the time, such organizations played an important part in gentlemanly civic and political advancement. Membership is limited to male descendants—usually first-born—of those original officers, plus a few exceptions; even the French have a chapter, due to the role they played in the revolution. The group is named for **Quinctius**

Cincinnatus, Roman leader whose life Washington's paralleled. The town of Cincinnati, Ohio, was named by a member of the society. Anderson House, where the Society of the Cincinnati is headquartered, is a Historic House Museum, and is not to be missed. Behind the stately Palladian facade is one of the city's finest townhomes, with lavish and opulent interiors filled with artistic treasures from the US, Europe and the Orient including a gallery of society members' portraits by famous American painters. The **Harold Leonard Stuart Memorial Library** of reference works on the American Revolution is *open to the public M-F 10am-4pm. Tours available for large groups by appointment. Admission free. Open Tu-Sa 1-4pm. 2118 Massachusetts Ave. NW. 785-2040/785-0540.*

The Phillips Collection

59 The Phillips Collection. In 1921 **Duncan Phillips** opened his 4-story brownstone home to the public, thus creating the first museum of modern art. Inside he had already established an exemplary collection starting with American Impressionists and expanding into French Impressionists and the post-Impressionists. Eventually **Duncan and Marjorie Phillips'** holdings spanned not only European and American modernism, but also *sources* of modernism such as **Goya, El Greco** and **Delacroix.**

Today the Phillips Gallery has preserved the private home atmosphere while displaying its inventory to best advantage. The museum is a delight for art lovers, who can stroll through the over-sized rooms, taking advantage of the many couches and chairs in which to rest and ponder particular works.

Phillips tried to create exhibition units, either of an artist's whole body of work or a comparison of several artists' pieces. He sought out interesting colors and unique qualities, encouraging lesser-known talents by being the first to collect their work. He insisted upon rearranging paintings to show off their best qualities—and did so even from his death bed.

About 2,500 pieces now occupy most of Phillips' original home and an adjoining building that was created in 1960. A 1984 restoration improved illumination and safety at the museum.

Degas, Monet, Van Gogh and **Cezanne** hold important positions throughout the museum, as do **Bonnard, Klee, Marin, Rothko, Dove** and **O'Keeffe.** Following Phillips' wishes, the museum sponsors exhibitions, publications and loans to other museums' special exhibits.

Admission free. Open Tu-Sa 10am-5pm, Su 2-7pm. Closed M. 1600 21st St. NW. 387-0961.

59 Cosmos Club (Townsend Mansion). (1900, **Carrere & Hastings**) A railway baron's wife commissioned this palace, which features one of the most ostentatious facades in the city. *Private club. 2121 Massachusetts Ave. NW.*

60 The Fonda del Sol Visual Arts & Media Center exhibits Hispanic American, Native American and African American art. *Open Tu-Sa noon-5:30pm. 2121 R St. NW. 483-2777.*

When a 1983 research group surveyed the **median education level** in the country, the Washington area managed to place 5 of its counties within the top 10: Falls Church came in as number 5, Montgomery as 6, Fairfax as 7, and Alexandria as number 10. The smartest people in the US live in Los Alamos County, location of the Los Alamos National Laboratory in New Mexico.

Introductions/Theaters/Narrative black
Hotels purple
Museums/Architecture blue
Parks/Open spaces green
Restaurants/Nightlife red
Shops/Galleries violet

60 Restaurant Nora. ☆ ☆ ☆ $$$$ Cozy and warm with large photos of fruits and vegetables hung on its brick walls, this is one of the cheeriest dining rooms in town. A favorite with journalists and other scriveners, Nora serves fresh, original American dishes. You'll discover new herbs and greens used to interesting effect in soups, salads, sauces and on fish. The homemade desserts—especially the pies—are a must. Nice wine list. *Original American. Open M-F 11:30am-2:30pm; M-Th 5:30-10:30pm, F till 11:30pm; Sa 6-11:30pm. Closed Su. Reservations suggested. No credit cards. 2132 Florida Ave. NW. 462-5143.*

61 Katmandu. ☆ ☆ ☆ $$ This enchanting restaurant is a *find* for the adventurous palate! The cooking of Nepal is one of the least spicy, most subtle of Asian cuisines. Meats and poultry are grilled and served with a yogurt sauce. Try the *shalgam* (turnip) curry, the fish or shrimp stew, or the pork fried in mustard oil. *Nepalese/Kashmiri. Open M-F 11:30am-2:30pm, 5:30-11pm; Sa & Su 5:30-11pm. Reservations required. Coat and tie recommended. 1800 Connecticut Ave. NW (at Florida and S Sts. NW). 483-6470.*

61 Timberlakes. ☆ ☆ $$ Always crowded, noisy and upbeat, this bar and grill boasts a wonderful cheeseburger, huge onion rings, fluffy omelettes and the like. *American bar/grill. Open M-Th 11:30am-midnight, F 11:30am-1am, Sa 10:30am-1am, Su 10:30am-midnight. Reservations accepted for parties of 6 or more. 1726 Connecticut Ave. NW (R St. NW). 483-2266.*

61 Food for Thought. ☆ $ One of the few vegetarian restaurants in town. Casual, cooperatively run, this is the place for big sandwiches of cheese, sprouts, and tomatoes on 7-grain bread, daily casseroles, and fresh fruit and vegetable salads. Live music on weekends. *Vegetarian. Open M-F 11:30am-midnight (except M from 3-5pm); Sa & Su 5pm-1am. No reservations. 1738 Connecticut Ave. NW (Florida Ave. NW). 797-1095.*

62 Baumgartner Galleries. European and American contemporary artists are shown in rotating exhibitions in this townhouse gallery. A specialty is the work of a school of Viennese magic realist painters led by the eccentric, prolific **Friedensreich Hundertwasser.** *Open Tu-Sa 11am-6pm. Closed Su & M. 2016 R St. NW. 232-6320.*

63 Fourways. ☆ ☆ ☆ $$$ A wide array of elegant and sometimes exquisite dishes—caviar with blini, seafoods of all sorts, gamebirds, vegetable concoctions—served in an elaborately restored old mansion. *Continental. Open M-Sa noon-2:30pm, 6-10:30pm; Su 11:30am-3pm, 6-10:30pm. Reservations suggested. Coat and tie recommended. 1701 20th St. NW (R St. NW). 483-3200.*

SUZANNE'S

63 Suzanne's. ☆ ☆ $$ From the ground floor gourmet carry-out shop to the chic and friendly little restaurant up a narrow flight of stairs, Suzanne's screams *trendy*. In the restaurant choose from a blackboard full of specials—meats wrapped in pastry, fresh pasta, fresh salmon, selected cheeses. The desserts are great, especially the chocolate chestnut cake. *American. Open M-Th 11:30am-10:30pm, F & Sa 11:30am-11:30pm. Closed Su. Reservations accepted. 1735 Connecticut Ave. NW (S St. NW). 483-4633.*

63 International Learning Center. Books, records and tapes in 120 languages, from Turkish epics to video courses in Swahili. *Open M-Sa 10am-7pm. 1715 Connecticut Ave. NW. 232-4111.*

63 Paru's Indian Vegetarian Restaurant. ☆ ☆ $ In this tiny self-service spot, sample Indian specialties like *masala dosa* (rolled pancakes filled with potato curry), *uddapam* (a huge tomato-onion pancake), assorted curries and the silky yogurt drink called *lassi*. *Indian Vegetarian. Open M-Sa 11:30am-9:30pm. Closed Su. No reservations. No credit cards. 2010 S St. NW (Connecticut Ave.). 483-5133.*

64 Lalibela. ☆ ☆ $$ Traditional Ethiopian cuisine: spicy stews of lamb, chicken, lentils and split peas, delicious unleavened bread used in place of silverware, mounds of cabbage and other cooked vegetables. Try *tej*, a honied wine, gaze into the fire, or look out the second-story bay windows onto Dupont Circle's street scene. *Ethiopian. Open daily 9am-2am. Reservations accepted. 2000 S St. NW (20th St. NW). 797-7460/797-7845.*

65 Barney Studio House. Part of the Smithsonian's National Museum of Art, the 1902 house built by **Alice Pike Barney** served as her home and studio. It features her work and early 20th-century artifacts. Recently renovated. *Tours by appointment, W & Th 11am-1pm. 2306 Massachusetts Ave. NW. 357-3095.*

66 Textile Museum. (1916, **John Russell Pope**) In 1896 **George H. Myers** purchased an Oriental rug for his college room and began a life-long fascination with the art of textiles—woven or knitted goods. In 1925 he turned his home, and its rich collection of rugs, blankets, fabrics, garments, upholstery, decorative trims—over 10,000 pieces, including 1,000 rugs—into this privately endowed showcase. The collection comes from all over the world, notably Europe, the Mediterranean and North Africa, the Orient and South America. Today the museum has expanded into the house next door, where there is also a 7,000-book resource library on textiles. *Tours are given Sa 11:30am-1pm,* and this is one of the best days to visit because the public is invited to bring in pieces for evaluation by experts—an opportunity to listen and learn.

Call the museum for information on its current special exhibit, lectures and demonstrations. The gift shop, housed in what was once Myers' library, offers textile gifts and publications. *Admission charge. Open Tu-Sa 10am-5pm, Su 1-5pm. 2320 S St. NW. 667-0441.*

66 Woodrow Wilson House. This National Historic Landmark serves as a museum commemorating our 28th president, whose accomplishments included creation of the Federal Reserve Board and participation in the establishment of the League of Nations. Wilson's distinguished career as author of 9 books, college professor, president of Princeton University and governor of New Jersey is covered in exhibits and photographs. Special museum events include walking tours of the surrounding Kalorama neighborhood, Christmas open house circa 1920, and Armistice Day services. *Admission charge. Open Tu-F 10am-2pm; Sa, Su, some holidays noon-4pm. 2340 S St. NW. 673-5517.*

67 Islamic Center. (1955, **Mario Rossi**) The Islamic nations that maintain embassies in Washington collaborated on a cultural and religious center for their staffs to use, and the result is one of the most interesting sights in town. Fine craftworks by Middle Eastern artisans—tile, glass, woodwork, bronze and carpets—furnish the white marble building; the walls are inlaid with turquoise and gold. The actual mosque is an independent structure in the center of a courtyard, oriented toward Mecca. A minaret rises 160 feet above the complex.

Moslems from over 40 countries comprise the center's congregation, which is among the most active in the country. The center publishes informative literature and conducts lectures. *Open daily 10am-4pm. 2551 Massachusetts Ave. NW. 332-8343.*

68 The Lindens. (1754, **Robert Hooper**) This New England-style Georgian house is actually the oldest building in DC. But it loses the title to the **Old Stone House** in Georgetown on a technicality: It wasn't *in* the district until 1934, when it was disassembled and moved from its original home in Danvers, Massachusetts. *2401 Kalorama Rd. NW.*

69 Woodward Apartments. (1913, **Harding & Upman**) An unspoiled turn-of-the-century apartment building with a strong European flavor *2311 Connecticut Ave. NW.*

70 Normandy Inn. *Moderate/expensive.* This classic European inn, which caters especially to visiting French dignitaries, will give you a taste of France in the heart of Washington. Its charm is everywhere, from the wine and cheese reception held every Tuesday evening, to its embassy-filled neighborhood. Enjoy the chic tea room and patio until midnight every evening. *2118 Wyoming Ave. NW. 483-1350.*

71 The Highland Hotel. *Moderate/expensive.* A warm, homey atmosphere reigns at this suites-only hotel. The plush accommodations are geared toward longer stays, offering convertible sofas, wet bars, and seating arrangements for dining or working. Frequent visitors should look into the **100 Club**—membership buys added perks of complimentary limo service, continental breakfasts, free evening cocktails and turned-down beds. *Washington Weekend* rates. *1914 Connecticut Ave. NW. 797-2000/800-424-2464.*

72 The Washington Hilton and Towers. *Moderate/expensive.* Two separate hotels, both providing Hilton-quality accommodations. **The Towers** VIP service, 2-top floor additions to the main building, offers many complimentary services that other hotels put on their tab—American breakfasts, afternoon tea, dinner cocktails and nightly turndown service. A large outdoor pool and 3 tennis courts complete the first-class picture. *1919 Connecticut Ave. NW. 483-3000/Telex: 248761 WHDC UR.*

72 El Caribe. ☆ ☆ ☆ $$ Small, very noisy, featuring distinctly Latin American decor and a strolling guitarist, this place offers the finest of Central and South American cuisines. *Latin American. Open M-Th 11:30am-11pm, F 11:30am-11:30pm, Sa 1-11:30pm, Su 1-11pm. Reservations suggested. 1828 Columbia Rd. NW (18th St. NW). 234-6969.*

72 Omega. ☆ ☆ $ This local favorite serves up huge portions of Cuban food at low prices. Start with appetizers—shrimp sauteed with garlic, fried squid, fried chicken wings—and then savor the zesty *paellas*, rabbit or lamb stew, roast chicken, main-course soups, or fried pork chops. *Cuban. Open Su, Tu-Th noon-10pm; F & Sa noon-11pm. Closed M. No reservations. 1858 Columbia Rd. NW (Belmont Rd. NW). 462-1732.*

72 Excalibur. A smallish, velvet-walled joint, featuring local jazz and blues talent. The dinner menu is steak and seafood, and very inexpensive. During happy hour, the varied clientele nurse strawberry-banana daiquiris while digging the moody blues of a jukebox. *Showtimes and cover charge vary. Open M-Tu 4pm-2am, F & Sa 4pm-3am, Su 8pm-2am. 1834 Columbia Rd. NW. 462-0415.*

73 Cubi XI. Abstract sculptor **David Smith** has used steel, nickel and chrome to powerful and startling effect. Standing 11 feet tall, the precariously balanced squares and rectangles of gleaming metal seem to hold the force of gravity temporarily at bay. *Universal North Building. 1875 Connecticut Ave. NW.*

73 New Orleans Cafe. ☆ ☆ $$ Narrow, noisy, with the kitchen right in the center of the place. Order a spicy Creole omelette (served with home fries, homemade biscuits and jam), crawfish balls, jambalaya (a rich seafood stew) or *pain perdu* (French toast made with French bread). The house coffee is a strong, milky brew. *Cajun/Creole. Open Su-Th 8:30am-10pm, F & Sa till 11pm. No reservations. 1790 Columbia Rd. NW. 234-5111.*

74 Middendorf Gallery. Occupying a light-filled former embassy building, this handsome gallery focuses on mainstream American painting, sculpture, prints and photographs. National avant garde trends can be studied here. The gallery also specializes in American Modernists from the first half of the century. *Open Tu-F 11am-6pm, Sa 11am-5pm. Closed Su & M. 2009 Columbia Rd. NW. 462-2009.*

75 Le Tam-Tam. ☆ ☆ $$ The meaty, peanut-laden cuisine of West Africa, served in a charming neighborhood restaurant/discotheque. Well-prepared French dishes also available. *West African. Open M-Th 11:30am-10:30pm; F & Sa till 10pm for dinner, later for drinks. Closed Su. Reservations recommended on weekends. 1910 18th St. NW. 483-0505.*

76 Kalorama Park. Pleasant oak-dotted park hosts the annual Hispanic Festival's celebration of traditional music and dance, held the last week in July. *Kalorama and Columbia Rds. NW.*

76 Adams-Morgan Spaghetti Garden. ☆ $ Family place serving cheap, hearty Italian fare. Outdoor roof-top dining in seasonable weather. *Italian. Open M-F 11:30am-2am, Sa 4pm-2am, Su 4-10pm. No reservations. 2317 18th St. NW (Belmont Rd. NW). 265-6665.*

76 La Fourchette. ☆ ☆ $$ French bistro replete with floor-to-ceiling murals of French cafe scenes. Daily specials include bouillabaisse and other rich soups, duck, rabbit, and lobster with cream and peppercorns. *French. Open M, Tu & Th 11:30am-10:30pm; F 11:30am-11pm; Sa & Su 4-10:30pm. Closed W. Reservations accepted. 2429 18th St. NW (Belmont Rd. NW). 332-3077.*

77 Millie and Al's. ☆ $ The neighborhood bar for casual conversation, golden oldies on the jukebox and good pizza. *Open M-Th 4pm-2am, F-Su noon-3am. No reservations. No credit cards. 2440 18th St. NW (Columbia Rd. NW). 387-8131.*

78 Red Sea. ☆ ☆ ☆ $ One of the best of DC's 8 Ethiopian restaurants, offers such dishes as *wot* (spicy stews of beef, lamb and chicken), *tibs* (beef with green chilis), tasty vegetables and lentil salads. All of it is eaten without benefit of silverware; use the spongy unleavened bread called *injera* to scoop up your dinner. Live music nightly. *Ethiopian. Open daily noon-2am. Reservations accepted. 2463 18th St. NW (Columbia Rd. NW). 483-5000.*

79 Inter-American Defense Board. (1906, **George Oakley Totten, Jr.**) Also known as the *Pink Palace*. A Gothic version of the Ducal Palace in Venice (note the windows), but the massing is somewhat awkward. *2600 16th St. NW.*

79 Unification Church (Formerly Church of Latter-Day Saints). (1933, **Young & Hansen**) For years, this small chapel was the Washington base of the Church of Latter-Day Saints. Sixteen-thousand buff-colored stones were reportedly hauled from Utah for the building, which echoes the Gothic Revival verticality of the Tabernacle in Salt Lake City. The Mormons have moved to larger and more flamboyant quarters on the outskirts of town, and the building is now home to **Sun Myung Moon's** Unification Church. *16th St. at Harvard Square NW.*

79 Calvert Cafe. ☆ $ Proprietress **Mama Ayesha** holds court in this dark, cozy bastion of Middle Eastern cuisine. Try the *hummus, baba ghanouj* appetizers, followed by main courses of eggplant with ground lamb and pine nuts, lamb or chicken dishes. Round out your meal with honey *baklava* or pistachio-filled pastry. *Middle Eastern. Open daily 11:30am-11:30pm. No reservations. 1967 Calvert St. NW. 232-5431.*

80 All Souls Unitarian Church. (1924, **Coolidge & Shattuck**) **Sir Christopher Wren's** design for St. Martin-in-the-Fields (located on London's Trafalgar Square) has been much copied, but critics hail this as one of the best recreations. In the Unitarian tradition, the simple interior is devoid of all religious icons. *Open Tu-F 9am-10pm; Su till 3pm. Services Su 11am. 16th & Harvard Sts. NW. 332-5266.*

81 Lutheran Church Center. (1885, **H.H. Richardson**; reconstruction 1902, **George Oakley Totten, Jr.**) It was originally another house that stood in the 1500 block of K Street, but when it was demolished in the late 1800s, Totten (a pupil of Richardson's) bought the remaining pieces from the wrecker and recomposed them here into a home of his own. The smooth, light-colored sandstone is a departure from the ruggedness typical of Richardson's other work. *Open M-F by appointment 9am-4pm. 2633 16th St. NW. 829-6727.*

82 Meridian Hill Park. Mrs. **John B. Henderson's** ambitious plan for the Meridian Hill neighborhood is epitomized by these 12 acres. Once the center of an ambitious plan to promote the area; now an inner-city no-man's-land. Outsiders walk in this neighborhood at their own risk. *Open year 'round. 16th & Euclid Sts. NW.*

83 Washington International Center (Meridian House). (1915, **John Russell Pope**) Though Pope later gained fame for monumental Classic Revival designs, his considerable finesse is evident in this rich Louis XVI delight. *1630 Crescent Pl. NW.*

84 Temple of the Scottish Rite. (1910, **John Russell Pope**) One of Pope's earliest contributions to *Monumental Washington*, the temple was inspired by the *Tomb of Mausolus* at Halicarnassus in Greece, one of the 7 wonders of the ancient world. The proportions of the building are based on numbers significant to Masonic mysticism and reflect an eclectic array of styles from Egyptian to Roman. The 2 huge sphinxes that guard the entrance to the shrine, each cut from a solid block of limestone, were sculpted in 1915 by **Alexander Weinman**; there are some stunning interior spaces to be seen here as well. *16th and S Sts. NW.*

85 El Bodegón. ☆ ☆ $$ Flamenco dancers, flowing sangria, a garrulous staff and crowded, festive dining rooms make this a particularly lively place. Good, thick soups, excellent seafood paella, chicken with sausage, ham and sliced potatoes in brown sauce, and an abundance of beef dishes. *Spanish. Open M-F 11:30am-2:30pm, 5:30-11pm; Sa 5:30-11pm. Closed Su. Reservations suggested. 1637 R St. NW. 667-1710.*

86 Source Theatre. Three stages offer a variety of works, from classics like **Tennessee Williams'** *The Glass Menagerie*, to premieres of new plays. *1809 14th St. NW at S St. 462-1073.*

Introductions/Theaters/Narrative black
Hotels purple
Museums/Architecture blue
Parks/Open spaces green
Restaurants/Nightlife red
Shops/Galleries violet

DC Bests

Art Buchwald
Syndicated Columnist

My house in Washington. It has tripled in value since Reagan became president.

The **Smithsonian Air and Space Museum**

The John F. Kennedy Center

RFK Stadium—when the Redskins are winning

The **Corcoran Gallery**

The **Phillips Gallery**

The **War Room** in the White House

The **Four Seasons** and **Madison** hotels

The **C&O Canal**

Rock Creek Park on Sunday

The **Maison Blanche** restaurant

Dumbarton Oaks

---

87 **Florida Avenue Grill.** ☆ ☆ ☆ $ Down-home Southern cooking in an old-fashioned diner. Breakfasts include scrapple (a Philadelphia specialty), home fries, grits and biscuits. For lunch and dinner, try the pan-fried chicken, spareribs or ham hocks, all served with greens or cabbage, sweet potatoes, beans or rice. The homemade corn muffins can't be beat. *Southern. Open M-Sa 6am-9pm. Closed Su. No reservations. No credit cards. 1100 Florida Ave. NW. 265-1586.*

88 **Le Droit Park.** Also known as **Malcolm X Park,** this once all-white area is now home to prominent blacks and a mecca for black academicians and artists, many associated with Howard University. U, T and 3rd Streets are lined with their large Romantic Revival homes and row houses, many designed between 1870-1890 by **James H. McGill.** The area is listed in the National Register of Historic Places. *Rhode Island to Elm St., 2nd to Florida and Georgia Aves.*

89 **Joplin's.** ☆ ☆ $$ This is a versatile place, serving Continental, traditional American and Southern specialities. Seafood of all kinds is best: crab soup, gumbo, fried catfish, a seafood sampler of breaded shrimp, crab cake, scallops and fish. Sunday brunch features shrimp creole, fried chicken, eggs, bacon and more. *Continental/American/Southern. Open Tu-F 11:30am-3pm, 6:30pm-1am; Sa 6:30pm-1am; Su 11am-3pm. Closed M. Reservations suggested on weekends. 2225 Georgia Ave., NW (in the Howard Inn). 462-5400.*

90 **Howard University. General Oliver O. Howard,** head of the Freedmen's Bureau and an outspoken champion of civil rights, founded the University as an educational institution for freed slaves in 1867. The original lecture building, Howard's own home, still stands on 607 Howard Place. Although open to applicants of any race, the 12,000-member student body spread over 17 colleges is primarily black. A symbol of black pride and cultural achievement, Howard University maintains the world's largest record of black history within its domain: The **Founders Library** houses the **Moorland-Spingarn Research Center,** where the **Channing Pollock Collection** chronicles African tribes, American slavery and the historical development of the country's black citizenry. *Open M-F 9am-5pm. 636-7253.*

Renowned for its dedication to the arts program, the **Howard University Gallery,** at the College of Fine Arts, holds Italian Renaissance paintings from the Kress Collections and a permanent display of African art, as well as works by outstanding black American artists. Special exhibits change regularly. *Open M-F 9am-5pm. 636-7040.*

The **Blackburn University Center** features a continuing schedule of films and live performances, open to the public, often at no charge. Call *636-5983* for information. Private campus tours arranged by calling 2 weeks in advance. *2400 6th St. NW. 636-6100.*

91 **Old Soldiers' Home.** (1843-1852) The oldest military retirement facility in the country is a Norman fortress, complete with crenellated battlements. The house was reportedly built with ransom money which **General Winfield Scott** took from Mexico City. Some of the newer buildings rival the original structure in presence. *Across from St. Paul's, Webster & 3rd Sts. NW.*

92 **Rock Creek Cemetery.** The city's oldest cemetery is filled with historic graves, including the **Adams Monument.** In 1890, **Augustus Saint-Gaudens** sculpted this haunting memorial to **Mrs. Henry Adams,** wife of the noted author. A large cloaked figure stares downward, the face lost in shadow. The setting was designed by **Stanford White.** It is a moving statue; many feel its nickname, *Grief,* is apt. *Off North Capitol St.*

92 **St. Paul's Episcopal Church.** (1775) The District's first church was built on this spot in 1775—the congregation had originally convened in 1712! Only the brick walls remain, due to a 1921 fire; now reconstructed, its Federal splendor includes several excellent stained-glass windows. *Services Su 8am, 9:30am, 11am (8am & 10am during summer). In Rock Creek Cemetery, Rock Creek Church & Webster Rds. NW. 726-2080.*

93 **Carter Barron Amphitheater.** Operated by the National Park Service, this open amphitheater seats 4,500, and features a 7-week summer festival with pop, rock and jazz music. *16th St. and Colorado Ave. NW in Rock Creek Park. 829-3202.*

The Washington Post, often considered one of the nation's most influential newspapers, was started in 1877 and immediately began to founder. In 1933 **Eugene Meyer,** a Wall Street tycoon and former governor of the Federal Reserve Board, bought the paper at a bankruptcy auction. Suddenly the Post began gaining recognition, first under Meyer and later under his son-in-law, **Philip Graham,** who, critics say, used the paper as his personal soap box. However, the Post really became a national force under the leadership of editor **Ben Bradlee** and publisher-owner **Katherine Graham,** Meyer's daughter, who took over after the death of her husband, Philip.

The Post is in large measure responsible for a renaissance in American journalism that started with the publication of the *Pentagon Papers* (discussing a secret study of US involvement in Vietnam) in 1971 and reached its apogee with the relentless investigative reporting of **Watergate** and its aftermath.

Actually, the New York Times beat the Post to the Pentagon Papers, but was stopped by a temporary restraining order instigated by the Nixon administration. The Post then got hold of the documents and printed excerpts before it too was restrained. An appeals court eventually decided that the press could reprint the documents.

Since the mid-70s, the Post has experienced a seesaw of triumph and defeat. In 1975 a pressman's strike over modernization erupted into violence. There have been libel suits and accusations of shoddy reporting; Post writer **Janet Cooke** won and then returned a Pulitzer Prize for a series of articles on a child heroin addict. The subject, it turned out, was a fictional composite, not a real person.

Yet the Post's reporting of Watergate has helped make journalism romantic again. In 1974—even before **Robert Redford** and **Dustin Hoffman** played reporters in the movie All the President's Men—there was a 15 percent jump in journalism school enrollment over the previous year.

5   NORTHEAST

Northeast Washington *is truly* vernacular *in Washington, a phrase sometimes used to distinguish the residential,* everyday *city from its better-known,* monumental *counterpart.*

In fact the whole eastern half of the area is *vernacular* in this same way, supporting the often-heard thesis that those who can tend to gravitate to a city's northwest. A number of exotic theses have been offered to account for this, including wind patterns, but none of them seem to explain it.

Both Northeast and Southeast Washington, as well as their adjoining suburbs, share in common a mix of middle and lower-middle class residents, as well as the poor. Today this population is predominantly black, but when the neighborhoods were new and settled by whites, they attracted the same economic groups. A number of areas in Northeast, such as **Trinidad**, were settled by the city's assimilating Italian and Greek populations, many of them policemen and firemen. **Riggs Park**, a Northeast neighborhood built after World War II, was originally settled by part of the area's large Jewish middle class.

Probably the best-known institution in Northeast is **Gallaudet College**, which has been pioneering instruction for the deaf since 1857. It sits on **Kendall Green**, land deeded to it by a member of Andrew Jackson's famous *kitchen cabinet.* Some of its innovations have been adopted by those with full hearing. For example, when its football team gathered to plan the next play, they naturally adopted the most efficient stance for the circumstances of signing. It seemed like such a good idea to everybody else, that it became an intrinsic part of the game. It is, of course, the *huddle.*

Generally speaking, this is not tourist country. Among its treasures, however, are **Kenilworth Aquatic Gardens**, and the **National Arboretum**. Set aside originally by the Department of Agriculture as a place to study whatever plant life would grow in the capital area, The Arboretum has developed into a delightfully serene place of escape from the city. A huge variety of trees and flowers are nurtured there, including a well-known display of rare **Bonsai trees**. However, the place is probably best known for its extraordinary profusion of azaleas, which in season draw the Arboretum's largest crowds. Administrators of the Arboretum are taking some pains to make visitors ever more welcome, and have moved their entrance from a previously impossible-to-find location to the well-travelled **New York Ave**.

There are also a number of major **Catholic** institutions in the Northeast, including **Catholic University**, where **Walter Kerr** taught drama for many years, the **Shrine of the Immaculate Conception**, built by an appeal to Catholic women nationwide, **Trinity College**, and the **Franciscan Monastery**, all of which are easily reached by the city's subway.

In 1611, **Lord De-La-Ware** stated the following: *"This is a goodly River called Patomack, upon the borders whereof there are growne the goodliest Trees for Masts, that may be found elsewhere in the World: Hempe better then English, growing wilde an aboundance: Mines of Antimonie and Leade."*

The names of the 18 settlers who were the original proprietors of Washington, DC, are carved into a small granite shaft in the President's Park south of the White House. The 4 panels next to the names symbolize corn, tobacco, wild turkey and herring—the settlers' only means of livelihood at the time.

1 **Chapel of Notre Dame, Trinity College**.
Byzantine chapel with 67-foot dome contains
Bancel Le Fargis mosaic of *Christ & Mary* in a
scene from Dante's *Divine Comedy. Michigan
Ave. & Franklin St. NE.*

2 **National Shrine of the Immaculate Conception**.
(1914-1939) The key word here is huge: At least
459 feet long, 157 feet wide and 329 feet high,
with a capacity to hold over 6,000 people. This
Catholic church stands as a magnificent
testimony to the faith of Marianism and its saint,
the Virgin Mary. Construction started in 1914,
when the Rector of Washington's Catholic
University obtained papal sanction for a new
monument dedicated to the *Heavenly Patroness
of the US* (as determined by **Pope Pius IX** in
1847). The final 1959 completion of the world's
seventh largest church—and the largest Catholic
church in the Western Hemisphere—showed a
contemporary massive cruciform structure
incorporating both Byzantine and Romanesque
elements. Thirty-two chapels in the upper church
contain bright mosaic altars, devoted to Marian
interpretations from all over the world. Light
streams through 200 windows of stained glass,
hitting an immense mosaic shrine whose
construction demanded the depletion of an entire
Italian quarry. Although the shrine's crypt gallery
holds a contemporary relic, **Pope Paul VI's**
crowning tiara, the ultimate masterpiece must be
Millard Sheet's colossal mosaic *Triumph Of The
Lamb,* affixed to the sanctuary dome.

Since every parish in the US contributed to the
building fund, the shrine now belongs to every
American Catholic. With this in mind, the church
administration actively encourages sacred
pilgrimages, and sacraments are celebrated daily
for pilgrims who come to the shrine. *30-minute
tours are given M-Sa 9-11am and 1-4pm, Su
1:30-4pm. Open daily 7am-5pm; mass hours vary;
call for information. Michigan Avenue at 4th St.
NE. 526-8300.*

3 **Catholic University**. The nearly 100-year-old
coeducational institution manifests a paradoxical
union of past and future. For instance, while
some students are studying the schools' highly
respected traditional ecclesiastical curriculum,
others are studying the science of storm control
in the school's high-tech Atmosphere and
Aerospace laboratories. Catholic University is
also renowned for the Hartke Theatre, which
presents period comedies and tragedies, often
with a definite religious theme. This is the only
university that belongs to the US hierarchy of the
Roman Catholic Church; founded in 1887 by
Maryland Cardinal James Gibbons, it retains an
eternal link with Deity in its schools of canon
law, sacred theology and diaconal services.
*Guided tours by appointment 3 weeks in
advance. Hartke Theatre's box office open M-F
10am-6pm. Call 529-3333 for ticket availability.
620 Michigan Ave. NE. 635-5000.*

4 **Colonel Brooks Tavern.** ☆ $ It's not easy to find
a restaurant in the Brookland area, so this
casual, reliable place is something of an oasis in
the desert. Burgers, good potatoes, egg dishes,
desserts. *American. Open daily 11:30am-2am. No
reservations. 901 Monroe St. NE. 529-4002.*

5 **Franciscan Monastery**. Officially the
*Commissariat of the Holy Land for the United
States,* this monastery provides a fascinating
insight to life behind holy walls. Its main function,
to preserve and maintain shrines in the Holy
Land through fundraising, has been possible due
to the enterprising minds of the *Order of the
Friars Minor,* the resident acolytes and keepers
of the beautiful grounds. A 45-minute tour of the
rose garden and the monastery's central part, an
early Italian Renaissance-church completed in
1899, includes faithful replicas of several Holy
Land shrines. Even a small, authentic
reproduction of a Roman catacomb has been
dug underneath the church, to demonstrate the
plight of early Christian worship. *1400 Quincy St.
NE. 526-6800.*

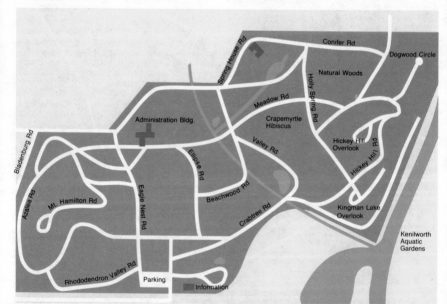

6 **National Arboretum**. It is easy to lose yourself
among the color splashes in this 440-acre
garden, where over 70,000 azaleas,
rhododendrons, wildflowers and ornamental
cherries bloom *en masse*. The National
Arboretum, established by Congress in 1927,
exists primarily to conduct research on trees and
shrubs, but locals claim it to be one of the most
memorable attractions of the capital. A variety of
rare plants and trees such as the *Siberian larch*
and the *Manchurian lilac* can be seen along the
9 footpaths leading through the principal plant
groups. The now nearly extinct *Franklin Tree,*
discovered in 1765 by a botanist friend of **Ben
Franklin,** is planted right on the Fern Valley trail.
A Russian statesman's connection to the
Arboretum is the *European little leaf linden,* given
to the people of the United States by former
Premier **Nikita Krushchev** in 1960.

Perhaps the most prestigious collection, valued
at $4.5 million, is the **National Bonsai
Collection,** given to the US as a 1976
Bicentennial gift from the people of Japan.
Housed in a specially constructed garden
pavilion adjacent to the Administration building,
the 53 trees of 34 species range from 30 to 350
years of age. The once-normal plants, artfully
trained to stunted growth in shallow pots, stand
no more than 1 or 2 feet in height. An elaborate
alarm system now protects the collection—after a
local student once pilfered a tree to decorate his
apartment. The plant was immediately returned
when the thief found the bonsai's value to be
$75,000! Another indoor boon to the vast
grounds is the **Herbarium,** filled with over
500,000 dried plants to maintain a technical
reference system.

There is a multi-purpose pavilion located at the lower end of the park, offering environmental educational programs, community exhibits and rollerskating. Dinghy boat rentals and larger outboarders are available from the yacht clubs dotting the river. *Open all year during daylight hours. Pennsylvania Ave. SE, East Capitol St. and Benning Road Bridge. 426-6706.*

Early summertime is the peak season for the arboretum, when daily crowds of 20,000 visitors view the blooming azaleas, flowering dogwood and crab apples. During winter, the 1,500 dwarf and slow-growing conifers assembled on a 5-acre hill dominate the scene, together with hollies; early spring is the time for jasmine and camelia blossoms. The arboretum continuously presents special demonstrations, films and flower shows. Group tours for 10 or more are arranged by calling 3 weeks in advance.

Admission free. Open 8am-5pm weekdays, 10am-5pm weekends and holidays. Closed Christmas. 24th & R Sts. NE. 472-9279.

7 Anacostia Park. Extending 8 miles along the Anacostia river, the 1,355-acre area qualifies more as a natural reserve than a conventional park, with mostly fertile marshland and small, sunny glades hidden in the forests. The northeastern part holds Kenilworth Aquatic Gardens; another area is designed as a bird sanctuary, where songbirds and wading birds like green heron and great blue heron inhabit the woods. During migrating season, a large number of ducks and geese also congregate in the park. You can walk almost anywhere, except to the upper reaches of the river, which are inaccessible due to their natural, wild state.

8 Gallaudet College. (1866, **Calvert Vaux & Frederick Law Olmsted**) **Edward Miner Gallaudet**, youngest son of deaf school patriarch **Thomas Hopkins Gallaudet**, helped create the beautiful Gothic-style college to serve as a higher learning institution for the deaf. Today, it is the world's only accredited liberal arts college, providing education for 1,500 hearing impaired students. The formal stone buildings epitomize the Victorian Gothic style; the campus grounds reflect Olmsted's master touch. *Tours of the campus are arranged in advance by appointment. Florida Ave. & 7th St. NW. 651-5100 or TDD 651-5104.*

9 Union Market, also known as the *Florida Ave. Farmer's Market,* is open year 'round and includes several warehouse-like wholesale centers that carry freshly butchered meats, fish, fresh produce, fruits and eggs. Emphasis on ethnic foods, such as the Italian products at **A. Litteri Inc.** where pastas, cheeses and sausages are sold by the pound. *Open M-F 8am-5:30pm, Sa 8am-3pm. 6th St. and Florida Ave. NE across from Gallaudet College.*

10 Trailways Bus Center. A new metal-and-glass terminal hidden north of Union Station in a quiet industrial neighborhood. *1st and L Sts. NE.*

DC Bests

Diana McLellan
Syndicated Columnist

Saturday shopping at the Eastern Market You go to Capitol Hill's bustling indoor-and-outdoor farmer's market to buy the freshest fish, poultry, sausage, eggs and vegetables. The greasy-spoon **Market Lunch** makes the finest crab-cakes, squash-rings and fresh lemonade in the East. Stand in line, then take them outside and gobble them at a picnic table on the sidewalk outside the huge, homely red brick building. It was was designed in the 1880s by **Adolph Cluss,** once **Karl Marx's** agent in Washington.

Seeing in the New Year at the Hay-Adams Hotel. Six big Georgian windows along that skinny ballroom look smack out at the White House across the street, brilliantly illuminated and decorated for Christmas. **Peter Duchin** plays. There are feathered headdresses, favors, a grand noise. Nearby is the **John Hay Room—** coziest year-round spot in the city for cocktails. It feels exactly like the hall of a great but cozy English or Irish country house. It costs.

Whistler's *Peacock Room,* **on show at the Freer Gallery.** Don't O.D. It makes you want to race right home and paint peacocks all over the rec room.

Wandering in the garden at Dumbarton Oaks in spring. A place to propose marriage. It was even better when, as students in the '50s, we used to sneak in at 3 a.m. to swim in the pool by moonlight. Nowadays, you can take your picnic next door to Montrose Park.

The Kennedy Center on a sunny day. Nothing is more beautiful than sitting at an outdoor cafe in the middle of all that white marble gazing down the tree-lined Potomac, drinking cold beer.

Swimming at the Washington Hilton's Racquet Club. It's mid-city, outdoors, and just a few yards from the spot where **John Hinckley** shot **Ronald Reagan.** But the **Gazebo** there serves something divine called *Maria's Health Salad* and ridiculous fruit-and-rum drinks; the pool, next to the tennis courts, is beautiful; and the fact that hotel guests may use it gives members - who include lots of shrinks, lawyers, lobbyists and journalists - plenty to grumble about in the shower.

The Hirshhorn Gallery and Sculpture Garden. The art was chosen, not because of artists' names, but because **Joe Hirshhorn** like it. The little guy had a great eye. Set aside a day.

Copenhaver's. This Washington stationer engraves everything perfectly for Ambassadors and Cabinet officers, and has since 1896. Your engraved calling cards or stationery are exactly *comme il faut.* Don't be frightened. The folks who run it have steered our very finest rubes along the path to Correctness.

Going to any play at the Folger Shakespeare Library's Theater. It's a precise copy of the *Globe Theater* in **Elizabeth I's** London. The productions are often stunning, the atmosphere magical. The *Folger Consort* sings madrigals here and plunges you into 14th century, where you wouldn't want to live, but it's nice to visit.

Eating Flounder Almondine for lunch at Pendleton's. It is perfect. I could eat it every day. Once, for two weeks, I did.

A 3-hour dinner at the Marrakesh Restaurant. It's in a horrible neighborhood, next to the Midas Muffler Shop. Inside, it's Ali Baba's cave—a wonderful place to go with friends and finger-eat your food. You are treated as a guest in an upper-crust Moroccan house. Nobody mentions prices. But relax, they're tiny.

Lunch at Le Pavillon. World-class nouvelle food, so beautiful it makes you want to weep. Let Janet decide what you eat. Let somebody else pay the bill.

The Iron Gate Inn. Romantic outside, in dappled sunlight beneath the grape arbor, or inside, by firelight. Middle-Eastern food.

Reeves Bakery. My mother took me here while shopping in downtown Washington; I took my daughter; she'll take her daughter. Reeves makes the best fresh strawberry pie in Washington, and the white-meat chicken sandwich on white bread, with home-made mayo and tiny sweet pickles, is dream about. It burned down in '83, but has been completely reconstructed.

(Diana McLellan writes *The Ear'* syndicated gossip column, and *'Diana Hears'* for The *Washington Times.* She has lived in Washington since the '50s, and in Capitol Hill since the '60s.)

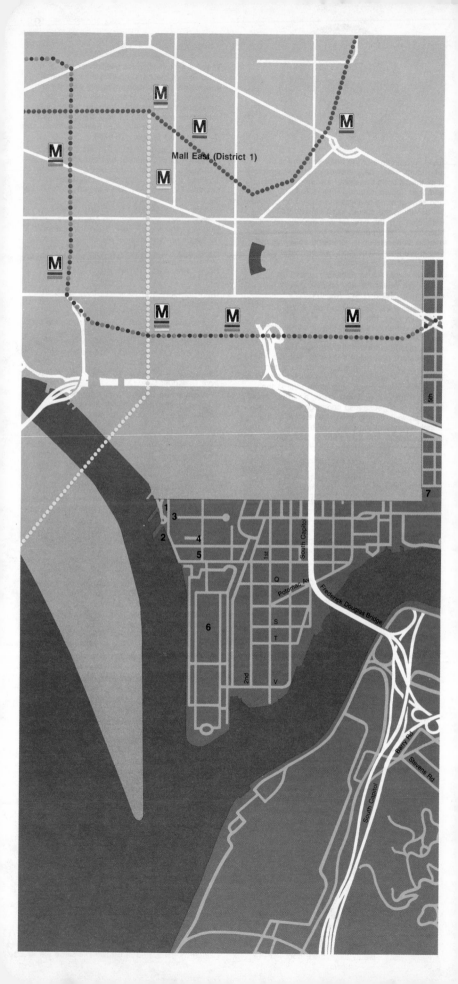

Mall East (District 1)

5th

7

1
3
2
4
5

1st

South Capitol

Q

Potomac Av

Frederick Douglas Bridge

S

T

2nd

V

6

Barry Rd

Stevens Rd

South Capitol

Northeast (District 5)

East Capitol

21

22

A

Kentucky Av

Independence Av

M

North Carolina Av

7th

19
18
17 16   8th   9th   10th   11th

M

15 14

South Carolina Av

Massachusetts Av

18th

C

D

20

12th   13th   14th   15th   16th   17th   E

23

19th

Pennsylvania Av

5th 6th   11

12   13

G

20th
21st

10

9   8

I

Ives Pl

Southeast Fwy

K

K

L

M

John Philip Sousa Bridge

7

Water

Nicholson

Anacostia Bridge

Naylor

Q   Fairlawn Av
18th   19th   23rd

Anacostia Fwy

Minnesota Av   22nd   25th

Anacostia Dr

Ridge Pl

R

Ridge Pl

S

23rd

Good Hope Rd

T

17th   18th

U

22nd

Good Hope Rd

V 13th   14th   15th   16th   Fendall

W

Pleasant

24

Shannon Ave

25

Fairfax

Howard Rd

Morris

High

Barry Rd

Suitland Parkway

Bangor

Sumner Rd

Bryan Pl   Pitts Pl

Stevens Rd

Wade Rd

Martin Luther King Av

Howard Rd

Anger Pl

Pomeroy Rd

Stanton Rd

Bruce Pl

Elvans Rd

Suitland Pkwy

M Indicates Metrorail Stops

Southeast Washington *is one of the least known, least-appreciated of the city's quadrants.*

The **Anacostia** section, across the Anacostia River, is in some respects an independent community—self contained, proud and even a little disdainful of the presumptuous residents of Washington's Northwest. In **Good Hope Road** and **Martin Luther King Avenue** it has its own **Main Streets.** In **Fort Stanton Park** and the banks of the Anacostia, it has its own serene relief from Washington's heat. In **Uniontown**, a community settled in the wake of the Civil War by freedmen, it has its own museum, the **Anacostia Neighborhood Museum.**

Southeast's population has changed a number of times in history. Right now, large areas west of the Anacostia River have been gentrified, while most of the quadrant across the river is, like the Northeast, a combination of middle-class, lower-middle, and poor, and overwhelmingly black. As it happens, the area contains, by chance and otherwise, numerous connections with the history of the black community, both local and national.

Fiery abolitionist leader **Frederick Douglass,** a former slave who came to be known as *the Sage of Anacostia,* remains the area's most honored hero. His then-suburban home across the Anacostia River, **Cedar Hill,** has been restored by the National Park Service and is open to the public. One of the bridges across the Anacostia is named in Douglass' honor.

Even near the Capitol, Southeast shows signs of an otherwise long-vanished Washington. The city, for example, once featured 3 major markets. The Central Market, the largest, is long gone, as is the Western Market. But **Eastern Market**, which has served that part of the city for generations, continues to do so.

Many well-known persons used this market over the years, including **John Philip Sousa,** one of Southeast's native sons (he even wrote a novel about the area). And many of its customers were—and doubtless are—employees of the **Navy Yard,** now primarily a museum. Ships and munitions are no longer made here, but the Navy Yard, together with the printing industry, was once one of the city's most important economic supports, and its vicinity one of the city's earliest neighborhoods.

What many area residents know best about Southeast is of course **RFK Stadium,** home of the **Washington Redskins,** who have not played before an unsold seat in over a decade. The football team, perhaps more than anything, is the one thing that binds Washington's unusually disparate population together.

Close to the stadium is the all-but-forgotten **Congressional Cemetery,** established by Congress in the days of slower transportation so that Congressmen and others who died in the city might have a decent resting place.

1 **The Gangplank.** ☆ $$ Just what you'd expect from a vast floating restaurant: a wonderful view, an ambitious menu of mostly satisfying seafood dishes, and an enthusiastic, efficient staff. *Seafood. Open M-Th 11:30am-10pm. F & Sa till 11pm; Su 11am-10pm. Reservations recommended. 600 Water St. SW. 554-5000.*

While a congressman, **John Lindsay** said, *"New York has total depth in every area. Washington has only politics; after that, the second biggest thing is marble."*

Introductions/Theaters/Narrative black
Hotels purple
Museums/Architecture blue
Parks/Open spaces green
Restaurants/Nightlife red
Shops/Galleries violet

WASHINGTON
BOAT LINES

2 **Washington Boat Lines.** As rivers go, the Potomac is not an extensively traveled one, but it is still possible to sightsee its quaint shoreline by taking a summertime cruise. The **First Lady,** a fancy replica of a big Mississippi riverboat, alternates with the **Diplomat** or the 150-passenger **Ambassador** on a 5-hour trip to Mount Vernon. Cruising past historic Alexandria and Fort Washington, the boat docks within walking distance of **George and Martha Washington's** beloved plantation. Ample time is offered to explore Mount Vernon's beautiful grounds and the house where the original First Couple spent many summers. The Diplomat and its smaller cousin Ambassador also make shorter trips on the river. The **Alexandria Connection** makes an afternoon stop in that old cobblestone city where George himself visited many of the now 200-year-old taverns and inns. Adult dance cruises on the 2 boats feature full bar and a live band under the stars, see the Lincoln Memorial and Georgetown from the river during the *Luncheon Buffet* cruise. Other trips include the First Lady's *Sunday/Holiday Brunch* cruise to Alexandria, and the *Spirit Of 76* pre-packaged, design-your-own tour: a Dutch-style canal boat available at $400/hour for up to 40 passengers. All boats depart from *Pier 4 at 6th and Water Sts., just off Maine Ave. next to the Gangplank restaurant. Departure times and ticket rates obtained by calling 554-8000.*

3 **Thomas Law House.** (1796, **William Lovering**) A classic 3-story Federal-style house, now used as a community center. *1252 6th St. SW.*

4 **Wheat Row.** (1790) Located in the shadow of the successful Harbor Square urban renewal project, Wheat Row is considered one of the best examples of the Federal style in the District. It was completely restored in 1966. *1313-1321 4th St. SW.*

5 **Titanic Memorial.** Sculpted in 1931 by **Gertrude Vanderbilt Whitney** in memory of the men who gave up their places in the lifeboats when the historic ocean liner sank. A granite figure stands with arms outstretched in the shape of a cross. The sculptor's own brother went down in 1915 when the *Lusitania* was sunk by the Kaiser's German Navy. *Washington Channel Park, 4th and P Sts. SW.*

6 **Fort Lesley J. McNair.** Over the years, the names and functions of this strategic military post have changed. In 1791, it was planned by L'Enfant as the main fortification point of the capital. As the **Washington Arsenal,** the fort was a major distribution center for government cannons and hand weapons in the early 1800s. Immediately after the 1814 *Battle of Bladensburg,* the British invaded the fort, only to lose 40 of their own men when a supply of gun powder accidentally exploded. Discouraged, the British left the ruined fort. The arsenal continued to store and also produce weapons; by the time of the Civil War, the fort contained more than 800 cannons, 50,000 rifles and hundreds of gun carriages. One more explosion was needed before the government deemed the arsenal unsafe: in 1864, an ignited rocket in a row of fireworks killed and maimed over 100 women who were making rifle cartridges in the

Marine Corps button design, circa 1804.

laboratory. The fort served as a warehouse and a small hospital until the **Army War College** (1908, **McKim, Mead & White**) was built on the mile-long peninsula. Later fused with the **Industrial College of the Armed Forces,** the college is still housed in its original, disciplined Beaux-Arts structure, under the name of **National Defense University.** The Inter-American Defense College and the headquarters of the US Army Military District of Washington are right next door; the Romanesque barracks and more sumptuous officers' quarters add a graceful note to the military primness. Although the buildings are not open to the public, a few outside cannons and the old soldiers' quarters have been preserved, making the beautiful grounds well worth a visit. *Open 7:30am-4pm. 4th & P Sts. SW.*

NAVY MEMORIAL MUSEUM ☆ ☆ ☆ ☆ ☆ ☆ WASHINGTON NAVY YARD

John Roach

Washington Navy Yard. (1800) Kids of all ages play and learn at the same time in this Historical Precinct, which served as the **Naval Gun Factory** during the entire 19th-century. The original planning and design was by the prolific **Benjamin Latrobe;** although various refurbishings have eroded his influence, the main gates (1804) still show his mark. It is speculated that he also designed the **Commandant's House.** Splendid officers' mansions once lined the waterfront here; now the functional factory and warehouse buildings draw tourists.

The **Navy Memorial Museum** gives a 200-year historical rundown of naval weapons, famous ships and entire battle scenes. The various exhibits have been designed for the young and energetic: gun turrets move, periscopes rise and the ships are open to the attacks of boisterous, young admirals. The authentic submarine room is not for the claustrophobic, who will prefer looking at large dioramas where heroes damn the torpedoes and go full speed ahead. Techniks will appreciate the inertial guidance systems, and the World War II uniforms by naval couturier **Captain Guy Molyneux** will delight the fashion conscious.

Those who hold the military in more solemn esteem can visit the **Marine Corps Museum** in the adjacent building. Here, honor is first and action second: flags and trophies are arranged in a proud, chronological display mixed with personal relics of famous mariners. Both museums put on parades and musical entertainment on Wednesday and Friday evenings from June through August. Call for reservations at least 3 weeks in advance.

Admission free. Navy Museum open M-F 9am-4pm, Sa-Su 10am-5pm. Marine Corps Museum open M-Sa 10am-4pm. 9th & M Sts. SE. Navy Museum 433-4882, Marine Corps Museum 433-3534.

Long before man took possession of Washington, the area was inhabited by much larger beasts—the colossal **dinosaurs**. In the 1920s, footprints and tail draggings older than 200 million years were discovered at Oak Hill, a private residence designed by **James Hoban** and **Thomas Jefferson** for their mutual friend **James Monroe**.

8 Marine Corps Barracks. America's first Marine post is still home to the *Eighth and Eye* Marines. The **Commandant's House** (1805), with its Classic overtones and crisp bay windows, is the only original building still standing on the grounds. *8th & I Sts. SE.*

9 La Casita of Capitol Hill. ☆ ☆ $ Mouthwatering Tex-Mex specials that come close to the real thing. Fuel-injected salsa is matched by crisp tacos or barbequed beef, then washed down with Mexican beer for the complete ranchero effect. *Mexican. Open daily 11am-3pm, 5-10pm. 723 8th St. SE. 543-9022.*

10 Broker. ☆ ☆ ☆ $$ This spacious, quiet dining room of blond wood and brick is renowned for its Sunday brunches, cheese and chocolate fondues, homemade bread and croissants and uniformly excellent Swiss and Continental cuisine. *Swiss-Continental. Open M-F 11:30am-2:30pm, 5-11pm; Sa 5-11pm; Su 11am-3pm, 5-11pm. Reservations suggested. Coat and tie recommended. 713 8th St. SE (G St. SE). 546-8300.*

11 Christ Church. (1806, **Benjamin Latrobe**) Quite likely the oldest church building in DC, and one of the first Gothic Revival designs in the country (though the design has been significantly altered). Many of Washington's important and famous have been members of the Episcopalian congregation. *620 G St. SE.*

12 Trattoria Alberto. ☆ ☆ $$ An honest-to-goodness trattoria, multi-leveled, friendly and slightly kitschy. Good, cheap wine; abundant portions of homemade pastas; tender and diverse veal dishes. *Italian. M-Th 11:30am-10:30pm, F till 11pm; Sa 5:30-11pm; Su 5-10:30pm. Reservations suggested. 506 8th St. SE (E St. SE). 544-2007.*

13 Knickerbocker Grill. $ All-you-can-eat dinner specials, plus a Sunday brunch of cold fish, omelets, salads, blintzes and other goodies. *American. Open M-Th 11am-11pm, F till midnight; Sa noon-midnight; Su 11am-9pm. 539 8th St. SE. 546-7766.*

14 Friendship Settlement (The Maples). (1975, **William Lovering**) Despite the fact that it has served many uses—from residence to hospital— its Federal-era character and integrity remain; past refurbishing efforts have been executed with taste and care. *619 D St. SE.*

15 Eastern Market. The most fashionable of the farmers' markets because of its proximity to Capitol Hill. This is a longtime Washington institution for out-of-the-crate veggies, fruits, meats, poultry (from chicken to pheasant), fish, spices, farm eggs, cider and homemade breads and cakes. *Open Tu-Sa 6:30am-6pm. 7th St. SE one block below Pennsylvania Ave. 534-2444.*

16 Machiavelli's. ☆ $ A fun place. The pizza's good, the jukebox plays Nat King Cole, Sinatra and classic rock and roll, and the decor really is art deco-ish. *Italian. Open daily 11:30am-11pm. 613 Pennsylvania Ave. SE. 543-1930.*

17 Capitol Hill Wine and Cheese. An excellent carry-out without the gourmet shop appeal. This shop combines its sandwich counter with an assortment of coffees, teas, and shelves of reliable domestic wines. The sandwiches are customized—smoked turkey, pate, rare roast beef and an awesome selection of cheeses are the raw materials for these towering works of edible art. *Open M-Sa 10am-7pm, Su noon-5pm. 611 Pennsylvania Ave. SE. 546-4600.*

18 Tunnicliff's Tavern. ☆ $ Scenes of the old Eastern Market are etched on the glass dividers that decorate this charming place. On alternate nights, Tunnicliff's features an oyster bar, mesquite-grilled meats and poultry, omelet specialties, and other treats. Outdoor dining out front in warmer weather. *American. Open M-Th 11:30am-10:30pm, F till 11pm, Sa-Su 8am-11pm. Reservations recommended. 222 7th St. SE (C St. SE). 546-3663.*

19 Provisions. Primarily a coffee-tea-specialty food shop. Customers can order thick sandwiches of turkey breast, imported cheese, curried tuna salad and other ingredients, or steaming cups of cappucino for take-out or to be consumed in a quaint dining niche. *Open M-F 7:30am-8pm, Sa till 6pm, Su 9am-4pm. 218 7th St. SE. 543-0694.*

20 Taverna the Greek Islands. ☆ $ Try the *moussaka*, lamb pie, stuffed grape leaves, kebabs and other specialties, as well as one of several varieties of Greek wine. *Greek. Open M-Sa 11am-11:30pm, Su 4-11pm. Reservations accepted for dinner. 307 Pennsylvania Ave. SE. 547-8360.*

20 Duddington's. $ A favorite with the preppy set. Stop here for a quick beer-burger-pizza. *American. Open daily 11:30am-2am. Reservations accepted. 319 Pennsylvania Ave. SE. 544-3500.*

20 Tune Inn. $ A Capitol Hill landmark. In addition to beers galore, this narrow storefront with the long counter serves crispy fried chicken, burgers and breakfasts at rock bottom prices. *Bar & grill. Open daily 8am-2am. No reservations. 331½ Pennsylvania Ave. SE. 543-2725.*

21 Lincoln Park. Two of the city's finest and most moving sculptures grace this compact city park. The **Emancipation Monument** shows a life-size **Abraham Lincoln** holding the **Emancipation Proclamation**. At Lincoln's feet a slave is just beginning to rise, his chains finally broken. Sculpted in 1876 by **Thomas Ball**, the man's face was modeled after a photo of **Archer Alexander**, the last person to be taken under the *Fugitive Slave Act*. All funds for the monument were donated by former slaves.

One of the city's happiest monuments is the sculpture of black educator/activist **Mary McLeod Bethune**. The former advisor to **Franklin Delano Roosevelt** is seen passing her legacy to 2 children; it reads in part *"I leave you a thirst for education. I leave you a respect for the use of power. I leave you faith. I leave you racial dignity. I leave you a desire to live harmoniously with your fellow man." East Capital St. NE, 11th-12th Sts. NE.*

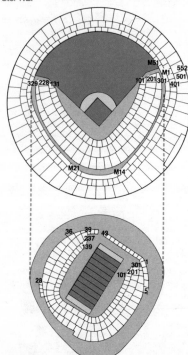

22 Starplex-RFK Stadium/DC Armory Hall. Two impressive plants, the **Robert F. Kennedy Stadium** (1962, **David Volkert & Associates**) and the historic **DC Armory Hall** (1947), comprise this huge concert, trade show and sports complex. The 5-tiered circular amphitheatre, home to the **Washington Redskins** and the **Diplomats**, provides 55,000 seats to sports fans who come to watch football or soccer played on 3½ acres of natural grass.

Rock concerts or religious convocations also attract sellout crowds to the arena. During the events, 35 concession stands operate at full speed, serving delicatessen and ethnic specialties in addition to regular fast food. Intermissions rapidly fill the **Sports Lounge** with fans, who watch action replays on several monitors and a 7-foot video screen. Added to these diversions is the Starplex **Hall of Stars**—heroes immortalized in paintings and photographs that line the walls of the Lounge.

Next to the Stadium is the Armory Hall, a huge domed structure with 2 levels totaling over 133,000 square feet. The column-free main hall hosts everything from *Holiday on Ice* to political conventions; Starplex technicians transform the hall into such different settings as ice rinks, circus arenas, boat shows and ballrooms. *Box office open 10am-6pm. 543-5667. Event information office open 9am-5:30pm. 2001 E. Capitol St. SE. 547-9077.*

23 Congressional Cemetery. *"Being interred beneath these grounds adds a new terror to death."* These words were once spoken by a US Senator to reflect the dull solemnity of the Congressional Cemetery, reserved for senators, diplomats and prominent members of Congress. The process of filling 100 burial reservations started in 1807; 70 years later, Capitol Hill architects **William Thornton** and **Robert Mills**, one Choctaw Chief and finally **John Philip Sousa** were the last ones to find their place under **Benjamin Latrobe's** stern pre-designed gravestones. Information and memorial maps given by the gatekeeper. *Open daily during daylight hours. 18th and E Sts. SE.*

24 Frederick Douglass Home (Cedar Hill). The simple white Victorian home, completed in 1854, was the abolitionist and statesman Frederick Douglass' residence from 1877 to his death in 1895. Douglass, who was born a slave on a Maryland plantation in 1817, escaped at the age of 21, to finally become an advisor to 4 presidents and an eloquent spokesman for the anti-slavery movement. His home, much restored to its original era, holds furniture and several gifts from his contemporaries, including **Harriet Beecher Stowe, Abraham Lincoln** and **William Lloyd Garrison**. One of the most unique features of Cedar Hill is the self-taught philosopher's personal library, containing over 1,200 volumes.

Cedar Hill rests on a hilltop; its large, airy porch, punctuated by Doric columns, offers breathtaking vistas of the Capitol and its downtown vicinity. The **Visitor Center** is located at the bottom of the grounds, in order to maintain the unobstructed view from the home.

An accurate and moving picture of Douglass' work is recaptured in a short film presentation, held at the Visitor Center, which also contains **Ed Dwight's** life-size statue of Douglass. Period-costumed guides conduct tours on request. Group tours can be arranged by calling the home. Limited parking provided. *Open daily 9am-4pm, Apr-Sept 9am-5pm. 1411 W St. SE. 426-5961.*

Radio Smithsonian, the Institution's half-hour weekly magazine show, is heard on 60 public broadcast (PBS) stations in 27 states.

25 Anacostia Neighborhood Museum. Housed in the former **Carver Theatre** of Anacostia, this local museum was founded in 1968 as a branch of the Smithsonian Institution. The government-funded exhibit center functions as a comprehensive arts and crafts facility for the predominantly black community of Anacostia, providing an excellent opportunity to view black history from a non-traditional perspective. Exhibits which change monthly, have included photographs of Harlem, black women achievers, and the history of Anacostia itself. Each exhibit attempts to include a spectrum of the various media in arts; borrowed artifacts from around the globe blend with special films, hands-on demonstrations of collage-making, silk screening and painting with watercolors. Half-hour self guided tours. Audio-visual and group tours for 10 or more are arranged by calling 48 hours in advance. *Open M-F 10am-6pm, Sa-Su 1-6pm. 2405 Martin Luther King, Jr. Ave. SE. 287-3369.*

SPORTS

When you're tired of hiking from memorial to monument and walking miles of museum hallways, go out and get some real exercise (or watch someone else work out). DC comes well equipped with spectator sports as well as places to run and play:

Football—The Washington Redskins are the local heroes, but don't count on actually seeing a game live. Season tickets have been sold out since 1966, an NFL record. Diehard football fans can catch a game at College Park, the Naval Academy or Howard University. USFL's Washington Federals play from March-July at RFK Stadium.

Baseball—Unfortunately, both major league teams have left the area in recent years. True fans shouldn't mind driving an hour or so out to Memorial Stadium in Baltimore to catch the Orioles—the 1983 champs. *1000 E. 33rd St.* The Minor League Alexandria Dukes put up an impressive battle each summer at Four-Mile Run Park in Alexandria, Virginia.

Hockey—The Washington Capitals glide through Capital Centre October-April.

Soccer—The Diplomats kick around RFK Stadium April-August.

Basketball—Former NBA champs Washington Bullets also play home games at Capital Centre.

American University's Eagles play at Fort Myer in Arlington; Georgetown's Hoyas reached the '83 NCAA finals.

DC and its environs offer you a chance to stretch your legs—horseback riding, biking, hiking, or jogging:

Golf—Late May attracts golf fans with the Kemper Open, at the Congressional Country Club in Bethesda.

Tennis—The Virginia Slims Tournament of Washington shows off women pros each January, while the men take over in July for the DC National Bank Tennis Classic.

Horseback Riding—DC: Rock Creek Park offers the most extensive riding paths—14 miles of wide graveled trails (See pg. 73). Rental horses and riding instruction are available at the Rock Creek Horse Center. 5200 Glover Rd., NW. Maps at Visitor Center.

Bicycling:

Lake Fairfax Park. Bike on all park roads, around the 30-acre lake, or up in the hills. *Lake Fairfax Dr. at Baron Cameron Ave.*

Long Branch Nature Area. Part of the Arlington County Bike Trail passes through here. *625 S. Carlyn Springs.*

Mount Vernon Bike Trail. Bike beside the Potomac. *George Washington Memorial Pkwy. south through Mt. Vernon Memorial Hwy.*

Potomac Overlook Regional Park. The 2-mile **Blue Trail** goes through much of the park, while the popular **Green Trail** is shorter. *Marcey Rd. at Military Rd.*

Prince William Forest Park. Bike all roads beside raccoon, grouse and white-tailed deer. Rentals available. *VA 619 south of I-95.*

Ice Skating:
DC:

Fort Dupont Park, Rockefeller Center and **the Federal Home Loan Bank Building** all offer popular rinks. **Rock Creek Park** and the **C&O Canal** have natural skating rinks in appropriate weather conditions only.

Maryland:

Cabin John Regional Park and **Wheaton Regional Park** both have artificial rinks.

Virginia:

Burke Lake Regional Park, Mason District Park and **Mt. Vernon District Park** also have artificial rinks.

Jogging:
DC:

Paved paths can be found in the **Mall, Ellipse** and **Tidal Basin,** but may be crowded. The Ellipse offers a 1½-mile or 1.5-mile course.

Rock Creek Park allows a cooler run in its shady areas. A parcourse completed in 1978 has 18 calisthenic stations challenging you along the 1.5-mile oval route.

Start in Georgetown down the **C&O Towpath** for a good workout, but watch for bikers and walkers.

Virginia:

Try the **W&O Railroad Trail** from Vienna east for a tough run.

Horseracing:

The local paper will give you all the information on which tracks are open. The following list offers a few tracks to choose from:

Virginia:

Charles Town Turf Club. Night thoroughbred racing. Restaurant facilities (reservations suggested.) *Charles Town, WVA. 304-737-2323.*

Maryland:

Laurel Race Course. Day thoroughbred and harness racing. Restaurant with reservations suggested. *Laurel, MD. 301-725-0400.*

Pimlico Race Course. Home of the Triple Crown's **Preakness** in mid-May. Also day thoroughbred racing. Restaurant. *Northern Pkwy Dr. Baltimore, MD. 301-542-9400.*

Rosecraft Raceway. Night harness racing. Dining available—make reservations. *6336 Rosecroft Dr., Oxon Hill, MD. Restaurant: 301-567-4045/ Information: 301-567-4000.*

Ocean Downs. Harness racing. *Berlin, MD. 301-641-0680.*

Bowie Race Course. Thoroughbred racing. *Bowie, MD. 301-262-8111.*

Introductions/Theaters/Narrative black
Hotels purple
Museums/Architecture blue
Parks/Open spaces green
Restaurants/Nightlife red
Shops/Galleries violet

In 1847, on what some call one of Washington's saddest days, nearly a third of the District of Columbia—all of DC that lay across the Potomac—retroceded back to the state of Virginia.

2

Theodore Roosevelt Br

1

M

Jefferson Davis Hwy

McClellan Dr

7

3rd Dr East

George Washington Memorial Pkwy

9

8

George Mason Memorial Bridge

10

M

Army Navy Dr

Joyce

Hayes

11th

M

Fern

Eads

M

16th
17th
18th
19th
20th
21st
22nd
23rd

11

12

13

14

16

24th
25th

26th

15

M

M Indicates Metrorail Stops

7   ARLINGTON

The land was returned for a number of reasons, including many Virginia residents' desire to regain their lost franchise and to allow the port of Alexandria, finally free of federal jurisdiction, to grow prosperous. Though some claimed the act was unconstitutional, the federal government felt that laggardly Washington would never amount to anything, and would have no use for the Virginia side of the district.

In the end, of course, the government retained control of the land, dictating the many uses to which it would be put, including **Arlington Cemetery**, the **Pentagon**, the **Iwo Jima Memorial** and the **Netherlands Carillon**. The bottom of the Potomac River was even dredged to make room for **Washington National Airport**.

The smallest US county—25.7 square miles—includes Clarendon, Crystal City, Fairlington, Rosslyn and **Shirlington.** Your visit to **Arlington County** will acquaint you with this facet of DC's history and development.

1   Arlington Memorial Bridge. (1926-1932, **McKim, Mead & White**) Although a bridge had been planned at this location for years, it took a massive traffic jam on Armistice Day, 1921, to get this one finally built. A long, low series of arches spans the Potomac with MM&W's usual Beaux-Arts flair.

2   Theodore Roosevelt Island and Memorial. In the Potomac River, between the Roosevelt and Key bridges, lie these gentle marshlands honoring the twenty-sixth president. The island's 88 acres allow red-tailed hawk, red and gray fox and marsh wrens to roam freely, along with groundhog, muskrat, great owls and wood duck. Old sycamore, oak, hickory and dogwood trees shade the 2½ miles of nature trails on the island.

Paul Manship's 17-foot bronze memorial statue of Roosevelt stands in front of 4 21-foot granite tablets, each inscribed with his thoughts on nature and The State. During summer months, surrounding fountains spurt 20-foot plumes. *Open daily 9:30 till dark; nature walks available. 703-285-2600.*

3   Tivoli. ☆ ☆ $$ All mirrors, elegance and gracious service, Tivoli offers fine Italian and Continental cuisine at reasonable prices. Choose from fresh fish, veal, pasta and other dishes; by all means sample a dessert. Nice Sunday brunch. *Italian/Continental. Open M-F 11:30am-2:30pm. Reservations suggested. Coat and tie recommended for dinner. 1700 Moore St., Rosslyn. 703-524-8900.*

4   Orleans House. ☆ $ An innovatively stocked salad bar as long as a boat is the centerpiece of this family restaurant. Standard entrees at low, low prices. *American. Open M-F 11am-11pm, Sa 4-11pm, Su till 10pm. No reservations accepted. 1213 Wilson Blvd., Rosslyn. 703-524-2929.*

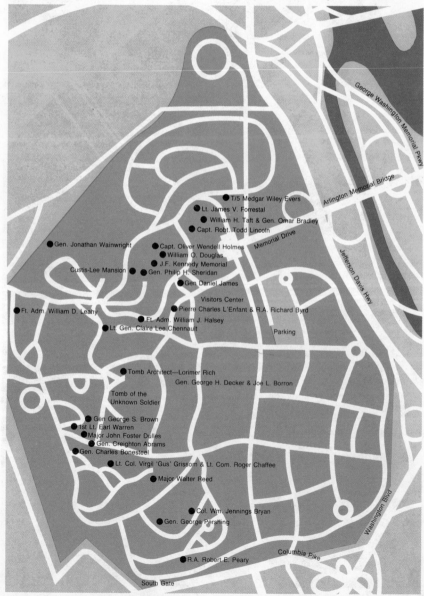

Best Western Westpark. *Expensive.* Located at Key Bridge, opposite Georgetown, this modern hotel is a short drive from DC and close to major interstate highways. A room on one of the top floors will assure you of a breathtaking view. *1900 N. Fort Myer Dr., Arlington. 703-527-4814.*

Arlington House and Arlington National Cemetery. The story of Arlington House (1802-1820, **George Hadfield**) is really the story of 2 great Virginia families—the Washingtons and the Lees—and their struggle to hold on to this 1,100-acre estate which overlooks the Potomac River and is now Arlington National Cemetery.

John Custis, Martha Washington's son, purchased the land in 1778. In 1802, his son, artist **George Washington Parke Custis** (adopted by George and Martha), started building the Greek-Revival mansion and, in turn, passed it along to daughter **Mary Anna Randolph Custis,** who married **Lieutenant Robert E. Lee** in 1831. The mansion took its more common name, the *Custis-Lee House,* from this famous marriage.

When the Union Army crossed the Potomac during the Civil War, it overran the mansion and forced the Lee family out. Then, in 1864, the federal government seized the land for unpaid taxes that had been questionably imposed. Finally, in 1883, the Supreme Court ruled to return the house to Lee's son, **George Washington Custis Lee.** He sold it back to the government for $150,000, to be used as a national mohument. Congress approved restoration for the ransacked house in 1925.

Extensive research and curatorial zeal have refurnished Arlington House as it was when it was the home of the Robert E. Lee family. Much of the furniture, artwork and housewares are the actual pieces used by the Lees; others are careful reproductions. Large portions of the double parlor set have survived and now furnish the **White Parlor; Nellie Custis'** music case is also here. The bed chamber in which Lee resigned from the US Army in 1861 is much as it was then. Copies of many of the paintings that once hung here, including an 1830 Italian *Madonna* by **William George Williams,** decorate the house. Original artworks include George Washington Park Custis' *Battle Of Monmouth,* originally intended for the Capitol but now hanging in the **Morning Room;** and the 1831 portrait of Mary Anna Randolph Custis by **August Hervieu** painted shortly before her wedding to Lee. Both floors of the house are open, and the glimpse into the lifestyle of pre-Civil War Southern gentility is a must for DC visitors.

Admission free. Open 9:30am-4pm in winter, 9:30am-6pm during summer. In Arlington Cemetery. 557-0613.

Arlington Cemetery. Lying across the Virginia hills, just over the Arlington Memorial Bridge is this serene testament to the US's military sacrifices: 1,100 acres of rolling hills dotted with simple headstones as far as the eye can see. Arlington National Cemetery is reserved for officers, enlistees and families of the US military and government. In 1868, General **John Logan** set 30 May aside to decorate Civil War graves, holding the first service at the Arlington House portico; this was the beginning of Memorial Day.

Authorities believe that space at the cemetery will run out about the year 2000, and have set strict requirements for interment. The 60,000-plus buried here represent the Revolutionary War, War of 1812, Civil War, Spanish-American War, World Wars I and II, and the conflicts in Korea and Vietnam.

The **Tomb of the Unknowns** (formerly, Tomb of the Unknown Soldier) remains the focus of sentiment and ceremony at Arlington National Cemetery. Cut from a single block of white marble, the tomb is decorated by sculpted wreaths and a 3-figure symbol for *Victory through Valor attaining Peace.* The inscription on the back panel reads *"Here Rests in Honored Glory an American Soldier Known but to God."* Entombed in the monument are the remains of 4 US servicemen: from World Wars I and II, and the Korean and Vietnam conflicts.

At all times, a soldier from *The Old Guard* of the Third US Infantry protects the tomb and periodically performs the engaging *Changing of the Guard.* This series of heal-clicking, rifle maneuvers and salutes takes place each half-hour during summer, every hour in winter and each 2 hours at night. The guard moves 21 steps, stops for 21 seconds, then retraces his route.

Mast of the Battleship Maine. The mast—its tower still in place—was raised in 1912 from the ship, which sank in 1898 in Havana Harbor. The mast is set in a granite base inscribed with the names of the 229 men who died in the mysterious explosion that preceded the Spanish-American War.

Arlington Memorial Amphitheater, a 4,000-seat theater that serves as a memorial to the Army, Navy and Marine Corps, was designed by Carrere & Hastings. Finished in white Vermont marble, it is reminiscent of Greek and Roman theaters.

The Tomb of Pierre Charles L'Enfant, the designer of DC's city grid, lies on a hillside overlooking Washington, just in front of Arlington House. His original plan is carved on the tomb.

An eternal flame and slate headstone mark **John F. Kennedy's** grave. The simple marble terrace yields a panoramic view of the city; one low wall reminds visitors of Kennedy's power with words, showing an inscription from his inaugural address. Flanking this site are the graves of Kennedy's 2 infants who died before him. Nearby in a grassy plot is **Robert F. Kennedy's** grave. A nearby granite wall and fountain memorialize the late Attorney General and US senator's words.

Netherlands Carillon. Located on the Marine Memorial grounds, this gift from the Netherlands has 49 stationary bells with a 4-octave range of notes. The smallest bell weighs 3,715 pounds, the largest weighs 12,654 pounds. Carillon concerts are *Saturdays at 2pm, Apr-Sep. 285-2600.*

Iwo Jima Memorial. Felix W. de Weldon's bronze recreation of **Joe Rosenthal's** Pulitzer Prize-winning photo. Five marines and a sailor raise the American flag on Mt. Suribachi, Iwo Jima. The 78-foot, 100-ton sculpture represents World War II, where over 5,000 Marines died.

The *Sunset Parade* each Tuesday at 7:30pm (May thru August) features the *Marine Silent Drill Team* and *Drum and Bugle Corps.* Call 433-4173 for information.

Confederate Memorial. Erected by the United Daughters of the Confederacy in 1914, **Moses Ezekiel's** baroque bronze monument honors the soldiers of the short-lived Confederate States of America. A female figure in the center stands for the *South in Peace,* while a frieze on the base portrays the South's women sending their men to fight. President **Woodrow Wilson** dedicated the statue in 1914.

Other soldiers are honored in splendor or simplicity throughout Arlington Cemetery. An equestrian statue stands over the grave of General **Philip Kearny,** the one-armed commander of the Union cavalry who was killed in action.

Quartermaster General **Montgomery C. Meigs,** who first suggested to Lincoln that Arlington should be a national cemetery, has a gravesite of the finest black marble. The rectangle holds the life-like figure of a young soldier lying dead on the battlefield—the image is preserved in bronze.

Highly polished granite decorates General **P.H. Sheridan's** grave. A bronze flag and medallion, the latter with a portrait of the general by **Samuel Kitson,** complete this ivy-surrounded memorial.

The **skyline of Washington** remains horizontal—not vertical like most large cities—because no building is allowed to stand taller than the Capitol.

Also prominent are, to the southeast, the graves of famed lawyer and orator **William Jennings Bryan**, who served as Secretary of State under Woodrow Wilson; and the grave of Rear Admiral **Robert E. Peary**, whose site is marked by a marble globe awarded by the National Geographic Society.

Other figures from American military and public life remembered at Arlington are: General **John J. Pershing**, **Richard E. Byrd**, **Walter Reed**, and **John Foster Dulles**.

Tourmobiles—the only vehicles allowed on the cemetery grounds—will take you on a guided tour. An express tour drives you directly to see the changing of the guard.

Admission free. Open 8am-5pm in the winter, 8am-7pm in summer. Stop for maps at the **Visitor Center.** *697-2131.*

7 **Fort Myer's** neat brick barracks house troops, chiefs of staff, a hospital and fire house. Its **Parade Ground** nearby has held demonstrations of aviation history's bests, including the **Wright Brothers** first public display of their plane in 1909.

A monument honors **Lt. T.E. Selfridge,** who was killed while flying with Orville Wright on a test flight. The US's first military planes were demonstrated here. *West of Arlington Cemetery.*

8 **Navy and Marine Memorial.** This simple, graceful representation of 7 seagulls in flight is acclaimed as one of the most visually stunning outdoor sculptures in a city brimful of sculpture and statues. **Ernesto Begni del Piatti** created the work, dedicated in 1930. Worth a special trip. *On Columbia Island just on the Virginia side of the Arlington Memorial Bridge.*

9 **Lyndon Baines Johnson Memorial Grove.** At the south end of **Lady Bird Johnson Park** stretch 15 acres of pines, flowering dogwoods and daffodils planted to commemorate the thirty-sixth president and his first lady. The memorial site, marked by a large Texas pink granite monolith, is surrounded by stones inscribed with quotations from Johnson. *Open daily.*

The Department of Defense

10 **The Pentagon.** The world's largest office building, the Pentagon has 3 times the floor space of the Empire State Building. The 5-sided structure—headquarters of the Department of Defense—covers 29 acres, with a 5-acre courtyard at its center. Built during World War II, the structure took only 16 months to complete. In spite of its 17.5 miles of corridors, no office is more than 7 minutes from any other.

Bookstore, bank, post office, men's store, jewelers, florist and grand concourse are all open to the public in this mini-city. Check out the barbershop's display of over 60 photos of military and political leaders, from MacArthur to Kennedy.

During an hour-long guided tour which leaves from the concourse, the guide walks backward the entire time. *Guided tours every hour M-F from 9am-12pm, every half hour 12pm-3:30pm. 695-1776.*

Introductions/Theaters/Narrative black
Hotels purple
Museums/Architecture blue
Parks/Open spaces green
Restaurants/Nightlife red
Shops/Galleries violet

11 **Woo Lae Oak.** ☆☆$ You might be slightly confused about what to order (they speak little English here), but you can't go wrong with an appetizer platter (a large one serves 4 or more), dumpling and noodle dishes, grilled meats, or hot pots of vegetables in spicy sauce. *Korean. Open daily 11am-11pm. Reservations suggested. 1500 S. Joyce St., Arlington. 703-521-3706.*

12 **Arlington County Visitors Center** offers information on hotels and restaurants and sites in DC and lower Virginia. *Open M-Sa 9am-5pm, Su 10am-4pm. 735 18th St. S. 703-521-0772.*

13 **Crystal City Underground.** Tucked neatly and quietly under an area of some 40 high-rise glass-and-concrete buildings that rise out of the flatlands near **National Airport** is this gem of a small mall, with winding cobblestone walkways and twisting alleys that charm shoppers from one boutique to the next. All paths seem to lead to the **Crystal Dinery,** with its dozen international food kiosks. Among the specialty shops are **Hodges Emporium** (892-5276), where a player piano entices browsers into an old-fashioned country store; **The Complement** (920-9700), for handbags and leather goods; **Cuff's Mens Shop**; **Ticketron** and a **Post Office**. *Open 7 days. Free parking underground after 6pm and on weekends. 1745 Jefferson Davis Hwy., Crystal City. 703-920-8500.*

13 **Crystal City Marriott Hotel.** *Moderate/expensive.* Located 5 minutes from National Airport, with round-the-clock limousine service. Two restaurants and a lounge. *1999 Jefferson Davis Highway, Rt. 1, Crystal City. 521-5500.*

14 **Marriott's Crystal Gateway.** *Expensive.* Crystal City's newest hotel is 10 minutes from National Airport. Shuttle service available. Terrace, atrium and underground shopping. The 17th floor offers the nicest rooms. *1700 Jefferson Davis Hwy., Crystal City. 703-920-3230/800-228-4290.*

15 **Hyatt Regency.** *Expensive.* Big shiny hostelry offers all you'd expect from a Hyatt, plus the convenience of this location near National Airport. Amenities include health club with pool, whirlpool and gym, and special weekend packages. Dine in one of the hotel's 3 restaurants. Meeting facilities. *2799 Jefferson Davis Hwy., Arlington. 703-486-1234.*

Within the hotel are:

Tidewater. ☆☆$$ The seafood here is fresh and varied, and specialties include an oyster bar, sushi, lobster and crab, along with fish, beef and lamb entrees. Nice wine bar. *Seafood. Open M-F 11am-2pm, 6-10pm; Sa 6-10pm. Closed Su. Reservations suggested.*

Skylights. ☆$$ The view is the main lure of this rooftop lounge and restaurant. Steak, pasta, prime rib and more; salads and sandwiches at lunchtime. Live music at cocktail hour and after 9pm. *American. Open M-F 11am-11pm; Sa & Su 6-11pm.*

16 **Washington National Airport,** handling domestic and commuter flights, is certainly the most convenient airport for visitors to Washington. Across the Potomac—just 3½ miles or 15-minutes from downtown DC, twice that time during rush hour. Cab fare and limo service is reasonable, and the airport is served by both Metrobus and Metrorail.

In order to meet strict noise control laws, WNA has a nighttime curfew that allows no landings or takeoffs after 10-10:30pm (the exception is the DC9 Super 80 which meets noise level requirements when landing). Despite the restrictions, WNA is the busiest of Washington's airports. There are 550 landings and takeoffs a day during the week, and in 1983 the airport served 14.4 million passengers.

Only 600 special agents are hired from the 10,000 hopefuls who apply to FBI's 59 field offices each year. The trainees, all college graduates between 23 and 35, receive 16 weeks of training, including over 100 hours of firearms instructions. An agent must then qualify in 8 yearly shooting tests.

The airport is somewhat sprawling. Ticketing areas are spread out. **Departure gates** are located, from left to right, at **North Terminal, North Concourse, Main Terminal, American Terminal** and **Northwest/TWA Terminal.** Don't let the names fool you. Several carriers leave from the NW/TWA and American terminals. A free **shuttle bus** is available between terminals.

Transportation is varied and inexpensive.

Driving: To get to the airport, take 14th St. to the George Washington Memorial Parkway. Parking is expensive. *Call 703-684-7766 for recorded information.*

Taxis are available at the exit of each terminal. A dispatcher is usually on duty until 11pm. The fare into downtown is about $7.

Metrorail rapid rail service is without a doubt the cheapest way to or from the airport. Both the yellow and blue lines stop at the station, which is just across from the North Terminal and easy walking distance from the Main Terminal. A free shuttle bus runs every 5-8 minutes between the terminals and the station. Metrorail allows you to transfer to any point served in the system, including Union Station.

Metrobus also serves the airport, though less frequently than Metrorail. *Bus stop in front of the Main Terminal.*

Limo service is provided by Washington Flyer, which serves 72 points in Washington, Maryland and Virginia, including Dulles and Baltimore Washington International. Service runs between 5am and midnight. Limos usually leave every half hour, less often after 10pm. Downtown stops are at several hotels: **Shoreham, Sheraton, Quality Inn, Capital Hill Hyatt Regency, Washington Hilton, Capital Hilton,** and **Mayflower.** There is a ticketing and information booth inside the Main Terminal adjacent to the United Airlines counter and another in the NW/TWA Terminal. *For 24-hour information, call 703-470-0640.*

General non-flight airport information 8:30am-5pm, 202-557-2045.

The **National Geographic** began accepting advertising in 1906, but banned all alcoholic drinks, tobacco and patent medicines. After the crash of 1929 it extended the ban to advertisements by financial and investment concerns as well.

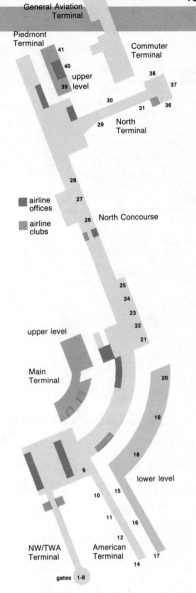

DC WEATHER

Spring (mid-March to mid-June) is beautiful in Washington. The cherry trees bloom during the first 2 weeks in April, causing the tourists to flock in and hotel rates rise considerably; you might want to consider this when making travel plans. Additionally, spring is a favorite time for travelers from abroad, and crowds are at their peak.

Summer is hot and humid, the city is a deeper green, and hotel prices generally drop as the humidity rises. The heat and smog should be considered before embarking on a trip, but also keep in mind that sudden daily thunderstorms often clear the air. The average high temperature in summer reaches 90°; but cooling off can be very enjoyable at the many outdoor concerts and performances that make DC a veritable summer festival.

Fall is an excellent time to travel in Washington, due to the temperate weather and moderate prices. The city is flooded with brilliant color from the abundant foliage, and the crowds are small and easily managed. The special events of summer are over, but the city's usual cultural season is beginning.

Winter highlights include the **December Pageant of Peace** and the inauguration in January (every 4 years). During winter, accomodations are easy to find and discounts are available. The normal low temperature reaches 27° in January.

	Jan	Feb	Mar	Apr	May	Jun
High	42.6	44.4	53.0	64.2	74.9	82.8
Low	27.4	28.0	35.0	44.2	54.5	63.4
Mean	35.0	36.2	44.0	54.2	64.7	73.1
	Jul	Aug	Sep	Oct	Nov	Dec
High	86.8	84.4	78.4	67.5	55.1	44.8
Low	68.0	66.1	59.6	48.0	37.9	29.8
Mean	77.4	75.3	69.0	57.8	46.5	37.3

Rainfall is evenly distributed throughout the year.

What to wear:

Month	Weather	Clothing.
Jan	Cold & moderate.	Heavy coat, hat, gloves, snowboots.
Feb	Late mild winter.	Heavy sweaters.
Mar	Warm spring.	Raingear, light jacket.
Jun		
Jul	Hot and humid.	Cool clothing.
Sep	Thunderstorms.	Swimwear, raingear.
Oct	Moderate to cool.	Heavy sweaters.
Nov		Jackets.
Dec	Late Cool to cold.	Same as Jan-Mar.

The **Capital Beltway's** 63 miles of highway encircle Washington, DC, linking the estimated 2 million people living in the nearby suburban areas of **Montgomery, Fairfax** and **Prince George** counties.

Much of the DC area's wealth is concentrated within the Beltway's northern arch—primarily in the residential communities of **Bethesda** and its renowned ultra-chic section, **Chevy Chase.** Several excellent specialty shopping areas are clustered around Bethesda and **Silver Spring.** The exclusive **White Flint** and **Mazza Gallerie** shopping centers are 2 worth visiting.

The southern Beltway in Virginia is dominated by historic sites, from colonial settlements to Civil War battlegrounds. A trip through rural Fairfax county—with Alexandria as your destination—will take you through a picturesque landscape that has changed little in the last 2 centuries.

1   **The Accotink Creek** meanders through 479 acres of a landscaped park area, ending in a pretty lake. A historical hiking trail follows the **Old Alexandria Railroad,** which once had its tracks running through the park. Canoes, paddleboats and rowboats can be rented at the marina facility, which also operates a mini-golf course and a seasonal snackbar. *Park open during daylight hours. Marina facility open 1 Mar-1 Dec 8am-dusk. 5660 Heming Ave., Springfield, VA. 703-569-3464.*

2   **Duck Chang's.** ☆ ☆ $ Prime duck is the specialty of this modest neighborhood place. *Chinese. Open M-Sa 11am-11pm. 4427 John Marr Dr. Annandale, VA. 703-941-9400.*

2   **Fritzbe's.** ☆ $ Suburban chic where the residents of Annandale and occasional Beltway farers feast on meats from the grill. Sunday Brunch. *American. Open M-Th 11:30am-1am, F & Sa till 2am; Su 10:30am-1am. 7250 Columbia Pike, Annandale, VA. 703-354-4560.*

3   **Falls Church.** The original wooden church was erected in 1733 near a road leading to the Potomac waterfalls; 60 years later a new structure was completed on the same site. Part of the church serves as a museum; weapons,

medical instruments and curios from the Civil War are exhibited. *Open daily 9am-3pm. 115 E. Fairfax St. Falls Church, VA. 703-532-7600.*

3   **Paradise East.** ☆ ☆ ☆ $ Korean barbecue. Once you've mastered basic chopstick skills, don't hesitate to order the various raw meat or seafood combinations—dip them in your own bubbling saucepan on the table and enjoy. Forks available upon request. *Korean. Open M-Sa 11am-11pm, Su 12:30-11pm. Lee Hwy., Falls Church, VA. 703-534-2552.*

4   **National Memorial Park.** A vast cemetery, noted for its gardens and sculptured fountains. The **Fountain of Faith,** the centerpiece of the grounds, was created by Swedish sculptor **Carl Milles.** Thirty-seven graceful bronze figures seem to hover in a spray of water, each face a portrait of one of the sculptor's deceased friends. The fountain represents the joy that awaits us after death. *Open M-F 9am-5pm, Sa & Su 10am-4pm. 7400 Lee Hwy., Falls Church, VA. 703-560-4400.*

5   **Tyson's Corner Center.** This center seems comfortable with its middle-income appeal. Major department stores are **Garfinckel's** (703-790-9292), **Bloomingdale's** (703-556-4600), **Hecht's** (703-893-4900) and **Woodward & Lothrop** (703-893-6400). Among its proven retail ingredients are **Britches** and **Britches Great Outdoors** (703-893-2083) for stylish neo-preppy professional and sports clothing; **Bailey, Banks and Biddle** (703-883-1400) for fine jewelry, crystal, china, silver and porcelains; and **This End Up** (703-734-5778) for home furnishings. *Mall hours M-F 10am-9:30pm, Su noon-5pm. Rt. 123 or Rt. 7, Tyson's Corner, VA 703-893-9400.*

The favorite pop of George Washington and his pals was not beer but scuppernong, a local wine with a plumlike flavor named after the Scuppernong River in North Carolina.

5 Tyson's Corner Marriott Hotel. *Moderate.* Adjacent to the shopping center, this hotel rhymes with the surrounding area—pleasant suburbia with a touch of class. Aside from the regular amenities—free HBO, valet service and restaurant—the second floor sports a health club, complete with indoor swimming pool, whirlpool, sauna and exercise room with locker facilities. *8028 Leesburg Pike, Tyson's Corner, VA. 703-734-3200.*

Courtesy of
Wolftrap
Foundation

6 Wolf Trap Farm Park. The 117-acre woodlands of concert/arts facility have brought the best of the arts to outdoor Virginia. The Wolf Trap Foundation chooses the performers, which have ranged from the **Metropolitan Opera,** lectures and workshops, and bluegrass festivals, to the **Alvin Ailey Dance Theatre** and a variety of comedians. The concert hall, **Feline Center,** is a fantastical wooden tent with magnificent acoustics. In 1982, the hall mysteriously burned to the ground, but reconstruction has been completed.

Tours of the Center and the park are available from the **Visitor Services Office.** *Open Jun-Sep. Tickets are required for most performances but Sunday afternoon concerts are free. 1551 Trap Rd., Vienna, VA. 703-255-1800.*

7 Giant Gourmet. A supermarket that excels in selection and quality, carrying freshly baked (in-house) breads and pastries, more than 500 wines and 60 imported beers, and exotic meats like camel and pheasant. *Open M-W 10am-8pm, Th-Sa 9am-9pm, Su 9am-6pm. 1445 Chain Bridge Rd., McLean, VA. 703-448-0800.*

7 La Mirabelle. ☆ ☆ $$ Elegance without pretense reigns at this classic French establishment, serving specialties *a la Escoffier* in a country-style atmosphere. *French. Open M-F 11:30am-2:30pm, M-Sa 5:30-9:30pm. 6645 Old Dominion Dr., McLean, VA. 703-893-8484.*

7 Kazan. ☆ ☆ $$ The tented ceiling and tuxedoed captains are in tune with the tab, slightly higher than at your usual ethnic hangout. The cuisine is a superior representative of what the Middle East has to offer, from Greek *moussaka* to Turkish *borek. Middle Eastern. Open M-Sa 11am-3pm, M-Th 5-10pm, F & Sa till 11pm. 6813 Redmond Dr., McLean, VA. 703-734-1960.*

8 Turkey Run Farm. Amazing look at an authentic pre-Revolutionary War farm, where costumed family (acting courtesy of staff members) performs heavy farm and housework with the help of original tools and utensils. *Admission free. Open W-Su 10am-4:30pm. Closed on rainy days. 6310 Old Georgetown Pike, McLean, VA. 703-442-7557.*

9 David Taylor Naval Ship and Research Center. US citizens over 14 years of age can visit this Navy laboratory, which spans acres and acres of the Maryland countryside. Inside the cavernous buildings are mile-long concrete water basins used to test the Navy's ship hulls. *Tours by appointment. George Washington Pkwy., Bethesda, MD. 202-227-1439.*

10 Clara Barton House. Last residence of the founder of the American Red Cross. In 1897, 86-year old Clara Barton moved to the Glen Echo house, originally built as a warehouse for Red Cross supplies. After removing some of the 72 concealed closets, deep enough to store wheelchairs, the indefatigable Clara expanded the house to 36 rooms. Her personal effects and furniture remain as they were during the heroine's last years. *Admission free. Guided tours upon request. Open daily 10am-5pm. 5801 Oxford Rd., Glen Echo, MD. 301-492-6245.*

MAZZA
GALLERIE

11 Mazza Gallerie. A posh shopping center aimed at the area's *nouveau riche.* Everything from designer sheets to fashionable children's wear is available to Chevy Chase's discriminating consumers. Mazza Gallerie's crown jewel is **Neiman-Marcus** *(966-9700),* 3 floors of all the fantastic goods an exclusive department store could offer. Underneath it all is the garden level, with 30 stores offering such diversity as **Pierre Deux'** fabrics and home accessories in 18th-century Provence prints *(244-6226)* and **B. Dalton Bookseller** *(362-7055)* stocking over 25,000 titles. On the upper level is **La Boutique Francaise** *(362-3762)* with Kenzo, Kansai and Castelbajac fashions, and **Pampillonia Jewelers** *(363-6305)* offering European custom-designed jewelry and little estate trinkets ranging from $50 to $50,000. There are also a few eating places. The basic McDonald's is here, as well as a well-appointed French dining room named **Cafe Maxime.** *Open M-F 11:30am-10pm, Sa till 6pm (244-7666).*

Pleasant Peasant *(364-2500)* is indeed a pleasant, informal Euro-American restaurant. *Open M-Sa 11:30am-3pm, Su-Th 5:30-11pm, F & Sa till midnight. 364-3500. Mall hours M-F 10am-8pm, Sa 10am-6pm. 5300 Wisconsin Ave. NW. Washington, DC 966-6114.*

11 Audubon Naturalist Society. (1828, **John Russell Pope**) Located on 40 acres of wildlife sanctuary, the Society makes its home in a Georgian mansion designed by the architect of the **Jefferson Memorial.** A 3/4 mile nature trail leads around the estate known as **Woodend.** Self-guided tours only. Gift shop. *Admission free. Open daily during daylight hours. 8940 Jones Mill Rd., Chevy Chase, MD. 301-652-9188.*

11 Imperial Palace. ☆ ☆ $ Traditional Hong Kong cuisine represented by mouth-watering chicken and seafood dishes. The kitchen occasionally ventures into Hunan and Szechuan territories. *Open Su-Th 11:30am-9:30pm, F & Sa till 10:30pm. 4515 Willard Ave., Chevy Chase, MD. 301-652-2920.*

11 Mr. L's. ☆ $$ An almost elegant Jewish deli 8 blocks from Chevy Chase Circle. Appetizers range in quality and variety; home-made whitefish or herring salad are of note, as is the hand-cut Nova Scotia salmon. *Open M-Th 9am-10pm, F & Sa till 11pm, Su 8am-9pm. 5018 Connecticut Ave. NW, Washington, DC. 244-4343.*

11 Brook Farm Inn of Magic. ☆ $$ Don't worry if your billfold disappears or your steak flies into the air—that's the kind of magic this rustic country inn likes to weave, as in-house magicians perform harmless tricks right at your table. The food, sometimes overshadowed by the entertainment, ranges from ribs to fresh seafood. *Open Tu-Su 6pm-midnight. 7101 Brookville Rd., Chevy Chase, MD. 301-652-8820.*

11 O'Brien's Pit Barbecue. ☆ ☆ $ Superbly authentic Texan pit barbecue offers hickory-fired ribs. Deserves more than just one lone star for taste. *American. Open S-Th 11am-10pm, F & Sa till 11pm. 7305 Waverly St., Bethesda, MD. 301-654-9004.*

11 The Fishery. ☆ ☆ $$ One of the best on the Beltway seafood circuit—half-shell oysters, smoked salmon cheesecake and good seafood-pasta dishes, with a slightly Mediterranean slant. *Seafood. Open Su-Th 11:30am-10pm, F & Sa till 11pm. 5511 Connecticut Ave. NW. Chevy Chase, MD. 363-2144.*

Introductions/Theaters/Narrative black
Hotels purple
Museums/Architecture blue
Parks/Open spaces green
Restaurants/Nightlife red
Shops/Galleries violet

11 La Miche/L'Hippocampe. ☆☆ $$ A people-watcher's paradise. The cafe-style menu goes beyond simple *croque monsieur*, with surprises like poached oysters topped with caviar or mussels in cream and almonds. *French. La Miche is open M-F 11:30am-2:30pm, M-Su 6-10pm. L'Hippocampe is open daily 11:30am-1am. 7905 Norfolk Ave., Bethesda, MD. 301-656-4499.*

11 Marriott Hotel Bethesda. *Moderate/expensive.* A step up from the usual suburban accommodations, this hotel features a large outdoor swimming pool, indoor lap pool, whirlpool, sauna and exercise room among its amenities. Three restaurants—Polynesian, Northern Italian and family-style American—ensure a variety in cuisines and prices. For an extra treat, ask about the *Executive Kings* room, an upgraded minisuite. *5151 Pooks Hill Rd., Bethesda, MD. 301-897-9400.*

11 White Flint Mall. Even the mannequins at this 3-tiered fashion mall have high cheekbones and that perfectly manicured look. **Bloomingdale's** *(301-984-4600)*, **I. Magnin** *(301-468-2900)* and **Lord & Taylor** *(301-770-9000)* are the big-leaguers anchoring more than 120 smaller shops and fashion boutiques in an interior of rosewood and copper terrazzo floors. Additional stores at White Flint include: **Black, Starr and Frost** *(301-770-1703)*, the oldest high-fashion jewelry outfit in the country; **Andre Bellini** *(301-231-9144)* stocks men's and women's imported; and **St. Laurent Rive Gauche** *(301-770-1133)* for *pret-a-porter* with a *haute couture* look. *Mall hours M-Sa 10am-9:30pm, Su noon-5pm. Rockville Pike and Nicholson Lane, Bethesda, MD. 301-468-5777.*

11 China Garden. ☆☆ $$ A favorite among Bethesda's sinophiles, who come to feast on exotics like lemon duck or crystal shrimp, Hong Kong-style. *Chinese. Open Su-Th 11:30am-10pm, F & Sa till 10:30pm. 4711 Montgomery Ave., Bethesda, MD. 301-657-4665.*

12 National Institutes of Health. Professionals affiliated with the medical sciences are welcome to visit the Center, where tours by appointment include films, slideshows and a model lab exhibition. The **National Library of Medicine,** adjacent to the Center, is the world's largest research library in a single professional field. *Open M-F 10am-4pm. Old Georgetown Rd. & Wisconsin Ave., Bethesda, MD. 301-496-4000.*

13 Temple of Latter-Day Saints. (1974, **Wilcox, Markham, Beecher & Fetzer;** landscape design, **Irwin Nelson**) Standing on a 57-acre hill in Maryland's countryside is this massive Art Deco temple, whose district must be the largest in the world. The $15 million temple is 248 feet long, 136 feet wide, and has a height equivalent to a 16-story commercial building. Its foundation is built on solid rock, to withstand any tests of the elements; the building itself is sheathed with 173,000 square feet of Alabama white marble, enough to cover 3½ football fields. Even the windows are made of marble, five-eighths of an inch thick and translucent, giving the interiors an ethereal quality. The fortress is topped with 6 gold-plated steel spires, the highest of which supports a gold leaf statue of the angel **Moroni.** The temple interior—open to members only—has a multitude of rooms on its 9 levels, reserved for important occasions such as weddings and baptisms. A formal 30-minute tour guided by volunteers passes through the **Visitors Center** where photographs, sculptures and a religious theater with life-like mannequins tell the story of Mormonism. *Open daily 10am-9pm. 9900 Stoneybrook Dr., Kensington, MD. 301-587-0911.*

13 Antique Row. More than 40 shops, some in malls and others in small buildings nearby, make up this collection of styles, periods and prices. Items range from Art Deco and railroad memorabilia to stained glass, folk art and vintage clothing. *Howard Ave. off Connecticut Ave., Kensington, MD.*

14 National Capital Trolley Museum. The museum, built as a replica of an old terminal, offers a loving look at trolley memorabilia from Austria, Germany and Washington, DC, itself. If you have a dollar for the ticket, a real trolley will take you on a 2 1/4-mile ride through the neighboring countryside. Gift shop. *Open Sa & Su noon-5pm, Jul-Aug noon-4pm. Closed 15 Dec-1 Jan. Bonifant Rd., Silver Spring, MD. 301-384-9797.*

15 Walter Reed Medical Center/Army Medical Museum contains specimens representing virtually any ailment that affects mankind. Emphasis is being placed on exhibits relating to pathology rather than medical instruments, but there is still an amazing collection of obscure devices used for bloodletting and vaccination, and a special selection of utensils based on medical superstition. A collection of amputated limbs from the Civil War occupies a special place in the museum's history.

Walter Reed's hospital facilities are located in a huge 7-story square (1979, **Stone Marracini & Patterson**). Another building worth noting is the windowless **Armed Forces Institute of Pathology** headquarters, built in the late 1940s as a prototype of *atomic bomb-proof* buildings that were envisioned to be the future standard for downtown Washington architecture. The development of the hydrogen bomb in the early 1950s made that vision—and this building—almost immediately obsolete.

The **Otis Historical Archives** are annexed to the Museum, and provide several voluminous collections for research and study, as well as an extensive photographic record of Civil War wounded. Individual and group tours by appointment only. *Open M-F 10am-5pm, F & Sa noon-5pm. 6825 16th St. NW., Washington, DC. 576-2348.*

15 Linden Hill Hotel & Racquet Club. *Moderate.* A variety of rooms—deluxe kings with sitting areas, 1-bedroom suites and 2-bedroom suites with kitchens—are available at this racquet and fitness establishment. The 16 wooded acres of Linden Hill offer 10 indoor/outdoor tennis courts with organized clinics run by pros on staff. Other relaxing diversions include an outdoor Olympic-size swimming pool, sauna and jacuzzi, jogging paths and a golf course nearby. *5400 Pooks Hill Rd., Bethesda, MD. 800-368-2706.*

16 Sheraton Inn NW. *Inexpensive.* Two-hundred rooms in Sheraton's well-appointed style. There is a regular American restaurant, as well as a Northern Italian dining room named **Mamma Regina's.** The health club—indoor pool, sauna and exercise room—is open to hotel patrons and guests. Special weekend rates. *8727 Colesville Rd., Silver Spring, MD. 301-589-5200.*

16 St. John's Catholic Church and Cemetery. (1790) Jesuit churchman **John Carroll** founded his private Evangelist Mission chapel on this site in 1774, where he served until his appointment as official head of the newly legislated US Roman Catholic Church 10 years later. The small frame building is an exact reproduction of the original structure, with all fixtures and sacraments intact. In essence, the church stands as a memorial to Maryland's influential Carroll family. *Open M-F 8:30am-4pm, Sa 8:30am-noon. Cemetery open during daylight hours. Forest Glen Rd. and Rosensteel Ave., Silver Spring, MD. 301-871-6500.*

16 Sakura Palace. ☆☆☆ $$ Great sushi bar in the dining area, flanked by *tatami* rooms for larger parties going completely Japanese. Fried, steamed, boiled and broiled complete dinners, including salt-broiled salmon, *tonkatsu*, tiny clams and Pacific oysters in season. *Japanese. Open Tu-F 11am-3pm, 5-10:30pm; Sa & Su 3-10:30pm. 7926 Georgia Ave., Silver Spring, MD. 301-587-7070.*

Introductions/Theaters/Narrative black
Hotels purple
Museums/Architecture blue
Parks/Open spaces green
Restaurants/Nightlife red
Shops/Galleries violet

16 Crisfield. ☆ ☆ ☆ $$ The bare cinder block decor belies the incredible seafood served at this unassuming fish house. Regional specialties like Chincoteague oysters, Maryland crab and fresh clams are offered on a menu that has been the same for the past 50 years. *American/seafood. No credit cards. Open Tu-Th 11am-10pm, F & Sa till 10:30pm, Su noon-9pm. 8012 Georgia Ave., Silver Spring, MD. 301-589-1306.*

17 University of Maryland. The main campus of this co-educational, state-supported facility has over 37,000 students and 2,000 faculty members; physics, mathematics and computer science are the departments that have earned Maryland U. a place among the country's top 10 public universities. *Guided tours by calling the Public Affairs office, South Administration Bldg. in advance. Open M-F 9am-4:30pm. College Park, MD. 301-454-5825.*

18 Agricultural Research Center. Seven thousand, five hundred acres of land, inhabited by cattle, swine and poultry, under research by the USDA. The center is devoted to solving such problems as environmental protection and global food supply. Self-guided tours allow visitors to wander at leisure among the research areas. *Admission free. Open M-F 8am-4:30pm. Powder Mill Rd., Beltsville, MD. 301-344-2483.*

19 Goddard Space Flight Center (NASA). NASA's museum, directly on its research facility, offers: a solar telescope for sunspot viewing, several dismantled rockets and other space objects, plus a range of outer space satellite transmissions to everyday TV weather maps. Film clips of NASA's adventures in space are screened non-stop; you can also watch outtakes from the pressure-cooker drama of ground control before a rocket take-off or landing. *Self-guided tours. Open W-Su 10am-4pm. Greenbelt, MD. 301-344-8101.*

20 Greenbelt Park. Only 12 miles from downtown Washington, this green pine forest is a haven for deer, red fox and raccoons; the streams are filled with small fish, and the air is fragrant with the scent of flowers. Twelve well-marked walking trails and picnic areas dot the 1,100 acres. *Open daily until dusk. Good Luck Rd., Greenbelt, MD. 301-344-3948.*

21 Kenilworth Aquatic Gardens. Fourteen acres of hydrophilic flora and fauna are contained in this hidden, seldom-visited Anacostia Park marshland. The garden was founded in 1882 by **W.B. Shaw,** a war veteran who began the collection with a few water lilies from Maine. The native trees—willow oaks, red maples and magnolias—provided natural shelter for the ponds, which attracted a variety of water dwellers. Muskrats, raccoons and opossums now coexist happily with species of frogs, toads and turtles. Plan for an early morning visit, since many of the night-blooming lotuses close during harsh daylight. Group tours on advance notice. *Open Memorial Day-Labor Day 7:30am-8pm, Sep-May 7:30am-6pm. Kenilworth Ave. and Douglas St. NE, Washington DC. 426-6905.*

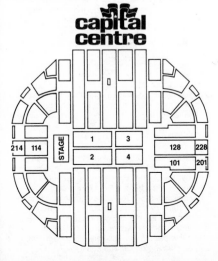

22 Capital Centre. One of America's foremost showcase auditoriums, the 20,000-seat arena has played host to some of the most popular contemporary events in the country. The steady procession of sports events includes hockey, all-star basketball tournaments and boxing. Other sellout events have included **Elvis Presley,** the **Rolling Stones** and **Bob Dylan** in monumental concerts. In 1981, the arena was the site of president-elect **Ronald Reagan's** inaugural gala.

There are 12 concession stands and 2 full-service restaurants on the premises: the elegant Continental-style **Capital Club** with reservations necessary 2 weeks in advance; and the **Showcase Pub & Eatery,** a deli-restaurant and bar seats on a first-come-first-serve basis. *Box office open daily 10am-5:30pm, and until 1 hour after start of event. 1 Harry Truman Dr., Landover, MD. 24-hour information, 301-350-3900.*

23 Wild World. Amusement park filled with the customary rides, shows and attractions guaranteed to drive youngsters wild and parents crazy. Assorted waterslides, an innovative children's pool, and **Wild Wave,** the world's largest wave pool provide big splashes of fun. A more spectatorial entertainment highlight is **Maxwell's High Dive Show** featuring clowns and professional divers who demonstrate their neck-breaking art several times daily. *Concessions available. Admission charge. Open daily late May-early Sep 10am-10pm. 13710 Central Ave., Largo, MD. 301-249-1500.*

24 Paul E. Garber Facility. The **National Air & Space Museum's** preservation and restoration facility exhibits 92 wondrous aircrafts together with models, kites and astronautical artifacts. Many of the antique foreign planes are war prizes, collected by the USAF at the end of WWII. More recent aviation achievements are equally represented: the Ryan X-13, the world's first vertical take-off jet; the Bell model 30, the first 2-bladed helicopter; and the 1960 Able-Baker nose cone from the Jupiter craft that carried 2 monkeys into space. *Admission free. Tours require 2 weeks advance reservations and run M-F at 10am, Sa & Su at 10am and 1pm. Old Silver Hill Rd., Suitland, MD. 301-357-1300.*

25 Andrews Air Force Base. Strategic military base enveloped in secrecy. Drop-in tours of the military community, shops and aircraft hangars are held *Tu & Th 8am Jul-Aug.* Tours by appointment only during all other months. Minimum age 8 years for children; US citizens only. *Admission free. Allentown Rd., Camp Springs, MD. 301-981-4511.*

26 Rosecroft Raceway. Fall and winter night harness racing with a view from the Continental restaurant. *Post times W-Sa 7:30pm, Su 6pm. Dining room open W-Sa 9am-11pm, Su 2:30-10pm. 6336 Rosecroft, Dr., Fort Washington, MD. Reservations: 567-4045/Information: 567-4000.*

27 Oxon Hill Farm. City folks can try the lifestyles of country bumpkins on this working farm, where home-woven charms abound. The cows are milked, the fields plowed, and all the farm animals provide plenty of diversions for incredulous asphalt-raised children. A forest, orchard and a vegetable garden complete the rosy rustic picture. *Admission free. Open 8:30am-5pm daily. Closed major holidays. 6411 Oxon Hill Rd., Oxon Hill, MD. 301-839-1177.*

28 George Washington's Grist Mill. A total reconstruction of one of the first president's many enterprises. From 1771 to the end of his days, the president operated the mill, capitalizing on Virginia's agricultural transition from tobacco to wheat. After Washington's death, the mill changed hands several times and was finally torn down by Quakers, who determined the property worthless and felled the walls to the ground. In 1932, exhaustive research, based on letters, journals and insurance policies, made it possible to re-erect this operating structure, making it into a Historical State Park. Self-guided tours or group tours by appointment. *Adult admission charge. Open daily 10am-6pm May-Sep. 5514 Mt. Vernon Memorial Hwy., Alexandria, VA. 703-780-3383.*

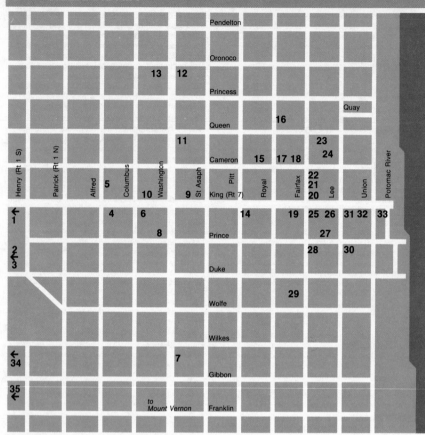

Very little in this historic seaport town has changed since Scotsman **John Alexander** purchased the land in 1669.

Established as a city in 1749, Alexandria became the principal trade, social and political center of Northern Virginia. It was the home of **Henry Light Horse Harry Lee** and his son **Robert Edward;** another important resident was **George Washington.** During the Civil War, Federal forces used the city as a base for campaigns in the area. Thus the city was spared a lot of the destruction typical of the conflict.

Old Town Alexandria's many beautiful examples of mid-Georgian and early Federal architecture have been preserved and are open to the public. The old merchant district—a couple of blocks on King St. between the River and St. Asaph's St. —has kept its heritage in many of the shops dating back to the 18th and 19th centuries. At least one day is needed to fully explore the area.

1   George Washington Masonic Memorial. An outstanding Freemasonry shrine modeled after the Pharaoh's lighthouse in Egyptian Alexandria. The 333-foot tower provides a bird's eye view of Alexandria and the Potomac River. *Admission free. Scheduled 30-minute tours. Open daily 9am-5pm. King St. and Callahan Dr. 703-683-2007.*

2   Fort Ward Museum and Park. The fifth largest Civil War fortification protecting Washington has been reconstructed with the help of photographs by Mathew Brady. Located in a 40-acre park with picnic facilities and an outdoor amphitheater. Soldiers in Civil War garb act out historic battles during summer weekends. *Admission free. Open Tu-Sa 9am-5pm, Su noon-5pm. 4301 W Braddock Rd. 703-838-4848.*

James Smithson's fortune, willed to the US government in 1835, amounted to $541,379.63.

3   Hard Times Cafe. ☆ $ Chili heaven, Cincinnati- or Texan-style. Come equipped with a hearty appetite—portions are humongous. *Regional American. Open M-Th 11:30am-10pm, F until 11pm, Sa noon-11pm, Su 4-10pm. 1404 King St. 703-683-5340.*

4   Taverna Cretekou. ☆ ☆ $$ Picturesque little restaurant, with a vine-covered courtyard in back. The grilled lamb, perfectly trimmed and seasoned with a lemon-herb mixture, is recommended. *Greek. Open Tu-F 11:30am-2:30pm, 5-10:30pm; Sa noon-4pm, 5-11:30pm; Su 11:30am-3pm, 5-9:30pm. 818 King St. 703-548-8688.*

5   Bittersweet. Carry-out menu, listing imaginative soups, pates, salads, chicken and steak entrees. *Regional nouvelle. Open M-F 11am-7pm, Sa until 6pm. 103 N. Alfred St. 703-549-2708.*

6   Geranio. ☆ ☆ $$ Comfortable, rustic *trattoria* for enjoying the gamut of classic Italian food. *Italian. Open M-F 11:30am-2:30pm, 6:30-10pm; Sa until 10:30pm. 722 King St. 703-548-0088.*

7   The Old Club. ☆ $$ George Washington often stopped by on his way to Mt. Vernon. The large homey dining room still pays him tribute in special Southern fare. *Regional American. Open Tu-Su 11:30am-3pm, Tu-Th 5-9pm, F & Sa until 10pm, Su until 9pm. 555 S. Washington St. 703-549-4555.*

8   Lyceum. (1839-1858; restoration **1974, Carrol Curtice)** Considered the historic headquarters of the city, the 2-story Grecian-style Lyceum presents Alexandria's history in etchings, daguerreotypes, photographs and color slides. *The Fashion Promenade* features costumed historians portraying colonial celebrities in amusing vignettes. *Admission free. Call for scheduled performances. Open daily 9am-5pm. 201 S. Washington St. 703-838-4497.*

Henry Africa's. ☆☆ $$$ French classics with some *nouvelle* surprises highlight the menu. The gorgeous art nouveau decor makes up for an occasional lapse in the kitchen. *French. Open Tu-Th 11:30am-2:30pm, 6:30-10:30pm, F & Sa until 11pm. 607 King St. 703-549-4010.*

0 Christ Church. (1767-1773; tower 1818, **James Wren**) **George Washington** paid $20 for his pew as a vestryman in this English country-style church. Much of the building, both inside and out, is original. Incumbent presidents attend services on the Sunday closest to Washington's birthday. *Open M-Sa 9am-5pm, Su during services and 2-5pm. 118 N. Washington St. 703-549-1450.*

1 Lloyd House and Library. (1793, **John Wise**) A perfect example of late Georgian architecture. After a succession of owners, Lloyd House was saved from demolition by Alexandria's preservationists. The interior has been restored for use by the **Alexandria Library**, which holds a large collection of books and documents on Virginia history. *Open M-F 9am-5pm, Sa 9am-5pm Sept-June; 9am-1pm July-Aug. 220 N. Washington St. 703-838-4577.*

2 Lee-Fendall House. Greek Revival mansion built by **Philip Lee's** grandson in 1785. The dining room was where *Light Horse Harry* **Lee** authored a farewell address to **George Washington**; several newborn Lees were delivered on the swooning couch of the upstairs lady's bedroom, and the children's room is full of antique toys left behind by many Lee generations. *Admission Charge. Open Tu-Sa 10am-4pm, Su noon-4pm. 429 N. Washington St. 703-548-1789.*

13 Boyhood Home of Robert E. Lee. The Lee family settled in the area before the War of 1812, and Robert E. Lee lived in this house until his West Point enrollment in 1825. Beautifully furnished with antiques and family artifacts, the brick house is a showcase of the early Federal period. *Admission charge. Open M-Sa 10am-4pm, Su noon-4pm. Closed mid-Dec to New Year. 607 Oronoco St. 703-548-8454.*

14 Holiday Inn of Old Town. *Moderate.* You wouldn't know there was a modern hotel behind these colonial brick walls. Comfortable rooms, a large indoor pool and a restaurant offering a great champagne brunch on Sundays. Pets and children under 18 in the same room free of charge. Shuttle service to National Airport every 30 minutes or upon request. *480 King St. 703-549-6080.*

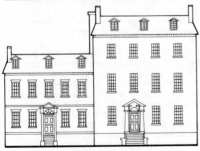

15 Gadsby's Tavern Museum. (tavern, 1752; hotel, 1792; **John Wise**) George Washington enjoyed his last birthday here; that day is still remembered in the traditional tavern *Birthday Ball*. The inn has been completely restored, to the point of including original china and silverware, although the original ballroom interior is a reproduction. *Admission charge. Open Tu-Sa 10am-5pm, Su 1-5pm. 134 N. Royal St. 703-838-4242.*

Adjacent to the museum, the almost 200-year-old **Gadsby's Tavern** restaurant (☆ $$) serves game specials, prime rib, veal, trifle and pecan pie. *American. Open M-Sa 11:30am-3pm, Su 11am-3pm, Su-Th 5:30-9pm, F & Sa till 10pm. 138 N. Royal St. 703-548-1288.*

The **first book published** by the Smithsonian Institution Press in 1848 was *Ancient Monuments of the Mississippi Valley*, by **E.G. Squires** and **E.H. Davis**.

16 G. Randall Fine Antiques specializes in late 17th- and 18th-century English furniture and accessories. Occasionally it carries outstanding American or English pieces of museum quality. *Open M-Sa 10am-5pm. 229 N. Royal St. 703-549-4432.*

17 Norford Inn. Three antique shops: **Eagle Antiques** (703-549-7611), **C&M Antiques** (703-548-9882) and **Two Harolds** (703-683-1883). The trio specializes in antique timepieces and clocks, as well as furniture, oil paintings, country kitchen primitives and glass. *311 Cameron St.*

18 Frankie Welch. The best in American fashions for women, including Frankie's nationally acclaimed designs of scarves and fabrics. *Open M-Sa 9:30am-5:30pm, Th till 7:30pm. 305 Cameron St. 703-549-0104.*

19 Stabler-Leadbeater Apothecary. (1792) It's a combination museum/antique shop which once filled prescriptions for famous Americans from **Martha Washington** to **Robert E. Lee.** The shelves are stocked with original prescription books and equipment. *Open M-Sa 10am-4:30pm. 107 S. Fairfax St. 703-836-3713.*

20 Ramsay House-Tourist Council of Alexandria. (1724) After selecting the area in 1749, Alexandria's founder **William Ramsay** simply shipped his house down the Potomac and hauled it in one piece to its proper lot. The oldest house in Alexandria still contains many of Ramsay's personal belongings, purchased during his career as a merchant trader. Several rooms of the house have been rebuilt to accommodate the **Alexandria Tourist Council**, providing free maps, hotel and group tour reservations, and lists of shops and restaurants in the area. *Open daily 9am-5pm. 221 King St. 703-549-0205.*

21 Antique Guild. Georgian silver, art nouveau and an occasional piece of furniture from the 17th century. *Open W-Sa 10am-5pm, Su 1-5pm. 113 N. Fairfax St. 703-836-1048.*

22 Carlyle House. (1752, **John Ariss**) Designed to resemble a Scottish manor house, the great mid-Georgian home was one of the first built in Alexandria. A number of the Carlyle family's personal effects and household items now on exhibit were found when archaeologists uncovered 5 privy shafts and trash chutes during the restoration. *Admission charge. Guided tours every half hour. Open Tu-Sa 10am-5pm, Su noon-5pm. 121 N. Fairfax St. 703-549-2997.*

23 Bilbo Baggins. ☆☆ $$ Chic wine bar and gourmet restaurant. Gourmet picnic lunches available for carryout. Live entertainment on the patio during warm evenings. *Nouvelle cuisine. M-Sa 11:30am-2:30pm, 5:30-10:30pm; Su 11:30am-3pm, 4:30-9:30pm. 208 Queen St. 703-683-0300.*

24 La Bergerie. ☆☆☆ $$$ Robust Basque specialties like seafood stew or the classic refinement of *filet de poisson* make La Bergerie an unusual restaurant and a definite must during an Alexandrian sojourn. *French. Open M-Sa 11:30am-2:30pm, M-Th 6-10:30pm, F & Sa till 11:30pm. 218 N. Lee St. 703-683-1007.*

25 The Coffee Bean is an institution in Old Town, providing umpteen varieties of coffees from a turn-of-the-century coffee roaster. *Open M-Sa 9:30am-6pm, Su 10am-5pm. 212 King St. 703-836-9242.*

26 Why Not? Would better be called *What Not?* Odds and ends, from handcrafted cotton carryalls to old Virginia recipe books, woven hats and Oshkosh overalls. *Open M-Sa 10am-5:30pm, Su noon-5pm. 200 King St. 703-548-4420.*

27 Athenaeum. Originally the *Bank of Old Dominion* (1851), it was purchased a century later by the **Northern Virginia Fine Arts Association** for an art museum and cultural activities center. Guest curators prepare loan exhibitions on antiques and local history. The museum also hosts lectures, readings, workshops, and films. *Admission free; donations encouraged. Open Tu-Sa 10m-4pm, Sa 104pm. 201 Prince St. 703-548-0035.*

28 Gentry Row. The houses on this mid-18th-century block form a collage of characteristic Georgian themes. All residences are private, except the Greek Revival-style Athenaeum (see above). *200 block of Prince St.*

29 Old Presbyterian Meeting House. The Scottish Presbyterians of Alexandria built this somber, staid Georgian church in 1774. **George Washington's** funeral services, canceled at Christ Church due to stormy weather, were held here. A weathered tombstone in the cemetery honors the **Unknown Soldier of the American Revolution.** *Open M-Sa 9am-4pm, Su noon-5pm. Services Su at 11am. 321 S. Fairfax St. 703-549-6670.*

30 Captain's Row. (early 1800s) The cobblestoned walk from the waterfront up Prince Street is known as *Captain's Row,* because of its charming homes built by old sea captains. The rooflines, proportions, materials and trim of these townhouses vary wildly, perhaps reflecting the independent spirits of the owners. *100 block Prince St.*

31 The Small Mall. This little arcade of shops includes: **Ampersand Books and Records** *(703-549-0840);* **The Gift Horse** *(703-836-1434)* for cut-glass items; *and* **Toys In The Attic** *(703-548-4110)* for old-fashioned quality kids' entertainment like toy lead soldiers. *Mall hours M-Sa 10am-10pm, Su noon-7pm. 118 King St. 703-549-0840.*

32 Serendipity. American craftswork and country accessories by 125 craftsmen from across the nation, from quilters and dollmakers to woodcrafters and tinsmiths. *Open M-Sa 10am-9pm, Su noon-6pm. Closed evenings Jan-Mar. 118 King St. 703-683-3555.*

33 Torpedo Factory. Works of more than 200 artists and craftsmen are represented in this old WWII factory, originally the major producer of Naval waterbombs. The 3 floors are filled with quality art created by the jewelers, sculptors, painters and textile designers who keep open workshops at the factory. Although everything is for sale, the artists are more intent on explaining rather than hard-selling their art. *Open daily 10am-5pm. 101 N. Union St. 703-838-4565.*

34 Thieves Market. More than 35 antique stores under one roof. Just about every collectable imaginable is sold, from furniture and Oriental rugs, to paintings, china, silver and old coins. *Open daily. 7704 Richmond Hwy. 703-360-4200.*

35 Pohick Church. (1769-74) **George Washington** and **George Mason** were on the small committee that designed this country church. The simple block of brick is set off with handsome quoins and pediments of Aquia Creek stone cut from Washington's own quarries. *US 1, south of Alexandria.*

CIVIL WAR SITES

As Civil War hostilities broke into open fighting, each side's capital city became a major target for the enemy. Washington, DC, served as the capital of the Union; Richmond, VA, just over 50 miles away, was capital of the Confederacy. Thus the early campaigns of the war centered in the area between and around these 2 cities:

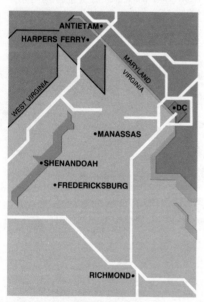

Fredericksburg & Spotsylvania National Military Park, Virginia. A 6,500-acre park commemorates the 100,000 soldiers who fell at the battles of **Fredericksburg, Spotsylvania, Chancellorsville** and **the Wilderness.** Both driving and hiking tours are available in each of the park's 7 areas. Costumed docents and narrative markers explain troop movements and the historic significance of each battle. *Admission free. Visitors Centers: US 1, Fredericksburg; and VA 3, Chancellorsville. Open 8:30am-6:30pm in summer, 9am-5pm rest of year. Take Beltway Exit 4 to Fredericksburg and follow the signs. 703-373-4461.*

By 1838, Fredericksburg was a prospering town for 1,797 white citizens, 1,124 slaves, and 287 free blacks.

Shenandoah National Park, Virginia. Important to the Southern Army for its agricultural riches, sympathetic inhabitants and strategic location, the valley served as a Confederate stronghold for the early part of the war. But Union troops attacked relentlessly, and dozens of battles shattered the farmland's serenity. See page 145 for more information on the Park and battlesites.

Manassas National Battlefield Park, Virginia. Also known as **Bull Run,** 2 of the war's bloodiest battles were fought on this small section of streams, woodlands and hills. At the first major battle of the Civil War, picnickers from nearby Washington, DC, daytripped out to watch the *military encounter;* neither spectators or soldiers expected the horror and panic that ensued. Troops clashed here again one year later when General **Robert E. Lee** sent **Stonewall Jackson** to protect Richmond-to-Shenandoah rail lines. Visitor Center (off Rt. 234) has audio-visual program explaining the military and historic aspects of both battles. *Admission free. Open daily 9am-6pm, till 5:30 in winter. Closed Christmas. Take Beltway Exit 9 to Rt. 234.*

Harpers Ferry National Historical Park, West Virginia. Site of **John Brown's** infamous raid on a Federal arsenal; he hoped to raise a private army to murder Southern sympathizers. The unsuccessful attack ended in the hanging of Brown and several of his men. The Harpers Ferry Visitor Center has a film on the historic town and Civil War activity here. The 1,500-acre park is *open daily; special programs during summer. Take Beltway Exit 35, then Rt. 340.*

Antietam National Battlefield, Maryland. Also known as **Sharpsburg.** Here the Union Army successfully halted Lee's drive north toward Pennsylvania. In the bloodiest day of the war, 23,000 men were left dead or wounded. Now 810 acres are set aside to commemorate the battle. *Admission free. Short slide show. Open daily during summer 8am-6pm, 8:30am-5pm rest of year. Closed major holidays. Take Beltway Exit 35, take Rt. Frederick, then Rt. 34 to Sharpsburg. Visitor Center is on MD 65 north of Sharpsburg. 301-432-5124.*

Collections were taken up among the soldiers of **Robert E. Lee's** army to relieve starvation and suffering among the people surviving the Battle of Fredericksburg in 1862. One Georgia regiment raised $500; General **Stonewall Jackson** personally gave $100, his headquarters $800; and **A.P. Hill's** division donated $10,000.

FAIRS & FESTIVALS

January

Jan 19   Robert E. Lee's Birthday, Alexandria. Reception held on the closest Saturday at the Robert E. Lee Boyhood Home and at Lee Fendall House in Alexandria. *North Washington at Oronoco Sts.*

February

Open House, Mount Vernon. On the third Monday in February, admission to Mount Vernon is free. *Take Washington Memorial Parkway to Mount Vernon.*

Open House, Fredericksburg. Admission free on the official Monday holiday to the Fredericksburg Museum, The Apothecary Shop, the Rising Sun Tavern and the Kenmore, Belmont and James Monroe Museum. *Visitors Center at Charlotte and Caroline Sts.*

Feb 22   George Washington's Birthday, Mt. Vernon. Party at Mary Washington House, *Mount Vernon.*

March

Sugar Maple Festivals. Virginia's Highland County opens its syrup-producing camps to visitors. Enjoy the Maple Queen contest, the Buckwheat Stomp and Maple Sugar Hoedown during the last 2 weekends in March. *West on US Route 250 to Monterey.*

April

Bay Bridge Walk, Annapolis. 1 Sunday each April attracts 10s of thousands each year. The 4.3-mile walk begins on the bridge's east side. *Route 2 to Colonial Parkway. 301-757-6000 for information.*

Apr 13   Thomas Jefferson's Birthday Commemoration, Charlottesville. University of Virginia honors Jefferson's birthday with the Thomas Jefferson Memorial Foundation awards in architecture & law. *Cabell Hall, University of Virginia. 804-924-3337.*

Charlottesville Dogwood Festival. The last Saturday in April hosts the festival and its Grand Feature Parade, from Water St. to Lane High School. Honor the Dogwood Queen at the coronation ball and barbeque, or enjoy lacrosse tournaments and a track meet. *US Route 29 south to Charlottesville. 804-295-3141 for more info.*

May

Shenandoah Apple Blossom Festival, Winchester, VA. Since 1924, Winchester has hosted the 4-day fesitval in early May, when small pink and white blossoms fill the orchards. Queen Shenandoah takes her crown, and the Shenandoah Apple Blossom Banjo and Fiddle contest winds up. *US Route 50 to Winchester. 703-662-3863.*

Preakness Festival, Baltimore. Pimlico Race Course sets off the Preakness Stakes, while also playing host to bicycle races, the Preakness parade and other racing festivities. *Hayward Ave. to Pimlico. 301-542-9400.*

June

June 14   Flag Day Celebration, Baltimore. Fort McHenry National Monument & Historic shrine, the site of an 1812 naval bombing, celebrates Flag Day with bands, a color presentation, speeches and military drills. *East Fort Ave. to the Fort. 301-837-1793.*

Perhaps because it is elected every 2 years rather than every 6, the House of Representatives marches more in step with the current electronic social drumbeat than does the Senate. In 1979 TV was allowed into the House. Six cameras are mounted in the gallery. The director and 3 cameramen give camera directions by remote control—from 2 stories below in the basement. The proceedings are carried via close-circuit TV to all congressional offices, allowing members to stay abreast while they're away. Clips are also made available free to the press and C-Span, a cable service, carries the proceedings. The Senate still votes by roll call and has declined to allow television access.

July

July 4   Wreath Laying Ceremony, Mount Vernon. Guard Fife and Drum Corps lead a procession from George Washington's Tomb. *703-780-2000.*

July 4   Charlottesville ceremonies. Monticello admission is free during the morning. Other festivities taking place throughout the city include softball tournament, concert at Ash Lawn, fireworks. *Route 53 to Monticello. 804-977-1783.*

July 14   Bastille Day Celebration, Annapolis. The annual festival at the Maryland Inn on Church Circle features French foods, mimes, musicians and dancing. *Route 450 to Church Circle. 301-263-2641.*

August

Late Aug   Shenandoah County Fair, Woodstock, Virginia. Livestock, old-time fiddle and banjo contests and harness races highlight this week-long fair. *Route 42 to the fairgrounds. 703-459-3867.*

September

Sep 12   Defender's Day Ceremony, Baltimore. Fort McHenry reenacts the bombardment each Sunday before Defender's Day. Fireworks, music and speeches top off the day. *East Fort Avenue off Hanover St. 301-962-4290.*

3rd Week   Baltimore City Fair. Baltimore's Inner Harbor's cultural neighborhoods come to life with exhibits of ethnic foods and entertainment. *Baltimore Washington Parkway to Pratt St. 301-837-4636.*

October

Maryland Oktoberfest, Baltimore. Folkdancers, oom-pah bands and alpine horn players gather at the Fifth Regiment Armory each 1st weekend of October. *Preston St. at Howard St. 301-837-4636.*

Dog Mart-Auction and Fair activities, Fredericksburg. The Dog Mart started in the 1600s, when Virginia settlers would meet with Indians to trade hunting dogs for gold. Now dogs of nearly every breed change owners and at the auction, following an elaborate dog and owner parade and informal dog show. *Route 17 to Fredericksburg Agricultural Fairgrounds. 703-373-1776.*

Oct 7   Anniversary of Edgar Allen Poe's Death—Commemoration, Baltimore. The first Sunday of October, the Westminster Presbyterian Church's wreath-laying ceremony take place at Poe's gravesite. Speeches and a reception follow. Also open house at the Poe House and Museum. *203 Amity St. 301-396-4866.*

November

Chesapeake Appreciation Days, Annapolis, Maryland. Sandy Point State Park celebrates the oyster season the weekend closest to Nov 1. Sailboat races, hot-air balloon races and seafood. *Route 50 past Annapolis. 301-974-1249/757-1841.*

December

Wolf Trap Carol Sing, Vienna, Virginia. The US Marine band and local choirs head up a sing-along Christmas presentation on the first Sunday in December.

In the dark basement of the Capitol, directly underneath the rotunda, there is a crypt that holds no corpse. The designers of the Capitol had hoped to reinter the remains of **George Washington** there. (Look for the mark on the Capitol floor where grill work would have allowed visitors to look down on the tomb.) Understandably, Washington's heirs protested, and the first president has stayed next to Martha in the family's simple tomb at Mt. Vernon.

The only thing to ever occupy the crypt is an ancient catafalque. The wooden platform covered with dark cloth has had a history of sad service. It's held the coffin for the lying-in-state ceremony.

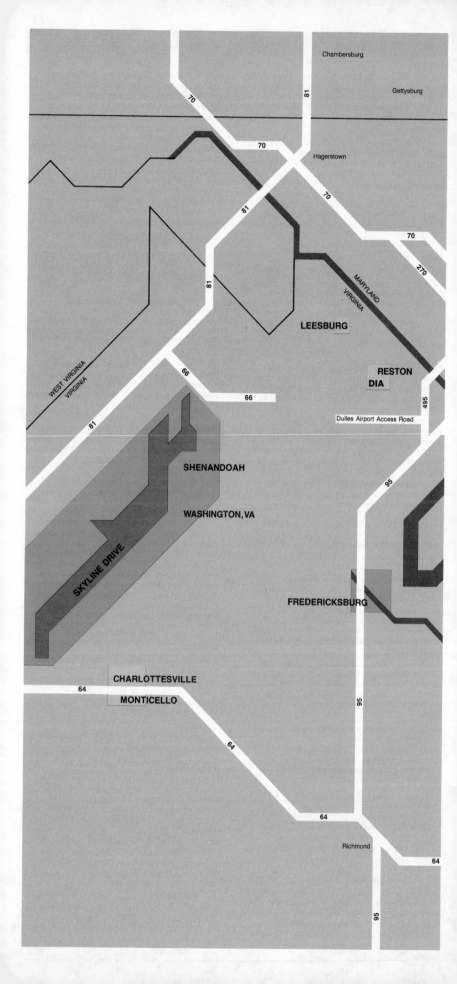

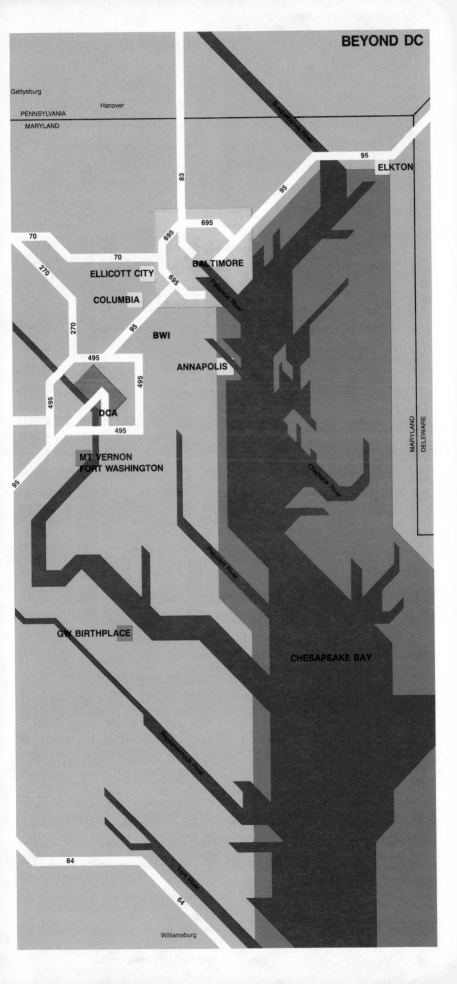

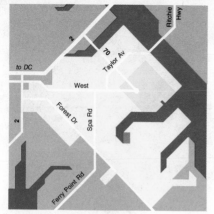

ANNAPOLIS

Annapolis, *just 30 miles away from DC, walks you through Colonial history with its splendid 18th-century homes, an old dock from the city's busy tobacco-export golden days, and the military sites of yesterday.*

First settled in 1649, the area was called Providence, then Anne Arundel Town. In 1694, Annapolis took its name from **Princess Anne,** *soon to be Queen of England. From November 1783 through August of the next year, the area served as the US Capital.*

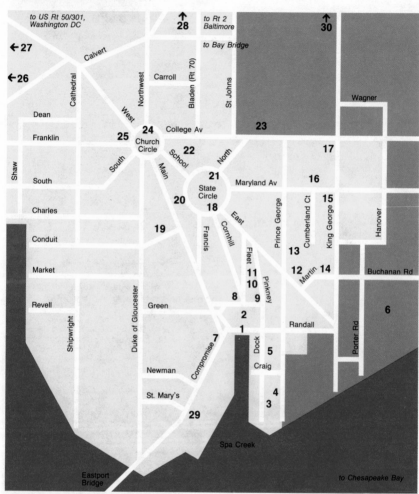

1 **City Dock.** The old dock marks the heart of the city, where the tobacco trade first took off. Street lamps in the waterfront's park are replicas of the oil lanterns from the 1800s. *At the harbor.*

1 **The Sign O' The Whale,** the brick building just west of the dock, is believed to have been the old Customs House. *At the harbor.*

2 **Market House at City Dock.** The first Market House here was built in 1788, the next in 1858. A renovated version opened in 1972. The market place's shops feature vegetables, bakery goods, and, of course, fish.

3 **Harbour House Restaurant.** ☆ ☆ $/$$ Modern version of an olde beamed-ceiling tavern. Seafood, prime rib and bouillabaisse specialities. A fine view overlooks the port. *Continental. Open daily 11am-10pm. City Dock, 301-268-0771.*

4 **Gibson's Lodging,** just off City Dock. *110 Prince George St. 301-268-5555.*

5 **Harbour Square.** Treat yourself to some wonderful chocolates before dashing off to the haberdashery among the square's half a dozen specialty shops. Jewelry, gifts and artwork could just finish off your day (and your wallet). *On the City Dock, open 7 days a week.*

6 **United States Naval Academy.** Established in 1845, buildings include the Chapel and French Renaissance-style **Bancroft Hall.** The Chapel houses the tomb of **John Paul Jones,** who is often called *the father of the US Navy.* Naval officers are memorialized in the chapel's stained glass windows; on either side lie anchors from the *New York,* a cruiser used to blockade Cuba in 1898.

Preble Hall's museum features 30,000 nautical relics, from ships models to uniforms, to oil paintings and engravings.

The **Visitor Information Center** at **Ricketts Hall** is open 9am-4pm daily. *Walking tours available. Gift Shop hours 10am-4pm daily. Visitor Gate, King George St. 301-267-6100.*

Victualling Warehouse Maritime Museum. the *Maritime Annapolis 1751-81* exhibit in this 18th-century building. Other displays focus on trade and commerce. Commissary stores stood here during the Revolution. *Admission charge. Open daily 11am-4:30pm. 77-79 Main St. 703-268-5576.*

Riordans. ☆ ☆ $$ This saloon and second-floor dining room is well-known for its reliable seafood and prime rib. *Open daily 11am-2am; Su brunch 10am-1pm. At City Dock, 301-263-5449.*

Tobacco Prise House. This restored warehouse exhibits tobacco-making tools and equipment. *Admission charge. Tickets at Victualling Warehouse. Open weekends Apr-Oct and by appointment. 4 Pinkney St.*

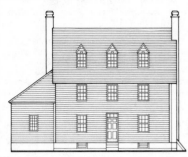

Shiplap House. Built in 1713 by **Edward Smith.** The Historic Annapolis group purchased and restored the building in 1958. *Not open to the public. 18 Pinkney St.*

The Barracks. Furnishings here show the lifestyle of Revolutionary War soldiers awaiting sea passage to battlesites. *Admission charge. Open weekends, Apr-Oct. 43 Pinkney St.*

Brice House. (1776, **James Brice**) This Georgian mansion is one of Annapolis' largest homes. Note the triple pediment windows above the main entrance and the huge chimneys. Recently restored using the original colors, this is a registered National Historic Landmark. *Not open to the public. 42 East St.*

William Paca House. (1765, **William Paca**) The signer of the Declaration of Independence and 3-time governor of Maryland built this 5-part mansion.

Now restored and refurnished, the building is used as a conference center for the US State Department. *Admission charge. Open Tu-Sa 10am-4pm; Su noon-4pm. Closed M except legal holidays. 186 Prince George St. 301-263-5553.*

William Paca Garden. Restored Colonial garden with sculptured terraces, waterways and other features authentically reconstructed. *Admission charge. Open M-F 10am-4pm; Su noon-5pm.*

Hammond Harwood House. William Buckland's 18th-century Georgian mansion features egg and dart molding and Ionic columns at the front door. Rose festoons frame the fan above the front window. *Admission charge. Open Tu-Sa 10am-5pm, Su 2pm-5pm. Closed in winter. Maryland Ave. at King George St. 301-269-1714.*

Chase-Lloyd House. Samuel Chase, signer of the Declaration of Independence, sold this unfinished house to **Edward Lloyd** in 1771. The piano which played the wedding march for **Mary Lloyd** and **Francis Scott Key** is still on exhibit. Now a ladies' retirement home. *Admission charge. Open daily except W & Su, 2-4pm. Maryland Ave. between Prince George and King George Sts. 301-263-2723.*

Ogle Hall. First occupied by Royal Governor **Samuel Ogle** in 1739, this hall was bought by the Naval Academy in 1949 to serve as a graduate guest home. *Closed to the public. 247 King George St.*

Old Treasury Building. Built in 1735 to store Bills of Credit, the brick building with arched ceilings serves as the tour office of Historic Annapolis Inc. *Open M-F 9am-4:30pm, 7 days in summer. State House Grounds at State Circle. 301-267-8149.*

19 Visitor's Center offers resources on the city and surrounding areas, tours and various buildings. *171 Conduct St. 301-268-8687.*

20 Gallery on the Circle. The Maryland Federation of Art operates this gallery with everchanging art exhibits. *Admission free. Open Tu-Sa 11am-5pm, Su 2-5pm. 18 State Circle. 268-4566.*

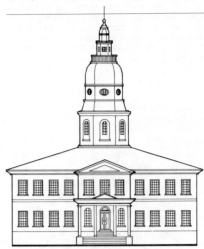

21 Maryland State House. This is the oldest US state capitol in continuous legislative use. Built between 1772 and 1779, a newer 1902 section houses senate and house chambers. **George Washington** resigned as commander-in-chief of the Continental Army in the Old Senate Chamber.

The structure's dome is the largest wooden dome in the US. Officials climb 149 steps twice daily to raise and lower the state flag. *Free guided tours. Open daily 9am-5pm. State Circle. 301-269-3400.*

22 Government House. This 1866 Victorian house belonging to the Naval Academy was converted to a Georgian-style structure in the 1930s. *School St. at State Circle.*

23 St. John's College. Opened in 1696 as one of the first US public schools, the college was used during the Civil War as a Northern parole and hospital center. **McDowell Hall,** built in 1742 as a residence for Governor **Thomas Bladen,** became known as *"Bladen's Folly"* for its grandiose style. *Campus bordered by Bladen and and King George Sts., College and Taylor Aves.*

The **Liberty Tree,** on the campus' nothern side, is a tulip poplar over 400 years old.

24 St. Anne's Church. The first church here was constructed in the 1600s; the present structure, built in 1858, is the third church built on this site. *Open 7am-6pm. Church Circle. 301-267-9333.*

25 Reynold's Tavern. This 1747 building served as **William Reynolds'** tavern and hat-making business. This burnt-blue brick colonial building was then used as a public library and is undergoing restoration. *Church Circle.*

26 London Town Publik House. This restored Colonial inn overlooks the South River. The only building remaining from an 18th-century town. *Open Tu-Sa 10am-4pm, Su noon-4pm. Closed Jan & Feb. 839 London Town Rd., Edgewater. 301-956-4900.*

27 Holiday Inn. *Moderate.* Plenty of rooms in this traditional hotel. Conveniently close to the historic district; equipped with HBO, meeting and banquet facilities. *210 Holiday Court. 301-224-3150.*

Introductions/Theaters/Narrative black
Hotels purple
Museums/Architecture blue
Parks/Open spaces green
Restaurants/Nightlife red
Shops/Galleries violet

ANNAPOLIS

28 Helen Avalynne Tawes Garden. The festive colors and sweet fragrances of the Eastern Shore's best gardens. *Admission & tours free. Open year 'round, dawn to dusk. Rowe Blvd. at Taylor Ave. 301-269-3656.*

29 Annapolis Hilton Inn. *Moderate/expensive.* Located in the historic district, some rooms have balconies overlooking the harbor; the **Penthouse Wardroom Restaurant, Skipper's Pub** and **Afterdeck Bar** are all there for refreshment. 135 rooms; special packages available. *Compromise St. at St. Mary's St. 301-268-7555.*

30 Les Survivants. ☆ ☆ $$ A creative and changing menu in a calm Annapolis setting. Outdoor deck dining in warm weather. *French. Open M-F 11:30am-2:30pm, 6-10pm; Sa 6-10pm; Su 11am-2pm. 609 Melvin Ave. 301-267-0999.*

COLUMBIA

Columbia. (Begun 1967) Columbia was conceived in the 1960s as an alternative to the urban lifestyle, and has since become one of the most successful planned communities in America. Eventually, 110,000 people will live on the 21-square-mile site. **The Rouse Company,** which is responsible for the city's development, brought educators, health professionals and sociologists into the design process, and set for itself a list of idealistic goals regarding the quality of life in the new town—goals which are particularly reflected in the innovative and exemplary educational and medical facilities available to residents of every age.

Comparisons between Columbia and not-too-distant Reston find a great number of similarities: clustered housing, proximity to nature, a wealth of recreational possibilities, and the presence of many high-tech companies as an economic base. Yet Columbia's larger population, somewhat greater density, and proximity to both Washington and Baltimore give it a bit more big-city feeling, and make it a very attractive option for residents of both cities who may be looking for a quieter pace. *Located in Howard County, MD, off I-95. 301-992-6000.*

ELLICOTT CITY

Ellicott City. Picturesque Maryland town was originally the site of a Quaker gristmill (1772). Today it attracts visitors with its many historic buildings (including **Benjamin Latrobe's Folly,** the great architect's 1835 viaduct), the B&O Railroad Terminal, the oldest in the country; the famed stretch of track where the **Tom Thumb** steam locomotive raced a horse—and won; and the town's special Christmas season celebration. *From Beltway Exit 30, take Rt. 29 to Old Frederic Rd., then to Ellicott City. Howard County Information Center, 301-992-2344.*

The famous **Senate Bean Soup,** a specialty of the Capitol, consists of white Boston beans soaked overnight and a generous piece of ham hock, all simmered for over 4 hours.

ELKTON

Elkton, Maryland, is the closest county seat south of New York, New Jersey and Pennsylvania. As such, the town flourished by marrying couples unwilling to wait the time other states required for marriage licenses. Cab drivers would meet incoming trains and—for a high fee—take couples first to a courthouse for a license, then to a parson for the wedding. Signs advertised *Marrying Parson* up and down Main Street. Business came to a halt in 1938, however, when Maryland passed a 48-hour waiting period for licenses.

Long before the capital became as much as a speck on L'Enfant's city map, Washington was an important center of activity to its original inhabitants, the American Indians of Chesapeake Bay. Mainly of **Algonquin** and **Nanticoke** linguistic stock, the 30 or 40 tribes occupied an extensive area stretching from the Virginia tidewater region and Potomac's peninsula and the bay, to the eastern country of Maryland. These permanent settlers lived in houses on small plots varying in size from 2 to 200 acres, their villages usually encircled by palisades and placed near fishing and hunting grounds. Almost all the areas used by the Native Americans have been traced to their original use; the valley beneath Capitol Hill was a source of fish, **Greenleaf Point** nearby was used as a council gathering place, and west of 16th Street at Arkansas Avenue was the location of a principal quarry workshop.

The Algonquins were a peaceful, somewhat artistic people, much devoted to spiritual ceremonies and acts of faith. Ritual burials and monotheistic praises to **Okee** (the one God) were principal activities. Among the subordinate tribes of the Nanticoke, sorcerers and medicine men enjoyed an elevated status.

The only known artisan efforts in these river communities consisted of pottery making. These utensils were crafted of soapstone taken from the country's greatest quarries only a few miles from the present site of the White House.

Captain John Smith's arrival in 1608 marks a slow but steady decline in the Native American population. Despite Smith's legendary marriage to Pocahontas, white settlers regarded the original inhabitants as second class citizens. Their land was exploited and their culture and customs disregarded. During the next 60 years, two-thirds of the 40 tribes disappeared due to smallpox, alcoholism, and actual expulsion—all brought on by the white settlers. But it wasn't only the Europeans who lead to this decline: the lower bay tribes—now weakened by the colonists' expansion, were continuously attacked by the Susquehannock tribe, an aggressive Iroquois people from the northern end of the bay. It was only at the turn of the 17th century that a few remaining tidewater Native Americans were rescued by the **Iroquoian League,** which now experienced the same threat of extinction from the white man.

What remained as a legacy to the first riparian civilization was the Native American place names: **Potomac, Piscataway, Accokeek, Pohick, Accotink. Anacostia** first appeared on an old map carried by Captain Smith, who himself called the village **Nacotchtant. Captain Henry Fleete** named the inhabitants **Nascotines,** later latinized by the Jesuits as **Anacostia.** Today, a small group of Native Americans reside in Washington, DC; most are assimilated yet highly conscious of their heritage and further their cause through the Bureau of Indian Affairs.

More than **54 miles of shoreline** and 100,000 acres of land belong to the 17 military installations in the metropolitan Washington area, within 10 miles of the Potomac estuary.

Originally the cost for building the **C&O Canal** was estimated at $2,000,000. At its completion in 1850, the tab was up to $11,000,000.

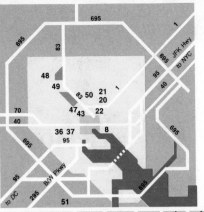

A rich Colonial history and new, shiny glass buildings have transformed **Baltimore** *back into the thriving city it was during the days of the* tall ships.

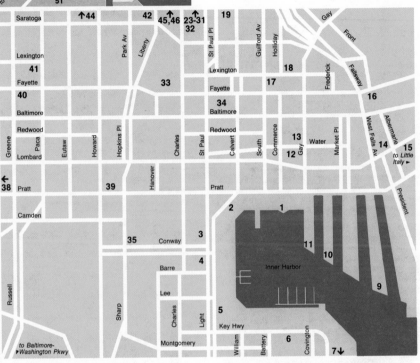

Founded in 1729, the once bustling seaport town began to deteriorate in the 1950s and by the 1960s was a prime target for urban renewal. Dismayed and alarmed by the city's disintegration, a group of businessmen formed the Greater Baltimore Committee and drew up plans for revitalization. With city governments' help—particularly Mayor **William Schaefer** in the 1970s—these plans have become reality.

The results? A sparkling inner harbor, spruced-up homes and a recharged downtown. The first makeover gave us **Charles Center,** a 15-building office and apartment complex which covers 33 acres of downtown Baltimore.

The second part of the plan involved developing the **Inner Harbor,** and the *piece de resistance* here is the **Rouse Company's Harborplace.** The $18 million project attracts thousands of visitors weekly with its 2 smooth glass pavilions topped with green aluminum roofs. The 2 marketplaces meet at a right angle, and from everywhere inside give a view of the water and its ships.

Other projects for the harbor have included the 30-story **World Trade Center** and the **Maryland Science Center.** The **National Aquarium** brings visitors face to face with fish and sea mammals—as close as possible without getting wet. The amazing concrete and glass structure juts out over **Pier 3.**

Enola Gay, the plane that dropped the first atomic bomb on Hiroshima, can be seen at the Smithsonian's airplane repair shop in Suitland, Maryland.

To further rehabilitate the city, homesteading programs have allowed people to buy abandoned homes for $1 and repair them, often turning simple row houses into valuable properties.

Backing up all of Baltimore's newfangled developments is a firm base in history. Now ranked as the 10th largest US city, Baltimore once enjoyed the height of power among seaport trade and commerce. The early 1800s brought wealth to the newly founded city. The Revolutionary War and the 1800s saw shipbuilding flourish, and the great Baltimore clippers were built.

Baltimore left its mark on US history as the meeting place of the Continental Congress in 1777. It can also boast of being the birth place of the *Star Spangled Banner,* created when **Francis Scott Key** saw the flag still flying after a British attack on **Fort McHenry.**

In 1827, Baltimore businessmen feared that the new Erie Canal would threaten their profitable trans-Allegheny traffic as goods and settlers moved westward from the East Coast cities and ports. In response, the Baltimore and Ohio Railroad, the first public railroad in North America, was established. The successful run of **Peter Cooper's** *Tom Thumb* train introduced steam locomotives to the B&O. A replica of it still stands at the **B&O Museum.** Faced with financial difficulties in 1965, the B&O joined forces with the Chesapeake & Ohio Railroad.

Historic Baltimore, with its new glimmering harbor and office buildings, can be proud of its history-making past and its positive steps towards a vibrant future. The port offers visitors a great chance to explore the best of urban America—old and new.

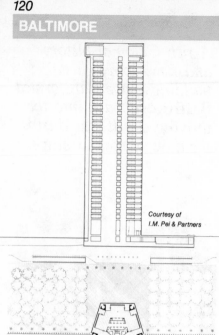

Courtesy of
I.M. Pei & Partners

1 World Trade Center. (1979, **I.M. Pei**) The world's tallest pentagonal highrise reflects Pei's fondness for strong geometries and is perhaps the most recognizable feature of Baltimore's new downtown skyline. There's a great observation deck on the 27th floor, called the *Top of the World:* you'll see the entire city, as well as creative displays of the port, its attractions and its people. Buttons, levers and viewers are all hands-on; this is the perfect place for kids and the first-time visitor to the city. *Admission charge. Open daily 10am-5pm; 7 Jul-Sept 10am-10pm. 401 E. Pratt St.* 301-837-4515.

The Information Kiosk on Inner Harbor's West Shore Promenade is a good place to stop when planning tours around Baltimore.

2 Harborplace. (1980, **Benjamin Thompson & Associates**) Acclaimed as the nucleus of the **Inner Harbor** renewal effort, the 2 glass-enclosed pavilions seem to float on the edge of Baltimore's inner harbor.

Put together with great attention to color and detail by **The Rouse Company,** the $18 million Harborplace offers 142,000 square feet of shops, taverns and eateries.

Two shimmering glass pavilions appear docked at the water's edge. The **Light Street Pavilion** features **Phillips' Harborplace, City Lights, The Sam Smith Market** and a variety of eating booths. The **Pratt Street Pavilion** hosts **The Taverna Athena, Black Pearl** and more restaurants and shops.

Also at Harborplace are:

The American Cafe. ☆ ☆ $$ Hip foods for the slick, high-tech generation—soups and croissants or Nouvelle American entrees. *Regional American/cafe. Open M-Th, Su 11-2am, F & Sa till 3am; Su brunch 11am-3pm. Light St. Pavilion.* 301-962-8817.

Phillips. ☆ ☆ $$ Great ocean-view patio seating, live Dixieland jazz on Sundays, and an assortment of some of the freshest crabs, mussels and clams in Baltimore. *Seafood. Open Su-Th 11am-11pm, F & Sa till midnight. No reservations. Light St. Pavilion.* 301-685-6600.

Jean Claude's Cafe. ☆ ☆ $$ More than just a regular bistro, Jean Claude's shines in its presentations of provincial lamb and veal dishes. *French. Open M-F 11:30am-2:30pm, Sa & Su till 3pm; M-Th 5:30-10:30pm, F & Sa till 11:30pm, Su till 9pm. No reservations. Light St. Pavilion.* 301-332-0950.

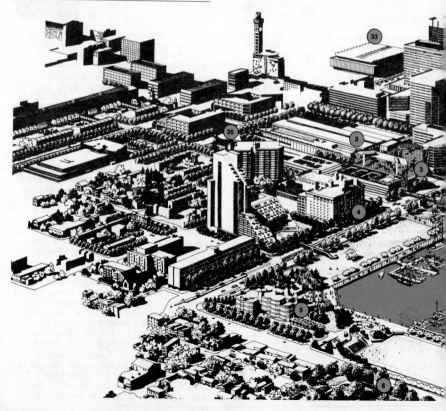

Gianni's. ☆ ☆ ☆ ☆ $$ The vibrant, irreverent art deco matches the playful kitchen's excellent preparation of Northern Italian delights. Order *fusilli*, pasta in a sweet cream *pesto* as an entree or as *antipasti*. *Northern Italian*. Open M-F 11:30am-3pm, daily 6pm-2am. Sa & Su brunch 11:30am-4pm. Pratt St. Pavilion. 301-837-1130.

Bamboo House. ☆ ☆ $ If you *must* have Chinese food while in Baltimore, try this top-class Szechuan haven. *Chinese*. Open M-Th 11:30am-10pm, F till 11pm; Sa noon-11pm, Su noon-10pm. Pratt St. Pavilion. 301-625-1191.

Some of the shops at Harborplace are:

Laura Ashley. Famous floral prints in fashion and home accessories. *Open M-Sa 10am-9:30pm, Su noon-6pm*. 301-539-0500.

Crabtree & Evelyn, for prepared or customized gift baskets. 301-547-0668.

The Limited for women's career and activewear. 301-547-1548.

Hats in the Belfry, with 500 different styles, topped by **Borsalino** and **Whittall & Javits** designs. 301-528-0060.

Grrreat Bears. High mama **VanderBear** is for sale with her whole family of **Poohs.** 301-244-8677.

Europa Imports. Polish weavings, Czech crystal, Italian glass and other handicrafts from 20 European nations. 301-332-0734.

Hyatt Regency Baltimore. *Moderate/expensive.* Special walkways connect this immense, glass-paneled hotel with Harborplace. The 490 rooms have access to 2 tennis courts, a health club and a large rooftop swimming pool. The upgraded **Regency Club** features fancy toiletries, morning paper, breakfast in bed, unlimited concierge assistance and free drinks. Lounge on the top floor. 300 Light St. 301-528-1234.

Within the hotel is:

The Trellis Garden ☆ ☆ $$$ Hyatt's innovative restaurant serves pasta salads, sushi and regional American specialties in a lush, elegant setting. *Reservations recommended, jackets required*. Open M-F 11:30am-2pm, Su-Th 6-10:30pm, F & Sa till 11pm. Light St. 301-528-1234.

Lacrosse. Baltimore is the USA's unofficial capital of Lacrosse. **The Lacrosse Foundation** and **Lacrosse Hall of Fame** are both located here. Home-team heroes, the **Johns Hopkins University** Lacrosse team, have captured several national titles. And it's a favorite game of the city's youth, who, as soon as they can hold a stick, are coached in the game's fine points.

The stick-and-ball game was derived from North America's native inhabitants such as the **Hurons,** who met in teams of one hundred to one thousand in sacred mock combat to play *baggataway*. Estimates date the beginning of the game to the 1400s. In the early 1800s the game was adapted by French settlers in Canada, who called it *lecross,* after the stick's resemblance to a bishop's crozier. By the 1870s a Lacrosse organization, with rules and standards, had been established. The game spread to college campuses, where it remains popular.

Lacrosse is a cousin of soccer, sharing that game's fast pace and back-and-forth field action. Two teams of players—10 for men, 12 for women— each play on a field 60-by-110 yards; goals are at each end with 80 yards betwen them. Players use a stick, or *crosse*, with a basket-like net at one end to catch and throw the ball down the field for a goal.

If you're visiting Baltimore during spring or summer, take time to learn why Lacrosse is a local passion. You can catch games on most pleasant evenings at local colleges or city parks. For more information, write *The Lacrosse Foundation, Newton H. White Athletic Center, Homewood, Baltimore, MD 21218,* or call *301-235-6882.*

Introductions/Theaters/Narrative black
Hotels purple
Museums/Architecture blue
Parks/Open spaces green
Restaurants/Nightlife red
Shops/Galleries violet

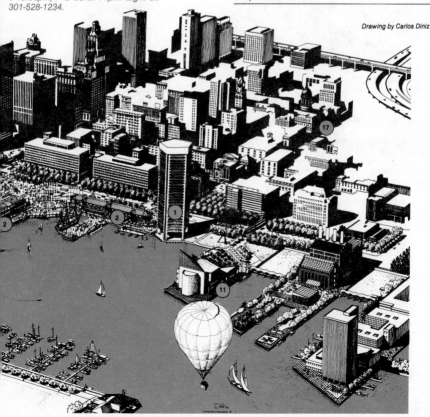

Drawing by Carlos Diniz

4 The McCormick & Co. Spice Factory has occupied the 9-story building on Light Street since 1921. Its free tour includes the half-hour movie *The Wonderful World of Flavor*, which describes spice packaging and marketing, the origin of spices and their importance in the 15th and 16th centuries. You can also see replicas of **William Shakespeare's** grammar school and **Anne Hathaway's** house, built in an Elizabethan courtyard by artist **Edwin Tunis**. Free coffee, tea and cookies at **Ye Old McCormick Tea House.** *Admission free. Tours M-F 10am, 1:30pm. Reservations suggested. 414 Light St. 301-547-6000.*

5 Maryland Science Center & Planetarium. (1976, **Edward Durell Stone**) An octagonal structure of soft pink brick encloses 5 permanent exhibits on Baltimore, the Chesapeake Bay and other scientific information. The center is the permanent home of the Maryland Academy of Sciences, founded in 1797. Traveling exhibits on the latest in Earth and Space achievements also find their way to this great institution. The **Davis Planetarium** creates a stellar voyage with 350 simultaneous projectors and the **Boyd Theatre** screens films and *live* experiments. Not to be missed. *Admission charge. Open M-Sa 10am-10pm, Su noon-8pm. 601 Light St. 301-685-2370/685-5225.*

6 Federal Hill Park. You'll get the best panoramic view of the harbor from this hill, which was occupied by the North during the Civil War. The Otterbein Homesteading Project below the park, an area of 18th-century homes, has been restored by modern urban homesteaders who each bought their homes for one symbolic dollar. *Open 7am-midnight. Battery St. and Key Hwy.*

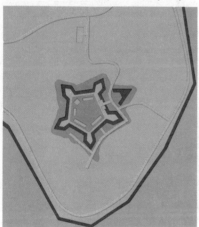

7 Fort McHenry. (1794-1805) **John Jacob Ulrich Rivardi** planned this star-shaped fort overlooking the harbor. The 20-foot-thick brick walls protected the compound from the British attact on 13 September 1814; the morning after, **Francis Scott Key** wrote the *National Anthem* when he saw that the US flag still flew.

The Visitor's Center offers films and exhibits on the fort and the national anthem. *Open daily except Christmas and New Year's, 9am-5pm; Memorial Day-Labor Day 9am-8pm. E. Fort Ave. 301-962-4290.*

8 Fell's Point. One of the first great maritime communities, much of this 18th-century area remains unchanged. Wharves, warehouses and port-related businesses sprang up soon after **William Fell** purchased the Point in 1731. Surviving buildings include the **Robert Long House, Brown's Wharf, Market Square, Public Market** and **Captain Pitt House.** Modern galleries, restaurants, shops and pubs round out your visit to Fell's Point. *Broadway to the Waterfront.*

In the wake of Baltimore's 1856 statewide elections, violent gangs like the *Plug Uglies* and the *Blood Tubs* controlled the streets.

Fell's Point shops and restaurants include:

Eat Bertha's Mussels. ☆ ☆ ☆ $$ Their namesake bumper stickers, ordering you to *Eat Bertha's Mussels*, speak the truth. Scottish tea on Wednesdays for a change of pace. *Seafood. Open Su-Th 11:30am-11pm, F & Sa till midnight. Reservations necessary for high tea. 734 S. Broadway. 301-327-5795.*

Unicorn Studios. Vintage stained glass, gold-leafed and expertly framed. *Open M-Sa 10am-6pm. 626 S. Broadway. 301-675-5412.*

Seaport Trading Company. Quirky mix of 19th-century antiques, wildlife decoys and *Harbor Sweets*—Baltimore's own chocolates. *Open M & Tu, Th-Sa 10am-5pm. Closed W & Su. 914-16 S. Wolfe St. 301-SEA-PORT.*

St. Honore. ☆ $$ Elegant pastries and *pates de maison* in addition to daily country-style specials. *French. Open M-Sa 11:30am-2:30pm, 5:30-10pm. 505 S. Broadway. 301-522-1100.*

Haussner's. ☆ ☆ ☆ $$ Heads-of-state are literally fixtures at this incredible restaurant, hoarding a big collection of Greco-Roman busts and antique paintings in the dining room. Once the gawking is over, settle down for a feast of rabbit with spaetzle, sauerbraten or seafood. *German-American. No dinner reservations. Open Tu-Sa 11am-11pm. 3236 Eastern Ave. 301-327-8365.*

9 Pier 6. Vaguely reminiscent of the opera house in Sydney, Australia, this new addition to the Inner Harbor is the largest of its kind in America. The open music pavilion seats 2,000 listeners both inside and outside its canvas-domed steel structure; pop, jazz and classical music are featured throughout the summer season. *Box office open Tu and Th 10am-6pm; W, F & Sa 10am-9pm. Pier 6 at Pratt St. 301-727-2766/ Telecharge 301-625-1400.*

10 USS Torsk. The submarine whose maiden voyage sank the last Japanese battleships of World War II. After that feat, the *Torsk* was fortified with a snorkel-equipped *GUPPY* machine; she went on to serve in the 1960 war in Lebanon and the 1962 naval blockade of Cuba. *Admission charge. Open Su-M, Th-Sa 10am-4:30pm. Inner Harbor. 301-396-3854.*

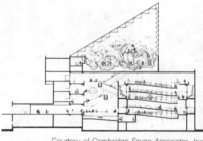

Courtesy of Cambridge Seven Associates, Inc.

11 National Aquarium. (1980, **Peter Chermayeff**) Sitting proudly on Pier 3 of the Inner Harbor, the aquarium gives the illusion of being under water; the greenhouse roofline resembling full sails. Inside, this $21 million structure gives visitors an eye-level view of over 6,000 specimens of fish, birds, reptiles, amphibians and sea mammals.

Moving walkways carry you to all 5 levels. A 63-foot finback whale skeleton hanging from the ceiling dives towards a central area. Four bottle-nosed dolphins swim in the dolphin pool, visible from nearly every point in the building. The sounds of the sea and cries of sea birds and sea lions surround you as you travel up the escalators.

The **Amazon Rain Forest** keeps 400 tropical plant species and 100 tropical birds in a steamy simulation of a South American jungle. Thirty species of fish, among them deadly piranhas, swim in a 64-foot-tall glass pyramid on top of the aquarium.

Baltimore's population was 267,000 in 1870.

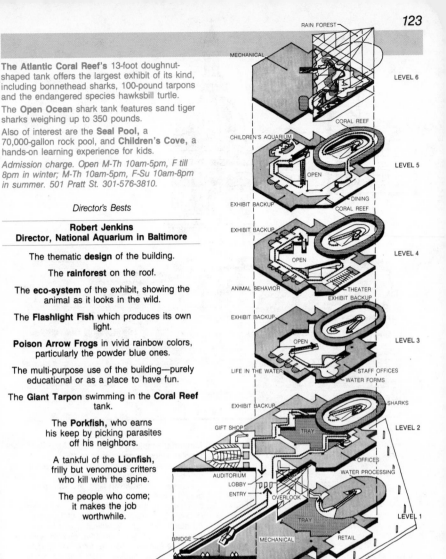

The **Atlantic Coral Reef's** 13-foot doughnut-shaped tank offers the largest exhibit of its kind, including bonnethead sharks, 100-pound tarpons and the endangered species hawksbill turtle.

The **Open Ocean** shark tank features sand tiger sharks weighing up to 350 pounds.

Also of interest are the **Seal Pool**, a 70,000-gallon rock pool, and **Children's Cove**, a hands-on learning experience for kids. *Admission charge. Open M-Th 10am-5pm, F till 8pm in winter; M-Th 10am-5pm, F-Su 10am-8pm in summer. 501 Pratt St. 301-576-3810.*

Director's Bests

Robert Jenkins
Director, National Aquarium in Baltimore

The thematic **design** of the building.

The **rainforest** on the roof.

The **eco-system** of the exhibit, showing the animal as it looks in the wild.

The **Flashlight Fish** which produces its own light.

Poison Arrow Frogs in vivid rainbow colors, particularly the powder blue ones.

The multi-purpose use of the building—purely educational or as a place to have fun.

The **Giant Tarpon** swimming in the **Coral Reef** tank.

The **Porkfish**, who earns his keep by picking parasites off his neighbors.

A tankful of the **Lionfish**, frilly but venomous critters who kill with the spine.

The people who come; it makes the job worthwhile.

Courtesy of Cambridge Seven Associates, Inc.

12 Customs House. Walk up the front steps to the big *call room,* used for 19th-century crew recruiting and enlistment for both World Wars. The 30-foot-by-68-foot canvas on the wall shows sailing vessels from ancient Egyptian papyrus boats to the Baltimore clipper. *Open M-F 8:30am-5pm. 40 S. Gay St. 301-962-2666.*

13 Holocaust Memorial. A pair of giant monoliths, each 75 feet long and 18 feet high, symbolize the nightmare that swept through Nazi Europe. Names of all World War II concentration camps are inscribed in the twin stones; the 6 rows of trees surrounding the memorial are dedicated to the 6 million Jews who perished. *Water and Gay Sts.*

14 Carroll Mansion. The last home of Declaration of Independence signer **Charles Carroll.** A fine variety of Empire furnishings and a spiral staircase still decorate this 1812 townhouse, which is considered one of early Baltimore's finest residences. *Open Tu-Su 10am-4pm. Lombard and Albemarle Sts. 301-396-4980.*

Introductions/Theaters/Narrative black
Hotels purple
Museums/Architecture blue
Parks/Open spaces green
Restaurants/Nightlife red
Shops/Galleries violet

15 Little Italy. Portuguese **Saint Anthony** protects this historical part of the city, spared from a 1904 fire that raged through most of downtown Baltimore. The neighborhood families proclaimed St. Anthony's Day as a holiday, and close the streets off for processions and celebrations 13 June.

Just as the homes of Little Italy are family-owned, the restaurants rarely change hands, and reflect the regions and styles of Italy's *buona cucina.* **Chiapparelli's** *(301-837-0309)* has great lobster and a lively atmosphere; **Trattoria Petrucci** *(301-752-4515)* specializes in mussels; and **Sabatino's** *(301-727-9414)* is an all-round favorite of the political set. The 200-block of South High Street is the main restaurant area; other listings are located on Eastern, Trinity and Fawn streets. Call for reservations and exact locations.

16 Shot Tower. This landmark, 246 feet high, was used between 1828 and 1892 to make gun shot. Over 1,100,000 handmade bricks were used to build it. A slide show inside the tower explains the process of dropping molten lead through a sieve from the top and into a barrel of cold water below. *Admission charge. Open daily 10am-4pm. 801 Fayette St. 301-539-8942.*

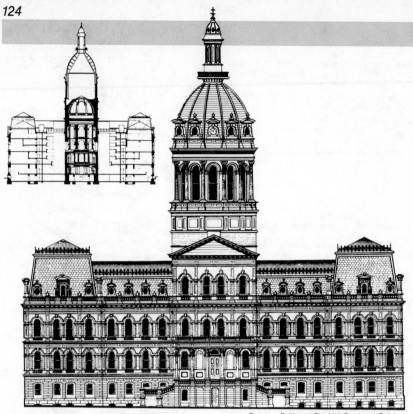

Courtesy Baltimore City Hall Courtyard Galleries

17 Baltimore City Hall. (1867-1875, **George A. Frederick**; restoration 1974, **Meyers, D'Aleo & Patton**) A Victorian wonder with local white marble, mansard roofs and a cast and wrought iron dome, designed by **Wendell Bollman**. The building's fine ironwork has been renovated and restored. Note the 110-foot rotunda and galleries of artwork depicting Baltimore's history. *Tours of offices by appointment; walking tours at 9am & 10am. Open M-F 9am-4pm. 100 N. Holliday St. Tours: 301-837-5424/Information: 301-396-3100.*

18 The Peale. Artist **Rembrandt Peale** first built this as his own **Baltimore Museum and Gallery of Fine Arts** in 1814. After serving temporarily as Baltimore's City Hall, the Peale went back to being America's oldest museum, with permanent exhibits of Baltimore's rowhouses and works by the artistic family Peale. *Admission free. Open Tu-Sa 10am-5pm, Su noon-5pm. 225 Holliday St. 301-396-3523.*

19 Prime Rib. ☆ ☆ ☆ $$$ An elegant, dimly lit restaurant where flawless service complements the superb entrees: succulent prime rib, steak and seafood. *American. Open M-Sa 5pm-midnight, Su till 11pm. Horizon House, 1101 Calvert St. 301-539-1804.*

20 Memorial Stadium. Home base of the **Baltimore Orioles** since its completion in 1954, the stadium has a capacity of up to 60,000 seats, depending on configurations for either baseball or football. Concession stands with light snacks are open during game time. Game tickets can be purchased at the stadium box office, *Fanfare (539-6920)* in Harborplace, and all *Ticketron* outlets in Baltimore, Washington and Virginia. *Box office open M-F 9am-5pm, and Sa 9am-1pm when the home teams are out of town. Ticket windows at the stadium open 2 hours before kickoff on game days. 33rd and Ellerslie Ave. 301-338-1300.*

21 Bo Brooks. ☆ ☆ ☆ $ Hammer your way through the best crabs in the city. Locals stand in line to feast on the little critters in all varieties: backfin, stuffed, fried, steamed or combined with the freshest oysters, mussels and clams available. *Seafood. No reservations on weekends. Open M-Sa 11:30am-4pm, 5:30pm-12:30am; Su 3:30-9:45pm. 5415 Belair Rd. 301-488-8144.*

If you can't get reservations or the lines are too long at Bo Brooks, try **Olde Obrycki's Crab House.** Same casual atmosphere and simple decor. *1729 E. Pratt St. 301-732-6399.*

22 Baltimore Museum of Art. (1929, **John Russell Pope**; expansion 1982, **Bower, Lewis & Thrower**) When Baltimore decided in the early 1900s that it greatly lacked a serious art museum, a commission quickly decided upon **Wyman Park** as the perfect site for one, and selected J.R. Pope—the man responsible for much of Monumental Washington—to design it.

Sights not to miss inside this massive Grecian temple include the **American Wing**, which occupies 3 floors and illustrates 18th- and 19th-century life; the **Wurtzburger Sculpture Garden**, with works by **Calder**, **Moore** and **Rodin**; the **Old Master Collection** of European paintings; **African and Oceanic Art**; and the **Cone Collection** of work from 1840-1940, including the largest collection of **Matisse paintings**. *Admission charge. Open Tu-F 10am-4pm, Th till 10, Sa & Su 11am-6pm. Art Museum Dr. at Charles St. 301-396-6337.*

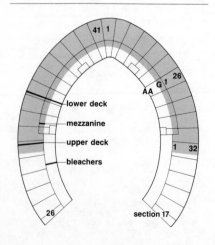

3 Danny's. ☆☆ $$$$ A traditional, somewhat overrated establishment for the high-brow set. The Dover sole is good, the wine list even better. *Continental. Reservations and jacket required. Open M-F 11:30am-3pm, 5-11pm; Sa till midnight. Charles and Biddle Sts. 301-539-1393.*

4 Belvedere. *Moderate/expensive.* Built on the site of an old mansion, the Belvedere is one of the most beautiful hotels in the Chesapeake Bay area. The marbled lobby with its sparkling chandeliers leads to 12 more floors of richly decorated rooms and the Ballroom, famous for its panoramic view of Baltimore. Amenities include a health club, small outdoor swimming pool, racquetball courts, valet, beauty salon and florist. *1 East Chase St. 301-332-1000.*

5 Brass Elephant. ☆☆ $$ The Northern Italian cuisine of this exquisitely restored 1860s townhouse runs from veal *Val d'Aostano* with truffles, to tender flounder prepared in 14 different ways. *Northern Italian. Open M-F 11:30am-2pm, M-Th 5:30-9:30pm, F & Sa till 10:30pm, Su 5-9pm. 924 Charles St. 301-547-8480.*

6 Great American Melting Pot. ☆ $ Art Deco-inspired night spot for Baltimore's artsy crowd. The menu lists anything from a decent Beef Wellington to fair tacos and salads. *Continental/cafe. Open Su-Th 11:30am-2am, F & Sa till 3am. 904 N. Charles St. 301-837-9797.*

7 Meredith Contemporary Art. A collection of platters, vases and baskets by **Kaette**, leading American ceramics artist. A small selection of good lithos and framed posters. *Open Tu-F 10am-5pm, Sa 11am-5pm. 805 N. Charles St. 301-837-3575.*

Drawing by Betty L. Heiges

8 Mt. Vernon Place. Once a forest known as *Howard's Woods*, this elegant square began with the **Washington Monument** (1815-1842, **Robert Mills**), the first monument to honor **George Washington**. The statue on top of the 178-foot marble Doric column shows Washington as he resigns from his position as general of the Revolutionary Army. For a quarter and a pretty view, you can climb all the 228 steps to the top. The **Mount Vernon Methodist Church** (1872, **Thomas Dixon** and **Charles Carson**) northwest of the Monument has green serpentine stone quarried in Baltimore County. **Leakin Hall** on *East Mount Vernon Place* was opened in 1927, as the Preparatory department of the Peabody Institute.

9 Peabody Institute. (1866, **Edmund G. Lind**) Founded by **George Peabody** in 1857, the institute was originally conceived of as a library, lecture series, art gallery and music academy. The conservatory grants 4 categories of degrees, and attracts 500-plus musicians each year.

The art collection has grown more extensive than the other arms of the academy. Among its more notable paintings are *Young Woman in Black* by **Mary Cassatt** and **Thomas Wilmer Dewing**'s *Lady With a Fan.* Also noteworthy are the gates outside of **North Hall,** bronze copies of the **Ghiberti** gates at the Baptistery in Florence.

Although the art collection is the main attraction, the **Peabody Library** should not be missed. Over 300,000 volumes are arranged on 6 levels of stacks, all connected by a central well that rises 61 feet to the ceiling. *1 E. Mount Vernon Pl. 301-659-8100.*

30 Walters Art Gallery. (1908, **Delano & Aldrich**) Engineer **William Walters** bequeathed his collection of 19th-century paintings, Chinese porcelains and other treasures to Baltimore in 1931. With it came the fine Palladian-style building, designed after a Renaissance palazzo in Genoa.

Among the gallery's treasures are artifacts from the Ancient Near East, Egyptian tomb paintings and papyrus scrolls and Roman sculptures. The museum store sells reproductions of museum works. *Admission free. Call for hours. 600 N. Charles St. 301-547-ARTS.*

31 Tio Pepe. ☆☆☆☆ $$$ Perhaps Baltimore's best restaurant. A large stuccoed cave serves incomparable pheasant *Alcantara* in grape sauce, sole with banana Hollandaise, or exquisite seafood paella. Say *Ole!* if you manage to get reservations after 2 weeks of trying. *Spanish/Continental. Open M-F 11:30am-2:30pm, 5-10:30pm; Sa till 11:30pm; Su 4-10:30pm. 10 E. Franklin St. 301-539-4675.*

32 Brown's Arcade. This Neo-Classical arcade—columns, arches, moldings and all—was reconstructed and bought for the city by Governor **William Brown** after Baltimore's *Sunday Morning Fire* in 1904. The ornate building has since the '70s been connected with charity ventures; part of the profits from its shops and restaurants goes to support the housing for the poor. *326 N. Charles St.*
Of note on the first floor are:

McGinn's. ☆ $ Irish pub with live music on weekends. Try the corn beef stew and the stout on tap. *Irish-American. Open daily 10am-1am. 301-539-7504.*

Brown's Cafe. ☆☆ $$ Feast on Baltimore's best pastries and croissants in the middle of a glass enclosed courtyard. *American. Open daily 7am-5pm. 301-675-9892.*

Femme. Classic day and evening wear in wool, linen and silk. Selected matching costume jewelry. *M-Sa 10am-6pm. 301-727-3131.*

Penny's. A collection of Dior's accessories—jewelry, lingerie and handbags. *Open M-Sa 10am-6pm. 301-752-3155.*

Shogun. ☆☆ $$ Super sushi bar or tatami-room for pre-Mechanic Theater dinners. *Japanese. Open Tu-Su 11am-midnight. 301-962-1130.*

33 Charles Center. A major development begun in 1956, the Center connects its 33 acres of apartments, shops and commercial buildings by an overhead walkway. Although the focus of Baltimore has shifted to the Inner Harbor, Charles Center still remains a vital area. **Hopkins Plaza,** the second open square in the center, is the forum for weekend festivals and concerts; check local papers for listings. Charles Center buildings include:

Baltimore Hilton. *Moderate.* Reliable and convenient, this Hilton high-rise has an outdoor pool, coffee shop, a lounge with nightly entertainment and an American cuisine restaurant where the service is good and the food acceptable. The rooms are some of the best in town: large, functional and pleasantly furnished. Color TV, valet/laundry and room service. *101 West Fayette St. 301-752-1100.*

Morris A. Mechanic Theatre. (1967, **John M. Johansen**) Sixteen hundred-seat testing ground for Broadway productions. The multi-faceted concrete building is Brutalist in inspiration. *Box office open M-Sa 10am-8:30pm, and special Sunday matinees 1-4pm. Hopkins Plaza. Telecharge 301-625-1400.*

In 1858-58, the harvest for Baltimore's *Crassotrea virginica* oysters amounted to a staggering 3,500,000 bushels.

33 Baltimore Civic Center. The 10,000-seat hall with its jagged roofline was Baltimore's main auditorium before the Convention Center was built. The site is where *Continental Congress* voted full military control to **George Washington** in 1776. The famous *Sunday Morning Fire* also began here in the cellar of the Hurst Company building. Check local listings for sports and entertainment events. *Open daily 10am-5pm. 201 W. Baltimore St. 301-659-7157.*

34 Baltimore Office of Promotion and Tourism. Maps, city information and brochures dispensed by 3 helpful ladies behind a counter. No hotel or tour reservations made. *Open M-F 9am-5pm. 110 W. Baltimore St. 301-752-8632.*

35 Otterbein Methodist Church. (1786) Built by German immigrants nearly 2 centuries ago, the Georgian building is now the oldest church in Baltimore. In the 1960s, it served as one of the anchors for the city's urban renewal plan. The interior is rather plain, except for the original stained glass windows. *Admission free. Open Apr-Oct Sa 10am-4pm. Tour reservations 2 weeks in advance. Conway and Sharp Sts. 301-685-4703.*

36 Mt. Clare Mansion. (1756-1760, **Charles Carroll**) Baltimore's oldest plantation home. Late 18th-century furniture and memorabilia of the Carroll family. *Admission charge. Open Tu-Sa 11am-4pm, Su 1-4pm. Washington & Monroe Sts. 301-837-3262.*

37 B&O Railroad Museum. (1851; roundhouse, 1883) Standing on the site of the nation's first passenger and freight railway station, the museum displays early locomotive brainstorms. Under the airy, windowed roof of the roundhouse and in the station building are such treasures as **Peter Cooper's** early **Tom Thumb** train, represented by a steam-powered replica. Also on display are an 1836 **Grasshopper locomotive** built here at the Mt. Clare shops, a red caboose from 1907 and a **Forty & Eight** boxcar.

The museum also features train memorabilia like hand-blown whiskey flasks and a collection of station clocks and railroad watches. *Admission charge. Open W-Su 10am-4pm. Closed M & Tu. Pratt & Poppleton Sts. 301-237-2387.*

Check out the harbor for **The Pride of Baltimore.** If she's in, you'll see the city's ambassador to the world. The clipper sails to international ports to promote new investments, local products and tourist business, all in the spirit of adventure and enterprise.

Upon seeing Chesapeake Bay, one of the very first Maryland colonists exclaimed that *"this baye is the most delightful water I ever saw between 2 sweet landes...."* And about the Patomeck: *"This is the sweetest and greatest river I have seene, so that the Thames is but a little finger to it."*

For Baltimore events call 301-837-INFO.

Introductions/Theaters/Narrative black
Hotels purple
Museums/Architecture blue
Parks/Open spaces green
Restaurants/Nightlife red
Shops/Galleries violet

38 Babe Ruth's Birthplace & Museum. The legendary baseball player is memorialized through pictures, paintings and professional memorabilia. The home is decorated in period furnishings. *Admission charge. Open W-Su 10:30am-3:15pm. 216 Emory St. 301-727-1539.*

39 P.J. Cricketts. ☆ ☆ $$ Choose between fine dining upstairs, or the casual atmosphere of the downstairs pub. Baby back ribs are the big push here, served with pasta, tacos or as *surf n' turf* with fresh crab cakes. *American. Open M-Th 11:30am-10pm, F till 12:30am; Sa 2pm-12:30am; Su 4-10pm. 206 W. Pratt St. 301-244-8900.*

40 Edgar Allan Poe's Grave. The master of scary suspense certainly picked his lot: Westminster church next to the graveyard is built directly on catacombs, where coffins with bones lie wide open. Tours to Poe's and the other grisly graves are held every first and third Friday evening and Sunday morning. Call for exact hours. *Admission charge. Fayette and Greene Sts. 301-528-7214.*

41 Lexington Market. Originally an open air market, the Lexington is the oldest of its kind in the country. Named for the Battle at Lexington, the land was donated in 1782 by General **John Eager Howard.** By the 1800s, wagons and farmers would come from all over to hawk their wares on Saturdays. A massive fire in 1949 destroyed the market, which was then rebuilt in 1952 and still attracts thousands with its meats, fresh seafoods and home-baked goods. *Open M-Sa 8:30am-6pm. 400 W. Lexington St.*

42 Marconi's. ☆ ☆ ☆ $$$ Baltimore's bastion of classic Italian cooking. The sweetbreads *bordelaise* are as famous as the lightly fried soft crabs; go for the *Baba au Rhum* or the *cannoli* at the end. *Italian. Open Tu-Sa noon-3:30pm, 5-8pm. Jackets required. No reservations.106 W. Saratoga St. 301-752-9286.*

Courtesy Enoch Pratt Free Library

43 Enoch Pratt Free Library. The city's principal library also maintains prints of old Baltimore, war posters and **H. L. Mencken** memorabilia. *Open M-Th 9am-9pm, F & Sa till 5pm, Su 1-5pm in winter. M-Sa only in summer. 400 Cathedral St. 301-396-5430.*

44 Inscribulus Books. Old and out-of-print books on history, art and the Civil War. Occasionally a real rarity shows up. *Open Tu-Sa 10am-5pm. 857 N. Howard St. 301-383-8845.*

45 Girards. Trendy disco/rock club, perhaps a little friendlier than the usual meat markets. Videoscreens flash lights and booming speakers deliver Top 40. *Admission charge. Open Sa-Th 9pm-2am, F happy hour from 5pm. 1001 Cathedral St. 301-837-3733/34.*

If you are lucky, you can see, hear and smell ghosts on board the **Constellation,** the world's oldest frigate. Sounds of running feet, the smell of gunpowder, and the fleeing shape of a man chased by the ship's commander sometimes take place below the gun deck. The struggle is merely the ghostly killing of a sailor who ran amuck during battle and was stabbed by the captain with a saber.

According to several eyewitnesses, the burial grounds of **Edgar Allan Poe** are haunted For the past 20 years, gravekeepers and visitors have seen the shadow of a young girl drifting around the subterranean grave. A ghost search conducted in 1976 revealed nothing — except distant footsteps somewhere inside the catacombs.

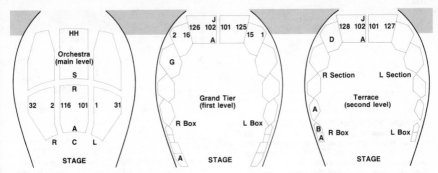

46 Joseph Meyerhoff Symphony Hall. (1982, architect **Pietro Belluschi**; acoustics, **Bolt, Beranek and Newman**) The dream of Baltimore Symphony Orchestra's maestro, **Sergiu Comissiona,** and its president, **Joseph Meyerhoff,** the hall presents the symphony in all its splendor.

The interior surfaces are curved for perfect acoustics; 420 tons of plaster coat the double-thick walls to protect the chamber from external noise. The building's uniquely round shape gives an unobstructed view of the stage. Its grand staircases, glass and brick touches further treat the eye. *1212 Cathedral St. 301-727-7300.*

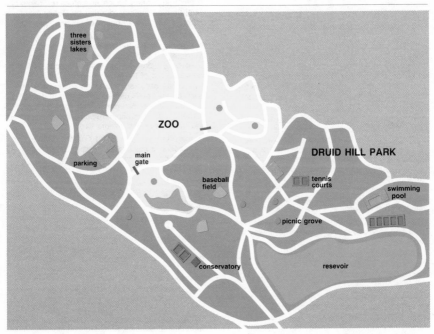

47 Druid Hill Park/Baltimore Zoo. What used to be a private estate in the 1800s is now Baltimore's largest public recreational area. Tennis courts and playgrounds are scattered throughout the 650-odd acres; the Victorian picnic shelters built in 1859 are still in use, and the Olympic pool is open during warm weather.

The Conservatory, a late 19th-century domed greenhouse, houses 3 massive seasonal floral displays. A permanent tropical collection of African violets, over 500 orchids and succulent cacti is located in a smaller greenhouse next door. *Admission free. Open daily 10am-4pm.*

Over 10,000 species of crawling, walking and swimming animals live on **Baltimore Zoo's** 150 acres. The lions and giraffes are housed in an open air exhibit; there is a hippo house and an area for rare breeds of antelope, and a house for **Dolly,** the affable African Elephant. The **Children's Zoo,** an area with rabbits, sheep and other tame pets, features pony rides, a mini-train and a carousel (admission charge). Feeding the animals is strictly prohibited, but you can watch the black-footed penguins get their fill daily at 3pm. Ophidiophiles should stop by the Reptile House outside the Zoo fence on Greenspring Ave. *Admission charge. Open daily 10am-4:20pm. Druid Park Lake Dr. exit, off I-83. 301-366-5466.*

48 Pimlico Racetrack. Home of the famed mid-May Preakness race, the second horse-racing spectacular of the Triple Crown. Watch the daily thoroughbred racing from the aprons, or reserve window seating in the restaurant. Post-time 1pm. *Open mid-March to first week of June M-Sa 11am-5pm. Park Heights & Belvedere Aves. 301-542-9400.*

49 Cylburn Arboretum. Built by wealthy Baltimore businessman **Jesse Tyson** between 1863 and 1883, this estate sprawls over 176 acres in the heart of Baltimore.

The **Arboretum,** run by the Bureau of Parks, contains rare trees, Japanese maples and native Maryland oaks. The many nature trails show off Maryland's flowering plants, trees and shrubs, left in their natural state. Also of interest: the **Horticultural Library, Children's Nature Museum, Fessenden Herbarium** and **Bird Museum.** *Admission free, trail and museum tours available. Museum open M-F 8am-4pm; grounds open daily 6am-9pm. 4915 Greenspring Ave. 301-396-0180.*

50 Villa Pace. Named after soprano **Rosa Ponselle's** debut aria, the Italianate mansion was the last home of the great American singer. Its opulent Renaissance furniture, the handpainted ceilings and the precious wall hangings are all in colors symbolic of Virgin Mary: red, gold, ivory and blue. Recitals are often held on the terrace or in the **Music Room;** Rosa's costumes and operatic memorabilia are displayed upstairs in her ornate dressing room. *Admission charge. Open W, Sa & Su noon-4pm. 1526 Greeenspring Valley Rd. 301-486-4616.*

PIER C

PIER D

BAGGAGE CLAIM/LOWER LEVEL
TICKETING/UPPER LEVEL

PIER B

PIER E

PIER A

ARRIVALS/LOWER ROADWAY
DEPARTURES/UPPER ROADWAY

51 Baltimore Washington International Airport is located 9 miles south of Baltimore and 32 miles north of Washington, a 45-60 minute drive. BWI used to be called *Friendship International* (and still is by some old-timers), but its new name, along with a major reconstruction job, reflects its growing importance in the region. The airport serves over 110 cities in the nation and world and handles 60 percent of all regional cargo.

The main terminal is a 2-level building with access roadways on each level. Ten monumental, red-tiled pillars support an airy *space frame roof* of glass and steel. Natural light filters into the terminal while the roof, which hangs over the pillars, effectively shelters arriving and departing passengers from the elements. The bi-level design effectively separates arriving and departing passengers. You can walk directly from individual airline entrances to a ticket counter no more than 50 feet away. From there all 40 departure gates are easily accessible. There are 5 departure piers, 3 of which are the long finger pier type. Loading bridges connect directly with the plane.

Arriving passengers go directly to the lower level where they find 2 baggage claim areas, customs, car rentals and ground transportation. Airport services include the usual complement of bars, restaurants and a duty-free shop. Twenty-four-hour-a-day language assistance is available. The Bank of Maryland has a branch in the airport and there is an American Express disbursing machine on the upper level. In Pier A there is a 24-hour snack bar.

When **driving** to the airport from DC, take Hwy. I-495 (the Beltway) to the Spellman Parkway to Route 46, which is the airport access road.

Taxi service is available to Baltimore and Washington. Fare is about $12 to Baltimore and $35 to DC. A dispatcher is always on duty. *Call 301-859-1100.*

Limo/van service is available to Baltimore and its suburbs from **Airport Commuter.** Buses leave every half hour from 5:15am to 9:15pm, then hourly until midnight. *Call 301-859-3000.*

Buses to DC are operated by **Airport Limo.** They leave every 40 minutes from 5:20am to 12:20am. The bus is reasonably priced but makes only one stop at the **Capital Hilton** at *16th and K streets. Call 301-859-7545.*

Trailways runs 8 buses a day to York and Harrisburg, Pennsylvania. Other services go to Annapolis and Fredericksburg. You can get information and tickets for all ground transportation at the **Central Ground Transportation Desk.** Someone is on duty 24-hours-a-day, or call *301-859-7545.*

Amtrak has a station 2 miles from the airport. Seventeen trains a day pass through on their way to Northeast Corridor cities like Washington, Philadelphia, New York and Boston. The airport runs a free shuttle bus to and from every train. Call 800-523-5700 for information.

General non-flight airport information, 859-7111 from Baltimore; from DC, 261-1000.

GREAT FALLS

Great Falls. This sudden break in the Potomac River's placid meanderings is a quarter-mile wide gorge where water tumbles over giant boulders with a primitive, powerful and breathtaking violence. The series of gurgling rapids drops the river a total of 76 feet, and in high spring the volume of water pouring over the cascades surpasses Niagara Falls.

The forest and swamps that follow along the Potomac's banks include spectacular displays of wildflowers in their seasonal blooms. The park

is a migration stop for many birds, and birdwatchers claim that this is one of the East Coast's best areas—bald eagles have even been spotted. The natural pools along the river attract deer, fox, muskrat, beaver, opossum and rabbit. An excellent system of hiking trails leads you through the woods and along the river. Picnic areas are located throughout the park (no open fires, please). The **Visitors Center** offers rotating exhibits about nature, conservation, safety, etc., and a helpful, friendly staff to answer questions and direct you to the season's special vistas.

In the late 1700s, **George Washington** came here to oversee the building of the **Potowmac Canal,** a bypass of the falls and other unnavigable parts of the river. Locks 1 through 5 and part of the canal are still visible, and the National Park Service, which maintains the area, is working constantly to prevent further deterioration. Ruins of the canal are located southeast of the Visitors Center. Also visible are a chimney, spring house and other remnants of **Matildaville,** the city founded by **Henry** *Light Horse Harry Lee* in honor of his first wife.

Note: This is an extremely beautiful yet extremely dangerous section of the river; currents are swift and the rock faces sheer. Everyone is urged to stay off the rocks near the river and out of the water near the falls; drownings occur several times yearly when the swift current pulls careless climbers and waders into the torrent. Parents: Watch your children! Experienced rock climbers with proper equipment can register at the Visitors Center.

Admission free. Take Exit 13 off the Beltway; park entrance is 6 miles west; Visitors Center is 1/4-mile past the entrance on the right. 703-759-2915.

RESTON

Reston. (Begun 1962) One of the nation's most remarkable *new towns,* Reston was envisioned by **Robert E. Simon** in the mid-1950s (Simon's initials form the basis of the city's name). It is a completely planned city, covering 11 1/2 square miles, and when it is completed in the 1990s, over 65,000 people will live around the 5 lakes that dominate the city plan.

Forty percent of all the land in Reston is open and/or public space. Homes are arranged in small neighborhood clusters, which are distributed evenly throughout the city; recreational amenities include golf courses, pools, ballparks, tennis courts, bridle paths and a **Nature Center.** Yet this picture of suburban serenity has been very successful in attracting high-tech industries, and the presence of such companies as GTE, AT&T, Sperry and the US Geological Survey has guaranteed at least one job per household in the city.

Reston's development is supervised by Mobil Land Development Corporation, which coordinates the design and construction of homes (ranging from small apartments to townhouses to mini-mansions, and built in a number of architectural styles), schools, business complexes and shopping centers—all with a splendid sensitivity to the woods and meadows that surround the town. *Located 5 miles east of Dulles Airport in Fairfax County, VA. 703-620-4730.*

Laws Antiques Complex. Thirty antique shops and some 75 flea market stands center around the **H. L.** *Sonny Laws* auction house. The auctions include 3-day catalogue affairs, first weekend of the month estate sales, and weekly Friday night disposals of household goods. One-stop shopping for antiques has been going on for more than 20 years here. Shops are open Thursdays through Sundays, the flea market operates the second and fourth Sundays of the month year 'round. *7209 Centreville Road, Manassas, VA. 703-631-0590.*

The first Germans arrived at Antietam Creek in 1726. Following an old Iroquois trail, they settled at Blue Ridge, past Shenandoah Valley.

Eero Saarinen and Associates

Loudoun County, home of **Dulles International Airport** offers you a look at history and peaceful respite from the more hectic streets of Washington. Named in 1757 for the **Earl of Loudoun,** a British commander in America, Loudoun's Blue Ridge foothills overlook the Potomac River. Visitors should take advantage of Loudoun's historical sites:

Leesburg. An outfitting post during the French and Indian Wars, Leesburg's walking tour includes museums, monuments and the Courthouse Square. Bluemont hosts a craft show each October, and White's Ferry is the last one on the Potomac.

Loudoun Museum features historical exhibits and a Visitor's Information Center. A slide presentation focusing on Loudoun's history is also available. *16 West Loudoun St. 703-777-6093.*

Morven Park. A 1,200-acre estate houses art treasures from around the world, a carriage museum and 2 nature trails. *Admission charge. Open 1 Apr-31 Oct 10am-5pm daily, Su 1-5pm. Old Waterford Rd.*

Oatlands is a Georgian mansion, the former home of the Carter and Eustis families. The National Trust for Historic Preservation runs the home, donated by the Eustis daughters as a memorial to their parents. *Admission charge. Open Apr-Oct, M-Sa 10am-5pm, Su 1-5pm. Rt 15, 6 miles south of Leesburg, VA. 703-777-3154.*

American Work Horse Museum features thousands of horse-equipment pieces, including harnesses, and blacksmith and veterinary equipment. *Museum open by appointment. Rt. 662 at Paeonian Springs. 703-338-6390.*

Ball's Bluff Cemetery honors the battle of Ball's Bluff, where North met South. *Two miles north of Leesburg, VA off Rt. 15.*

Dulles Marriott. *Moderate.* Closest hotel to the airport. Round-the-clock limousine service. Special weekend rate. *Sterling, VA. 703-471-9500/800-228-9290.*

Holiday Inn Dulles Airport. *Inexpensive.* Convenient airport location with 24-hour limousine service. *1000 Sully Rd., Sterling, VA. 703-471-7411/800-465-4329.*

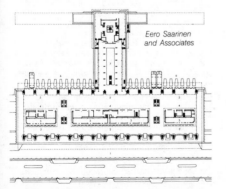

Eero Saarinen and Associates

Dulles International Airport, handling domestic and international flights, is located in Virginia, 26 miles or about a 35-minute drive from downtown Washington. It was built upon orders from Congress and is owned and operated by the Federal Government.

One rarely has a good word to say about airports. They are confusing at worst and invisible at best. Yet Dulles stands out. Completed in 1962, with a terminal designed by **Eero Saarinen,** the airport still seems modern. Dulles was the first major airport designed with the jet plane in mind; it's sleek and simple, a near perfect marriage of form and function.

The object at Dulles was to build a facility that was efficient for both passengers and planes. After much analysis, Saarinen found that people wasted time and energy getting to the planes and planes wasted valuable fuel taxiing to passengers. His solution, mobile lounges, were revolutionary.

The mobile lounge was conceived as an extension of the terminal building. They are actually comfortable, streamlined buses that link up directly with the departure gate. Passengers board the bus and are driven out to the plane where a moveable passenger bridge joins the aircraft, allowing passengers to embark without taking a step outdoors.

The mobile lounge allows for a compact terminal building instead of the finger pier construction common at most other airports. At Dulles you can enter the building, check in and get on a mobile lounge while walking less than 200 feet.

Dulles is designed to keep arriving and departing passengers separate. Departure gates and check-in counters are on the main floor, as are lounges, restaurants, an observation deck, drugstore and barber shop. Though most airport facilities close after 11pm, there is a 24-hour snack bar.

International arrivals, customs, baggage claim, ground transportation, a duty-free shop and 24-hour car rentals are on the ground floor. You will also find information and foreign language assistance services, a post office, bank, and American Express disbursing machine.

There is no public transportation to Dulles. You must either drive, take a cab, or use the limousine service.

Driving: A 13.5-mile limited access highway runs east from the airport. It connects with Rt. 123, I-495 (the Beltway) and Hwy. I-66. Highway I-66 will take you over the Theodore Roosevelt Bridge and into downtown DC in about 30-35 minutes.

Taxis: There is a dispatcher on duty 24 hours a day. The taxi fleet is new and as you approach, the dispatcher will give you a brochure, in 5 languages, with estimated rates to points in DC, Maryland and Virginia. The cabs are metered. Fare into DC can cost as much as $35. *(703-471-5555)*

Limo: Washington Flyer runs bus and limo service to Washington, Maryland and Virginia, also Baltimore-Washington Airport and Washington National Airport. Service runs frequently between 5am and midnight, and the fare is reasonable. Hotels served in DC are the **Shoreham, Sheraton Park, Capital Hilton, Mayflower** and the **Washington Hilton.** All routes terminate at the Washington Hilton, which is also the major pick-up point for trips to the airport. There are 2 ticketing and information booths at the top of the ramps leading to the ground transportation loading and pick-up area. For 24-hour information on stops and schedules call *703-471-0640/685-1400.*

General non-flight airport information, 703-471-7596/471-4242.

In 1982, a couple from Maryland's Eastern Shore sighted and videotaped a 30-foot-long, dragonlike creature at Chesapeake Bay's Love Point. The humpbacked aquatic monster was instantly named **Chessie,** after its illustrious relative in Loch Ness, Scotland.

Colonel Fielding Lewis, Kenmore's illustrious owner, has been seen putting around in Revolution-wear just like his 250-year-old self. He favors dim corridors and his study, where he checks out the dusty ledgers for ghastly financial errors.

CHESAPEAKE BAY AND THE EASTERN SHORE

The tentacles of this great waterway saw the birth of America. Here we struggled to survive and prosper, here we nurtured all that is unique about us. But our survival was assured long ago. Now the question is, can the Chesapeake survive us?

The history. Important chapters of our history have been written on the shores of fertile Chesapeake Bay and her tributaries, from the founding of Jamestown—the first permanent English settlement in America—to the ending of the Revolutionary War at Yorktown, to the testing of WWII naval landing boats in the 1940s. The waters that run into the Chesapeake pass by the steel country of Pennsylvania, the farmland of Virginia, the corridors of power in Washington, DC, and the ports of Baltimore, Annapolis and Newport News.

But even before a single colonist set foot in the region, it was bustling with activity. The *Delmarva Peninsula*, as it is known to geologists, was alternately covered with jungle and choked with ice. Muskrat and fox live on the land where saber-toothed tigers and mastodons once roamed. And then there were the Native Americans. We all know of the American Indian girl who, in 1608, saved explorer **John Smith** from a gruesome death. But, comparatively speaking, **Pocahontas** was a latecomer. There may very well have been Indians in the region 10,000 years ago, and scientific dating techniques have shown that at least 5,550 years ago the Indians were enjoying the same oysters we gobble down in swank Eastern seaboard restaurants. They would leave large piles of shells known as *midden heaps*—the biggest and oldest heap was found 20 feet deep and covered 30 acres near the Potomac.

Some who came to settle the land were adventurers looking for a quick profit far from royal interference. Others, like those led by the **Calvert** clan, came in search of religious freedom. In 1632 the Calverts were granted 12 million acres—all of Maryland and half of Pennsylvania—plenty of room in which to practice tolerence. These ideals—free trade and freedom of belief—faced many challenges in the new world, but they ultimately forged themselves into the American character.

The geology. Maryland looks eaten away on a map, like something voracious has chomped up through the state and divided it into two parts. The jagged *bite* is the Chesapeake Bay.

The Bay is a drowned river. When the glaciers melted 18,000 years ago, the sea rose to fill the valley of the Susquehanna River. The River had flowed south from western New York 400 miles away, its valley and the valleys of all the rivers joining it became Chesapeake Bay. The 48 rivers and 102 branches and tributaries together are navigable for 1,750 miles. Maryland's 24 rivers give her more river frontage than any other state.

The Chesapeake Bay is both a bay and an estuary, a place where fresh water mingles with salty tidal water. It is 195 miles long and varies from 22 miles wide at the Potomac River, to four miles wide at Annapolis. Its surface area is 4,316 square miles (one-third the size of Maryland itself) and it drains a total land area of 64,170 square miles. At any moment it contains about 18 trillion gallons of water; about 45 billion gallons flow in and out of it each day.

The land around the bay is sinking about one foot per 100 years. Each year the Bay swallows about 326 acres from the shore. Whole islands have divided or disappeared. In 1850 Sharp's Island had 600 acres; by 1944 only six acres of marsh were left. Now even that is gone, leaving a solitary lighthouse. Further south, James Island has lost 150 acres in this century alone.

So dredging to maintain a navigable channel has been necessary since the early 1800s. Erosion or

sedimentation is constantly filling it in. Towns which were once ports are now land-locked or claim only a trickle of water. (Easton, though, was saved by mud in 1812 when a British invasion ran aground in the Tred Avon River.) The shipping channel through the Bay is 161 miles long and 42 feet deep, but the Bay's average depth is less than 28 feet. Here and there are deep stagnant pools formed millions of years ago. One pool near Bloody Point is 174 feet deep.

The weather. Nature's tumults have always marked the Bay. Every generation seems to have its great storm; the most recent was Hurricane Agnes in 1972. That storm shed tremendous quantities of rainwater on the Bay, lowered its salinity, and devasted the shellfish industry. Agnes was one of the worst natural disasters in American history, and the Bay is still recovering from it.

But severe weather is now much less common. Winters especially seem milder, ice has become less a hazard—or convenience. Once you could walk or ride all the way down (1856) or across (1780) the iced-over Bay—but not within the last 50 years.

The industry. The Chesapeake is America's great fish store. More than 10,000 fishermen make their living from the Bay, bringing in an astounding annual harvest. In good years more than 29 million pounds of hard-shell crabs, 2 million pounds of soft-shell crabs, 2 million bushels of oysters, 400,000 bushels of soft clams, and 112,000 bushels of hard clams are plucked from the Bay by a wide range of methods, some dating to the 1600s.

495

WASHINGTON

95

95

0   15 M

0   24 K

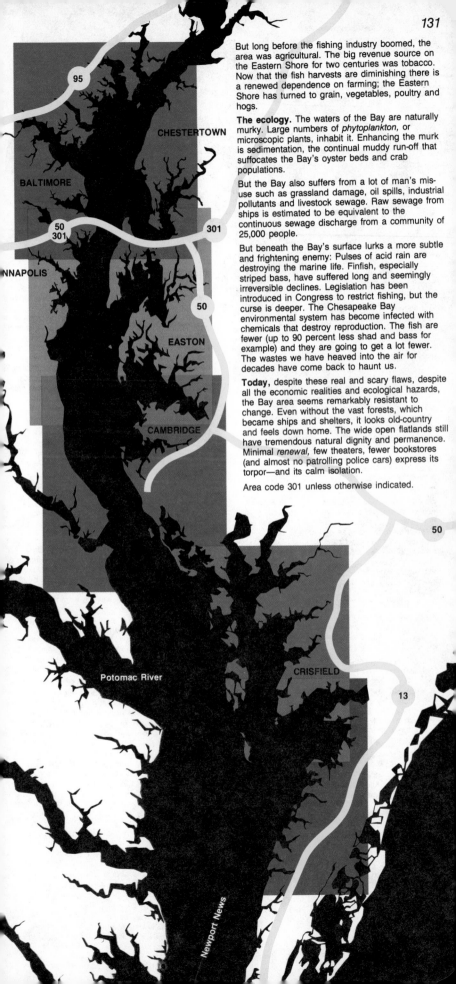

But long before the fishing industry boomed, the area was agricultural. The big revenue source on the Eastern Shore for two centuries was tobacco. Now that the fish harvests are diminishing there is a renewed dependence on farming; the Eastern Shore has turned to grain, vegetables, poultry and hogs.

The ecology. The waters of the Bay are naturally murky. Large numbers of *phytoplankton,* or microscopic plants, inhabit it. Enhancing the murk is sedimentation, the continual muddy run-off that suffocates the Bay's oyster beds and crab populations.

But the Bay also suffers from a lot of man's mis-use such as grassland damage, oil spills, industrial pollutants and livestock sewage. Raw sewage from ships is estimated to be equivalent to the continuous sewage discharge from a community of 25,000 people.

But beneath the Bay's surface lurks a more subtle and frightening enemy: Pulses of acid rain are destroying the marine life. Finfish, especially striped bass, have suffered long and seemingly irreversible declines. Legislation has been introduced in Congress to restrict fishing, but the curse is deeper. The Chesapeake Bay environmental system has become infected with chemicals that destroy reproduction. The fish are fewer (up to 90 percent less shad and bass for example) and they are going to get a lot fewer. The wastes we have heaved into the air for decades have come back to haunt us.

Today, despite these real and scary flaws, despite all the economic realities and ecological hazards, the Bay area seems remarkably resistant to change. Even without the vast forests, which became ships and shelters, it looks old-country and feels down home. The wide open flatlands still have tremendous natural dignity and permanence. Minimal *renewal,* few theaters, fewer bookstores (and almost no patrolling police cars) express its torpor—and its calm isolation.

Area code 301 unless otherwise indicated.

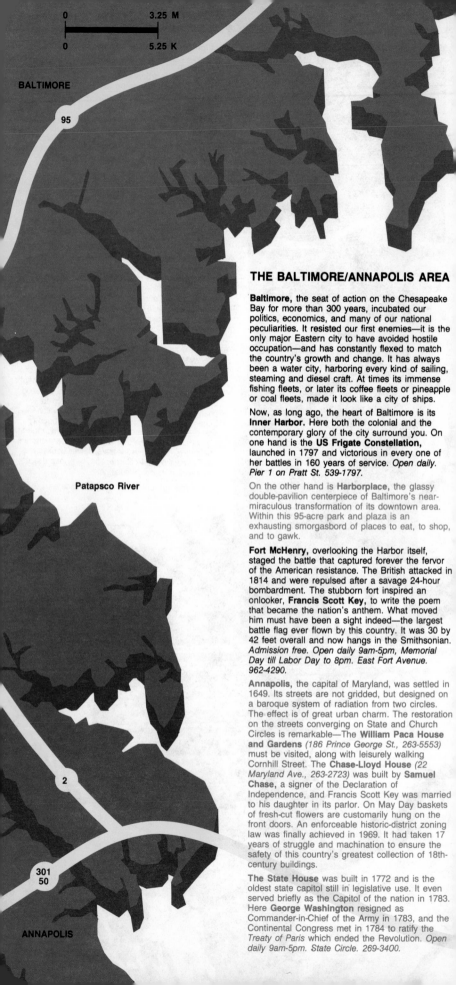

BALTIMORE

95

Patapsco River

2

301
50

ANNAPOLIS

THE BALTIMORE/ANNAPOLIS AREA

Baltimore, the seat of action on the Chesapeake Bay for more than 300 years, incubated our politics, economics, and many of our national peculiarities. It resisted our first enemies—it is the only major Eastern city to have avoided hostile occupation—and has constantly flexed to match the country's growth and change. It has always been a water city, harboring every kind of sailing, steaming and diesel craft. At times its immense fishing fleets, or later its coffee fleets or pineapple or coal fleets, made it look like a city of ships.

Now, as long ago, the heart of Baltimore is its **Inner Harbor.** Here both the colonial and the contemporary glory of the city surround you. On one hand is the **US Frigate Constellation,** launched in 1797 and victorious in every one of her battles in 160 years of service. *Open daily. Pier 1 on Pratt St. 539-1797.*

On the other hand is **Harborplace,** the glassy double-pavilion centerpiece of Baltimore's near-miraculous transformation of its downtown area. Within this 95-acre park and plaza is an exhausting smorgasbord of places to eat, to shop, and to gawk.

Fort McHenry, overlooking the Harbor itself, staged the battle that captured forever the fervor of the American resistance. The British attacked in 1814 and were repulsed after a savage 24-hour bombardment. The stubborn fort inspired an onlooker, **Francis Scott Key,** to write the poem that became the nation's anthem. What moved him must have been a sight indeed—the largest battle flag ever flown by this country. It was 30 by 42 feet overall and now hangs in the Smithsonian. *Admission free. Open daily 9am-5pm, Memorial Day till Labor Day to 8pm. East Fort Avenue. 962-4290.*

Annapolis, the capital of Maryland, was settled in 1649. Its streets are not gridded, but designed on a baroque system of radiation from two circles. The effect is of great urban charm. The restoration on the streets converging on State and Church Circles is remarkable—The **William Paca House and Gardens** *(186 Prince George St., 263-5553)* must be visited, along with leisurely walking Cornhill Street. The **Chase-Lloyd House** *(22 Maryland Ave., 263-2723)* was built by **Samuel Chase,** a signer of the Declaration of Independence, and Francis Scott Key was married to his daughter in its parlor. On May Day baskets of fresh-cut flowers are customarily hung on the front doors. An enforceable historic-district zoning law was finally achieved in 1969. It had taken 17 years of struggle and machination to ensure the safety of this country's greatest collection of 18th-century buildings.

The State House was built in 1772 and is the oldest state capitol still in legislative use. It even served briefly as the Capitol of the nation in 1783. Here **George Washington** resigned as Commander-in-Chief of the Army in 1783, and the Continental Congress met in 1784 to ratify the *Treaty of Paris* which ended the Revolution. *Open daily 9am-5pm. State Circle. 269-3400.*

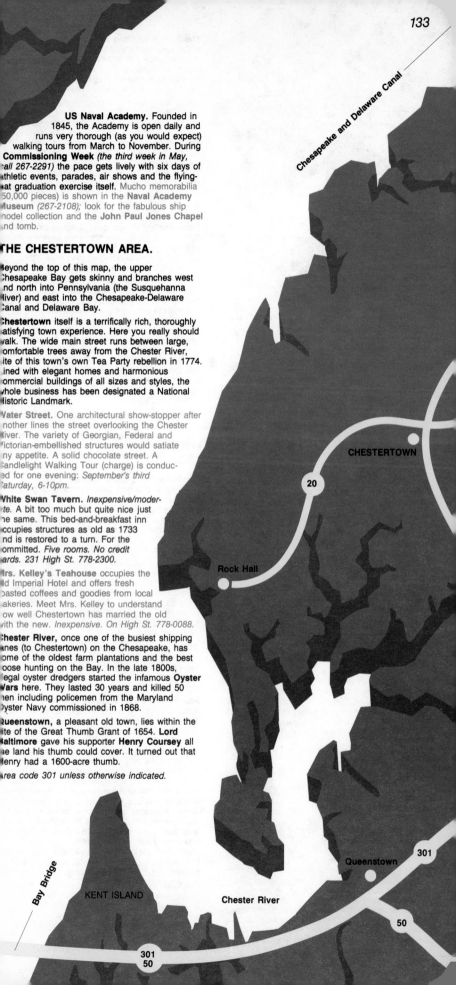

US Naval Academy. Founded in 1845, the Academy is open daily and runs very thorough (as you would expect) walking tours from March to November. During **Commissioning Week** *(the third week in May, call 267-2291)* the pace gets lively with six days of athletic events, parades, air shows and the flying-hat graduation exercise itself. Mucho memorabilia (50,000 pieces) is shown in the **Naval Academy Museum** *(267-2108);* look for the fabulous ship model collection and the **John Paul Jones Chapel** and tomb.

THE CHESTERTOWN AREA.

Beyond the top of this map, the upper Chesapeake Bay gets skinny and branches west and north into Pennsylvania (the Susquehanna River) and east into the Chesapeake-Delaware Canal and Delaware Bay.

Chestertown itself is a terrifically rich, thoroughly satisfying town experience. Here you really should walk. The wide main street runs between large, comfortable trees away from the Chester River, site of this town's own Tea Party rebellion in 1774. Lined with elegant homes and harmonious commercial buildings of all sizes and styles, the whole business has been designated a National Historic Landmark.

Water Street. One architectural show-stopper after another lines the street overlooking the Chester River. The variety of Georgian, Federal and Victorian-embellished structures would satiate any appetite. A solid chocolate street. A Candlelight Walking Tour (charge) is conducted for one evening: *September's third Saturday, 6-10pm.*

White Swan Tavern. *Inexpensive/moderate.* A bit too much but quite nice just the same. This bed-and-breakfast inn occupies structures as old as 1733 and is restored to a turn. For the committed. *Five rooms. No credit cards. 231 High St. 778-2300.*

Mrs. Kelley's Teahouse occupies the old Imperial Hotel and offers fresh roasted coffees and goodies from local bakeries. Meet Mrs. Kelley to understand how well Chestertown has married the old with the new. *Inexpensive. On High St. 778-0088.*

Chester River, once one of the busiest shipping lanes (to Chestertown) on the Chesapeake, has some of the oldest farm plantations and the best goose hunting on the Bay. In the late 1800s, illegal oyster dredgers started the infamous **Oyster Wars** here. They lasted 30 years and killed 50 men including policemen from the Maryland Oyster Navy commissioned in 1868.

Queenstown, a pleasant old town, lies within the site of the Great Thumb Grant of 1654. **Lord Baltimore** gave his supporter **Henry Coursey** all the land his thumb could cover. It turned out that Henry had a 1600-acre thumb.

Area code 301 unless otherwise indicated.

Chesapeake and Delaware Canal

CHESTERTOWN

20

Rock Hall

Bay Bridge

KENT ISLAND

Chester River

Queenstown

301

50

301
50

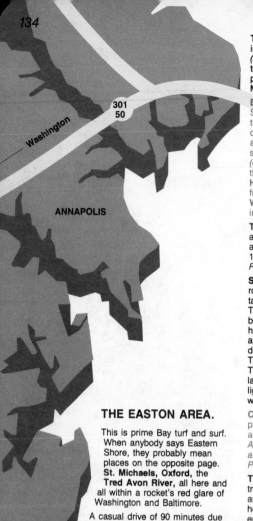

The Annual Jousting Tournament has been held in Cordova near Wye Mills in August since 1868 *(for information call 822-4606)*. The medieval sport took hold in Maryland around 1840 and was proclaimed the state's official sport in 1962. Maryland is the only state to have an official sport.

Easton itself was once the capital of the Eastern Shore. Still a trading, banking and cultural center, the slow infusion of wealthy riverfront property owners has brought chic to town. Old, spruced-up and new Colonial buildings grace the streets surrounding the 1711 **Talbot Country Courthouse** *(on Washington St., open M-F 8:30am-4:30pm).* To the south is the **Third Haven Quaker Meeting House,** considered America's oldest religious frame building. **Lord Baltimore** attended and **William Penn** preached on its broad lawns. Built in 1682, *South Washington St.*

Tidewater Inn *(inexpensive)* is not so old (1949) and quite large, but still somehow pays a cunning allegiance to the old Colonial *publick* house look. 120 rooms. *Restaurant open daily 6am-10pm. Reservations. Dover and Harrison Sts. 822-1300.*

St. Michaels Peninsula. On out the crooked neck road (Maryland has incredibly fine road conditions) takes you to **St. Michaels,** ship-builder to the Bay. The town is undergoing low-watt restoration, but behind the ferns and quaint signs is still an honest, working village. The old Baltimore clipper and log canoe shipyards are gone, but the fishing docks are operating and can be closely inspected. The British attacked the town at night in 1813. The town blacked itself out (a warfare first), hung lanterns in nearby trees and the British shot at the lights instead. Ah, where would our history be without the British?

Chesapeake Maritime Museum has all 28 principal types of Bay boats, watermen's tools, and the screwpile lighthouse from Cooper Strait. *Admission charge. Open Mar-Dec 10am-4pm; Jan and Feb on weekends only, 10am-4pm. Navy Point. 745-2916.*

The Inn at Perry Cabin *(moderate)* has tremendous grounds, seasonal flocks of geese, and four dining rooms within a wedding cake house topped with cupolas. The great Negro emancipator Frederick Douglass lived here—in the slave quarters. *Six rooms. Restaurant open daily 11am-3:30pm and 5:30-10pm. Reservations. Major credit cards. Rt. 33. 745-5178.*

Harrison's Chesapeake House *(inexpensive),* the locals will tell you, has the Bay's best seafood. Direct and simple fare (try the *Angels on Horseback),* served with bustle. And they'll put you up in an honest little room your Uncle Murray would like. *42 rooms. Restaurant open daily 6:30am-10pm. Reservations. Major credit cards. Tilghman Island. 886-2123.*

Oxford existed long before Baltimore but it seems to have fallen asleep. It was once Maryland's largest port with a heavy tobacco trade, but now an exquisite quiet prevails. Oxford is suspended in time, so much the better for cozy town lovers.

Robert Morris Inn. *Moderate/expensive.* The most notable inn on the Eastern Shore dates back to 1710. It still has a grand air despite 275 years of continual enlargement. Robert Morris built it in a manner befitting the town's leading citizen (he was later killed by wadding from a ship's guns fired in his honor, the only man known to be killed by his own salute) and his son Robert Morris, Jr., risked all his savings on the new concept of a United States and financed the Revolution. Anyway, their house is now a nice inn with a nice restaurant. **James Michener** rated its crab cakes 9.2 (out of 10) because they bulged out the sides, but alas, they don't bulge anymore. 36 rooms. A separate Lodge on the River has quieter, larger rooms. *Restaurant open daily for breakfast 8-11am, lunch 11:30am-4pm, dinner 5-9pm, Su dinner 1-8pm. South Morris St. on the Tred Avon River. 226-5111.*

Masthead Club. *Moderate.* A dark-horse (maybe a bit too dark) but a must. The place looks so-so, but everything is prepared and delivered with elegance and flair. *Open Tu-Su noon-2pm, 6:30-9pm. Reservations advisable. 101 Mill St. 226-5303.*

Area code 301 unless otherwise indicated.

THE EASTON AREA.

This is prime Bay turf and surf. When anybody says Eastern Shore, they probably mean places on the opposite page. **St. Michaels, Oxford,** the **Tred Avon River,** all here and all within a rocket's red glare of Washington and Baltimore.

A casual drive of 90 minutes due east from Washington's Capitol building takes you over the Bay Bridge, down Route 50 to **Easton** and out a bit west to the tip of St. Michaels peninsula. You pass through all that is characteristic of the Eastern Shore. The immense sky presses the landscape flat and diminishes large, isolated farmhouses to dots in the distance. The countryside is grandly open. Glimpses of the Bay itself beyond the fields stretch the pool table to eternity—the world is really flat after all.

The Chesapeake Bay Bridge isn't one bridge, it's two. Built in 1952 and 1973, they are among the largest continuous overwater steel structures in the world. Stolid engineering determinism probably made the style and structure of the two spans completely different, but anyway, after 350 years of boat crossings, a leap from shore to shore can't now be made in minutes.

Wye Mills has, obviously, a mill (which ground grain for Washington's troops during the Revolution and is still operating) and one terrific tree. Something there is about a tree...the **Wye Oak** stands 104 feet high, 160 feet wide, 32 feet around the trunk, and is 440 years old. All by itself it was made the Wye Oak State Park, the only one-tree state forest in the country.

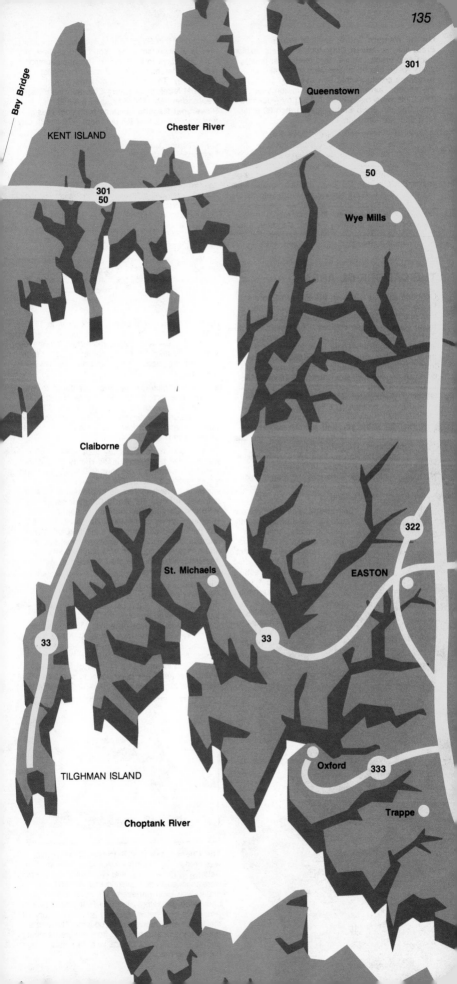

On the Western Shore, south of Prince Frederick, is Calvert Cliffs where you can explore the Bay's prehistoric life. Bird teeth (yes, teeth), shark teeth, crocodile jaws, and whale skulls reveal the creatures that flew over and swam in the ancient Calvert Sea 10 to 12 million years ago. The Cliffs were discovered in 1608 by (you-know-who) Captain John Smith; they stretch 30 miles long and 120 feet high.

Another few miles south is the Cove Point Lighthouse. Built in 1828, it is the oldest brick tower lighthouse on the Bay. *(Open daily 9am-4pm, 326-3254.)* Then on to Solomons on the Patuxent River, where you have the choice of roaming a pleasant old town, the busy oyster fleet docks, or the Calvert Marine Museum with its exhibits on slave ships, naval battles, marine biology, boat building and the watermen's trade. Lots of models and Leroy Pepper Langley, a real live working model maker. *Admission free. Open M-F 10am-4:30pm, Sa & Su 1-4:30pm. Main St. 326-3719.*

THE CAMBRIDGE AREA

Continue zipping south on the Eastern Shore's Route 50 across the Choptank River and into Cambridge. After seeing the town (which you must) you have three choices. Due west on Route 343 is continuous Eastern Shore landscape, on and on through handsome land, tiny towns, and by an odd little windmill built in 1850. Southwest from Cambridge on Route 16 is Taylors Island, ditto but no windmill. But branch off 16 onto 335 at Church Creek (settled in the 1670s) and you will enter Blackwater National Wildlife Refuge and marsh heaven. The road ends on Hooper Island (actually three bridge-connected islands) where you find yourself surrounded by the almost disturbing beauty of the tidal wetlands. They stretch to the Bay on all sides, broken by little inlets, coated with spiky-silky grass. In the evening, the low light enhances the muted color tones and the wind brings a pulse to the land.

Cambridge itself is a polyglot, sitting on land bought from the Choptank Indians for 42 cloaks. The Edward Hopper (sunny, silent Sunday) main drag (Race Street) branches off into supremely mixed Colonial-Georgian-Victorian neigh-

borhoods (High Street) punctuated by some weird breeds of uncertain origin. You could say it works but you'd have to be tolerant. The encroaching highway interchanges signal major redevelopment on the way. This little city holds the annual National Muskrat Skinning Championship *(last weekend in Feb, 397-3517),* and a series of Powerboat Regatta Classics *(with corn roasts and crab feasts, Jun through Sept, 476-5113).* City does as city looks.

Cator House Restaurant. ☆ ☆ $$$ Perfect for Cambridge: new, classy, and out of place. They have a nice *Lobster Fra Diabolo* (Fettucine has arrived on the Eastern Shore). Lots of usual stuff with French names and teepee napkins. *Franco-Italian. Open M-F 11:30am-2:30pm, 4pm-midnight; Sa 11:30am-midnight; Su 1pm-midnight. Reservations. Major credit cards. Gay and Muse Sts. 221-0300.*

Old Trinity Church. On Route 16 six miles west of Cambridge is the oldest active church in the United States. Built around 1675, it suffered some Gothic modernizing but was restored 30 years ago. As was common, its cemetery surrounds it. Why do you suppose they wanted the graves so close? *Open daily except Tu, Mar-Dec 9am-5pm. Church Creek. 228-2940.*

Harriet Tubman was born a black slave in 1820 in Bucktown. A wildly successful slave-runner—for the good guys—she guided more than 300 slaves from the Eastern Shore to freedom in Canada. In 10 years she made 19 trips and not one slave was caught.

Salisbury is distractingly urban compared to the rest of the Shore; it can disturb your countryside tune. If so, you will be grateful for Route 50's detour around the city's skirts—the most damaging visual aspects are a few quicky food joints and a Sheraton Inn.

On the other hand, Salisbury does spell relief. It was founded by Colonel Isaac Handy (who called it Handy's Landing more than 250 years ago) and it was leveled twice by fire. It has shown great vitality in its revivals, spurts of development, and activities. It holds the World Championship Wildfowl Carving Competition in April *(write to Wildfowl Carving Competition, Salisbury, MD).* It has park band concerts, art exhibits, Civil War reenactments, rodeos, auto shows, boat shows, and a nice little zoo with wild ponies from Assateague Island. *Call the Chamber of Commerce, 749-0144.*

Blackwater National Wildlife Refuge. Eighty thousand Canada geese and 30,000 ducks call this place home in the fall. Also hiding here are four endangered species: the bald eagle, Delmarva fox squirrel, peregrine falcon, and the red-cockaded woodpecker. Vidal Martinez runs an enthusiastic Visitor Center, even if he is from the Bronx. There is a five-mile Wildlife Drive, observation tower, and a number of foot trails. Lots of nature. *Trails open dawn to dusk, the Visitor Center 7:30am-4pm. Rt. 335. 228-2677.*

The Chesapeake Bay Retriever, legend says, was created by mating a male otter with an Irish Setter. Or, more likely, that Newfoundland puppies were rescued from a sinking ship in 1807 and mated with local retrievers. Whatever their checkered genealogy, the Bay Retriever is one of America's only native sporting breeds, and one of the few breeds native to the country. The dog's dense undercoat protects it from severe weather and its reddish color blends with its natural habitat, the marshes.

2
4

Calvert Cliffs

Cove Point

Solomons

235

● St. Mary's City

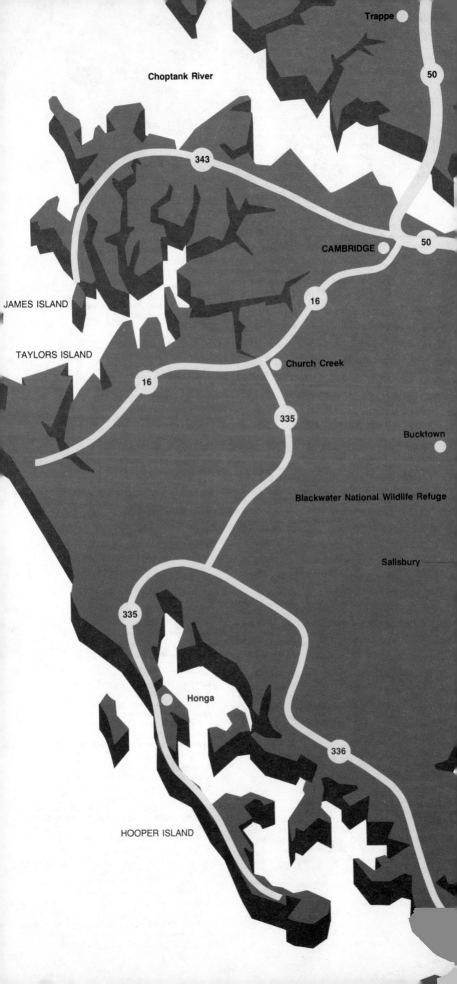

The Bay's marine life is tremendously varied. There are normal or pink or green oysters, clams, blue crabs, and 238 recorded varieties of finfish. Some are biggies like 100-plus-pound drumfish, and, in Colonial times, sturgeon 12 feet long. There are hogchokers (the American sole) and toadfish (ugly, but tasty). Bull sharks and brown sharks (some more than eight feet long), eels, seals, porpoises, and stinging jellyfish, a species 500 million years old. Whales bred in the Bay during the Miocene Age, some still drop in. Marine Turtles (diamondback terrapins) were enormous and enumerous in the 1700s, in fact so plentiful and cheap that slaves were given little else until laws were passed limiting their turtle meals to one a week.

Oysters were abundant beyond the Colonists' dreams. They first tasted them in 1607 when they surprised Indians in the middle of an oyster roast. In 1610 oysters were found 13 inches long—one-oyster dinners.

An oyster pumps around 50 gallons of water a day, extracting oxygen, proteins, carbohydrates, fats, salts, and minerals. A natural final-stage sewage treatment plant. If healthy, the Bay can provide 2.3 million bushels of oysters a year; in its present condition it gives up less than a million. They are caught by a variety of methods: tonging, dredging, and diving. Oysters take 30 months to grow to market size, a time that controlled breeding can halve. But its enemies are many. Man-made pollutants like acid rain, oil spills and indiscriminate sewage dumping have been devastating, but so has the Bay's natural pollutant, ever-encroaching sediment.

Crabs shed their shells 18 to 20 times in their two-year (female) to three-year (male) life spans. They have been found as big as 14 inches across; fishermen say they are biggest and tastiest when the moon is full. In 1915, 50.5 million pounds were harvested, today the annual yield is around 33 million, two-thirds the national total. Around fishing docks you will see wood-lattice shedder floats in which crabs are kept until they drop their hard shells. While soft they are packed in seaweed and ice and shipped live to market.

The migrating habits of these creatures are fascinating. When a bunch were let loose up near the Chesapeake-Delaware Canal the speedy creatures scrambled east and west at a rate of four miles a day. Some crawled 97 miles in 27 days. Because they would shed any kind of tag with their shells they are now branded with laser beams.

THE CRISFIELD AREA

As you continue south into Somerset County, the blue-collar Eastern Shore emerges. Fishing and farming are the orders of life. The land continues flat, if possible flatter, always blending into the plane of the Bay. Absolutely effortless bicycle country.

Princess Anne, the county seat since 1744, is venerable and dignified with magnificent sycamores lining its streets. The Manokin River once made it a busy port but it is no longer navigable—in fact it is no longer at all. Gone. The town now cans and pickles things and raises chickens. It has inhabited structures dating as early as 1705, but most of the architecture is Federal and Victorian. Many can be toured during **Olde Princess Anne Days** on the second weekend in October *(for information call the Chamber of Commerce, 968-2500).*

The Teackle Mansion, an elegant five-part brick house built in 1801, is a little Late Georgian and a little Tudor. It figures prominently in an ante-bellum novel about the Eastern Shore's most notorious slave kidnapper and smuggler, **Lucretia Patty Cannon**. There is a candlelight walking tour in December. *On Mansion St. 651-1705.*

Washington Hotel *(inexpensive)* is an oldie built in 1744. It sits unpretentiously in the middle of town offering unpretentious accommodations and most definitely unpretentious meals. *10 rooms. Restaurant and coffee shop open M-Sa 6am-9pm. Somerset Ave. 651-2525.*

Deal Island is one of the last refuges for the sailing Skipjack. Hop down from Princess Anne on Route 353, past the church cemeteries lined with cement sarcophagi lying on top of the waterlogged land, to **Wenona.** Here the boats can be seen close at hand.

Skipjacks are the Bay's most famous throwbacks. The use of power in collecting deep-water oysters is limited by the state so these boats continue doing what similar boats have done for 300 years. There were once 150 Skipjacks at Deal Island. But as the oysters diminished, so have the boats; they now number around a dozen. Flat-bottomed and sloop-rigged, from 30 to 60 feet long, always white with a hefty raked mast and coarse work sails, they are arresting sights. They use iron-pronged, jaw-like dredges to scrape oysters off the bottom. Look just beneath the bowsprit for the *trailboard* carvings of the boat's name embellished with gold leaf and bright colors.

Crisfield is a factory town. Somber but honest, it looks like the hard-working town it is. In season the vacationers somehow mix well with the workers. Find the shell-shedding tanks behind the packing houses and watch nature's process of turning hard-shell crabs into soft-shell crabs.

And, ta-da, there are crab races during the **National Hard Crab Derby and Fair** in September, a three-day affair with fireworks, bands and carnivals *(for information call 968-2500).* If the excitement is too much, take a day-cruise or ferry *(for information call 651-2968) to nearby* **Smith Island** (10 miles away, discovered by **Captain John Smith** in 1608) or **Tangier Island**—places where time is running late.

The Captain's Galley restaurant (☆$) suits the town—straight-up meals on kitchen table settings. Sort of a sea-side truck stop with quite good oyster stew. *Open daily 8am-10pm. Main St. in Crisfield. 968-1636.*

Aunt Em's ($) looks awful, an All-American highway food stop. For some reason they make an extra effort on clam chowder. *Open M-Sa 5am-8pm. Richardson Ave. 968-0353.*

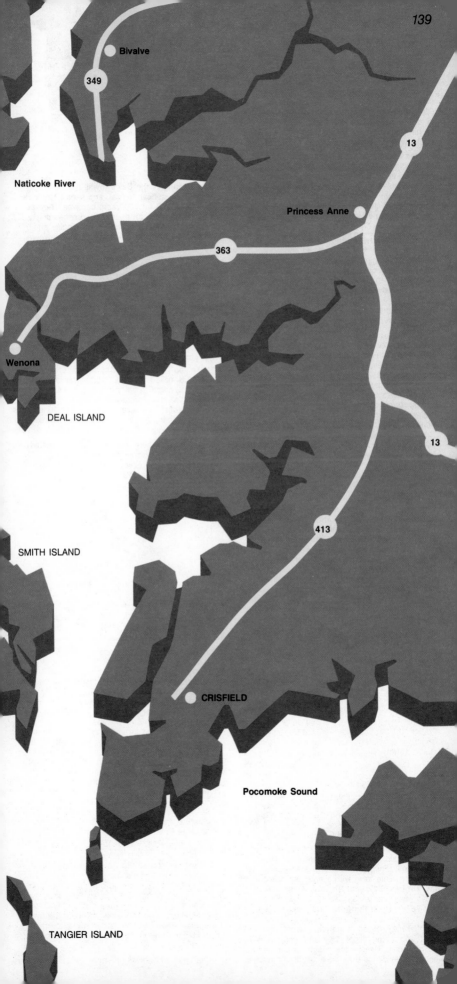

THE LOWER CHESAPEAKE

Captain John Smith cross-hatched the Bay with his sailing treks. He fished ("That abundance of fish, lying so thicke with their heads above the water as for want of nets we attempted to catch them with a frying pan."), he mapped, he named (**Tangier Island** after his enemies the Tangier pirates and **Stingray Point** after eating one which bit him), and he shot (or claimed he shot) 148 ducks with three shots. Busy, busy.

Pirates appeared in the Chesapeake as soon as there was anything to steal. They were first recorded in 1610 only three years after Jamestown was colonized. In 1685, **Roger Makeele** and his crew of 13 men and four women crime-waved the Bay, in 1717 **Blackbeard** blockaded the mouth of the Bay at Cape Henry and demanded tribute for passage.

Piracy begat **privateering.** The only difference was the government encouraged and honored it instead of hanging for it. Privateers formed a very effective navy during the Revolutionary War and in the War of 1812 their fleet of 126 ships captured 556 British ships. They certainly weren't wanting for style, one Captain **Thomas Boyle** announced to London that he was blockading the entire coast of Britain and Ireland with his one schooner and 16 guns.

The boats have always mirrored the Bay's activity. Before the quick schooners of the privateers, sailing log canoes were fashioned from Indian dugouts; they evolved into larger versions called *brogans* and *bugeyes.* There were *shallops, deals, wherries, bateaux,* and *scows* (all utility, fishing, or *church* boats), *sloops, clippers, skipjacks* and *rams* for increasingly serious pirating, fishing and trade. The most famous of these was the **Baltimore Clipper,** built like a souped-up schooner in the late 1700s. It was long, low, extremely raked and very fast—it became very popular among pirates and slavers. Around 1860, in came decent laws and out went the Clippers—they just couldn't carry enough honest cargo.

Steamboat lines criss-crossed the Chesapeake from 1787 (when James Rumsey ran one up the Potomac) to 1959, when the last two side-wheeling steamers were last used to break the Bay's ice. Some steamers could be quite long (200 feet) but they were always slender—the Chesapeake and Delaware Canal restricted their width to no more than 24 feet, the width of the locks. In the late 1800s the steamers were the last word in classy travel. They served cheap, extraordinary meals with their own silverware (which turn up still in local antique shops) in genteel, paneled salons and cabins.

But a steamer's career could be mixed. The **Chauncey M. Depew** was built in 1913 for the Maine Central Railroad, used as a day cruiser on the Hudson River, then as a troop carrier in World War II, back to the Bay and then to Bermuda as a cruiser, back to the Bay to be scuttled, then raised and turned into a dock-locked restaurant. The Bay steamboat **President Warfield** became the **Exodus** in 1947. It carried 4,554 Jews from France to Palestine, although her capacity was only 540. She later caught fire, sank in Haifa Harbor, and was sold for scrap.

Below Crisfield, as you enter **Virginia,** the Eastern Shore thins to a scraggly finger pointing at Cape Henry and **Newport News.** The terrain approaches the desolate. Flat City. The huge forests of the 1600s were long ago turned into boats and villages, leaving the land open and agricultural by default. Violent gales could carry ships deep ashore into the diminishing woods.

Accomac, the county seat, has more restored colonial buildings than any town of its size. **Onancock** (*Foggy Place* to the Algonquin Indians) is a pearly little town with a museum operated by the **Virginia Historical Society.** *Admission charge. Open Mar-Dec, Tu-Sa 10am-4pm. Kerr Place. 804-787-2460.* In **Pungoteague,** seven miles south, three men performed *Ye Beare and Ye Cub,* the first play staged in the New World. It was in 1665 and, being illegal, they were charged with *acting a play.* Despite the costumes and script shown in evidence they were declared innocent.

SMITH ISLAND

The naming of the Bay's towns has been variously historical, logical, and exotic. **Hadlock** was called **TB** for 130 years because **Thomas Bell,** a man with an exaggerated sense of property, burned his initials into shingles and plastered them on the town's trees. Elsewhere there are towns called **Gratitude** (after a steamboat), **Bivalve** and **Shelltown** (origins obvious) and **Accident** (origin uncertain). **Two Johns Landing** on the Choptank River came from an 1880 vaudeville team of two 300-pound men who lived there—both named John. **Plaindealing Creek** was named by the Indians after the honesty of the Quakers they traded with—evidently they found incidents of honesty so rare they felt they should be commemorated.

Forty-five miles below Accomac the peninsula of the Eastern Shore ends. Hopping the mouth of the Bay is the **Chesapeake Bay Bridge and Tunnel.** It is 17.6 miles long including two mile-long tunnels beneath the ship channels, one high bridge, and four 8-acre islands. *"One of the seven wonders of the modern world",* it takes 23 minutes to cross *(charge)* and has a restaurant and fishing pier on the way.

If you continue your tour north up the Western Shore back to Washington, **Williamsburg, Jamestown,** and **Fredericksburg** would be just minutes off your path.

Lighthouses were first used in 1791. By 1910 more than 100 had been built. But these and the few lightships used were not satisfactory. They were either too far from the danger they marked or too low. So, the **screwpile** method of on-water construction was developed. Pilings were corkscrewed down into the soft, mucky Bay bottom until they formed a stable base and stone rip-rap was added to protect the pilings. Neat little hexagonal cottage-lighthouses were built on top, poised on girders above the water like fantasy houses on spider legs. There were once 40 of these, only three are left. The 110-year-old **Thomas Point Light** near Annapolis still works. The other two are retired, one to the Maritime Museum in St. Michaels, the other to the Calvert Marine Museum in Solomons. All other operating lights are unmanned, automated affairs except for the **Cove Point Lighthouse** north of the Patuxent River. Two Coast Guardsmen and their families run it—the last family light station on the Bay.

Animal life around the Bay, beyond the usual, includes wolves menacing the villages in the 1600s. Talbot County paid a bounty of 100 pounds of tobacco for each wolf's head. Only three herds of **miniature elk** (Sika deer) exist in this country, one of them is on **James Island** near the Little Choptank River. **Poplar Island** was once a black cat fur farm until the Bay iced over and they all ran off.

Area code 301 unless otherwise indicated.

413

CRISFIELD

MARYLAND

Pocomoke Sound

VIRGINIA

TANGIER ISLAND

316

Onancock

718

13

180

Pungoteague

178

Chesapeake Bay Bridge and Tunnel

Maps by Joyce Rothschild
Illustrations by Mary Anne McLean
Text by Peter Bradford

Hadlock

MOUNT VERNON

Mount Vernon. The contemporary presidential home is characterized by privacy and security. Sliding iron gates, video cameras and guard posts protect the presidential stretch of beach or length of riding trail. But in the early days of the republic what presidential homes held in common were wheat and tobacco fields, mills, smokehouses and stables. In a time of broad personal mastery, a gifted leader was often able to administer a nation, lead troops in battle, design a building and run a profitable farm. **George Washington** exemplified this spirit and his estate at Mount Vernon is its testimony.

In its prime, Mount Vernon comprised 8,000 acres divided into 5 working farms. It was self-sufficient in almost every way. There were orchards, a grist mill and facilities for making textiles and leather goods.

"No estate in United America is more pleasantly situated than this house," wrote Washington, but during the years he was Mount Vernon's proprietor he was allowed little time there. First there were the French and Indian Wars, then the Revolutionary War, which kept Washington away for 8 years. When he returned he was determined to be a successful planter. He experimented with crop rotation and compared notes with like-minded growers. His harvests were good, and he even won a *"premium for raising the largest jackass"* from the Agricultural Society of South Carolina. But only 4 years later he went to Philadelphia as a delegate to the **Constitutional Convention** and then served 2 terms as president. Finally, in 1797 he returned home, where he lived contentedly until his death—2 years later.

The current estate, a more manageable 500 acres, is probably the best preserved 18th-century plantation in the country, and in the summer as many as 10,000 people a day come to enjoy it. The best strategy is to arrive early and tour the mansion before visiting the outbuildings and grounds.

The inside of the white Georgian mansion has been lovingly restored. All wallpaper, drapery and upholstery are exact replicas and the original colors have been repainted on the walls. (The colonial palette was much bolder than you'd expect.) Note the Palladian window in the **Banquet Hall** and in the **Little Parlor**, a harpsicord Washington imported to the tune of £1000, for his adopted daughter **Nellie**. One of the upstairs bedrooms holds a trunk Washington carried with him during the Revolutionary War and the bed in which he died. Washington was 6 feet, 2 inches and had the extra-long bed made to order.

Nine of the outbuildings are open, including the spinning room and open-hearth kitchen house. (In days when fires were common and virtually unstoppable, the kitchen was often set apart from the main house.) You can visit the stable where a rare 18th-century coach is on display and a small museum with exhibits of Washingtoniana, Colonial silver and china. In the reconstructed greenhouse/slave quarters there is a fascinating exhibit about archaeology at Mount Vernon.

George Washington called Fredericksburg *"the place of my growing infancy."*

On either side of the gracious bowling green are period gardens with flowers, vegetables and boxwood hedges. Note the partially submerged walls called *ha has* that separate tended lawns and gardens from pasture. It's a pleasant walk down to the family vaults where George and Martha are buried.

Admission charge. Open daily Nov-Feb 9am-4pm, Mar-Oct till 5pm. Metrobus/Tourmobile tours Jun-Sep. Washington Boat Lines cruises (see entry District 6). Mt. Vernon located at southern end of the George Washington Parkway. 703-780-2000.

GW BIRTHPLACE

George Washington Birthplace National Monument (Wakefield). George really slept here...and like a baby—he was born on this verdant farm in 1732. It all started in the winter of 1665 when George's great grandfather, **John**, was sailing up river in a ship carrying Virginia tobacco to England. The ship sank and while it was being refitted, John was taken in by the charms of the countryside and a local planter's daughter. He stayed. John's grandson, **Augustine**, built the plantation at **Pope's Creek**, called *Wakefield*. Here George was born and lived as a child, and later for several years as a teenager.

The original estate burned down on Christmas Day 1779, but the National Park Service has done a fine job recreating the plantation as it might have been. There is a reconstructed kitchen house and spinning house. The **Memorial House** is a faithful rendition of an 18th-century plantation home. Vegetable and kitchen herb gardens are planted with period accuracy.

Today Wakefield is maintained as a demonstration Colonial farm. Using, for the most part, 18th-century methods, they grow wheat, flax corn and tobacco, crops this plantation once produced.

Many of the animals here were common Colonial varieties like red Devon cattle, English game hens and razorback hogs. Costumed employees give demonstrations in spinning, weaving, and if staffing permits, in blacksmithing, carpentry and ox-driving.

Picnic areas are available and a hiking trail, which leads you through a cedar grove, to the banks of Pope Creek where Washington often went hunting. There is an introductory film at the **Visitors Center**.

Admission free. Open daily 9am-5pm. Closed Christmas, New Year's. Group tours available. Guided tours on the half hour. Located 37 miles south of Fredericksburg, VA. Rt. 3 to Rt. 204. Continue for 2 miles. A granite obelisk marks the entrance. From DC take the Beltway to Rt. 5 (Exit 7), go to Rt. 301 which turns into VA. Rt. 3. 304-224-0196.

FORT WASHINGTON

Fort Washington. The fort that now occupies this site is the successor to the original **Fort Warburton**, destroyed by British fires in 1814. The present structure completed by L'Enfant in 1824 was manned as a river defense post, at times with the strength of nearly 350 men. High brick and stone walls enclose the 833-square-foot fort; the entrance has a drawbridge suspended over a dry moat, preventing attacks from the enemy. The ramparts, the casement positions and the water battery 60 feet below the main fort could deliver lethal bombardments from 3 levels. Also on view are the officers' quarters and the soldier barracks nearby, where volunteer guides in period costumes give musket demonstrations during peak season. Several trails lead to picnic areas in the 300-acre historical park surrounding the fort. Tours on request. *Admission free. Open daily 7:30am-dusk. Fort Washington Rd., Fort Washington. 301-292-2112.*

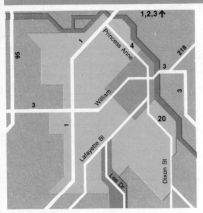

Fredericksburg sits like a giant dollhouse on the south shore of the **Rappahannock River.** The frontier port town was barely 10 years old when sandstone miner **Augustine Washington** moved his family to **Ferry Farm** on the north side of the Rappahannock in 1738. The farm became George Washington's boyhood home, where he lived until his appointment as the official land surveyor of Culpeper County.

During the American Revolution, Fredericksburg became a center for heavy arms manufacturing. Unscathed by this war, the Southern town continued its prosperous existence until 1860, when the peace was abruptly shattered by another conflict. Fredericksburg was thrown into the firing line of the Civil War, resulting in massive losses and tremendous physical destruction. Although the battles permanently scarred many of the surrounding areas, several of **Old Town's** Colonial homes were mended or rebuilt. Today, hundreds of 18th- and 19th-century buildings are still used as shops, museums and private residences in the historic blocks along the river.

1 Belmont. American artist **Gari Melchers** spent his last 16 years in the splendor of this 27-acre estate, filled with European antiques and paintings by **Breugel, Morisot** and **Puvis de Chavannes.** Melchers' private studio, now converted into a gallery display area, exhibits more than 50 of his impressionistic works, including a version of *The Last Supper.* The artist's tools as well as medals and honorary certificates are also on view. *Admission charge. Open 1-5pm daily. Closed Tu & Th. Rt. 1001, Falmouth, VA. 703-373-3634.*

2 Joe & Mo's Eugate. ☆ $$ The place for hip burghers and country squires, who come to rub shoulders with out-of-towners in tour buses. Hearty prime rib and snazzy brass decor. Weekend live entertainment. *American. Open M-Sa 5-10pm. 720 Cambridge St. on US 1N. 703-371-0484.*

3 Renato's Italian Restaurant. ☆ ☆ $$ Homemade pasta, excellent seafood and veal specialties are served in this red velvet and red vinyl establishment. Local crooners a la **Sinatra** and **Tony Bennett** appear regularly. *Northern Italian. Open M-F 11am-3pm, daily 4-10pm. 1300 Jefferson Davis Hwy. 703-371-8228*

4 Fredericksburg Colonial Inn. *Inexpensive.* Thirty-four rooms and 6 suites furnished in antiques from 1850 make this old-fashioned inn a faithful rendition of a pre-Civil War hostelry. All accommodations have queen sized 4-poster beds and Colonial marble top washstands; the *Stonewall Jackson Room,* also called the *Honeymoon Suite,* features a canopy bed and a pretty love settee in the sitting room. Private baths, refrigerators, radios and color TVs are added touches of comfort. *1707 Princess Anne St. 703-371-5666.*

Introductions/Theaters/Narrative black
Hotels purple
Museums/Architecture blue
Parks/Open spaces green
Restaurants/Nightlife red
Shops/Galleries violet

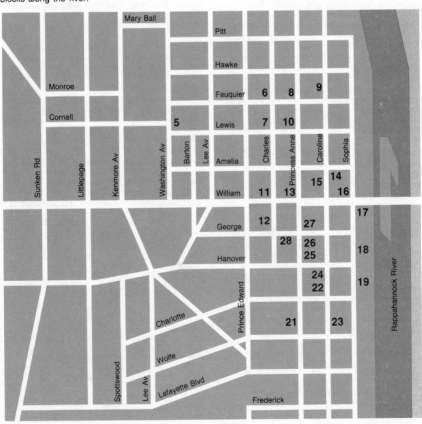

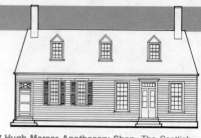

5 Kenmore 1752. The home of **George Washington's** sister **Betty Lewis** is perhaps the most beautiful mid-Georgian mansion in Fredericksburg—some of its rooms are considered to be among the country's most elegant. Richly ornamented plaster ceilings (tradition says that Washington helped direct their design) complement the elegant mahogany furniture; the carved stone portico overlooking the boxwood garden is grander than any other in town. Tea and gingerbread served in the Colonial kitchen. *Admission charge. Open daily Nov-Mar 9am-4pm, Apr-Oct till 5pm. 1201 Washington Ave. 703-373-3381.*

6 St. James House. George Washington bought the site from his brother-in-law, **Fielding Lewis,** in 1761. A few years later, he sold it to his mother's attorney, who built the tiny gambrel-roofed house. The garden and the interior have been restored with priceless European antiques to reflect handsome 18th-century living. *Admission charge. Open by appointment last week of Apr and 1st week of Oct. 1300 Charles St. 703-373-1776.*

7 Mary Washington House. Another quaint piece of family real estate, this one bought for Mary herself by her son **George.** Here, Mary spent her last 17 years among favorite possessions from the Ferry Farm home. The old sun dial was placed in the English garden; her old Bible box was brought along, as well as the *"best dressing glass"*—an 18th-century Chippendale mirror. *Admission charge. Open 1 Apr-31 Oct daily 9am-5pm; remaining months 9am-4pm. 1200 Charles St. 703-373-1569.*

8 Smythe's Cottage Restaurant. ☆ ☆ $$ Stuffed pork chops with fresh brandied apples, Virginia ham and peanut soup served in a pre-Civil War setting. Fresh seafood and steaks round out the menu. Reservations suggested. *Regional American. Open daily 11:30am-3pm; Su-Th 5:30-9pm, F & Sa till 10pm. 303 Fauquier St. 703-373-1645.*

9 Rising Sun Tavern. (1761, **Charles Washington**) The revolutionary leaders of Virginia often plotted anti-British activities at this gathering place, owned by **George Washington's** brother Charles. The remarkable collection of original fixtures has again been put to use in the **Tap Room,** where spiced tea is served by a costumed tavern maiden. *Admission charge. Open Jan-Feb daily 10am-4pm, Mar 9am-4pm, Apr-Oct 9am-5pm, Nov-Dec 9am-4pm. 1306 Caroline St. 703-371-1494.*

10 Kenmore Inn. *Inexpensive.* Beautiful ante-bellum bed-and-breakfast inn. Each of the individually decorated rooms has a private bath. Luncheon or British-style afternoon tea is taken at the small restaurant on the premises. *1200 Princess Anne St. 703-371-7622.*

11 Slave auction block. Pre-Civil War remnant from the *Dark Ages of America. William and Charles Sts.*

12 James Monroe Museum & Library. Monroe's first law office made into a showcase of his Louis XVI furnishings. The ultimate piece is the desk where the famous *Monroe Doctrine* was signed; other items of interest include Mrs. Monroe's gems and lavish wardrobe. Thousands of books and manuscripts in the library tell us everything we want to know about Monroe and his era. *Admission charge. Open daily 9am-5pm. 908 Charles St. 703-373-8421.*

13 La Petite Auberge. ☆ ☆ ☆ $$ The city's one and only French restaurant. Ample portions of country specials in rich sauces. Robust reds from the wine list recommended. *French. Open M-F 11:30am-2:30pm, M-Sa 4:30-10pm. 311 William St. 703-371-2727.*

14 Anrapo's Antiques. Early 18th- to mid-19th-century European dressers, buffets and dining sets share quarters with new mahogany reproductions from France. Largest and finest furniture collection on *Antique Row. Open M-Sa 10am-5pm. Su noon-5pm. 1027 Caroline St. 703-371-7176.*

15 Hugh Mercer Apothecary Shop. The Scottish doctor-turned-general treated Colonial ailments with snakeroot and crab claws from this 200-year old drugstore. Silver pills in apothecary jars painted from the inside are a few of the more palatable antidotes displayed. *Admission charge. 1020 Caroline St. 703-373-3362.*

16 John Hile, Silversmiths. Mr. Hile's handwrought sterling silver jewelry sparkles with malachites, agates and jasper. *Open Tu-F 9am-4pm. 103-1/2 William St. 703-373-9480.*

17 Old Stone Warehouse. (pre-1760; renovated 1975) Four stories of Civil War relics are housed in this Colonial tobacco warehouse. The underground area, once used for loading cargo aboard ships, is now a basement dig for wild boar tusks, fragments of pottery and the like. The present ground level is really the second story: Sophia St. was raised early in this century and the first floor was buried in the effort. Excavated Civil War items for sale in the souvenir shop. *Admission charge. Open daily 9am-5pm. 923 Sophia St. 703-371-4375.*

18 The Silversmith's House. Saved from demolition by local historians, the 18th-century town smith's home is now headquarters of the *Fredericksburg Center for the Creative Arts.* Monthly exhibits by living artists and craftsmen, film series and a weaver's studio in the basement are the main attractions. Call for schedule of events. *Admission free, donations accepted. Open Tu-Sa 10am-4pm. 813 Sophia St. 703-373-5646.*

19 Copper Shop. Father-and-son team hammering out 6 patented versions of the *Fredericksburg Lamp,* chandelier or tabletop size. The city gives them to visiting dignitaries—now you can have one too. *Open M-Sa 9:30am-5pm, Su noon-5pm. 701 Sophia St. 703-371-4455.*

20 Fredericksburg Pewter. Classic wine goblets, plates and bowls. Cottage industry at its best, emanating from the backyard of a home. *Open M-F 1-5pm, Sa 10:30am-5pm. 309 Princess Elizabeth St. 703-371-0585.*

21 Homespun Elegance. Complete country house furnishings, from swag curtains to rugs in American Primitive and traditional designs. Large assortment of counted cross stitch and candlewicking kits for sale. *Open M-Sa 10am-4pm. 602 Caroline St. 703-371-6377.*

22 Fredericksburg Visitors Center. A practical pit stop for the Fredericksburg explorer, this center offers block admission tickets, maps, hotel and restaurant information. A short action film of the city's bloody Civil War involvement is shown upon request. *Open M-F 8:30am-5pm, Sa & Su 9am-5pm. 706 Caroline St. 703-373-1776.*

23 Chimneys Publick House. ☆ ☆ $$ (1772, **John Glassell**) Duck, game pie and Beef Wellington are the specialties of this fine Colonial eatery. The Georgian-style house, named for its massive brick chimneys at each end, was the childhood home of **Nell Arthur.** Inside, the original mantels and wainscoting add to the authenticity. *Regional American. Open daily 11:30am-3pm, Tu-Su 5:30-9:30pm. 623 Caroline St. 703-371-2850.*

24 Little Women. This little nifty back alley store features goods exclusively crafted by the artistic people of Fredericksburg. Mostly on consignment, the assortment ranges from homemade chocolate to stuffed animals. *Open M-Sa 10am-4:30pm. 710 Caroline St. 703-371-3322.*

The legend of George Washington's cherry tree originated in Fredericksburg.

Masonic Lodge. One of the oldest lodges in America. This is where **George Washington** was initiated as a Mason in 1752; the Bible and minute book used to record this event are displayed together with his portrait. *Admission charge. Open daily Nov-Mar 9am-4pm, Apr-Oct till 5pm. 803 Princess Anne St. 703-373-5885.*

Courthouse. (1852, **James Renwick**) A Gothic Revival replacement of an 18th-century structure. Though the one-room interior has been divided into offices, the original walnut ceilings supported by handcarved bridgework still grace the courtroom. **Mary Washington's** will and old city documents can be found in the Clerk's Office below. *Admission free. Open M-F 9am-5pm. 809 Princess Anne St. 703-373-7781.*

St. George's Episcopal Church. (1849) This 19th-century Gothic church is graced with stained glass windows dedicated by the DAR to **Mary Washington**, including 3 signed by **Louis Comfort Tiffany**. Several friends and relatives of the Washington clan are buried in the cemetery: **Martha Washington's** father, **Betty Washington's** husband **Fielding Lewis,** and **John Paul Jones'** brother **William.** *Admission free. Open daily 7am-5pm. 905 Princess Anne St. 703-373-4133.*

Presbyterian Church. (1833) A target for Civil War bombardments in 1862, the Greek Revival structure still has cannonballs stuck in its pillars and scars in the belfry walls. The original bell was melted into cannons, pews were torn loose to make coffins, and **Clara Barton** nursed the Yankee soldiers who lay dying inside. *Admission free. Open daily 8:30am-3pm. 304 George St. 703-373-7057.*

9 National Cemetery. Three-fourths of the 15,243 Federal soldiers buried here are listed as unknown. The monuments and plaques throughout the somber grounds commemorate various Confederate divisions and military units. *Open during daylight hours. Marye's Heights, corner of Sunken Rd. and Lafayette Blvd.*

0 Fredericksburg Battlefield Visitors Center. Information center and starting point for covering the 1862 **Battle of Fredericksburg.** An electric map presentation takes you through the bastions and bombardments, and an old-fashioned diorama shows the destruction of the inner city buildings. Maps for driving tours are available; guided walks through the park are held on weekends. *Admission free. Open M-F 9am-5pm, Sa & Su till 6pm. 1013 Lafayette Blvd. 703-373-6122.*

1 P.K.'s Restaurant and Lounge. ☆☆$$ Small-town, romantic atmosphere with Victorian accents. Baked stuffed shrimp or succulent ribs are favorite entrees, finished off with homemade chocolate-walnut pie *a la mode*. Reservations suggested. *American. Open M-Sa 11:30am-2:30pm, 5-10pm. Westwood Shopping Center, Rt. 3 and I-95. 703-371-3344.*

2 Sheraton Fredericksburg Resort. *Moderate.* Four-hundred landscaped acres offering 3 tennis courts, an 18-hole golf course and fishing grounds for the outdoor enthusiast. Cable TV, large outdoor pool and 3 restaurants are the additional amenities of this 196-room hotel. *Rt. 3 and I-95. 703-786-8321.*

Aquia Church in Stafford, 20 miles north of Fredericksburg, has been the site of a female ghost since the American Revolution. The legend tells of a young woman who was murdered by highwaymen while praying in the church. After sundown, heavy breathing, sounds of struggle and the shuffling of feet can be heard inside the church; from the outside, the terrified woman is seen by the window wailing for help.

Introductions/Theaters/Narrative black
Hotels purple
Museums/Architecture blue
Parks/Open spaces green
Restaurants/Nightlife red
Shops/Galleries violet

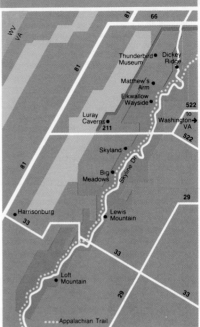

Shenandoah Valley National Park. Overlooking the Shenandoah River along 80 miles of Blue Ridge Mountains lies Shenandoah National Park. In the autumn the park shows off its fiery colors on oak, hickory and hemlock trees. Spring and summer come to life with a rainbow of wild flowers and blossoming trees, carpeting the park's 190,000 woody acres. The 105-mile-long Skyline Drive winds through the park near the crest of the Blue Ridge Mountains, through Rockfish Gap, to converge with the Blue Ridge Parkway.

Encircled by the Blue Ridge Mountains on the east and the Alleghenies to the west, the Shenandoah Valley runs deep with native and early American history. Its Indian name means *Daughter of the Stars,* perhaps alluding to the Indian belief that the valley was once a lake around which the stars sang every thousand years. The valley's half billion years of development glow in its primitive volcanic rock, as old as any in existence. For a few million years, the area was smoothed by winds, uplifted and worn down again. The river's *wind gaps,* where it diverted other channels into its own waters, still lie in the Blue Ridge, now far above the river's floor. So splendid were nature's ways here that **George Washington,** a major landowner, insisted all his tenants plant 4 acres of apple trees, as the peaceful orchards in the valley now attest.

The **Shenandoah National Park,** established in 1935, marks what was, during frontier days, the major route west.

Skyline Drive's numbered mileposts guide you to historic and scenic features. Some spots you'll encounter include:

Dickey Ridge Visitor Center—picnic sites and Ranger information. (*Milepost 4.6*)

Mathews Arm—camping and picnic areas. (*Milepost 22.3*)

Elkwallow Wayside—rest stop, trout fishing. (*Milepost 24.1*)

Skyland Lodge—horseback riding, lodging. (*Milepost 41.7*)

Byrd Visitor Center—museum and information.

Big Meadows, Wayside and Lodge—rest stop, store, stables, fishing. (*Milepost 51.3*)

Lewis Mountain—camping. (*Milepost 57.6*)

Loft Mountain—picnic area, restaurant, camping. (*Milepost 79.8*)

Several companies offer canoe trips along the Shenandoah River. The park is open all year 'round, except in extreme weather. *703-999-2266.*

SHENANDOAH

Called *the Bread Basket of the Confederacy*, the Shenandoah Valley served as the chief supply site for **Robert E. Lee's** army during much of the Civil War, and was a crucial battlefield for both North and South. In 1960, the Virginia Civil War Commission placed *Circle Tour* markers at major battle sites throughout the valley, including:

Winchester: Changing hands 72 times during the war, Winchester saw more fighting than any area west of Richmond. Visit the **Stonewall Jackson Home,** his headquarters in a Gothic-style house which now displays Jackson memorabilia; the **Confederate Monument;** **General Philip Sheridan's** headquarters; and Stonewall Cemetery.

Cedar Creek: Here Confederate soldiers tried for the last time to win over the valley. Visit **Belle Meade mansion,** where **James and Dolley Madison** honeymooned; **Front Royal,** where Jackson's men captured 750 Federal Soldiers; the **Soldier's Circle Monument;** and **the Battle of Front Royal Monument.**

Thoroughfare Gap: Where Confederate troops scored a victorious 1862 battle.

Strasburg: This village, which divides the valley in half, was used by both sides as a sentry outpost.

Edinburg: Headquarters for the Southern cavalry briefly in 1862, it was burned by the North in 1864.

New Market: A Civil War museum rests on an 1864 battlefield where the South overtook Union lines.

Harrisonburg: Jackson often met with his troops here in 1862.

Cross Keys: The 1862 Northern attack failed here.

Port Republic: The South won a battle here following Cross Keys, but suffered heavy casualties.

Bath County: Entrenchments remain at Millboro Springs.

Waynesboro: The last battle for the North's control of Virginia took place here.

Lexington: Site of the **Virginia Military Institute** and the **Jackson Home.**

Also in Shenandoah: The **Thunderbird Museum and Archeological Park** lies 7 miles south of **Front Royal.** The museum guides you through 12,000 years of history via its archaeological excavations. Exhibits of early American Indian tools include 11,500-year-old clove spear points.

The **Corral Site,** an ongoing excavation, is open from spring to fall. In the summer, archaeologists will explain the current diggings.

Three miles of **nature trails** wind through intricate rock formations and caves. Maps mark 13 stations of historical interest. *Admission charge.*

Near Skyline Drive, **Luray Caverns** boasts shiny stone columns and cavern walls that reflect every color imaginable. Discovered in 1878, the caverns have fascinated millions of visitors.

The **Great Stalacpipe Organ** fills the cavern's *Cathedral Room* with symphonic tunes made from *playing* the stalactites which hang from the cave's ceiling. The nation's only stalacpipe organ can be played either from the organ or with automatic controls. *Open daily 9am-6pm; hours vary with the season. Off US 211.*

Inns of the Shenandoah Valley, an organization of 12 independent bed & breakfast inns, provides varied accommodations in several rural and historical places. Try the **Belle Grae Inn,** a former Victorian mansion in Staunton, or the **Jordan Hollow Farm Inn,** a 45-acre horse farm in Stanley. For more information write or call the **Historic Lexington Visitor Center,** *107 E. Washington St., Lexington, VA 24450. 703-463-3777.*

Washington, Virginia. Not only were there 8 other national capitals before Washington, DC, there was even another town called Washington, and as the residents of that Virginia hamlet (population 250) like to tell you, **George Washington** had much more to do with it than with his namesake to the northwest.

As a 17-year-old surveyor, George Washington and his 2 assistants layed out the town plan that is pretty much the same today: 2 main streets bisected by 5 shorter cross streets. This was done 43 years before DC became the capital. And if by chance you should have any doubts about the town's authenticity, visit the stone monument where a plaque proudly proclaims *"The town of Washington Virginia, The First Washington of All, Surveyed and Plotted by George Washington...."*

Washington, Virginia, is typical of all that is good about small northern Virginia towns. Moreover, it has scrupulously avoided the developers and their cousins, the gift shop owners, who seem to be taking over the rest of the state. It's in sight of the foothills that knock up against the Blue Ridge mountains, and nestled between farms, peach orchards and apple orchards where many owners will let you pick your own and pay by the bushel. Many of the farms have remained in the same family for over 200 years. In the village are several antique stores, art galleries, cabinet making studios and a charming 1833 courthouse where justice is still handed down. An 1800s tavern has been converted into a free museum with rooms recreating an 18th-century kitchen and a one-room schoolhouse.

The **Inn at Little Washington** (☆ ☆ ☆ ☆ $$$) is the place to go for serious culinary delight. Furnished like an Old English country inn, the restaurant has made a first rate reputation for itself serving imaginative offerings in what is called the *new American* style of cooking. Most meat and produce comes directly from local farms and gardens. The home-baked desserts are not to be missed. Cocktails are served outside by a reflecting pool and 10 rooms are opening in late 1984 for those wishing to explore the historic area or who are simply too blissed out on the food to drive home to DC. **Rooms are pricy but include a sumptuous breakfast.** *American. Open W & Th 6-9:30pm, F 6-10pm, Sa 5:30-10:30pm, Su 4-9:30pm. Closed M & Tu. Take 66 West from DC. At Gainesville turn onto 211. Go through Warrenton to Massey's corner. Continue 3 miles further and head right for Washington. 703-675-3800.*

PLANTATION TOUR

Stratford Hall. (1730) Perhaps the grandest manor house in the area, it was the boyhood home of **Robert E. Lee.** *Open daily 9am-4:30pm except Christmas. State Rt. 214, east of Fredericksburg. 804-493-8038.*

Morven Park. (1781) Greek Revival plantation house features rooms furnished in wide spectrum of historical styles. *Open Apr-Oct M-Sa 10am-5pm, Su 1-5pm. 2 miles north of Leesburg on Old Waterford Rd.*

Hampton National Historic Site. (1780s) Over 2 dozen buildings depict life in the heyday of the plantation system. Impressive Late Georgian main house. *Open daily 11am-4:30pm. North of Baltimore, off US 695 (the Beltway). 301-823-7054.*

Sully Plantation. (1794) Recently restored complex was home of **Robert E. Lee's** uncle. *Open W-M 10am-5pm. State Rt. 28, near Dulles Airport. 703-437-1794.*

Oatlands. (early 1800s) Well-preserved Greek Revival mansion is now a major equestrian center. *Open Apr-Oct M-Sa 10am-5pm, Su 1-5pm. 6 miles south of Leesburg on State Rt. 7. 703-777-3174.*

Sotterley. (1713) Working plantation. A highlight is the intricately carved woodwork throughout the farmhouse. *Open daily Jun-Sep 11am-5pm. Hollywood, MD. 301-373-2280.*

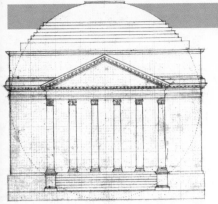

Charlottesville, *one of the nicer places in the United States to live and visit, is nestled on the eastern slope of the Blue Ridge Mountains in the area of Virginia known as Piedmont, 120 miles southwest of Washington.*

This quiet town of 40,000 is the home of the **University of Virginia,** and, more importantly, of the University's founder, **Thomas Jefferson.** The country's third president was a gentleman farmer, writer, architect, educator, lawyer, gadgeteer, sometimes politician, a dabbler in the arts and sciences, in short, America's favorite frontier Renaissance man. Charlottesville is *Mr. Jefferson's Country*—a lovely place of mild winters and long beautiful springs and autumns. Here one finds rolling fenced fields, white porticoes, red brick houses, flowering trees, boxwood gardens surrounded by vistas of pale blue mountains; it is as close as one comes to an American *Arcadia.* This physical amenity together with the area's *sense of history* and its heritage of attractive old buildings has drawn a wide variety of retired diplomats, businessmen and teachers as well as a fair assortment of rich people seeking expansive *second homes.* The University of Virginia adds to this special atmosphere so that for most, save diehard urbanists and the very poor, there is a sense of *privilege*—historical, social, educational and environmental—about being able to live here...much like a year-round resort.

Like the mythical towns of our country's collective memory, Charlottesville seems the sort of place where it is possible to live the ideal American life and at the same time to *get away from it all.* It is a setting for children, dogs and family outings; for discussions about horticulture and horses as well as about basketball and books. Significantly it is also a place where *History* is given more than lip service. **Madison, Monroe, Mason, Washington, Henry, Lee, Jackson, George Rogers Clark,** but especially Jefferson, seem a part of one's life here. His great buildings, the **Rotunda** and the **Lawn** and **Monticello,** are not just historic landmarks but cultural icons still with some potency—symbols, if you will, of a core of beliefs, styles and images not yet dead. A sense of a *living past* is present here to a much greater extent than is usually found in other American communities. In this sense Charlottesville, considered a liberal frontier by tidewater Virginians in Colonial times, is both closer to certain European settings in feeling and sense of place and somewhat more removed from the current American.

Among the most revered artifacts of this peculiar cultural framework are old buildings. Architecture in the Virginia colony was the central art form and is everywhere, something an educated gentleman knew about, as well as practiced; an emblem of refinement and worth. (Probably a quarter of the books on prominent display today in a bookshop in this part of Virginia deal either with Virginia history or historic buildings.) This love of old buildings and gardens extends also to furniture, china, draperies, silverware, flowers, trees—all things that adorned a Virginian's home. In such a setting historic preservation has traditionally held a central place so that old buildings and not new ones are the center of attention and emulation, even today.

The University of Virginia stands literally and symbolically at the center of the region. Founded and designed by Jefferson in 1819 (when he was 70 years old!) the original complex of buildings, what Jefferson called his *academical village,* is generally conceded to be the most significant contribution to American architecture since the founding of the Republic. By any standard it is an architectural masterpiece, the first example of the Greco/Roman Revival in the United States and the model for campuses and countless civic buildings all over the country. Today Jefferson's complex is internationally recognized as a pilgrimage for all serious students of architecture, an *"ideal city: of gardens and buildings, the clearest built statement of the ideas of the American Enlightenment,"* which like its Oxford and Cambridge counterparts, is as vibrant and alive and used today as when it was conceived.

On a nearby hill, like a custodian of value, stands Monticello, Jefferson's villa and the citadel of his beliefs, another of our culture's seminal buildings. Here American pragmatism and invention are melded with Palladio and French Revolutionary architecture in an extraordinarily inventive if ideosyncratic way. Monticello is both quirky and sublime, a *little mountain* of American classicism erected in the wilderness. One can sense here, better perhaps than anywhere else, Jefferson's many-sided personality: his values, priorities and obsessions. For the architectural buff there are 2 other houses near Charlottesville from the hand of our only architect/president, **Edgemont** and **Barboursville,** the latter a Piranesiesque ruin now surrounded by a thriving Italian-owned vineyard and what are probably the largest tree boxes in North America.

To the west lies the **Skyline Drive,** a great tourist route which is breathtaking in spring and autumn, and the **Shenandoah Valley,** a place still seemingly removed from the 20th century and not unlike parts of the Austrian Tyrol.

The drive from Washington to Charlottesville via Route 29 can be broken at **Warrenton** where a fine meal can be had at **The Depot.** The return can be made on R-20, through **Orange,** the **Battle of the Wilderness National Park,** and historic **Fredericksburg,** the site of another epic Civil War battle. Two exceptional houses— George Mason's **Gunston Hall,** with the first Palladian interior in the New World and a wonderful garden, and **Stratford,** the extraordinarily powerful Lee plantation on the Potomac (my favorite American house), are within an easy drive off of Route 495 and should be seen.

Washington, Virginia, a tiny town west of Warrenton in horse country, boasts a superb inn with one of the finest restaurants in the region. And, of course, for those seeking the luxurious resort, there are the 2 famous mountain spas, *The Homestead* at Hot Springs, Virginia, and *The Greenbrier* at White Sulphur Springs in West Virginia, just over the border. Both are superbly run and equipped and come as close as anything in America to the great spa/resorts of Europe.

All in all Piedmont, Virginia, Mr. Jefferson's country, offers an ideal escape from the growing contemporary squalor of metropolitan Washington, an alternative environment in which buildings and nature still exist in harmonious balance. Driving on the backroads during the dogwood season can almost make up for what you have to drive through to get there.

Mr. Jefferson's Country
Jaquelin Robertson
Dean, School of Architecture
University of Virginia

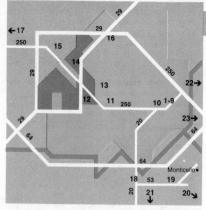

1 **Albemarle County Courthouse/Court Square.**
The centerpiece of the downtown historic district
is the old courthouse (1803, additions 1859 and
1867). It was the political and business hub of
old Charlottesville, and a passerby in the early
1800s might very well have seen Jefferson,
Madison and Monroe chatting together on the
green. It was also the shared church of the
town's 4 faiths. Jefferson wrote, *"In our
village...there is a good degree of religion with a
small spice of fanaticism. We have 4 sects, but
without either church or meeting house. The
courthouse is the common temple, one Sunday of
each month. Here Episcopalian, Presbyterian,
Methodist and Baptist meet together...listen with
attention and devotion to each others preachers,
and all mix in a society of perfect harmony."* Feel
free to walk into the building. Court still meets in
the original chambers. *Open M-F 9am-4:30pm.
501 E. Jefferson St., Court Square.*

2 **Albemarle County Historical Society.** There is
a library specializing in local history and
genealogical research. They answer thousands
of letters a year from people hoping to find an
old family link to **Thomas Jefferson** or
Pochohontas, and have files on at least 1,200
families. There is also a small museum, not often
open, with local artwork, photographs, some old
weapons and tools. The Society is staffed by
volunteers; if there are enough personnel they will
show you around. Call first. *Library open M, W-F
1am-4pm; Tu & Sa 10am-noon. 220 Court
Square. 804-296-1492.*

3 **Jackson Monument.** Old **Stonewall Jackson** is
full of fire and brimstone despite the bronzing.
He rides **Little Sorrel** (1921, **Charles Keck**). *NE
corner, Jefferson and E Sts.*

4 **Lee Monument.** General **Robert E. Lee** sits
astride his horse, **Traveller,** hat in hand.
Designed by **Henry Schrady,** who did the **Grant
Memorial** in DC. Completed after Schrady's
death by **Leo Lentelli.** *Jefferson St., between 1st
and 2nd Sts.*

4 **Walking Tour.** The immediate area is filled with
18th- and 19th-century buildings. However, most
are privately maintained, many as lawyer's
offices. A walking tour map with dates and brief
descriptions is available from the **Visitors Center**
(see number 19) or from **Downtown
Charlottesville Inc.** at *416 E. Main St.,
804-296-8548.* Among the sights is the site of
Old Swan Tavern owned by **Jack Jouett,** the
man who rode all night to warn Jefferson of the
approaching British. The building is now
occupied by the **Red Land Club,** an exclusive
men's club.

5 **McGuffey Art Center.** This 1916 schoolhouse
has been converted into a complex of artists'
studios. Painters, sculpters, glassblowers, potters
and guitarmakers all work here. There's a gallery
and sales area. The public is welcome to wander
about the studios and chat with the artists.
*Admission free. Open Tu-Sa 10am-5pm, Su
1-5pm. 201 2nd St. 804-295-7973.*

6 **Fellini's.** ☆ $$ Northern Italy in Old Dominion.
Homemade pasta, bread and some really intense
chocolate desserts. Try hay and straw—green
and white fettuccini with prosciutto. The steaks
and home-grown veal are good. Ask about the
weeknight meal and movie special—fixed-price

dinner and ticket to the adjacent **Vinegar Hill
Theater,** where old classic films are shown.
*Italian. Open Tu-Su 6-10pm. Credit cards
accepted. 200 W. Market St. 804-295-8003.*

7 **The Mall.** Seven blocks of Main Street that have
been paved with brick and reserved for walkers.
There are fountains, flowers and renovated turn-
of-the-century buildings housing boutiques,
antiques, gift and specialty shops, as well as
restaurants and outdoor cafes. Check out
Williams Corner Book Store, and **Rubiyat** for
handmade one-of-a-kind women's clothes.
Outdoor concerts Jul & Aug Tu 8pm.

*Charlottesville's downtown is compact, and
encompassable, so don't be afraid to explore
both sides of the street. Often what looks like a
residential stretch is broken up with isolated, but
delightful, shops and restaurants.*

8 **C&O.** ☆ ☆ ☆ $$/$$$ Inside a rather nondescript
building with a Pepsi sign hanging off it is one of
Charlottesville's best restaurants. The upstairs is
known for its game, rabbit, duck, fresh fish and
superb sauces. Creamy white interior, intimate
setting, coat, tie and reservations required.
Downstairs, lunch is more casual and less
expensive: quiche, salads and changing specials.
There's a separate room with music nightly.
*American. Open for dinner M-Sa, seating 6pm &
10pm. 515 E. Water St. 804-971-7044.*

9 **Eastern Standard.** ☆ ☆ $$ A bit of New York chic
on the Mall. Light, airy 1920s decor. Ella and
Billy Holiday croon in the background. Funky
mismatched china, but excellent and eclectic
food. Try veal in banana peels, oriental chicken
curry or oysters in caviar sauce. Fresh flowers
abound and the best English trifle in town.
*American. Open 11am-2:30pm, 6-10pm; till 11pm
on weekends. Reservations suggested. Credit
cards accepted. 102 Preston Ave., west end of
Mall. 804-295-8668.*

10 **Le Snail.** ☆ ☆ ☆ $$/$$$ The Viennese chef
prepares excellent Continental/French food in a
charming renovated old house. Try the fresh fish,
beef Wellington or baby rack of lamb. *Four-
course-fixed price dinner available. Reservations
suggested, jacket required. Open M-Sa 6-9:30pm.
320 W. Main St. 804-295-4456.*

10 **Blue Moon Diner.** ☆ $ Classic stainless steel
diner interior. Small, but fun. Good burgers,
omelettes, blueberry muffins and pancakes at
cheapo prices. Packed for brunch. The best R&B
jukebox in town. *American. Open Sa, Su & M
8am-4pm, Tu-F 7am-7pm. 512 W. Main St.
804-293-3408.*

11 **The Corner.** This section centered at University
Avenue and Elliwood Street is the student
shopping strip; expect to find a hodgepodge of
casual dining spots, bookstores and boutiques.
For soup, salad and sandwich fare, check out
Graffiti's or the patio at **Martha's Cafe. Eljo's** is
the preppy clothing store of choice, and
Mincer's Pipe Shop is a Corner institution—the
crowded establishment is tobacconist, bookstore
and purveyor of university paraphernalia.

11 **The Virginian.** ☆ $/$$ Old wooden booths,
blackboard menus and a boisterous crowd at the
bar. Food is dependable: burgers, stir-fry,
international specials. Brunch could be eggs
Benedict, Florentine, Chesapeake—or French
toast with fried apples on the side. *American.
Open M-F 9am-2pm, Sa & Su 10am-2pm. 1521
Main St. 804-293-2606.*

11 **Lena's Dance.** ☆ $/$$ Not fancy, but generous
Tex-Mex and Creole cooking in a cozy, old-
fashioned house. Porch and patio dining in good
weather and a young, casual crowd inside. Bar's
upstairs. The shrimp Creole is fine and the
enchiladas a bargain. *Mexican. Open for lunch
M-F, daily for dinner. 20 Elliwood Ave.
804-293-3600.*

Introductions/Theaters/Narrative black
Hotels purple
Museums/Architecture blue
Parks/Open spaces green
Restaurants/Nightlife red
Shops/Galleries violet

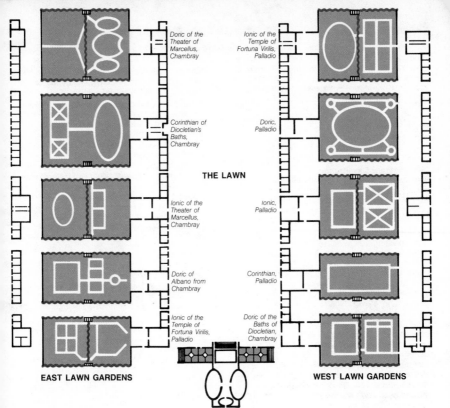

Doric of the
Theater of
Marcellus,
Chambray

Corinthian of
Diocletian's
Baths,
Chambray

Ionic of the
Theater of
Marcellus,
Chambray

Doric of
Albano from
Chambray

Ionic of the
Temple of
Fortuna Virilis,
Palladio

Ionic of the
Temple of
Fortuna Virilis,
Palladio

Doric,
Palladio

Ionic,
Palladio

Corinthian,
Palladio

Doric of the
Baths of
Diocletian,
Chambray

THE LAWN

EAST LAWN GARDENS

WEST LAWN GARDENS

2 University of Virginia. When Jefferson's *academical village* opened in 1825 there were 68 students and 10 professors. Now it's a small city with over 17,000 students and 2,200 faculty members. It's the town's biggest single employer and it dominates the social scene. Charlottesville is full of students who decided not to leave. They joke that you can't get a job as a waiter around here without a Ph.D or at the very least a master's degree. There's a strong preppy contingent at UVA, with the attendant fraternities, beer parties and sun dresses. But equally strong is the tradition of liberal academic excellence with nationally acclaimed graduate programs.

UVA was the project of Jefferson's old age, and he lovingly planned every aspect of it from the fund raising, to the design of the buildings, to the selection of the faculty, curriculum, and library books. His school was to be run by the teachers and have affiliation with no church or religion. All courses would be electives. Students of all ages would mix and live in a village setting among their teachers. There was no American precedent for what Jefferson created—the prototype of a modern university.

The Lawn. The terraced lawn was the center of the old campus. It's flanked on both sides by low rows of student rooms broken up at intervals by 2-story pavilions, the whole fronted by a colonnade. Students lived in the rooms while faculty lived upstairs in the pavilions and taught downstairs. Students still live in the 54 lawn rooms which have fireplaces but no bathrooms. It's considered a great honor and is attained by a highly competitive and political process.

A natural didactician, Jefferson decorated each pavilion with an order from a different Roman temple. He meant to expose all students, particularly those who might never travel abroad, to a classical notion of good taste.

Behind the pavilions are gardens that are enclosed by characteristic Jeffersonian **Serpentine Walls.** Though only one brick thick, their curved design gives them great strength. Behind the East and West Gardens are rows of additional student housing called **The Ranges.** These rows are broken up by 6 *hotels.* Now administrative offices, they were once dining halls. A different language was to be spoken at table in each one.

West end of Main St. Tour information, see **Rotunda.**

The Rotunda. Considered Jefferson's most perfect building. It housed the library and was the focal point of the campus. Its plan, basically a sphere inscribed in a cylinder, is derived from the Pantheon; its dome is exactly half the size of the original in Rome. Jefferson's interior design called for 3 floors, the first 2 with graceful oval rooms, and the top, a dome room that would house books, and, he hoped, a planetarium with gilded models of the stars on the ceiling.

In 1895 the interior was destroyed by fire. Reigning architectural monarch **Stanford White** was called in to remodel, which he did, completely discarding Jefferson's plan. He removed the oval rooms and an entire floor while adding clunky Victorian columns and a gallery. Luckily the original rotunda was one of the best documented buildings in America. In 1973-1976, White's work was gutted and the building restored. As you enter the dome room you can see bookcases behind the pillars, but these vanish as you move towards the center. Allegedly Jefferson envisioned student dances in the room and didn't want the young scholars to be reminded of their work while having fun.

While school is in session 5 daily tours (free) are given by informed student guides. Off session, 2 tours are given. Call 924-7969.

McGuffey Ash. A spectacular old tree—it takes 4 people, arms linked, to encircle its trunk. Planted in 1826 by the University's first professor of moral philosophy. He was succeeded by **William Holmes McGuffey,** who, according to legend, would sit under the tree and read to local youths. Their lack of aptitude was the inspiration for his famous *Readers. Garden behind Pavilion 9.*

Poe Room. Room 13 in **The Ranges**—but of course! Furnished with the most common style of period furniture probably what **Edgar Allan Poe** would have had as a student. Poe only stayed at UVA for 10 months—he ran up big gambling debts, which he couldn't pay, and was asked to leave.

Jefferson's design was practical as well as pretty. Decentralized, modular dormitories and teaching pavilions meant that in case of fire or epidemic the whole university needn't shut down.

Bayly Art Museum. A small, intimate museum whose eclectic collection offers the afternoon browser a taste of everything. Special collections are: *Art in the Age of Jefferson,* representative neo-Classical European paintings; an *Oriental collection;* and *Contemporary American Realists* featuring such artists as **Alfred Leslie, William Bailey** and **Jack Beal.** Frequent traveling exhibitions. *Admission free. Open daily 1-5pm. Rugby Rd. half a block from the lawn of UVA. 804-924-3592.*

14 **Best Western Cavalier Inn.**
Inexpensive/moderate. Conveniently located one block from the University of Virginia; 118 rooms with tv and air conditioning. Pool, restaurant serving sandwiches and salads. Clean, generic. *Corner University & Emmet Sts. 804-296-8111.*

15 **Ivy Inn.** ☆ ☆ $$ Dine in one of the 6 rooms of this renovated 1830s house furnished *a la* Williamsburg. Specials are Virginia duckling, veal, seafood kettle of steamed shellfish and drawn butter. Bread and desserts are homemade. Relax and take your time. The owner believes 3 hours for a dinner among friends is reasonable. *Regional American. Open M-F 11:30am-2pm, dinner M-Sa seating between 5-8:30pm. 2244 Old Ivy Rd. 804-977-1222.*

16 **English Inn of Charlottesville.** *Moderate.* Despite the name, a relatively new hotel. Sixty-seven rooms, 21 suites with wet bar, 2 conference rooms, indoor pool, sauna, whirlpool and weight room. Lounge and restaurant serve standard hotel fare. Breakfast complimentary for hotel guests. *2000 Morton Dr. south of the 250 bypass, Rt. 29 N.*

17 **Boars Head Inn.** *Moderate/expensive.* Probably the best-known hostelry in this area. One hundred and seventy-five rooms and suites built around an old mill and set in rolling lake country. Swimming, indoor and outdoor tennis, racquetball, weights, sauna, fishing and biking all available. Impeccable old-fashioned service. Two conference rooms and a ballroom available for groups. Ask for a suite with fireplace and lake view. The wood-paneled tavern with fireplace serves standard American fare for lunch and dinner. The **Mill Room** is a large wood-beamed dining room with Colonial-costumed waiters and waitresses. Pleasant setting, particularly the glassed-in **Garden Room** (☆ $$/$$$). Filling but average American/Continental food—though the beef Wellington is worthy of a special mention. *Lunch, dinner 6-9:30pm. Ednam Rd. off 250 west, 2½ miles from Charlottesville.*

18 **Western Virginia Visitors Center.** Sometimes called the *Bicentennial Visitors Center,* the *Thomas Jefferson Visitors Center* and sometimes just *that brick building near* **Piedmont Virginia Community College.**

A good place to stop on your way into town for brochures and information on the countryside as well as Charlottesville—neat things like balloon rides, where to go hunting, riding or pick your own berries and vegetables. Hotel and restaurant reservation service. *Rt. 20 south, junction with I-64. Open daily 9am-5pm. 804-977-1793/293-6789.*

19 **Michie Tavern.** Originally the boyhood home of **Patrick**—*give me liberty or give me death*—**Henry.** It was later sold to Mr. Michie (pronounced *micky*), who, realizing he was on the busiest stage coach route in town, expanded

---

On 4th July 1826 **John Adams** was dying. Not knowing that **Thomas Jefferson** was dying that very same day in Virginia he said, *"Independence forever, Jefferson survives."* These were his last words.

"I think this is the most extraordinary collection of talent, of human knowledge, that has ever been gathered together at the White House, with the possible exception of when Thomas Jefferson dined alone."

John F. Kennedy, *White House dinner honoring Nobel Prize winners, April 1962.*

---

and opened a tavern. **Jefferson, Madison, Monroe, Lafayette** and **Andrew Jackson** all ate here at one time or another, but by the turn of the century the tavern fell into disuse.

When Monticello opened to the public in 1924, the tavern owners saw a golden opportunity. They moved the tavern stone by stone to its present location half a mile from Jefferson's home. Though it was only a 17-mile trip, it took 3 years to complete reconstruction.

The tavern is now a museum with a fine collection of pre-Revolutionary War furnishings. In the **Gentleman's Parlor,** note the old-time equivalent of a drive-thru window where waiting coachmen could be served. There is also a ladies' parlor, ballroom, dining room and furnished bedroom. Many of the outbuildings have been preserved and are open, including a kitchen house, smokehouse (still in use), privvy and a dairy. Next to the grist mill is the **General Store** where local handicrafts, antiques and glassware are for sale. After viewing Monticello and Castle Hill, Michie Tavern provides an enlightening view of how the common man lived. *Admission charge. Guided tours. Open daily 9am-5pm.*

The restaurant or *Ordinary* ($) serves a Colonial buffet lunch in converted slave quarters. Southern fried chicken, black-eyed peas, corn bread, nothing fancy but satisfying. Price is good and includes extra helpings. There may be a 5-10 minute wait. *Regional American. Open daily 11:15am-3pm. Rt. 53, 2.5 miles southeast of Charlottesville. 804-977-1234.*

20 **Ash Lawn** was the home of **James Monroe** from 1799 to 1826, but Monroe wasn't around much to enjoy the place. He served as senator, governor and Minister to France, England and Spain. Then he served 2 terms as president.

It was **Thomas Jefferson,** Monroe's law teacher for several years and his mentor for many more, who suggested that Monroe move to Albemarle County close to Monticello. Ever planning and improving, Jefferson was eager to create a *"society to our tastes,"* in the neighborhood. While Monroe was in France, Jefferson personally selected the site for his friend's house and sent over his own gardeners to seed the orchards.

The large yellow house is quite simple on the outside, but beautifully appointed on the inside—a dichotomy that prompted Monroe to refer to his home as his *"cabin-castle."* Sadly, Monroe was broke after 40 years of working for the government and had to sell the home upon finishing his term as president.

Visitors can tour 5 rooms of the main house, the basement, warming kitchen and 2 rooms of a Victorian-era addition. The furniture is all antique, much of it Monroe's own from either Ash Lawn or from the Monroe tenancy in the White House.

Stroll through the pastures, woods and boxwood gardens where you may very likely meet up with a cow or one of the 24 peacocks who live on the plantation. The peacock was popular in Colonial times as a game bird and—because of its singularly loud and ugly voice—as a watch bird. There have been some archaeological digs at the old icehouse and servants quarters that have turned up coins and pottery. If one is going on during your visit you are welcome to watch.

From April to October costumed personnel give spinning, caning and basket weaving demonstrations. A summer festival from July through mid-August includes performances in the garden of 18th-century operas on weekends and Tuesday and Wednesday evenings. On Sundays, children's programs of dance and puppet shows are presented. In early July there is an excellent **Colonial Craft Festival,** call 293-9539 for more information. Picnic facilities and guided tours.

Admission charge. Open daily Mar-Oct 9am-6pm Feb-Nov 10am-5pm. Closed Thanksgiving, Christmas & New Year's. 2½ miles from Monticello. Take Rt. 53 to county Rt. 795.

21 Scottsville. A lovely 20-mile drive south from Charlottesville on Route 20. This sleepy town, chock-a-block with Federal, Republic and ante-bellum buildings, was once the county seat. River traffic kept it busy as early settlers pushed west, but its heyday came in the middle 1800s when it was the center of business on the **James River Kanawha Canal.** During the Civil War, Sheridan, Custer and 10,000 Union troops came in and blew up all the locks. Even now it is not uncommon for residents working in their gardens to turn up a Civil War cannonball. Try and visit the **Scottsville Museum** with its collection of antiques, Indian relics, antique dolls and local folk art. *Open Apr 15-Nov 15, Sa & Su only. Call 804-286-3201.*

James River Runners. Rent a canoe or a big fat inner tube for the afternoon. The service takes people up river and lets them float or paddle down. The **James River** and its tributary, the **Rockfish,** offer class 1 and 2 white water—fun but not too hard for a novice. The crystal clear water is a favorite hangout for small mouth bass, and it is not uncommon to see deer, wild turkey and beaver on the banks. *Open daily. Take Rt. 20 to Scottsville, Rt. 726 south, left on Rt. 625 to the river. 804-286-2338.*

Hatton Ferry. The last pole drawn ferry in the state offers rides across the James River for free. *Call 804-286-3201 or James River Runners for information. Rt. 20 to Scottsville, take Rt. 726 south to Rt. 625, then to the river.*

Schulyer and all the area around Scottsville is **Walton Country.** Author **Earl Hammer, Jr.,** grew up in Schulyer. If there aren't too many Toyotas and Datsuns around, it can look like **John Boy** might come loping around the corner at any moment. *Take Rt. 6 out of Scottsville, turn left on Rt. 800. Continue 2 miles to Schulyer.*

22 Castle Hill. Home to some of Virginia's most prominent families over the past 2 centuries. It's still occupied, but now the elegant first floor and sumptuous grounds are open to the public.

Actually 2 houses, the original Colonial clapboard house was built in 1764 by Dr. **Thomas Walker.** In 1824 his granddaughter built a very formal Federal-style addition. The first floor is furnished exquisitely with Colonial, Federal and Empire pieces. As you walk through the house, notice that the ceilings are 2 feet lower in the Colonial section.

The original owner of the house, Dr. Walker, was **Thomas Jefferson's** guardian and, according to the best version of the local legend, he helped save his young ward's life in a most ingenious manner. During the Revolutionary War, Walker was warned that the British, lead by **Colonel Tarlton,** were moving on Monticello to arrest Jefferson. Walker was also on the British arrest list, but when they arrived to take him, he greeted them with Southern hospitality and served them a lavish meal. This delaying tactic allowed Jefferson and half the Virginia Legislature, who had been visiting Walker at the time, to sneak out the back door and ride to safety. Another local legend concerns Walker's great granddaughter, who was drowned at sea. Allegedly her ghost haunts the **Colonial Parlor** and has been known to ask certain visitors to leave.

There is a 30-minute guided tour of the house, but you should also allow time to tour the grounds, with their giant boxwoods and terraced garden. Picnic facilities available. *Admission charge. Open daily 1 Mar-30 Nov, 10am-5pm. Call 804-293-7297.*

Castle Hill is 13 miles from Charlottesville. Coming from DC, take I-66 west to Rt. 20. Go south on 29 to Culpeper, then take Rt. 15 south to Gordonville. Take Rt. 231 south 8 miles to Castle Hill, which will be on your right. From Charlottesville, take Rt. 250 E. to Shadwell. Turn left on Rt. 22 E. until you can pick up Rt. 231. Castle Hill is 2 miles north on your left.

23 Prospect Hill. ☆☆$$ Romantic country inn and delightful, quirky restaurant in a restored manor house. Guests are greeted at the door with wine and invited to sit by the fire or stroll in the gardens. A bell summons all to dinner. There is no menu; the evening's 4-course dinner is always a surprise but is always good and usually French. Host leads all in short grace before the meal. *French. Open W-Sa. Reservations required.*

The inn *(moderate/expensive)* has 3 rooms in the main house and 4 converted slave cabins, one with whirlpool. Furnishings range from elegant to rustic/cozy. Country breakfast included. *14 miles east of Charlottesville, on Rt. 250, near Zion crossroads. 703-967-0844.*

Historic Garden Week. This unique chance to glimpse gracious Virginia living takes place in April, timed to coincide with the colorful explosion of spring foliage. Expertly maintained gardens, some in restored 18th- and 19th-century estates, are open to the public. Special events include candlelight tours of the lawn at **UVA** and **Ash Lawn.** Homes change each year. *Call Chamber of Commerce 804-295-3141 or Visitors Center 293-6789 for information, brochures and reservations.*

Polo Matches. The sport of kings is played May through November. Bring food for a tailgate picnic and enjoy the game. **Farmington Hunt Club,** *May-July F 7 & 9pm. Located on Garth Rd. off Rt. 601.* 804-979-0293. **Forest Lodge,** *Apr, June-Nov, matches on F & Su. I-64 to 5th St. exit, Rt. 631 south for 3½ miles.* 804-293-6265, 804-979-0293.

Guesthouse Bed and Breakfast Inc. A service that specializes in dispensing southern hospitality and romantic country weekends. The more than 20 homes and one dozen suites and cottages (many that are on the annual garden tour) range from cozy guest rooms with a bath down the hall to suites in restored 19th-century homes to cottages on rolling country horse farms. All come with breakfast, weekly rates. Very private accommodations are available. On the other hand, enjoying your host's hospitality and knowledge of the area can be half the fun, so the service tries harder than most to match guests with appropriate homes. Expect to spend some time on the phone. 804-979-7264/979-8327.

Foxfield Races. Spring and fall running of nationally known steeplechase events. *Foxfield Race Course, Garth Rd. 804-293-9501/293-8160.*

Virginia Byways. As you cruise around Virginia look for the bright blue Virginia Byway sign with the picture of a cardinal and dogwood blossoms on it. These signs mark alternate, generally less traveled roads that either lead to special attractions or are themselves the attraction, winding through farmland, river valley and blue ridge foothills.

Common rules of an 18th-century tavern: No tinkerers or razor grinders taken in, all organ grinders to sleep in the washhouse. No more than 5 in a bed and no boots worn in bed.

Rambunctious students were fond of riding on horseback past The Rotunda and shooting out the clock. Consequently UVA became the first university to have a bullet-proof clock.

In the famous painting *Washington Crossing the Delaware,* a young **James Monroe** is pictured behind Washington, holding the flag.

Introductions/Theaters/Narrative black
Hotels purple
Museums/Architecture blue
Parks/Open spaces green
Restaurants/Nightlife red
Shops/Galleries violet

Monticello. Thomas Jefferson *left testimony to his public self in history books, but to glimpse the private man, one must look to his home.*

No other structure so fully embodies the character of its owner. It is graceful, learned, spacious, generous, ingenious and quirky. And it is totally Jefferson. He picked the site, he designed the plan and its endless modifications. He supervised every aspect of the construction, planted the gardens, picked the furniture and designed the draperies. The timber came from his woods; even the bricks and the nails were produced on his own land.

Thought to be the best American architect of his day, Jefferson was self-taught. Rejecting the prevailing Georgian style, he was drawn to the harmony and mathematical perfection he saw in classical Roman buildings. Monticello is decorated with the classic orders drawn directly from the books of **Palladio**, the great Renaissance scholar and architect. (One of Jefferson's beloved architecture primers is preserved in the Library of Congress, and, not surprisingly, it shows signs of hard use.)

He began work on Monticello, *little mountain* in Italian, in 1769 when he was 26 years old. Three years later, when he moved into his house on a snowy night, with his new bride, only one small building, the **Honeymoon Cottage** had a roof on it. If he wasn't away on public duty, he was modifying the plans; construction continued for the next 40 years, long after his wife had died.

When Jefferson returned from France in 1789, the house was almost complete. But he had been smitten by the domed pavilions he saw abroad and the Parisian townhouses with their emphasis on privacy and comfort. *"Architecture is my delight,"* he said, *"and putting up and pulling down one of my favorite amusements."* Still, it took a very bold man to tear down half a house and begin again. He added a dome, a new front, 13 rooms. The new second story bedrooms had floor-level windows tied together by a single frame with the ground floor windows. This creates the illusion that the house has one story and is much smaller than it is.

Jefferson was an inveterate entertainer who even in straitened circumstances might order 150 bottles of his favorite wine. That side of him is seen in 18-foot-high, light-filled public rooms where lavish dinners, weddings and spirited musicales were held.

But Monticello was also the home to which Jefferson came for quiet contemplation, so his own suite, seldom visited by friends or family, provided great privacy. In it is his alcove bed and his study where he read and wrote thousands of letters. The bedroom leads to a library and the glassed-in piazza where Jefferson nursed his seedlings. Monticello also reveals Jefferson the gadgeteer, the lover of mechanical ingenuity. There is a clock that tells the day as well as week. In his study is a writing table with a revolving top and the polygraph which makes a copy of a letter as the original is being written. While Jefferson didn't invent the machine, he did modify it. He owned several and was so fond of the innovation, he even lent his name to an advertisement. There are dumbwaiters hidden in the dining room mantlepiece and under the parlor doors is a hidden chain and sprocket mechanism that allows both doors to swing open when only one is pushed.

The house is practical as well as pleasing. There is brick nogging (insulation) between floor and ceiling, and double doors to preserve heat. The natural incline of the hilltop is used to hide the service dependencies half underground. These extensions contained servant quarters, stables, kitchen and smokehouse. Connected to the cellar by an all-weather passageway, the roofs of these wings become broad terraces that connect to the main floor of the house.

There has been much work on the grounds of the estate in recent years. Jefferson kept extensive notes on the over 250 varieties of vegetables and herbs he planted in terraced beds, organized according to whether the plant was used for root, leaf or fruit. These are being replanted with the help of his notes. Excavation also continues on *mulberry row*, the industrial strip of the estate where 19 buildings once stood, including stables, a nailery and a carpentry shop. Work goes on reviving his groves, vineyards and berry squares as well

After almost 40 years of public service Jefferson finally retired to Monticello. Though toward the end he was beset by debts and an army of uninvited guests, it's easy to see how he might be happy here and why he might say, *"All my wishes end where I hope my days will end at Monticello."*

Admission charge. A shuttle bus runs between parking lot and house, or to return, walk to graveyard and take nature trail to parking lot. Guided tours last 25 minutes and begin every 5 minutes. Allow 2 hours for house, dependencies, garden and grounds. Guided tours of gardens at 3pm. Open Mar 31-Oct 8am-5pm, Nov 30-Apr 9am-4:30pm. 3 miles southeast of Charlottesville on Rt. 53. 804-295-8181/295-2657.

The Albermarle County in which Jefferson grew up was the western frontier of the nation. That expansive mindset helped set the tone of his ever-exploring, restless personality.

As a young man he mastered Greek, Latin, French, Anglo-Saxon, the natural sciences and mathematics. He was a good violinist, an excellent horseman and a decent dancer. It's said he may have been one of the last men to have embraced all the learning of his age—he was certainly one of the few men, then or now, to make practical use of calculus.

He went on to study law and had a successful practice, earning $3,000 one year, and within 2 years increasing his caseload from 154 to 405 Yet Jefferson, not a forceful public speaker, disliked a trade whose task it was to *"question everything, yield nothing, and talk by the hour."*

He was 6-feet, 2 inches tall with broad, angular features, a freckled complexion, a strong but loose build and rather unkempt reddish hair. Just as his rough looks contrasted with the subtle and supple mind within, so was much of his personal conduct contradictory. At the White House he employed 14 servants and a French chef, yet he occasionally did his own shopping. Though he tried for years to curb slavery through legal means, he owned at least 150 slaves himself, only a few of whom he freed in his will.

Wishing more to reform the law than profit by it, he quit the profession in 1774 and, at a most volatile moment, entered the political fray.

He was a man of tremendous energy, who even into his 70s rode 3 hours a day and wrote for 4 or 5 more. When a friend once asked him to prescribe a course of study for self-improvement, Jefferson recommended readings in science, ethics, and religion—and all before eating breakfast! With such vitality even the leanest summary of his career would sound extraordinary.

Deeply resentful of British rule, Jefferson made a name for himself in the Virginia House of Burgesses, going on to represent his state in the Continental Congress. While living in rented rooms in Philadelphia, and attending meetings all day, he managed to write the Declaration of Independence in just over 2 weeks. He was 33 years old.

He became governor of Virginia and later minister to France. In Europe he took notes on architecture, farming, new inventions, anything he thought would be useful in America. He went so far as to smuggle protected grain seeds out of Europe. He was a tinkerer, believing everything could be improved, from the design of a plow—he held a patent on an improved moldboard—to the laws that govern human conduct. He worked doggedly in Virginia to guarantee religious freedom and reform the laws of inheritance.

Though Jefferson disliked cities and missed **Monticello** every day he was away from it, he served as secretary of state under **Washington,** vice president under **Adams,** and finally, for 2 terms, as president.

He was radical as a theorist, but could be pragmatic in action. He believed that government had a strictly limited authority, yet as president he stretched that authority to the utmost in engineering the *Louisiana Purchase,* perhaps the most important single event in United States history. Characteristically, Jefferson dispatched **Lewis and Clark** posthaste to explore the area and send back samples of everything—from berries to the bones of extinct animals.

He was a savvy, astute politician, who often lobbied through others while keeping clear of the fray, yet he was singularly untalented when it came to his own finances. His constant rebuilding of Monticello and lavish political entertaining, at his own expense, kept him forever in debt. When he left the presidency, he was forced to sell his 7,000-volume personal library to the government (for $23,950) to meet his obligations. (Whereupon he immediately resumed collecting books.) In describing the difference between his own views and those of his Federalist adversaries, who supported a strong central government, Jefferson wrote *"One feared the ignorance of the people, the other, the selfishness of the rulers without them."* Here may lie the key to his philosophy, which was much more than a cold cribbing from **Locke** and **Montesquieu** or a simple state rights versus federal rights polemic. Jefferson had an unbridled belief in the good judgment of man and his perfectability. He believed men could chose for themselves what church to attend and what government to obey. He believed education allows men to actively participate in their fate. Above all, he believed in freedom, as his own words make clear, *"I have sworn upon the altar of God eternal hostility against every form of tyranny over the minds of men."*

ARCHITECTURE

Monumental Musts

Bates Lowry
Director, National Building Museum

The Lincoln Memorial—the most perfect architectural monument anywhere! Aside from honoring the Great Emancipator, its beautiful proportions and delicate detailing create a harmonious whole of such serene, yet majestic, effect that all can see why classic architecture was so long considered the finest model for the architect to follow.

For an amusing architectural mirage, **look down 16th Street** from Meridian Hill toward the White House. At this point the dome of the Jefferson Memorial joins the roof of the Executive Mansion to create a more Palladian Presidential Palace.

The Federal Triangle Buildings—a first class product of Beaux-Arts training in design and planning and the most colossal example ever to be built. Although, unfortunately still not completed, there are many lessons for future architects to follow in the way the enormous facades are articulated by the strategic repetition of colonnades and pedimented pavilion blocks (note the echoing of these motifs in the IRS and Commerce buildings). The great sweeping hemicycles in the center of the design are particularly handsome and if the circular plaza intended on 13th Street had been completed it would now be the architectural center and wonder of DC.

Attention should be given to all the details embellishing these buildings, particularly the decorative metal grills and lamp fixtures. Unfortunately, only a few of the interiors of these buildings can be visited (the Art Deco decoration of the Justice Building is one of DC's forbidden fruits for the architecture buff) but step into the green marbled entry hall of the Commerce Building; visit the elaborately sculpted rotundas and entry hall of the Interstate Commerce Commission Building, and enjoy the Imperial Splendor of the Auditorium (note particularly the hanging chandeliers and richly coffered ceilings along the window walls).

The **view from the south end** of the White House lawn never loses its appeal. From here the not very noble White House does, nevertheless, appear so and the fact that this impression is due, in good part, to the original, sensitive landscape design worked out by Thomas Jefferson adds to the pleasure of the experience.

In Chinatown, still to be seen in the area along and off of H Street between 7th and 5th Streets, are some of the original dwellings built to house the government functionaries when they moved here in 1800 from Philadelphia. Although not in themselves remarkable buildings, they should be noted for their diminutive size because only then can one appreciate what a powerful, colossal impact must have been made in those early days by such public buildings as the Bulfinch dome of the Capitol, the great colonnade of the Treasury and the massive, gigantic portico of the Patent Office. (Now the home of the Portrait Gallery, one enters it at basement level, its majestic flight of steps having been cut off in 1936 to widen F Street which, ironically, has now been turned into a pedestrian mall.)

A **trip to the roof terrace of the Washington Hotel** brings one the best and most comfortable public views of southwest DC as well as glimpses of the White House and its garden over the roof of the Treasury. An especially pleasing panorama of the red tile roofs of the Federal Triangle buildings makes the overall plan of this vast complex clear.

"...The greatest building in the world," according to architect **Philip Johnson**, is the Old Patent Office, now home of the National Museum of American Art & National Portrait Gallery.

The Vietnam Memorial—the most emotion-provoking memorial in DC. Its black granite gash into the lush green of the Mall aptly symbolizes what a terrible, self-inflicted wound that conflict was for our country. A continuous stream of quiet visitors brushing their fingers over the inscribed name of their lost son, friend or husband is a poignant part of the monument which becomes, by that act, an enormous braille tablet allowing those unable to see the dead to make contact with them. The tributes often left there—cowboy boots, last letters and guitars—are carefully collected at the end of each day and stored away.

The Old Executive Office Building is a must on many lists simply due to the exuberance of its design which appears to have been freely poured out of a cornucopia filled with pediments, columns, cornices and other architectural delights. But the architectural buff should also ponder the lesson to be learned about *style* by taking into account the fact that the ground plan of this building is almost identical to that of the very staid Treasury Building on the other side of the White House.

The most impressive, breath-taking architectural interior anywhere in the world is to be experienced in the vast but carefully articulated space of the Great Hall of the old Pension Building (National Building Museum). The experience is made all the more striking because the close-up impression of the exterior is of a long, low structure that in no way suggests the enormous height and length of the hall within.

Finally, **all who have endured the traffic fracas of DC** and cursed its city planner should reflect on the incredible boldness and vision of its designer. When L'Enfant proposed his audacious scheme, he truly found only one supporter, George Washington. It was the military and political father of our country who insisted upon this plan being put into execution. He truly was a visionary figure who foresaw how great would become the union of the little 13 colonies and believed that only a capital city many times larger than any one then existing on the Continent would be appropriate for that nation. That his name should have been given to the Federal City was an entirely appropriate decision. Unfortunately, a comparable honor has not yet been accorded its planner.

On the exterior of
The National Building Museum

The **3 *missing* bricks under each window** actually planned as openings for fresh air to penetrate the building. The air was channeled under the window sills, over the heating units and into the offices from which it then flowed through the open arches leading into the central courtyard and up to the windows of the clerestory 100 feet above the ground floor.

The **alternating triangular and curved entablatures** of the second story windows, the massive projecting cornice and the sculptured friezes on the second and third story levels, all of which are derived from the design of the 16th century Feranese Palace in Rome, the chosen model for the architect's designs of the Pension Building. In using this style as a model, Meigs was ahead of his time. The building most cited as marking a return of the Italian Renaissance Style is the Boston Public Library by McKim, Mead and White, 1888-95.

The Old Executive Office Building next to the White House still bears traces of **General Douglas MacArthur**. To lighten the facade of the colossal structure, MacArthur placed stone planters with flowers and shrubs in a parallel row from the north steps down to Pennsylvania Avenue. Although this former State, War and Navy Department building has a new name, the planters stand as a memorial to the great general.

DC Bests

Lois Craig
**Associate Dean,
School of Architecture and Planning
Massachusetts Institute of Technology**

I lived in that city for some 25 years, so in a way I know too much. At first the obvious buildings came to mind, the foreground city of official Washington with its high steps, grey colonnades, and long vistas. There is, of course, another Washington of residences, of lavish greenery, and of a fair share of urban problems, design and otherwise. And there is the city that **Henry James** remarked, *"the quite majestic fact of the city of Conversation."* This last city can be put together in the mind's eye only over time and in many places, private and public.

Finally I decided that the advantage of long domicile is the possibility of sharing with visitors a knowledge of mostly accessible but hidden places, places behind or beyond the postcard views. So I selected mostly *inside* places:

Elizabethan Theater of the
Folger Shakespeare Library

Whistler's **Peacock Room** at the
Freer Gallery

Main Reading Room at the
Library of Congress

Old house of the **Phillips Gallery**
and its drawing room for a Sunday
afternoon concert

Great Hall of the **Pension Building**

Members dining room at the
Smithsonian Castle (worth finding a member for
the star-studded ceiling)

Exhibition hall of the
Arts and Industries Building

Model Room of the
National Portrait Gallery

Lincoln Room of the
National Museum of American Art

Second floor of the **Renwick Gallery**

Interdepartmental Auditorium of the
Federal Triangle Arena Stage, for a
performance

Rooftop lounge of the **Washington Hotel,** in
the summer and for a special view of the
monumental city

Metro subway stations, especially one with a
long descent—e.g., at Dupont Circle

**National Cathedral for Christmas Eve
service** or Sunday vespers

Interiors of **Old State War & Navy
Building** and of the **Department of Justice,**
largely inaccessible.

Dumbarton Oaks Pre-Columbian Museum

The last entry is part of my favorite place-of-places, where I often walk, to read, to look, to meet friends, to watch children.
Between 30th and 32nd at R Streets NW one finds Oak Hill Cemetery with its old gatehouse and Renwick Chapel; **Montrose Park** with its rolling English landscape; **Lovers Lane,** which leads to Dumbarton Oaks Park, a walking park particularly beautiful in the spring when the narcissi are in bloom; **Dumbarton Oaks House and Gardens,** particularly notable for its formal gardens but also for its Byzantine and Pre-Columbian art collection, the latter housed in the contemporary jewel box of the Pre-Columbian Museum, located in a wooded corner of the grounds. The foregoing complex is bordered by 2 special Washington places—by **Georgetown** with its residential streets and courtyard gardens that recall the Southern city; and by **Rock Creek Park,** which winds through Northwest Washington and yields its own special spots for picnicking and hiking as well as the **National Zoo** with its collection of fanciful animal houses.

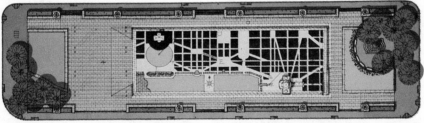

For a good overview of **Pierre L'Enfant's** design of Washington, DC, visit **Western Plaza,** the block-long park that duplicates L'Enfant's layout in miniature. **Venturi, Rauch and Scott Brown** designed the park. *(See District 1, number 39.)*

Embassy Row. This concentrated diplomatic community, stretching along both sides of a bend in Rock Creek, includes representatives from over 130 foreign governments. While security is tight at most embassies and chanceries, several are worth a drive-by look for their interesting facades. For a quick tour of *the Row,* drive from Sheridan Circle to the Naval Observatory; keep your eyes open for the multicolored flags and coats-of-arms that mark foreign offices.

The **Indonesian Embassy** is in the 60-room **McLean Mansion** *(2020 Massachusetts Ave. NW).* Parts of the house are literally paved in gold; it was an incredibly expensive home in 1903, even for a mining tycoon.

Moran House (the **Pakistan Embassy**), and, next door, **Fahnestock House** (formerly the **Chinese Embassy**) are 2 gems from the Sheridan Circle neighborhood's heyday. (1908, **George Oakley Totten;** 1909, **Nathan C. Wyeth**) *2311 & 2314 Massachusetts Ave.*

At *2701 Massachusetts Ave. NW,* look for the **Indian Embassy's** famous door guards: twin carved elephants.

Many of the contents of the former **Iranian Embassy,** *3005 Massachusetts Ave. NW,* were auctioned to pay Iranian government debts abandoned when the Shah was deposed.

Queen Elizabeth II's regal **British Embassy,** as straight and stately as one might expect, is at *3100 Massachusetts Ave. NW.*

The new **Canadian Chancery** is at *6th St. and Pennsylvania Ave.*

The **USSR Consulate** is located on a hill, allegedly to facilitate electronic eavesdropping *(1825 Phelps Pl.).*

In 1846, when **Charles Dickens** visited Washington, he made the following remark: *"It is sometimes called the city of magnificent distances, but it might with greater propriety be termed the city of magnificent intentions."* He wasn't discussing politics but architecture, and went on to describe the city as a place with *"spacious avenues that begin in nothing and lead nowhere; streets, miles long, that want houses, roads and inhabitants; and public buildings that need only a public to be complete."*

L'ENFANT'S PLAN

From a speech by Joseph Passonneau

On 29 March 1791, **Pierre L'Enfant's** letter to **George Washington** described, leading from Georgetown to a bridge on the Anacostia *"...a large and direct avenue...planted with double rows of trees...a street laid out on a dimension proportioned to the greatness which...the Capital of a powerful Empire ought to manifest."* That street is Pennsylvania Avenue, 160 feet wide per L'Enfant's instructions, and finally almost 200 years later planted with double and triple rows of trees.

In his *Observations Explanatory of the Plan,* L'Enfant said that *"The positions of the different Grand Edifices, and for the several Grand Squares...were first determined on the most advantageous ground, commanding the most extensive prospects..."* and in a memorandum to Washington he described **Jenkin's Hill,** the location of the *Federal House* (the Capitol building), as standing *"...really as a pedestal waiting for a superstructure...(no other location) could bear competition with this."*

Because *"...Avenues of direct communication (were) to connect the separate and most distant Objects with the Principal (Objects)...,"* the street laid out on a dimension proportioned to the greatness of a powerful Empire connected the Capitol and the President's House. Pennsylvania Avenue is bent a bit at the White House because, according to Washington's notes, the President's House was moved westward to take advantage of high ground and the view down the Potomac.

L'Enfant had surveyor **Andrew Ellicott** draw *"...a true Meridian line by celestial observation, which passes through the Area intended for the Congress house; this line he crossed by another due East and West..."* The true Meridian is North and South Capitol Street and the line due east and west is the center line of the **Mall** and East Capitol Street. The east and west line and the north and south line through the President's House (16th Street) intersected at *"The equestrian figure of George Washington, a monument voted in 1783 by the late Continental Congress. These lines were accurately measured, and made the bases on which the whole plan was executed."*

From this arrangement of large and direct avenue, *Grand Edifices,* several *Grand Squares,* true *Meridian* and *due east and west line,* the rest of the Plan followed in logical sequences. Eighth Street, half-way between the President's House and the Congress House was also an important locus of places. It is the center line of 3 of *"The Squares...proposed to be divided among the several States...";* it was the location, opposite the President's House, of the **National Church;** its intersection with Pennsylvania Avenue was adorned with *"...a grand fountain, intended with a constant spout of Water;"* and its intersection with the banks of the Potomac was the location of the *Naval Itinery Column,* which was certainly intended as the American prime meridian, this being half a century before Greenwich was adopted worldwide as *the* prime meridian.

Twenty-third Street is Nineteenth Street's twin on the opposite side of the President's House, and 13th and 19th are the subharmonics to the basic rhythm set up by North/South Capitol, 8th and 23rd. (One must go to the site to see why the sub-harmonic between 8th and North Capitol is missing: It would have been located in the depression now occupied by the North/South Freeway Connector, and all of these *monumental avenues* were to be located on *advantageous ground, commanding the most extensive prospect.* In its place, and *out of synch,* are **John Marshall Place** and **Judiciary Square,** on high ground with a commanding prospect of the Mall.)

Courtesy Library of Congress

L'ENFANT'S PLAN

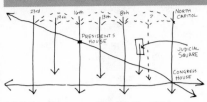

All of the 18th-century Baroque city plans proposed arrays of avenues radiating from the principal places. But, except for Karlsruhe, Germany, Washington is the only city in which these plans were fully realized. New York Avenue is the twin of Pennsylvania Avenue, both radiating from the President's House; Maryland is the twin of Pennsylvania but radiating from the Congress House. Connecticut, Vermont and F Street complete the *star* around the President's House; New Jersey and Delaware complete the *star* about the Congress House.

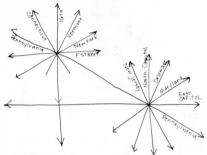

Massachusetts Avenue connects Dupont Circle (high ground at the intersection of Connecticut Avenue and 19th Streets) and Mount Vernon Square (the intersection of New York Avenue and 8th Street); east of North Capitol Massachusetts bends south to intersect East Capitol in **Lincoln Square** at the Itinerary Column (exactly one mile east of the Congress House, from which all land distances were to be measured). New Hampshire connects Dupont Circle and Washington Circle (high ground at the intersection of Pennsylvania Avenue and 23rd Street). K Street connects Washington Circle and Mount Vernon Square. And so on.

Overlaid on, and *in addition to,* this network of avenues is a grid of conventional streets each 90 feet wide.

The logic of the Plan has many consequences, a few of which are:

> Over 50 percent of central Washington is in public rights-of-way; this is more street space than exists in any other major city in the world.

> Central Washington is a city designed for pedestrians, 2-legged and 4-legged. Every pedestrian-sized precinct is focused on a public square, and every major street is regularly interrupted by public open spaces about a 5-minute walk apart. The city is, or should be, a pedestrian's dream; but it is a modern traffic planner's nightmare.

> The angled avenues and irregular grids create a multitude of oddly shaped blocks and intersections; these provide a variety of dilemmas for private architects and for public urban designers. L'Enfant had begun to tackle that problem in ways that could have produced lovely results; but he was done in before he could finish the job.

> The topographic, ceremonial and geometric logic of the Plan is easily accessible. It reflected a capacious, 18th-century, enlightened view of the world, with the private and public life in a fine equilibrium. That original, crystalline structure has been largely obscured. This is too bad, and it need not continue to be the case.

L'Enfant's city covered an area roughly the size of Paris in 1800. It took over a century for that space to be filled with buildings. In the meantime Washington was the subject for cheap shots by visitors, particularly Europeans and particularly Englishmen. *"The City of Magnificent Distances...,"* *"the great Serbonian Bog,"* *"...with shrines unbuilt and heroes yet unborn...."* And so on. Dickens described it this way, *"Take the worst parts of (London)...the straggling outskirts of Paris...make it scorching hot in the morning, and freezing cold in the afternoon, with an occasional tornado of wind and dust...and that's Washington. Such as it is, it is likely to remain."*

Despite its proposed arched way and 160-foot breadth, East Capitol Street never became a retail street. The pull of Georgetown and the White House was too strong, and Washington early developed along the axis between the 2 Grand Edifices. But by the time of the Civil War most of the L'Enfant city was still unoccupied. Buildings were strung out towards Georgetown a couple of blocks on either side of Pennsylvania Avenue, and along 7th Street north about to N Street. In the Southwest, the area about 3 blocks south of the Mall was built up, and there was a settlement north of the Navy yard in Southeast Washington. Northeast Washington was still open country. What is now P Street was the northern edge of Georgetown.

Washington was, and remains, a company town. In the 19th century it was for Congressmen a temporary home; during the summer most returned to their families in other cities. Pennsylvania Avenue was bordered with hotels, rooming houses, and other houses; F Street and Seventh Street were the retail streets. The city was seen, by many people, as a temporary place in another way; until the end of the century there were frequent movements to relocate the seat of government west of the Appalachian Mountains or, later, west of the Mississippi.

But the seeds of the modern metropolis were germinating. The **Henry Fords** and the **Otises** would have more effect on the shape of the modern city than would architects and city planners, and the **Boss Shepherds** * and the **Thomas Crappers** would have more effect on the health of populations than all of medical science before the development of antibiotics. The private automobile would permit cities to spread out over extraordinary distance at very low densities, the high speed elevator would permit concentrations of activity in certain locations at densities previously undreamed of, and modern sanitation would help ensure that there would be people to inhabit the suburbs and the skyscrapers.

And Washington would, uniquely, be shaped by changing roles for national governments, and by America's changing position in the world of nations.

*In 1848, **Andrew Jackson Downing**, a landscape architect, laid out the White House grounds and the Mall as English landscape gardens, and in the 1880s the elder **Frederick Law Olmsted** designed the Capitol grounds which remain today one of the great urban design accomplishments. But **Alexander Robey** *(Boss)* **Shepherd**, in the early 1870s briefly head of the Department of Public Works, had more effect on the city than either. In 2 years he regraded the streets, added pavement and curbs, rebuilt bridges, built water and sewer mains, planted trees, added street lights. The dusty village took on some of the character of a modern city. Shepherd also bankrupted the city. Like L'Enfant before them, both Downing and Shepherd were fired before they could finish their work.

> *"Washington...is the symbol of America. By its dignity and architectural inspiration...we encourage that elevation of thought and character which comes from great architecture."*
> **Herbert Hoover,**
> 1929

> *"Auspicious Heaven shall fill with Fav'ring Gales, Where e'er Columbia spreads her swelling sails."*
> **Phillis Wheatley,** 1784.

*Courtesy of
Dunlap
Society*

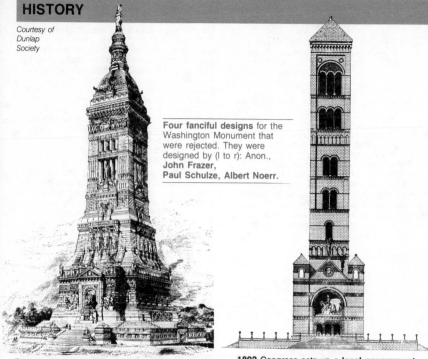

Four fanciful designs for the Washington Monument that were rejected. They were designed by (l to r): Anon., **John Frazer, Paul Schulze, Albert Noerr.**

Prior to the Europeans' settlement in the Potomac River area during the mid-1600s, the only known human inhabitants were the Piscataway Indians.

1749 Settlers found Alexandria, the area's first town.

1765 James Smithson, founder of the Smithsonian Institution, is born in France.

1790 Alexander Hamilton successfully leads a campaign in Congress to place the nation's permanent capital in a southern state. In exchange, the southern states agree to accept a tax overcharge.

1791 At Congress' request, President **George Washington** chooses the exact site for the capital city. With city designer **Pierre Charles L'Enfant's** help, each of the major federal buildings is given a location. Virginia and Maryland deed the necessary land to the federal government.

1792 Architect **James Hoban** wins $500 and a city lot for his winning entry in the competition to design the President's House.

September 18, 1793 George Washington lays the cornerstone for the **Capitol building.**

1800 President **John Adams** and his wife **Abigail** move into the not-yet-finished President's House. At Adams' insistence, Congress moves from its temporary Philadelphia headquarters to its new permanent home on Capitol Hill. Approximately 5,000 non-Indians have settled in the area.

November 1, 1800 First joint session of **Congress** is called to order on the Hill.

1801 Thomas Jefferson's presidential inauguration marks the first one held in the new federal capital.

1802 Congress sets up a **local government** consisting of a mayor and a council to help govern the city. Washington residents gain the right to elect the city council.

1814 During the **War of 1812,** British soldiers invade the city, burning many of the just-built federal buildings, including the Capitol and the President's House. With only moments to spare, First Lady **Dolley Madison** rescues many of the Executive Mansion's treasures, including **Gilbert Stuart's** portrait of Washington, before fleeing by carriage.

1816 James Hoban is brought back to restore the President's House in time for **James Monroe** to take residence in 1817.

1819 Most of the damage done by the British in 1814 has been repaired. Congress moves back into the Capitol.

1820 Washingtonians win the right to elect their own mayor but still have no say in congressional or presidential elections. **Maria Hester Monroe** weds **Sam Gouverneur** in the Executive Mansion's first wedding ceremony. The **Chesapeake & Ohio Canal** opens, linking the capital with Cumberland, Maryland. More than 500 boats regularly use the canal, creating the city's earliest freeway system.

1821 George Washington University is founded.

July 4, 1826 Thomas Jefferson and John Adams die.

1829 Daniel Webster and **Henry Clay** appoint the first Congressional page.

1833 Fire destroys the Treasury. The restored building spreads across Pennsylvania Avenue, interrupting the view between the President's House and the Capitol.

1835 The **United States inherits** James Smithson's fortune. Congress does not decide for 8 years whether the US will accept the bequest.

1841 William Henry Harrison dies after one month in office. **John Tyler** becomes the 10th US president.

1846 Virginia regains the land deeded to the nation for the capital city when the city's growth fails to meet earlier expectations. Population is approximately 50,000. Congress decides to accept James Smithson's half-million dollar fortune and establishes the **Smithsonian Institution.** Architect **James Renwick, Jr.,** begins building the red brick castle which will house the Institution.

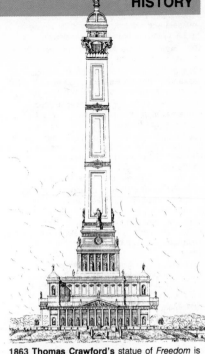

1848 Funded by private donations, **construction begins** on the marble obelisk which will memorialize George Washington.

1850 A South Carolina congressman reads a **prophetic warning** to his northern colleagues on Capitol Hill: *"...let the (southern) states we represent agree to separate and part in peace. If you are unwilling we should part in peace, tell us so, and we shall know what to do, when you reduce the question to submission or resistance."*

1853 Clark Mill's equestrian bronze of **Andrew Jackson** finds a home in Lafayette Square. A second fire (the first was set by the British in 1814) virtually destroys the **Library of Congress.**

1855 Washington Monument funds run out, and the construction stops at 55 feet.

1857 The Smithsonian begins using balloons to collect weather data; the *Washington Evening Star* reports this information daily.

1860 On the **128th anniversary of George Washington's** birthday, **Clark Miller's** statue of the first president is unveiled in Washington Circle. South Carolina leads **secession of southern states.**

1861-1865 As the government grows in time of war, so grows the capital city. The **population soars** from 60,000 to 120,000, thanks in part to the thousands of freed blacks who move to Washington in search of a new life and federal protection. An enormous housing shortage develops.

1861 The **fall of Ft. Sumter** and the ensuing **Civil War** turn Washington into an army camp. Soldiers are quartered in the East Room of the Executive Mansion, and the Capitol Rotunda becomes a field hospital. At night, Washingtonians can see rebel campfires across the Potomac. Smithsonian Secretary **Joseph Henry** successfully encourages Lincoln to support hot air balloon pioneer **Thaddeus Lowe's** idea of using balloons to observe military operations.

February 5, 1862 The press criticizes **President Lincoln** and his wife **Mary** for throwing a gala reception at the Executive Mansion while war bitterly divides the nation. The press fails to mention that both of the Lincolns had protested against the party and that upstairs the 2 younger Lincoln sons were gravely ill. Five days later 11-year old Willie Lincoln dies.

January 1, 1863 Lincoln signs the **Emancipation Proclamation** in his Cabinet room (later this room is turned into the Lincoln Bedroom).

1863 Thomas Crawford's statue of *Freedom* is lifted to the top of the Capitol dome, climaxing a decade of building on the Capitol.

1864 Arlington National Cemetery is established.

1865 The **13th Amendment** abolishes slavery.

April 14, 1865 Lincoln is fatally shot while attending a performance of *Our American Cousin* at the **Ford Theatre.**

1867 Howard University is founded.

1868 President **Andrew Johnson** is impeached by the House, but acquitted in the Senate by one vote.

1871 Congress sets up a territorial government for the **District of Columbia,** headed by a president-appointed governor. A building for the State, War, and Navy departments is authorized.

1874 Congress revamps the local government again, this time putting 3 commissioners, appointed by the president, in charge.

1877 Lucy Hayes sponsors the first **Easter egg-rolling contest.** Black spokesman **Frederick Douglass** creates a stir when he moves into a whites-only section of Anacostia (Cedar Hill) and becomes a District of Columbia US Marshal.

1881 A second Smithsonian building (later called the **Arts and Industries Building**) opens in time for **James Garfield's** presidential inauguration.

July 2, 1881 President Garfield is assassinated in Washington's railroad terminal. **Chester Arthur** succeeds Garfield and begins redecorating the presidential residence with Victorian decor.

1884 The **Washington Monument** is finally completed. Unfortunately, after construction was shut down in 1855 for lack of funds, the original quarry ran out of marble, so the color of the top 500 feet of the monument does not quite match the lower 55 feet.

1886 Forty-nine-year-old President **Grover Cleveland** marries 21-year old **Frances Folsom** in the Blue Room, making Cleveland the first and only president to be married in the Executive Mansion.

1887 L'Enfant's original manuscript of the **Plan Of The City Of Washington** is rediscovered. Study shows that its guidelines have been carelessly ignored.

1890 City acquires **Rock Creek Park** where the **National Zoo** will be built.

1897 Library of Congress building is completed (an annex is added in 1939).

September 14, 1901 President **William McKinley** dies from a gunshot wound inflicted 8 days earlier. **Theodore Roosevelt** becomes president and officially adopts *White House* as the name for the presidential residence.

1902 Steel magnate **Andrew Carnegie** endows the Carnegie Institute.

1904 Smithsonian Institution board member **Alexander Graham Bell** brings **James Smithson's** remains to DC from Italy.

1907 Construction begins on **Washington Cathedral** atop Mount St. Albans. (President Wilson is later buried here.)

1909 Belatedly acknowledging the hard work of the city's original architect **Pierre Charles L'Enfant**, DC moves his remains to a grave site on the Custis-Lee estate overlooking the Potomac. The presidential **Oval Office** is built.

1910 President **William Taft** appoints the first Commission of Fine Arts and assigns it the task of supervising all subsequent city development.

1912 The mayor of Tokyo presents First Lady **Helen Taft** with a gift of Japanese cherry trees which she plants in the recently drained **Tidal Basin.**

1914 **World War I** begins in Europe. Alley dwelling is prohibited in the city after September, 1918, but this proves inoperative due to the housing shortage brought on by World War I.

1916 Montana elects 36-year old **Jeannette Rankin** to Congress—only 4 years before American women are given the right to vote in national elections.

1917 The **US officially enters World War I,** and war once again brings a boost in population for the nation's capital. By 1918 the city's population has topped 450,000. The automobile has nudged out the horse and buggy, and the Mall is turned into a parking lot.

1919 President **Woodrow Wilson** wins the Nobel Peace prize for attempting a just settlement of World War I and advocating the **League of Nations.**

1922 Dedication of the **Lincoln Memorial** causes many Washingtonians to show a newfound respect for the Commission of Fine Arts. The commission chooses **Henry Bacon** as the monument's architect and **Daniel Chester French** as the creator of what will become one of the most recognizable and best loved sculptures in the world.

1923 **Freer Gallery of Art** opens.

1924 **Washington Senators** win the World Series against the New York Giants, 4 games to 3.

1930-1940 New government jobs created to ease the **burden of the Depression** cause a third population boom. By the time the US enters **World War II**, the city boasts 665,000 residents.

1932 Arkansas' **Hattie Wyatt Caraway** wins a Senate seat—the first woman to enter the Senate by election, not appointment.

1937 **Washington Redskins** win the National Football League championship 28-21 against the Chicago Bears.

1939 In a year that produced *Gone With the Wind, The Wizard Of Oz,* and *Stagecoach,* the capital city premieres *Mr. Smith Goes To Washington,* starring **Jimmy Stewart.** Sensing an unfavorable reception, the film's director **Frank Capra** sneaks out during the screening.

1940 **Washington Redskins** lose the National Football League championship game 73-0 to the Chicago Bears.

1941 On behalf of the American people, President **Franklin Roosevelt** accepts the **National Gallery of Art,** a gift from the estate of **A.W. Mellon.** After the Japanese bombing of **Pearl Harbor,** FDR makes his *Day That Will Live In Infamy* speech from the White House. The US enters World War II.

1942 **Washington Redskins** win National Football League championship against the Chicago Bears, 14-6.

1945 FDR dies; Harry Truman becomes president. The war finally ends, but the world has entered the age of nuclear weapons.

1948-1952 **President Truman** and his family move into Blair House while the White House undergoes a major renovation.

1950-1952 US becomes involved in the **Korean conflict.**

1950 **Population peaks** at 800,000, then drops as people migrate to the suburbs.

1954 In response to a Supreme Court decision (*Brown v. Board Of Education Of Topeka*), Washington becomes the **first major city to integrate** its schools.

1959 **Francis Cardinal Spellman** dedicates the **National Shrine of the Immaculate Conception.**

1960 **National Museum of American History** moves into its current home.

1961 The Constitution's **23rd Amendment** gives Washington, DC, residents the right to vote for president and vice president. **The Arena,** a theater-in-the-round built by private subscriptions, opens near the river front.

1961-1963 Jacqueline Kennedy's restoration of the White House furnishings becomes a media event, climaxed by her 1962 nationally televised tour of the Executive Mansion's refurbished first floor.

August 28, 1963 In the shadow of the Lincoln Memorial, an interracial crowd of more than 200,000 demonstrators gathers peaceably to demand equal justice for all citizens under the law. **Martin Luther King, Jr.,** one year away from a Nobel Peace prize, delivers his impassioned *I Have A Dream* speech, emphasizing his faith that one day all men will be brothers.

November 22, 1963 President **John Kennedy** is killed in Dallas, Texas. **Lyndon Johnson** moves into the White House and, in 1964, establishes a Commission for the Preservation of the White House. The commission facilitates donations to the White House and ensures that the Executive Mansion will be maintained in museum-quality condition.

1964 Washingtonians vote in their first presidential election.

1965 Construction begins on the **John F. Kennedy Center for the Performing Arts** (opens in 1971).

1966 The **Hirshhorn Museum and Sculpture Garden** is dedicated (opens in 1974).

1968 Following **the assassination of Martin Luther King, Jr.,** the *April Riots* plague Washington, DC, resulting in 7 people killed, 1,166 injured, and 7,370 arrested. Over 15,000 troops are required to quell the rioting. The **Ford Theater** reopens.

1972 Campaign workers for Republican president **Richard Nixon** break into the Democratic political headquarters at the **Watergate** apartment-office complex. The subsequent scandal leads to Nixon's 1974 resignation. The **National Zoo** receives 2 **giant pandas** from the People's Republic of China.

1973 Secretary of State **Henry Kissinger** wins the Nobel Peace prize for his work in negotiating the Vietnam War cease-fire agreement. For the first time in 100 years, Washingtonians decide, through elections, who will run their local government.

1974 **Walter E. Washington** wins Washington, DC's first mayoral election in over 100 years.

1976 *All The President's Men,* based on 2 *Washington Post* reporters' investigation of the Watergate break-in, wins the Academy Award for best picture. The world's most popular museum, the **National Air and Space Museum,** opens on the Mall in time for the Bicentennial celebration. The Smithsonian sponsors a special exhibition dramatizing Revolutionary War times.

1978 The **East Building** of the **National Gallery of Art** opens.

1983 **Washington Redskins** win Superbowl XVII. The event draws the largest TV audience ever for a live broadcast.

Late 1980s **Washington National Cathedral** expected to be completed.

TRANSPORTATION

English diplomats used to get extra pay for working in Washington, which was considered a tropical hardship post.

It was hot and hard to get around. It still gets muggy in the summer, but getting around town isn't hard anymore—in fact, it can be an adventure!

Washington is a city of commuters and tourists (a large percentage of the work force lives outside the District of Columbia). To accommodate them, **Washington Metropolitan Area Transit Authority** (WMATA, or *Metro* for short) has developed an extensive and complementary bus and rail system. The showpiece of the system is Metrorail (1976, **Harry Weese**). It's not called a subway, since so much of it is above ground, but the underground stations are the prime object of interest. Tunnel support and service structure are combined in innovative arches, which are made both lighter and more aesthetically pleasing by large coffers that echo the Classical ceilings found throughout the city. The coffers hold sound-absorbing material and air quality control systems that make the interior airy and quiet. Fluorescent lights are sunk into the floor near the wall, gently illuminating the entire arch. Surfaces are reportedly graffiti-proof.

Daily over 300,000 passengers take advantage of its clean, fast and reliable service. Federally funded construction began in 1969 and will continue into the 1990s. Five lines and 51 stations are currently in service. The system serves Downtown and outlying suburban areas and links up with **Union Station** (the city's railroad terminal) and **Washington National Airport**. For the visitor, the system is great good fortune as it stops near most points of interest from A to Z—or Arlington to the zoo.

Metrorail has won numerous awards. Most recently it was cited by the American Institute of Architects, who said its comprehensive design set a national standard.

The sleek trains run above the ground, on the ground and in Downtown deep underground. On the street, station entrances are marked by a tall brown pylon. A large letter **M**, the system logo, is displayed on all 4 sides. Beneath the logo, brightly colored stripes indicate which lines serve the station, e.g., blue line/yellow line. (Though all trains have official names based on their starting and destination points, most locals refer to them by color.)

To get to the train, passengers descend long, dramatic escalators. The one in **Dupont Circle** is one of the longest in the world. You arrive at the mezzanine or ticketing part of the station which has large colored maps of the system and kiosks where free pamphlet-sized maps are available. Maps of bus routes that serve the station are also available here. There are ticketing machines and a booth with an attendant on duty.

The trains themselves are spotless, air conditioned and quiet. Though the entire system could be run automatically by computer, there is an operator in each train, and each car has an intercom allowing you to talk to the operator in case of trouble. Stops are announced over the PA system.

So, you're wondering if perhaps this silver lining has a cloud in it? It does: a fare system so confusing at first that it must have been designed by moonlighters from the IRS. The price you pay depends upon where you get on, where you get off and what time of day you travel. Basic fare is about 65 cents, but going a long way at peak hours can cost you over $2.

To deal with the cumbersome price hierarchy, Metrorail has created the *Farecard*. It's about the size of a credit card, and like a credit card has a magnetic stripe on the back. When you enter the station, you buy your Farecard from a machine. You press buttons to indicate the amount you want to spend. Machines accept 6 coins, $1 and $5 bills. You can put up to $20 worth of travel on a Farecard.

Before entering the platform you will pass an entrance turnstile. Insert your card. The time and place is recorded and the Farecard is returned. When you get off the train and prepare to leave the station you will pass through an exit turnstile. Insert the Farecard. The correct value of the trip will be subtracted. If there is value remaining, your card will be returned. If there isn't enough value on the card you will be directed to an *Addfare* machine. Insert your card. The machine tells you how much is needed to make up the difference. Put in the money, retrieve the card and pass through the turnstile. Do not throw away your card on the train! Not only is this littering, it can be expensive.

The Farecard system is not as bad as it sounds. There are pictures and directions on the machines, and if you're confused you can ask the attendant.

There's one more detail: Once you're through the turnstile you can get a free transfer from a machine. If you plan to take a bus after the train, the transfer gives you free fare within DC and reduces the bus fare to outlying areas. You don't need a transfer or a Farecard to change lines once you are within the system.

Metrorail hours:
M-F—6am-midnight
Sa—8am-6pm
Su—10am-6pm
Slightly higher rush-hour rates are in effect weekdays between 6am and 9:30am and again between 3pm and 6:30pm.

Bus and rail routing and schedule information, 637-2437.

Timetables by mail: 637-1261/Metro Transit Police: 637-2121/Lost and Found: 637-1195, or 637-1196.

Each station has an elevator that wheelchair-bound passengers may use instead of the escalator.

Metrobus is also run by WMATA. At peak hours over 1,400 buses busily ply some 790 routes in Washington, suburban Maryland and Virginia. Buses work their way deep into suburban areas and bring passengers into town or to Metrorail stations.

Although many people take the bus, the system is complicated, and most people know only the routes they take frequently. With that in mind, it's best to get a map. Comprehensive system maps can be bought for $1 at most drugstores and grocery shops. Metrorail stations have free maps of particular bus routes serving the station. If you call WMATA at 202-637-1261 and tell them where you will be going, they can send you maps. If you're already in town, call 637-2437 between 6am and 11:30pm for complete bus and rail routing information. (You may be on hold for a while, but someone will pick up eventually.)

(continued page 164)

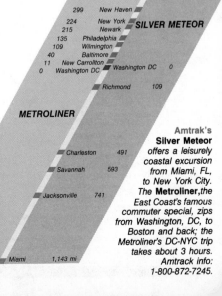

455 mi — Boston
412 — Providence
299 — New Haven
224 — New York
215 — Newark
135 — Philadelphia
109 — Wilmington
40 — Baltimore
11 — New Carrollton
0 — Washington DC — **SILVER METEOR** — Washington DC — 0
Richmond — 109

METROLINER

Charleston — 491
Savannah — 593
Jacksonville — 741
Miami — 1,143 mi

Amtrak's **Silver Meteor** offers a leisurely coastal excursion from Miami, FL, to New York City. The **Metroliner**, the East Coast's famous commuter special, zips from Washington, DC, to Boston and back; the Metroliner's DC-NYC trip takes about 3 hours. Amtrack info: 1-800-872-7245.

METRO SYSTEM MAP

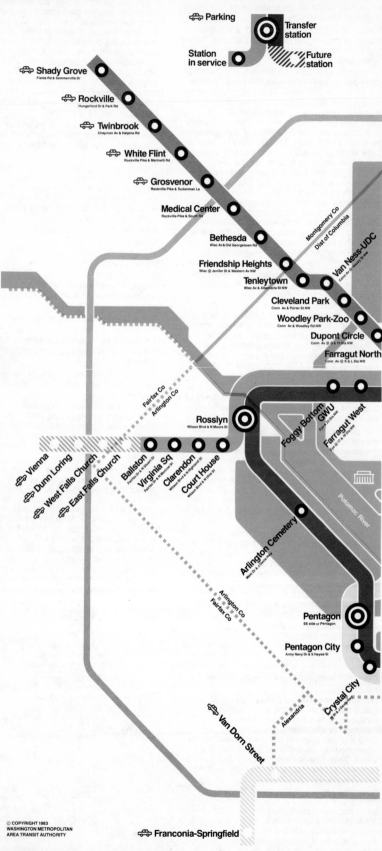

Parking

Station in service

Transfer station

Future station

Shady Grove
Fields Rd & Sommerville Dr

Rockville
Hungerford Dr & Park Rd

Twinbrook
Chapman Av & Halpine Rd

White Flint
Rockville Pike & Marinelli Rd

Grosvenor
Rockville Pike & Tuckerman La

Medical Center
Rockville Pike & South Rd

Bethesda
Wisc Av & Old Georgetown Rd

Friendship Heights
Wisc @ Jenifer St & Western Av NW

Tenleytown
Wisc Av & Albemarle St NW

Cleveland Park
Conn Av & Porter St NW

Woodley Park-Zoo
Conn Av & Woodley Rd NW

Dupont Circle
Conn Av @ Q & 19 Sts NW

Farragut North
Conn Av @ K & L Sts NW

Van Ness-UDC
Conn Av @ Veazey St NW

Montgomery Co
Dist of Columbia

Fairfax Co
Arlington Co

Rosslyn
Wilson Blvd & N Moore St

Vienna

Dunn Loring

West Falls Church

East Falls Church

Ballston
Fairfax Dr & N Stuart St

Virginia Sq
Fairfax Dr & N Monroe St

Clarendon
Wilson Blvd & Highland St

Court House
Wilson Blvd & N Uhle St

Foggy Bottom
GWU
23rd & I Sts NW

Farragut West
Eye @ 17 & 18 Sts NW

Potomac River

Arlington Cemetery
Mem Dr & J Davis Hwy

Arlington Co
Fairfax Co

Pentagon
SE side of Pentagon

Pentagon City
Army Navy Dr & S Hayes St

Van Dorn Street

Alexandria

Crystal City
18th & S Clark St NW

© COPYRIGHT 1983
WASHINGTON METROPOLITAN
AREA TRANSIT AUTHORITY

Franconia-Springfield

This copyrighted map was reproduced by permission of the Office of Public Affairs of the Washington Metropolitan Area Transit Authority.

METRO SYSTEM MAP

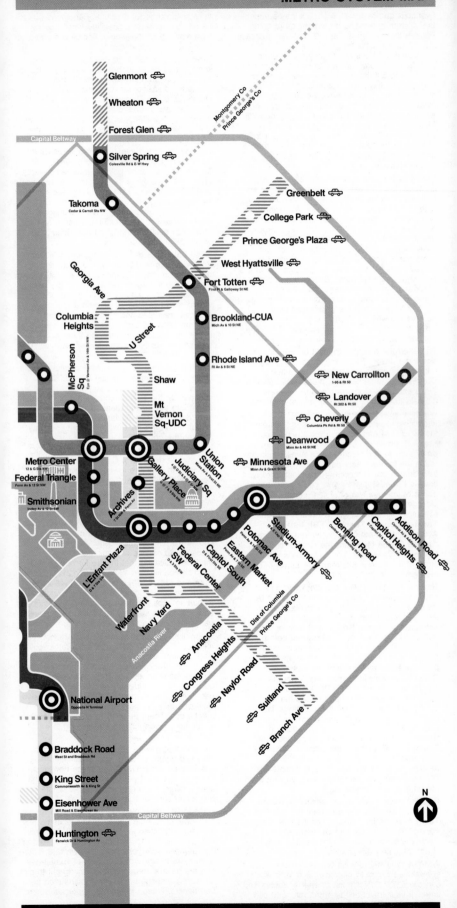

Glenmont

Wheaton

Forest Glen

Capital Beltway

Silver Spring
Colesville Rd & E-W Hwy

Takoma
Cedar & Carroll Sts NW

Greenbelt

College Park

Prince George's Plaza

West Hyattsville

Fort Totten
First Pl & Galloway St NE

Georgia Ave

Columbia
Heights

U Street

Brookland-CUA
Mich Av & 10 St NE

McPherson
Sq
Eye @ Vermont Av & 14th St NW

Shaw

Rhode Island Ave
RI Av & 8 St NE

New Carrollton
I-95 & Rt 50

Landover
Rt 202 & Rt 50

Mt
Vernon
Sq-UDC

Cheverly
Columbia Pk Rd & Rt 50

Deanwood
Minn Av & 48 St NE

Metro Center
12 & G Sts NW

Federal Triangle
Penn Av & 12 St NW

Smithsonian
Indep Av & 12 St SW

Gallery Place
4 @ 7 & 9 Sts NW

Judiciary Sq
4 @ D & E Sts NW

Union
Station
Mass Av & First St NE

Minnesota Ave
Minn Av & Grant St NE

Archives
7 St NW & Penn Ave

Stadium-Armory
19 & C Sts SE

Benning Road
Central Ave & Benning Rd NE

Capitol Heights
E Capitol St & Southern Ave

Addison Road

L'Enfant Plaza
D & 7th SW

Potomac Ave
Penn Av & 14 St SE

Eastern Market
8 & D First Sts SE

Federal Center
SW
D & 3 Sts SW

Capitol South
D & First Sts SE

Waterfront

Navy Yard

Anacostia River

Anacostia

Congress Heights

Dist of Columbia
Prince George's Co

Naylor Road

Suitland

Branch Ave

National Airport
Opposite N Terminal

Braddock Road
West St and Braddock Rd

King Street
Commonwealth Av & King St

Eisenhower Ave
Mill Road & Eisenhower Av

Capital Beltway

Huntington
Fenwick Dr & Huntington Av

Montgomery Co
Prince George's Co

N

TRANSPORTATION

Like taxis and Metrorail, Metrobus has a variable fare system depending on where you're going. Fares within DC are a flat rate, but they increase rapidly as you pass through zones in Maryland or Virginia. All fares are slightly higher during rush hour. The easiest way to know how much to pay is to tell the driver where you're going and ask him the price. There is no shame in this; locals do it all the time. Be sure you have exact change. The driver will take dollar bills, but won't make change. If you have just gotten off Metrorail, *make sure you picked up a free transfer* in the station. This can give you a free bus ride in the District. Buses also issue free transfers, but they are only good on other buses, not on Metrorail.

During rush hour the buses can be slow and crowded, but off peak hours they're a great way to travel. They're slightly cheaper than Metrorail, tend to take you closer to where you want to go, and provide a great view. Be sure before you get on a bus that it's a local or, if it's an express, that it stops where you need to go. Most express buses say so on the destination marker, but some don't. However, if the route number is printed on a red field you can be sure the bus is running an express route. District buses and buses that go into Maryland have 2-digit numbers or a letter followed by a number, e.g., 32, M8. Virginia buses are identified by a number followed by a letter, e.g., 11A. Destination markers indicate the end of the line, not necessarily the streets followed to get there.

To get off the bus, pull the red or grey cord to signal the driver. The newer buses have a yellow rubber strip which you press. If you have any questions about schedules, please call WMATA. While each bus stops running at a different time, it's safe to assume that most stop at midnight.

We have selected several routes that might be interesting to visitors. The **30 series**, including the 30, 32, 34 and 36, will probably be most useful. They all run essentially the same route on Wisconsin and Pennsylvania Aves., until they reach the far southeast part of the District, where they branch off. The northern destination of all 4 lines is **Friendship Heights.** You'll pass these points of interest: **National Cathedral, Georgetown,** the **White House, Blair House,** executive office buildings, **Treasury, National Theater, Federal Triangle, FBI, National Archives, National Gallery, Hirshhorn, National Air and Space Museum,** the **Capitol** and **Library of Congress.** You'll also pass within a block of the **Folger Shakespeare Library.** This bus remains in the District.

Routes 13A and 13B make clockwise and counterclockwise loops respectively. The 13A leaves from the Pentagon in Virginia. It stops at **Arlington Cemetery** before crossing the **Arlington Memorial Bridge** and heading into DC. You pass the **Lincoln Memorial** before turning right on Constitution Ave. and going parallel to the Mall. Traveling down the **Mall,** you pass the **National Academy of Sciences, Constitution Gardens (Vietnam Veterans Memorial),** the **Reflecting Pool, the Ellipse** and the **White House.** The bus crosses the Mall at 7th St. and goes west on Independence before heading back toward the **Pentagon** on 14th St. During the last part of the trip you pass the **Bureau of Engraving and Printing,** the **Tidal Basin, East Potomac Park** and the **Jefferson Memorial.** Route 13B makes the same trip in reverse. Because the bus runs in Virginia and DC, your fare may vary depending on where you get on and how far you go.

Route 11A provides all-day service to **Mount Vernon.** Along the way it passes through **Old Town Alexandria.** You can get the bus in the **Federal Triangle,** on 10th St. between Pennsylvania and Constitution Aves. Travel time is approximately 45 minutes.

WMATA regularly runs lift buses that are specially equipped to handle wheelchairs. You can call 637-2437 for a list of specific routes and times. If your travel needs aren't met, you can call Metrobus' *On-Call Service* at 637-1825 and they will arrange for a specially equipped bus to be on your route at a specified time. Reservations are first-come, first-served and must be made a day in advance.

Driving: If you decide to use a car, here are some things to remember. The city is laid out in a grid. Numbered streets run north and south and lettered streets run east and west. Lettered streets go up to W, and there is no J street. These streets are bisected by wide avenues running on the diagonal, and they're named after states. Where several intersect you frequently find traffic circles.

The city is divided into 4 quarters: **Northeast, Northwest, Southeast,** and **Southwest,** with the **Capitol** as the center point. Numbered streets start from 1 on either side of the north-south axis and lettered streets start from A on either side of the east-west axis. All addresses in the District include the quadrant, e.g., NW. If someone doesn't give you the quadrant, be sure and ask for it. You could spend hours searching in the wrong neighborhood.

Rush hour auto traffic is from 7am to 9:30am and from 4pm to 6:30pm. Try to avoid driving during these times. Despite a modern rail system and the fourth largest bus system in the nation, commuters from outside the District choke the streets with their cars. Traffic on some one-way streets is reversed and many 2-way streets become one-way. Left hand turns are banned at many intersections, and though there is a right turn on red—except where posted—it doesn't seem to help.

If you must drive, be particularly careful in traffic circles. These move very fast indeed. Know where you're going before you enter. To continue on the avenue you started on it's best to get into the far right lane. If you miss your turn, don't try anything fancy. Go around again or pull off on the next exit and work your way through the grid.

Parking tickets are given out frequently in DC and they're expensive. Cars parked incorrectly during rush hour are towed, and it may cost upwards of $50 to get the car back.

Taxis: As far as taxis are concerned, Washington seems to fall comfortably between the bobbing yellow sea of Manhattan and the arid wasteland of Los Angeles. With 8,000 cabs in operation it's not hard to get a cab—unless of course it's raining. Many kinds of cars are pressed into service as cabs, but all have markers indicating that they're for hire. The 3 main companies are **Yellow (544-1212), Diamond (387-6200),** and **Capitol (546-2400).** There are several other suburban operators. Suburban cabs can take you into the District and back out to the suburbs, but they cannot carry passengers within DC. These cabs are metered.

The majority of cabs in the District are not metered. Fares are calculated on a rather quirky zone system, with zones radiating outward from the center of town. How much you pay depends on how many zones you cross. As Zone 1 is quite big and includes many tourist attractions, a cab ride in this district can be fairly inexpensive. However, drivers make up for this with surcharges. There is an extra charge for each additional passenger and for traveling in rush hour.

Drivers must have a zone map posted in the cab, and if you tell them your destination they are obligated to tell you in advance how much the trip will cost. It pays to be familiar with the zones. Often walking a block further before you hail a cab can save you as much as 75 cents.

Cabs in DC are allowed to stop and pick up additional passengers as long as it doesn't take the original passenger out of his way. Not only are cabs allowed to do this, they like to, so don't be surprised. Everyone pays his own fare. There is no extra cost to you. Because of surcharges and the drivers' frequently exercised right to pick up extra passengers, Washingtonians tend to be bad tippers. Fifteen percent is appreciated here, but not taken for granted.

Taxi complaints, *727-5401.*

INDEX

INDEX

New to DC:

The Regent. *Luxury.* A brand new and exquisite addition to a city where playing host to visiting dignitaries is a refined art. The Regent is even more luxurious than its counterparts in NYC & Chicago (the acclaimed Mayfair Regents). Enjoy Continental nouvelle cuisine in the hotel's **Mayfair Restaurant.** Manager **Jan Mestriner** ably choreographs the intricate workings of this inviting hotel. *24th & M Sts. NW. 429-0100/800-545-4000.*

DC PHONE NUMBERS

(all 202 area code unless indicated)

EMERGENCY

FIRE	**911**
POLICE	**911**
AMBULANCE	**911**
STATE POLICE	727-1000
COAST GUARD	426-2158
FBI	324-3000
SECRET SERVICE	535-5100
VIRGINIA POLICE	323-4500
ALEXANDRIA POLICE	703-838-4444
EMERGENCY MEDICAL	857-1100
DENTAL REFERRAL	686-0803
POISON CONTROL	625-3333
DULLES AIRPORT	703-471-7596/
General Office	471-7596
TRAVELERS AID	347-0101

RECORDED MESSAGES

White House	456-7041
Dial-A-Museum	357-2020
Dial-A-Park	426-6975
Smithsonian Information	357-1300
Democratic Floor Information, House	225-7400
Democratic Floor Information, Senate	224-8541
Republican Floor Information, Senate	224-8601
Republican Floor Information, House	225-7430

RECREATION

Capitol	224-3121
Daily Tourist Info	737-8866/789-7000
DC Dept. of Recreation	673-7660
Dial-A-Museum	357-2020
Dial-A-Park	426-6975
Dial-A-Phenomenon	357-2000
Grayline Tours	479-5986
National Park Calendar	426-6700
Smithsonian Visitors Center	357-2700
Tourmobile Sightseeing	554-7950
Washington Area Convention and Visitors Association	789-7000
Washington Monument	426-6839
Smithsonian Performing Arts Division	287-3357

Richard Saul Wurman

Janet Smith *Administrative Director*
Michael Everitt *Design Director*

Joy Aiken *Managing Editor*
Allison Goodman *Art Director*

Contributing Editors
Charles Freund *Introductions*
Don Oldenburg *Shopping/Nightlife*
Sara Reeder Ortiz *Architecture*
Ben Ruhe *Galleries*
Pamela H. Sommers *Restaurants*
Arna Vodenos *Hotels*

Writing & Editing
Christine Drakenhall, *Assistant Editor*
Linda Lenhoff, *Assistant Editor*
Doree Lovell
Shelly Moore
Jonathan Shestack
Devorah Rosen

Art & Production
Cathy Gurvis, *Senior*
Lee Buckley
Hugh Enockson
Juliet Jacobson
M.L. Peacor
Jill Yesko

Typesetting
Linda Lenhoff, *Senior*
John Huszar
Sara Reeder Ortiz
George Quioan
Eileen Yamada

Proofreading
Luisa Larona
Monte Mann
Shelly Moore
Denen Schumacher
Andrea Walters

Office
Kathy Rapp
George Ochoa
Randy Walburger
Britta Wilson

Printing
Craftsman Press/Seattle WA
Bill Dorich

Photocomposition
Graphic House/Glendora CA
Frank Kiluk

Joel Katz *Cover Photography*

Special Thanks:
Axonometric drawings of Central Washington by **Joseph Passonneau & Partners;** the monumental buildings were drawn by **Jeffery Wolf,** other buildings by Jeffery Wolf and Staff. This work was financed in part by the **National Endowment for the Arts.**

Metrorail map on page 162 was reproduced by permission of the Office of Public Affairs of the **Washington Metropolitan Area Transit Authority.**

Drawings on pages 24, 40, 61, 65, 120-121 by **Carlos Diniz & Associates**

Marion Barry, Jr., Mayor, Washington, D.C.
Daniel Boorstin, Director, Library of Congress
Walter J. Boyne, Director, National Museum of Air & Space Museum
J. Carter Brown, Director, National Gallery of Art
Art Buchwald, syndicated columnist
Elliott Carroll, FAIA, Executive Assistant, Architect of the Capitol
Lois Craig, Associate Dean, School of Architecture and Planning, MIT
Dr. Charles C. Eldridge, Director, National Museum of American Art
Alan Fern, Director, National Portrait Gallery
Lloyd E. Herman, Director, Renwick Gallery
Abram Lerner, Director, Hirshhorn Museum and Sculpture Garden
Bates Lowry, Director, National Building Museum
Roger G. Kennedy, National Museum of American History
Diana McLellan, syndicated columnist
John Naisbitt, author
Jacquelin Robertson, Dean, School of Architecture, Univeristy of Virginia
Warren Robbins, Director, National Museum of African Art
Duke Zeibert, restaurateur

ACCESSPRESS Ltd. gratefully acknowledges the assistance of:
American Institute of Architects Foundation
Architect of the Capitol, Florian Thayn
Arena Stage
Arlington National Cemetery
Elizabeth Armstrong
Baltimore City Hall Courtyard Galleries
Baltimore Streetcar Museum Inc.
B&O Railroad Museum
Bureau of Engraving & Printing, Jeanne Howard
Carter Barron Amphitheater
Cooper Lecky Partnership, Architects
Corcoran Gallery of Art
Decatur House
Department of Defense
Dunlap Society, Jan Peden
Dumbarton Oaks
Enoch Pratt Free Library
Jim Goodman
Michael Graham
John Greer
Hillwood
Harborplace
Howard University
I.M. Pei and Partners
Intelsat
Federal Bureau of Investigation
Georgetown University
George Washington University
Kennedy Center
Library of Congress, Mary Ison
Maryland Hall of Records Commission
Mount Vernon Place United Methodist Church
National Building Museum
National Aquarium Society
National Geographic Society, Howard Paine
National Park Service, Ford's Theatre
Navy Memorial Museum
Organization of American States
Pavilion at the Old Post Office
Phillips Collection
Pimlico Race Course
RFK Stadium
Rouse Company
Shepley Bulfinch Richardson and Abbott, Inc.
Smithsonian Institution
  Anacostia Neighborhood Museum
  Archives of American Art
  Arts & Industries Building
  Freer Gallery of Art
  Hirshhorn Museum & Sculpture Garden
  National Air & Space Museum
  National Museum of African Art
  National Museum of American Art,
    Margery Byers
  National Museum of American History,
    Joyce Lancaster
  National Museum of Natural History
  National Portrait Gallery
  National Zoological Park
  Renwick Gallery
Textile Museum
University of Virginia
US Department of Agriculture
US Marine Corps Historical Center
Venturi, Rauch and Scott Brown
Vietnam Memorial Fund
Warner Associates, Ltd.
Washington Cathedral
Washington Convention Center, Alan Grip
Washington Metropolitan Area Transit Authority, Larry Glick
Washington Visitors & Convention Association, Marie Tibor
Watergate
White House
Robert Jenkins, Director, Baltimore National Aquarium

ACCESSPRESS Ltd.
Richard Saul Wurman
Frank Stanton
Co-owners

Sales & Marketing
P.O. Box 30706
Los Angeles, CA 90030

Editorial Offices
2690 Beachwood Drive
Los Angeles, CA 90068
213 461 0251

ACCESSPRESS Ltd.
P.O. Box 30706
Los Angeles, CA 90030

ACCESSPRESS Ltd.
P.O. Box 30706
Los Angeles, CA 90030

The creative adventure continues

ACCESSGUIDES

The ultimate guides

1st: Circle the price in the table below which corresponds to your order desires:
2nd: Circle shipping and handling charge per title:

	1 copy	**2** copies	**5** copies	**10** copies
NYCACCESS	$11.95	$20	$50	$95
SAN FRANCISCOACCESS	$9.95	$18	$45	$85
LAACCESS	$9.95	$18	$45	$85
HAWAIIACCESS	$9.95	$18	$45	$85
DCACCESS	$9.95	$18	$45	$85
NEW ORLEANSACCESS	$2.50	$4	$12	$20
BASEBALLACCESS	$4.95	$9	$24	$45
TOKYOACCESS *(September '84)*	$9.95	$18	$45	$85
DOGACCESS	$2.50	$4	$12	$20
for shipping and handling:	*$1.50*	*$2.25*	*$3*	*$5*

3rd: Add the circled prices. $_____. *(California only add 6.5% sales tax.)*
4th: Write your name and address here: *(Please include shipping and handling.)*

_____
Name

_____
Address

_____
City, State & Zip Code

5th: Send a check or money order
with this coupon to:

ACCESSPRESS Ltd.
P.O. Box 30706
Los Angeles, CA 90030

*Please allow 4-6 weeks
for delivery*

1st: Circle the price in the table below which corresponds to your order desires:
2nd: Circle shipping and handling charge per title:

	1 copy	**2** copies	**5** copies	**10** copies
NYCACCESS	$11.95	$20	$50	$95
SAN FRANCISCOACCESS	$9.95	$18	$45	$85
LAACCESS	$9.95	$18	$45	$85
HAWAIIACCESS	$9.95	$18	$45	$85
DCACCESS	$9.95	$18	$45	$85
NEW ORLEANSACCESS	$2.50	$4	$12	$20
BASEBALLACCESS	$4.95	$9	$24	$45
TOKYOACCESS *(September '84)*	$9.95	$18	$45	$85
DOGACCESS	$2.50	$4	$12	$20
for shipping and handling:	*$1.50*	*$2.25*	*$3*	*$5*

3rd: Add the circled prices. $_____. *(California only add 6.5% sales tax.)*
4th: Write your name and address here: *(Please include shipping and handling.)*

_____
Name

_____
Address

_____
City, State & Zip Code

5th: Send a check or money order
with this coupon to:

ACCESSPRESS Ltd.
P.O. Box 30706
Los Angeles, CA 90030

*Please allow 4-6 weeks
for delivery.*

At **ACCESS PRESS** Ltd., our enterprise is fired by a curiosity about *what people do, where they like to go,* and *how they see.* At best, this book will help you see some things that you have always seen, but never *seen.*

Our investigations into the world around us have led to the creation of the **ACCESS** series of guides, including **LA**ACCESS, **SAN FRANCISCO**ACCESS, **HAWAII**ACCESS, **FOOTBALL**ACCESS, **NYC**ACCESS, **D.C.**ACCESS, **NEW ORLEANS**ACCESS, **BASEBALL**ACCESS and 1984**OLYMPIC**ACCESS.

Our books benefit greatly from the reactions of our readers, so we welcome your comments, criticisms, and suggestions—any ideas that can help us do what we do better!

_____

_____

_____

_____